Studies in Human Geography

Also published on behalf of the Social Science Research Council by Heinemann Educational Books:

Forecasting and the Social Sciences, edited by Michael Young

Social Indicators and Social Policy, edited by Andrew Shonfield and Stella Shaw

REVIEWS OF CURRENT RESEARCH

1. *Research in Political Science*

2. *Research on International Organization*

3. *Research in Social Anthropology*

4. *Social Research on Automation*

5. *Research on Poverty*

6. *Comparability and Social Research*

7. *The Population Census*

8. *Longitudinal Studies and the Social Sciences*

9. *Research in Economic and Social History*

10. *Research in Human Geography*

Studies in Human Geography

Edited by

MICHAEL CHISHOLM
and BRIAN RODGERS

Published for the
Social Science Research Council
by
HEINEMANN EDUCATIONAL BOOKS · LONDON

Heinemann Educational Books Ltd
LONDON EDINBURGH MELBOURNE AUCKLAND TORONTO
HONG KONG SINGAPORE KUALA LUMPUR
IBADAN NAIROBI JOHANNESBURG NEW DELHI

ISBN 0 435 35165 6

Published by
Heinemann Educational Books Ltd
48 Charles Street, London W1X 8AH
Printed in Great Britain by
Morrison & Gibb Ltd, London and Edinburgh

Preface

The Social Science Research Council is charged to foster research in the social sciences. Among the various means available to pursue this objective is the publicising of research activities, both substantive findings and questions in search of an answer. It is in this context that the present volume of essays has been produced, to focus attention on the substantive contribution of geographers to several fields of study. The intention is two-fold. First, for non-geographers, to provide a synopsis of current activities and, hopefully, to stimulate an interest in a number of intriguing problems. Second, for practising geographers, the present volume is analogous to the review papers in *Progress in Geography* (edited by C. Board *et al.*) but the exposition is deliberately kept as non-technical as possible.

The Human Geography Committe of the SSRC took the initiative in getting this volume compiled but it was only through the generosity of the Council in providing funds that the enterprise could be undertaken. We are immensely indebted to the Council, as also to all the contributors for the trouble they have taken.

M. C.
B. R.

1972

Contributors

Michael Chisholm, Professor of Economic and Social Geography, University of Bristol

Brian Rodgers, Professor of Geography, University of Manchester

Michael Wise, Professor of Geography, London School of Economics and Political Science

David Grigg, Reader in Geography, University of Sheffield

John Clarke, Professor of Geography, University of Durham

Ross Davies, Lecturer in Geography, University of Newcastle upon Tyne

Harold Carter, Gregynog Professor of Human Geography, University College of Wales, Aberystwyth

Brian Robson, Lecturer in Geography, University of Cambridge

Gerald Manners, Reader in Geography, University College London

John House, Professor of Geography, University of Newcastle upon Tyne.

Contents

Preface
MICHAEL CHISHOLM and BRIAN RODGERS   v

List of figures   viii

List of tables   ix

1. *Introduction*   1
   MICHAEL WISE

2. *Geographical studies of economic development with special reference to agriculture*   18
   DAVID GRIGG

3. *Population in movement*   85
   JOHN CLARKE

4. *The location of service activities*   125
   ROSS DAVIES

5. *Structure and scale in the city system*   172
   HAROLD CARTER

6. *A view on the urban scene*   203
   BRIAN ROBSON

7. *Regional development, with particular reference to Britain*   242
   GERALD MANNERS

8. *Geographers, decision takers and policy makers*   272
   JOHN HOUSE

Diagrams and Maps

FIGURE 2.1 Per caput national income 1963–68 in US dollars   20

FIGURE 2.2 Daily supply of calories, per caput   24

FIGURE 2.3 Per caput daily supply of calories as a percentage of requirements, 1964–68   25

FIGURE 2.4 Calories derived from cereals, potatoes and sugar as a percentage of total calorie intake, 1964–68   26

FIGURE 2.5 Daily supply of total protein (grammes)   28

FIGURE 2.6 Average annual rate of increase in population, 1963–68   37

FIGURE 3.1 Population potential and central tendency in Sierra Leone, 1963   90

FIGURE 3.2 Net migration as a factor of population change in various sizes of areal units in England and Wales   91

FIGURE 3.3 A Cartesian co-ordinate graph of the components of population change in the local authority areas of Norfolk, 1951–61   92

FIGURE 3.4 Semi-logarithmic dispersion graph of sex-ratios in the local authority areas of Norfolk, 1961   94

FIGURE 3.5 Types of city-size distribution in African countries   95

FIGURE 3.6 Lorenz curves of population densities in seven selected African countries   99

FIGURE 3.7 Models of demographic transition   101

FIGURE 3.8 Patterns of age and sex structure in Sierra Leone, 1963   108

FIGURE 4.1 The nesting arrangements of trade areas   129

FIGURE 4.2 Christaller's alternative central place systems   130

FIGURE 4.3 The Löschian complex landscape   131

FIGURE 4.4 Probability contours for consumers shopping in three centres   137

FIGURE 4.5 The central business district core-frame concept   149

FIGURE 4.6 The internal structure of central area core retailing facilities   151

FIGURE 4.7 Graph representation of factors affecting consumer space preferences   160–1

FIGURE 5.1 The rank-size rule   176

FIGURE 5.2   The urban hierarchy in England and Wales   178
FIGURE 5.3   The urban hierarchy in the Rhondda valleys   184
FIGURE 5.4   The growth of a system of cities   185
FIGURE 5.5   The process of cumulative causation at the root of
             agglomeration trends   189
FIGURE 5.6   The upper ranks of the urban hierarchy in England
             and Wales and the linkages with London and
             A-ranked centres   192
FIGURE 5.7   Indexes of specialization by distance from the
             nearest metropolis   194
FIGURE 6.1   Social areas in Chicago   221
FIGURE 6.2   The inter-relationship of aggregate and individual
             scales   223
FIGURE 6.3   Household life cycles and the age profiles of areas 229

Tables

TABLE 1   The urban population of England and Wales,
          1801–1911   33
TABLE 2   World urban growth 1920–60   34
TABLE 3   Variation in the percentage distribution of age groups
          among local authorities in the British Isles, 1961   93
TABLE 4   Rank correlation coefficients for various indices of
          centrality in the North West   143
TABLE 5   Berry's classification of business service configurations 145
TABLE 6   A step-by-step approach to retail forecasting for one
          town   156
TABLE 7   An hierarchy of central places   181

1 Introduction

MICHAEL WISE

The intention in writing this volume is to review some of the areas of research in human geography in which major contributions have been made in recent years, and to relate these contributions to work accomplished in other disciplines. The review, it must be emphasized, is necessarily a selective one and is not intended to be comprehensive. The themes of the various contributions have been chosen to illustrate the nature and direction of recent changes in the subject and it should not be thought that the omission of a theme implies the absence of recent major contributions. Nor, in this Introduction, will an attempt be made fully to summarize the nature of recent trends in research, since such a review has recently been published for the Social Science Research Council (Chisholm, 1971a) while, additionally, the series of volumes entitled *Progress in Geography* (Board, Chorley, Haggett and Stoddart, 1969–) provides further insight into current thought in a number of crucial fields of study. Rather, this introduction offers a personal impression of recent changes in human geography as a field of study from the viewpoint of one whose first training in the subject was gained in one of the typically small university departments of geography in the years before 1939.

Rapid change has, of course, been characteristic of almost all branches of geography in the post-war years. The rate of change quickened perceptibly in the 1960s: indeed, Professor K. C. Edwards (one of the first to apply geographical methods to the analysis of planning problems) is amongst those who have discussed the 'revolutionary advances' of the last ten years, especially in social and economic geography and, very notably, in the methodology of the subject (Edwards, 1967).

Whether or not, when viewed in retrospect, the years since about 1960 will be seen as a 'revolutionary' phase in the history of the subject one cannot yet say: but certainly there has been the feeling amongst most academic geographers in Britain that the changes in attitudes, approaches and methods compared to those of the pre-war and immediate post-war periods have been sufficient to justify their description as 'revolutionary'.

Significant change would, of course, be expected in a subject that has grown greatly in its scale of activity within the universities and polytechnics since the end of the 1939–45 war. The increase in the number of undergraduate and postgraduate students, and the related growth of university staffs and research activities (Chisholm, 1971) has made possible a much greater degree of specialization of teaching and research both by departments and by individuals. Whereas, formerly, most geography teachers had to a considerable degree to be 'generalists', a much greater specialization of interest within human geography has been possible in recent years. Coupled with the rapid expansion of activity that has been characteristic generally of the social sciences, and the greater opportunities for inter-disciplinary contact that have emerged, it is perhaps not surprising to find increasing attention being paid to the social and economic aspects of geography, associated also with an enhanced sharpness of focus upon research problems and methods.

However, the changes appear to run more deeply and to relate to the goals and objectives of geographical study. Professor Edwards, for example, commented that one of the significant features of the revolutionary change, as he saw it, had been a shift in objectives away from the older view of geography as the study of 'the earth as the home of man'. This had been the key to the outlook of men like H. J. Mackinder and A. J. Herbertson, pioneers of the study of human geography in Britain. Their 'new geography', fashioned in the period between about 1885 and 1910, had been based on a 'holistic' or 'integrating' view of geography as the study of the relationships between societies and those elements of the physical environment that varied from place to place. The impetus given by their earlier 'revolutionary' activities which had, indeed, established geography as a discipline in British universities and schools, and of the teaching of other pioneers such as P. M. Roxby and H. J. Fleure, had continued to the time of the Second World War and had greatly influenced the training of the generation of university teachers active at the time of the first post-1945 expansion of British universities. Characteristic of the present trend, however, has been the diminution or even the elimination of interest in the physical geography base of human activities, as a result of the specialization of research activity upon the spatial inter-actions of social, economic and political phenomena. Thus, the decline in interest in the 'control' exerted by the physical environment has been matched by more thorough enquiry into the geographical, or spatial, organizing activities of societies and individuals. So the study of the social and economic processes of spatial organization and change became in its own right a field of study. Such an approach, directed more keenly at the nature of social and economic environments, has seemed particularly appropriate in an age of urban growth and at a time when the shaping and administration of public policies for the geographical environment has become a major focus of interest. The intricacy of the problems of understanding the changing man-made environment in terms not only of physical structures and landscapes (using that term in its narrow sense), but also of the movements of people, goods and services, of the inter-actions between places and areas, and of the perceptual processes of groups and the results of their decision-making, has thus provided a special field of study. While still related to the older and more general study of geography, it may be recognized as a subset of objectives, activities and techniques which has led to new links with other fields of study.

Thus a significant number of research workers in human geography would now replace the 'older' outlook based on the examination of relationships between societies and the physical environment with one based on the relationships between spatial forms and organizations and the socio-economic environment.

The change goes still a little further. The geographers of the earlier revolution, notably Mackinder, recognized the difficulty that their own advocacy of a holistic approach was likely to create: that of a conflict between, on the one hand, what Mackinder referred to as the 'crying need of humanity' for synthetic studies of society-environment relationships by areas or regions and, on the other, the intellectual satisfaction of studying in depth the problems raised by the distributions of individual phenomena; land forms, cities, industries, mineral resources, etc. Mackinder's view had been that 'the object of the geographer is to understand the concrete complexity, not to abstract and reduce to simplicity'. Geography was 'a comprehensive idealistic science' and he saw its rôle as that of a natural counterpoise 'for the materialism of the specialist sciences' (Mackinder, 1935). It was not that geography was not a specialist subject, for there was a specialism 'proper to the strictest conception of synthetic geography', but it was a different kind of specialism which presented 'regions to be philosophically viewed in all their aspects interlocked'. This was the nature of the tradition that influenced the early training of many geographers, like myself, still active in university teaching.

Richard Hartshorne's *The Nature of Geography*, first published in 1939, proved a further powerful influence. Systematic and regional geography were viewed as intimately related and essential to each other. The ultimate purpose of geography, 'the study of the areal differentiation of the world', was 'most clearly expressed in regional geography', and only by maintaining its relation to regional geography could systematic geography hold to the purpose of geography and not disappear into the other sciences. Regional geography, on the other hand, would be sterile 'without the continuous fertilization of generic concepts and principles from systematic geography'. It was irrelevant to argue the relative importance of regional and systematic geography: both were essential to the 'integrated dualism' of the subject. Geographical study, if it were to be complete, was required 'not only to study those features and relationships that can be expressed in generic concepts but a great number of features and relationships that are essentially unique'.

It may well have been, as Haggett indeed suggests (Haggett, 1965), an increasing realization of the uneasy relationship between regional geography and systematic geography that produced the attack upon the 'exceptionalist tradition' in geography in the 1950s. Schaefer's paper of 1953 undoubtedly provided a new stimulus, though Bunge (1962) found, through his vividly expressed book, a receptive audience among younger geographers especially, who were seeking a clearer conceptual framework for the development of geography as a social science than had been provided for them by the regional method. Both Schaefer and Bunge found 'uniqueness' an unsatisfactory basis: it was necessary for systematic geography to develop its own theoretical base and for regional geography to search for generic concepts. Such contributions stimulated a fresh interest in the methodology of the subject, and started a re-examination of the methodology of geography in relation to the social and natural sciences. It may not be an exaggeration to suggest that the new revolution was comparable in effect to that initiated by Mackinder and his fellow revolutionaries of the 1880s and 1890s. The philosophy of geography as a 'point of view', as an integrating and synthesizing science, was rejected: it was 'theory that formed the hallmark of a discipline' (Harvey, 1969).

How far could geography as a science be identified by its theory? If existing theory was inadequate, the immediate task was to apply scientific method to the systematic aspects of the discipline to seek adequate generalizing concepts, to develop law-statements and to test them. A theoretical basis was, of course, not entirely absent: it was to be found especially in the systematic aspects of the subject. Though it had not been entirely neglected by British geographers (Smailes, 1946; Dickinson, 1947), the full possibilities of Christaller's theory of central places had not been widely appreciated. The theory of location of economic activity, with von Thünen's work as its base, was another point of attack (Chisholm, 1962). The theory of city structure and form was a third. How far could generalizations be made concerning similarities, rather than differences, in the distributions and relationships of phenomena over the earth's surface? Further, while geographers had been accustomed to describe and to interpret, the collapse of geographical determinism in the 1920s and the dying away of argument after the more recent discussion of modified determinist viewpoints in the 1950s (Martin, 1951; Spate, 1952) had left open the problem of finding a satisfactory basis for explanation. How far then could a satisfactory explanatory philosophy be identified and developed? (Harvey, 1969.)

It is unnecessary at this stage to pursue these questions further. They underlie the chapters that follow: in these chapters may be found evidence of the kinds of investigation that have been stimulated and the reader may assess for himself the success that has been attained. It should be remembered that the time has been short: the essays in this volume report on the beginning of change and on first steps.

QUANTIFICATION AND MODEL BUILDING

Mention must now be made of some of the clearer indications of the change in character and in outlook of much work in human geography. First has been the development, and the associated acceptance into teaching and research, of techniques for the more exact measurement of spatial distributions and of the relationships between different distributions. True, pioneer work in this direction in both geography and statistics may be traced back into the inter-war period, for example in the studies of location of industry and employment by Smith (1942). More recently, human geography has profited greatly from advances in statistical methods and from the more widespread teaching of statistics. The change in teaching in university departments has been a dramatic one: some, at least, of the older practical work in cartography for undergraduates has been curtailed and is now supplemented by a training in statistical techniques appropriate to the analysis of spatial patterns, for which a number of suitable textbooks now exist. In a number of university departments there are also appropriate courses at graduate level. So great has been the change that it is often said that within little more than a decade geography has passed through a 'quantitative revolution'. Through the analysis and measurement of patterns, problems central to the discipline are identified: the matching or correlation of patterns is a further need. Accessibility and centrality must be assessed. Such problems provide basic studies for the field of work that has become known as 'spatial' or 'locational analysis'.

However, the quantitative revolution has implied much more than the application to distributional problems of statistical techniques. It must also be thought of as having effected a major change in the organization and content of human geography. In this respect Haggett's *Locational Analysis in Human Geography* (1965) has undoubtedly exercised a significant influence, confirming trends that were already in progress and initiating fresh ventures. The reader was invited to organize both thought and practical study around location models concerned respectively with movement, networks, nodes, hierarchies and surfaces. As Haggett himself pointed out, the conceptual scheme which ties together these elements is derived from systems theory. The influence of systems analysis has been felt also, it may be noted, in physical geography. The operation of systems in space at different levels of scale has certainly become a major concern in human geography, and it may be that the growth of this field will open up yet new applications for the subject.

The trends which have been already indicated have been greatly assisted by the eagerness with which geographers have turned to the use of the computer: indeed, amongst social scientists, geographers have become one of the larger groups of users of computer time. The eagerness extends to both teaching and research. The development of the computer has provided opportunity and facility both to order and to analyse geographical data in new ways. Haggett (1969) has reviewed the research response of geographers to this new situation, stressing the newly gained ability to employ multivariate methods and the addition of new techniques such as trend surface analysis to the more traditional isoline methods. A most promising development has been initiated in computergraphics, already profitably applied to planning problems at national, regional and sub-regional scales (Willatts, 1971).

Further gains have been recorded in the simulation of processes, the use of computer simulation models to project images of spatial structures. Particularly important has been the use of such models in establishing and testing generalizations of urban spatial structures. But little use has yet been made of the computer for coding and assembling world-wide data or for developing models of regional growth. In reply to the question, 'What new mutations in geography will the computer environment induce?' Haggett replied '. . . though our problems may remain the traditional ones—areal differentiations, inter-regional comparison, regional analogues, spatial patterns, environmental reactions —the computer may allow us to throw those problems further forward in time from a concern with past and present geographies to those of the future'. The prospect of gaining insight into 'various desirable and undesirable geographies that might be' is indeed challenging.

Thus the computer has become a part of the everyday life of many departments of geography and first-year geography students find themselves immediately engaged in problem solving with the use of computer methods. Profitable use of the computer in both teaching and research has been slowed not by lack of enthusiasm for experiment but by shortage of funds for the training and employment of programmers and for the purchase of special equipment. In this respect, the advancement of the social sciences is slowed by the relative paucity of funds allocated for equipment purchases and for technical assistance: relatively small expenditures on these items could bring immense gains in the quality of both teaching and research. But clearly such additional resources cannot be made universally available and it is likely that a further degree of specialization between departments will emerge, with activity in advanced fields of spatial analysis concentrated at selected centres.

It will be clear from many of the essays which follow that concern with measurement, statistical method and the use of the computer, are not the only hallmarks of the recent 'revolution'. In the search for patterns, for order and for general statements, the rôle of 'models' has been greatly enhanced. Indeed it may not be unfair to characterize much of the work of the 1960s as that of a 'model based geography'. Chorley and Haggett (1967) certainly claimed that the use of models and the rôle of model building marked a significant difference between recent trends in research and those reflected in pre-existing work, and that through the use of models in the main fields of human geography a degree of communality of ideas could be identified. Recent literature in this field of activity within geography certainly suggests that the methodological isolation which was alleged to be a feature of older work in the subject is a circumstance of the past. Well apparent are the links with mathematics and physics, as well as with the development of ideas and methods in systems analysis and operational research. The degree of generality conferred by models is, of course, a main attraction: equally important is the rigour imposed by the method upon the model builder. Through the discarding of detail, models assist the identification of the primary factors influencing the phenomena under consideration: the clarity afforded by a model should enable the consequence of the past upon the present and the future to be more clearly understood (Cowan, Ireland and Fine, 1967). Much model building has centred on problems of urban life and change, where opportunities for contributing an analytical approach of value to planners in evaluating alternative policies have been especially apparent.

From a planning point of view, the value of model building as a means of describing city structures, of monitoring change and of estimating the effects of changes in urban structure or in planning policy needs no stressing. Many examples now exist of progress in this field, some of the work being carried out in specialized research units (*Regional Studies* special issue, 1969; Wilson, 1969). Interesting results are also likely to emerge from the testing of models of regional development against experience in developing countries. Indeed, it may be argued that through the use of models the problem of linking the systematic and regional aspects of the subject may be essayed in a new way: general tendencies may be tested against locationally unique situations. Certainly, a new basis may be given to the task of forecasting the future geographical shape of regions, a task in which Peter Hall's *London 2000* marked an exciting beginning, and one in which future applications of geography may prove of immense significance.

One aspect of current work remains to be mentioned: it arises especially from the increased concern with processes of spatial change. A major influence on recent work in Britain has been the Swedish geographer and social scientist, Torsten Hägerstrand. Hägerstrand's contributions, based on detailed empirical research, have been made mainly through studies of migration and of the diffusion of innovations (Hägerstrand, 1957, 1967). The theme has been expressed by Allen Pred (1967) in a postscript to Hägerstrand's *Innovation Diffusion as a Spatial Process:* 'Geographic expressions of human behavior, whether they aggregatively reflect patterns of movement or spatial distributions, must be viewed in terms of the information available to the individual decision-maker and thereby analysed in terms of the "social network" of interpersonal communications through which the information circulates'. The examination of the processes of decision making by individuals and groups, leading to the creation of new geographical patterns or to the modification of existing patterns, has become an important field of activity. Information has been sought not only on the conscious factors involved in arriving at decisions on locations but also on the conceptions of the geographical environment held by the decision makers. Thus, complementary to the search for generalization and the testing of general theories of spatial structure and location has been the emergence of a 'behavioural' geography. Its concern has included the effects of group or of institutional arrangements on the decision making process, the relevance of individual images of reality upon decisions to migrate, to change the location of a firm, or to choose an area for residence. Through the study of individually recorded 'time-budgets' more has been learned about how individuals and groups use space and generalizations have been more firmly established about patterns of regular movement within cities. Through the examination of 'mental maps' we are acquiring more information about individual and group perceptions of environment: such studies have practical as well as academic significance, for the real improvement of environment must depend upon a fuller understanding of individual appreciations of the environment—not merely upon the geographer's or the planner's appreciation. Thus the field of behavioural studies in geography is one in which important development may confidently be expected, particularly as further links are established with colleagues in other social sciences.

Reference has now been made to a number of the signs of recent change in outlook and method in human geography in Britain. The more specialized focus on the organization of spatial patterns coupled with an increased degree of conceptualization and a concern with more precise measurement are clear signs. We may recognize a tendency to organize enquiry about the study of locations rather than about the relationships between societies and the physical environment. There is an emphasis on the processes of geographical change. A search for more rigorous scientific methods and a desire to strengthen theory have been apparent. There is, in my view, no doubt that the discipline has been greatly strengthened. However, an untrue picture would be drawn if it were suggested that there has been an unanimous endorsement of all the trends that have been indicated.

There has been disquiet, for example, that in the enthusiasm for a 'spatial analysis' approach and for research at inter-disciplinary frontiers, the traditional core of the subject, the study of man-land relationships in their varied regional settings, together with its association with the 'region' as the principal organizing concept in human geography, has been neglected (Fisher, 1970). For many parts of the world, precise statistical information is either not readily available or not suitable for use in sophisticated statistical procedures. While, in the urban environments of advanced countries, soil and climate may seem remote influences, yet great cities are still dependent on the natural world and relationships with the physical environment must not be neglected, particularly in an age of concern at global environmental conditions. How far, it may be argued, is the new approach a sound one for organizing the study of the problems of 'developing' countries where the constraints on social and economic development inherent in the physical environment need an assessment that can best be provided through integrated studies? It has also been argued that the reaction against regionally organized studies has been carried too far. Partly, such a reaction was undoubtedly against a stereotyped method of regional synthesis rather than a devaluation of the regional concept itself: partly, the older form of regional geography, which rested upon a personal interpretation of the life of a region founded upon the critical assembly and selection of facts, was felt to lack the rigour of scientific method, the exactness of statement, the penetration into spatial change within the grasp of the 'new' geography.

The present 'revolution', possibly from speed and enthusiasm, may sometimes have been carried too far. It is not necessary to demolish the best of older traditions to establish the value of new, and there can be no doubt that the new approaches have added in a major way both to thought and practice. Equally, the best of the regional syntheses, employing historical methods of enquiry, qualities of critical assembly of data, informed skill in the formulation and discussion of ideas, a disciplined interpretation of trends, clarity in literary and carto-graphical presentation, make lasting contributions to knowledge of the world in which we live and to the forces of change. It is also necessary to guard against the tendency that sometimes appears within the subject to denigrate the 'descriptive' rôle of the geographer and to undervalue the intellectual problems involved in providing those descriptions of the varied patterns of life and activity over the earth's surface that society expects its geographers to provide. Undoubtedly, the use of the new methods will in time enable us to provide more accurate and more deeply informative descriptions. At the present time, a major problem for research is to employ the new methods to link analyses of present spatial patterns with analyses of changes in patterns through time. It is a difficult task: it is necessary to work both in the time dimension and in the spatial dimension. We must examine processes operating through the years and assess their relevance for changes in areal patterns of social and economic activities, for distances, movements and inter-connections between places.

Happily, there are many signs that the application of improved methods of enquiry is bringing fresh life to old problems: that the process of testing new generalizations is being carried on in areas far removed in character as well as in distance from those of the original studies. There is optimism too that the use of spatial analytic procedures applied to 'regions' will produce regional studies that, while not lacking the distinguished character of their classical predecessors, will have enhanced value as a basis for regional and environmental planning. Possible lines for a new relationship between the social science and the physical aspects of geography have been sketched (Chorley, 1971). Even more difficult to attain, perhaps, may be a return to working on a world scale. Mackinder argued that environmental planning on a world scale was the ultimate goal of geographical study, and his words strike a new relevance in our age of international concern with environmental problems.

TWO VIEWS OF CHANGES IN GEOGRAPHY

One way of bringing home the nature of the change that has been discussed, particularly in its impact upon research activity, is to compare two assessments of research tasks and needs. The first was made at a time when the new trends had hardly begun to make themselves felt; Stamp (1957) called his review an 'agenda for the future'. The second and more recent review of research tasks was made by Chisholm (1971a, b), as Chairman of the Human Geography Committee of the Social Science Research Council. It would be interesting, incidentally, to make a similar comparison for geography in the United States of America between the review made in 1954 for the Association of American Geographers entitled *American Geography: Inventory and Prospect* (James and Jones, 1954), and the recent report of the geography panel of the Behavioral and Social Sciences Survey (Taaffe, 1970), and to consider how far the changes in the United Kingdom and in the United States have proceeded along similar lines and how far there have been common influences.

For Stamp, the scientific method was one based on exhaustive survey and collection of data followed by systematic analysis. The study of land use, his own personal concern, involved inter-disciplinary work, too, with the geologist, botanist, soil surveyor and farm economist. It was, he argued, 'in the cartographical representation of data that the unique contribution of the geographer' lay. Once the data were organized in maps, the work of correlation and interpretation became possible: new questions were thrown up for research. He was 'a little alarmed by the view that the geographer must add to his training a considerable knowledge of statistics and statistical method, of theoretical economics and of modern sociology'. And so his first appeal was for a major effort to be applied to uniform mapping of data—especially to complete the mapping on the world scale of population and land resources. He called for co-operation in the production of standardized population maps to reveal the principal features of world population change. Similarly, completion in a uniform way of the World Land Use Survey was an important task. Stamp referred to differences of emphasis in the International Geographical Union Commission on World Land Use between those who sought to perfect the tools to be used and those, including himself, who were convinced that 'the time is ripe for solid work to be done with the tools we already have'.

Turning to the fields which awaited attention at home, Stamp referred again to the need for survey: there was a large amount of conscientious, systematic mapping to be undertaken. Particularly needed was a detailed survey of the British coasts with possibilities for land reclamation in mind; a geographical survey of vegetation was overdue. His experience as a member of the Royal Commission on Common Land had revealed the lack of exact information on the distribution of commons and led him to argue the case for maps showing land ownership and the boundaries of farm units. Stamp went on to consider the need for studies of building materials and for cartographic work in economic geography before concluding on the theme of the wide and largely untapped market that lay open for good geographical writing.

Progress has, of course, been made on some at least of the items in Stamp's agenda. Examples that spring to mind are Howe's *National Atlas of Disease Mortality* (1963) and the land use and vegetation mapping undertaken by Miss Alice Coleman's Second Land Utilization Survey of Great Britain. Outside Britain, the work of land use mapping has been carried on by the World Land Use Survey Commission of the International Geographical Union, though not perhaps in quite the way Stamp had in mind. Stamp would certainly have regarded the *Atlas of London* (Jones and Sinclair, 1968) as an important contribution to the mapping of the population and social characteristics of a great city region.

Strict comparison between Stamp's agenda and Chisholm's statement of 'Priority research areas in human geography' (Chisholm, 1971a and b), is, of course, not possible. Chisholm was writing from a viewpoint as Chairman of the Human Geography Committee of the Social Science Research Council. Furthermore, the Human Geography Committee of SSRC was looking specifically for fields of research activity that were seen to be important but which had not received so much attention from geographers as might have been expected. Nevertheless, setting the two groups of suggestions, as it were, side by side, it is possible to detect a change in tone and, in the later suggestions, a new kind of spirit at work.

Seven fields were named. These were perception studies, the measurement of space perception and space preferences; the simulation of spatial systems by means of simulation models; the forecasting of future spatial environments; regional taxonomy, the efficient division of space into operational units for particular purposes, and especially the application of statistical procedures to this task; the need in an age now aroused to problems of pollution and conservation for the determination and measurement of environmental standards; the spatial aspects of population growth and change; and, lastly, the study of the processes of social and economic change, not only to identify constraints to development but also to seek out fruitful courses of action.

Clearly, in one or two of these fields, for example, population growth and change, there is a degree of similarity with items on Stamp's agenda. However, an emphasis on statistical rather than on cartographic procedures is evident: there is reference to new fields of work such as perception studies; the study of process looms larger than the carrying out of surveys. Most important, perhaps, is the implicit rejection of the earlier view of the synthetic rôle of geography, reliant on other disciplines, and its replacement by a view of geography as a highly disciplined study in itself, equipped with techniques other than cartographic, and working in relation with other disciplines.

The discussion on Chisholm's suggestions was carried further by a Working Party of the Institute of British Geographers (Coppock, 1971). The Working Party commented on the omission of reference to time and place, making clear their view that many of the proposals were equally appropriate in the past and in the present, in the United Kingdom and in other lands. They also gave much greater emphasis to the need to encourage the employment by geographers of the computer and of spatial statistics. In addition to stressing the desirability of interdisciplinary co-operation, they attempted a rather different method of organizing the topics, employing three heads, namely: behavioural studies, simulation studies and spatial statistics.

Thus the change of tone becomes still more evident. True, other voices have expressed the view that the recent suggestions neglect to emphasize the contribution that geographical studies should increasingly be making in the examination of the environmental constraints to development in the countries of the Third World. Attention has also been drawn to the continuing importance, especially for developing countries, of fact-finding surveys. It may be, however, that we are now entering a phase in which survey data will be gained increasingly from remote sensing, using aircraft or earth satellites. This point is also made in the recent survey of research tasks made in the United States of America (Taaffe, 1970). If well handled, our powers to gather data concerning, let us say, land use, urban change, soil or mineral resources, will rapidly increase. If this is so, the need will become apparent for a closer relationship between departments of human geography and those departments and institutions concerned with the technical aspects of survey and information gathering by satellites and other means. The possibilities for a fuller understanding of the human geography of the world and for the fruitful application of knowledge and skill in the amelioration of major human problems appear to be immense. Probably a combined operation between disciplines is needed to speed progress in this direction and a new organizational framework may be necessary.

CONCLUDING REMARKS

Little emphasis need be given in this Introduction to the strength of the applied aspects of work by British geographers, for this is fully treated in the contributions from House and Manners in particular. Though it should be noted that there exists a widespread feeling amongst geographers that, despite achievements such as those noted by our contributors, the resources of geography and of geographers are still under-employed in the study of both national and international problems and in discussions leading to the formation of public policy. True, many geographers are professionally employed in national and local government service, but, in an age in which communities and governments are becoming increasingly concerned with the quality of environment and with the relevant problems of planning geographical distributions, it is likely that the potential contribution to be gained from involving geographers in closer participation has not yet been fully realized. This may be due, in part, as House suggests, to a failure on the part of administrators to realize the significance of problems expressed in spatial terms.

This Introduction would be incomplete if it failed to refer to the high international standing of British geographers at the present time. For this there are many reasons. The work of Sir Dudley Stamp as President of the International Geographical Union must not be over-looked: indeed, on his death British geographers combined to produce a volume of tribute that stands in its own right as an important review of the recent progress of research in the fields of land use, resource and environmental analysis (Institute of British Geographers 1968). The 20th International Congress held in Great Britain in 1964 brought geographers from overseas into close contact with the activities of university and government centres of geographical research in all parts of the country. British geography was widely seen to be vigorously engaged in a period of reconsidering old ideas, and absorbing new concepts and techniques. British geographers have continued to be active as members of commissions of the International Geographical Union. The example of the Anglo-Polish seminars in stimulating international discussion of research needs and techniques, a series which began under the sponsorship of the Institute of British Geo-graphers in 1959, has been followed by practical proposals for Indo-British, Anglo-Rumanian, Anglo-German and Anglo-Hungarian seminars. Further arrangements are under discussion. The contribu-tions made by the geographical societies of Great Britain in the progress of the last fifteen years is a theme worthy of separate discussion. A large number of British geographers has moved overseas to univer-sities in the countries of the Commonwealth and to the United States, carrying with them the new spirit of activity. Perhaps the most important of all, the record of publication both of empirical findings and of work embodying new ideas is the best evidence of the extent to which British geographers are joining and, in a number of fields, leading research discussion and activity at the international level.

In short, the essays in this volume reflect recent work in a subject which has been passing through a phase of critical re-appraisal and vigorous development. On the foundations laid during this phase, new structures are being built in the theory of geography and in the testing of theory, and new applications are being opened for the application of findings to the improvement of the environment in many lands.

REFERENCES

Board, C., Chorley, R. J., Haggett, P. and Stoddart, D. R. (1969—) *Progress in Geography*, Arnold.

Bunge, W. (1962) 'Theoretical geography', *Lund Studies in Geography*, Series C, No.1

Chisholm, M. (1962) *Rural Settlement and Land Use: an essay in location*, Hutchinson.

Chisholm, M. (1971a) *Research in Human Geography*, A Social Science Research Council Review, Heinemann.

Chisholm, M. (1971b) 'Priority research areas in human geography', SSRC *Newsletter*, **11**, March 1971, 15–16.

Chorley, R. J. (1971) 'The rôle and relations of physical geography', in *Progress in Geography*, **3.**

Chorley, R. J. and Haggett, P. (Eds.) (1967) *Models in Geography*, Methuen.

Coppock, J. T. (1971) 'Priority research areas in human geography: IBG Working Party Report', *Area*, **3**, 100–103.

Cowan, P., Ireland, J. and Fine, D. (1967) 'Approaches to urban model building', *Regional Studies*, **1**, 163–172.

Dickinson, R. E. (1947) *City, Region and Regionalism*, Routledge and Kegan Paul.

Edwards, K. C. (1967) 'The broadening vista', *Geography*, **52**, 245–259.

Fisher, C. A. (1970) 'Whither regional geography?', *Geography*, **55**, 373–389.

Hägerstrand, T. (1967) *Innovation Diffusion as a Spatial Process*, University of Chicago Press.

Hägerstrand, T. (1957) 'Migration and area', in Hannerberg, D., Hägerstrand, T. and Odering, B. (Eds.) 'Migration in Sweden', *Lund Studies in Geography*, Series B, No. 13.

Haggett, P. (1965) *Locational Analysis in Human Geography*, Arnold.

Haggett, P. (1969) 'On geographical research in a computer environment', *Geographical Journal*, **135**, 497–507.

Hall, P. (1963) *London 2000*, Faber and Faber.

Hartshorne, R. (1939) 'The nature of geography', *Annals of the Association of American Geographers*, XXIX, 3 and 4, Sept. and Dec., later issued as *The Nature of Geography*.

Harvey, D. (1969) *Explanation in Geography*, Arnold.

Howe, G. M. (1963) *National Atlas of Disease Mortality in the United Kingdom*, Nelson; revised edition, 1970.

Institute of British Geographers (1968) *Land Use and Resources; Studies in Applied Georgaphy*, Special Publication No. 1.

James, P. E. and Jones, C. F. (1954) *American Geography, Inventory and Prospect*, Syracuse University Press.

Jones, E. and Sinclair, D. J. (1968) *Atlas of London*, Pergamon.

Mackinder, H. J. (1935) 'Progress of geography in the field and in the study during the reign of His Majesty King George the Fifth', *Geographical Journal*, LXXXVI, July 1935.

Martin, A. F. (1951) 'The necessity for determinism: a metaphysical problem

INTRODUCTION 17

confronting geographers', *Transactions of the Institute of British Geographers*, **17**, 1–11.

Pred, A. (1967) Postscript to Hägerstrand, T., *Innovation Diffusion as a Spatial Process*, University of Chicago Press.

Regional Studies (1969) Special issue: 'Urban and regional models in British planning research', **3**, No. 3, Dec. 1969.

Schaefer, F. K. (1953) 'Exceptionalism in geography: a methodological examination', *Annals of the Association of American Geographers*, **43**, 226–249.

Smailes, A. E. (1946) 'On the urban mesh of England and Wales', *Transactions of the Institute of British Geographers*, **11**, 85–101.

Smith, W. (1942) *The Distribution of Population and the Location of Industry on Merseyside*, University Press of Liverpool.

Spate, O. H. K. (1952) 'Toynbee and Huntington: a study in determinism', *Geographical Journal*, **118**, 406–424.

Stamp, L. D. (1957) 'Geographical agenda: a review of some tasks awaiting geographical attention', *Transactions of the Institute of British Geographers*, **23**, 1–17.

Taaffe, E. J. (Ed.) (1970) *Geography*, The Behavioral and Social Sciences Survey, Prentice-Hall.

Willatts, E. C. (1971) 'Planning and geography in the last three decades', *Geographical Journal*, **137**, 311–338.

Wilson, A. G. (1969) 'Research for regional planning', *Regional Studies*, **3**, 3–14.

2 Geographical studies of economic development with special reference to agriculture

DAVID GRIGG

Interest in economic development is recent, dating mainly from the end of the Second World War. There are two major problems: by what means are the underdeveloped nations to become more prosperous; and how and why did the present rich industrialized nations achieve their transformation? At first these problems were thought to be mainly the concern of economists, but there has been growing recognition—not least among economists themselves—that economic development involves a radical transformation of attitudes and institutions. Thus anthropologists, sociologists and political scientists have all increasingly contributed to the study of economic development, which, it is clear, can hardly be regarded as a well defined discipline, but rather a group of problems to which solutions can be offered by a variety of disciplines.

In a sense geographers, concerned with differences between places, have always been interested in economic development. Indeed conventional regional geography, now sadly in disfavour with so many geographers, has always provided the background information upon which any sensible plan for development must be based, and against which any model of economic development must be tested (Fisher, C. A., 1970; McLoughlin, 1966). But the interest of geographers in economic development in a narrower sense is much more recent, dating from the mid-1950s. Since then an increasing proportion of the work of geographers has become orientated to problems of development. A number of text-books on economic development has been written (Lacoste, 1965; Fryer, 1965, 1970; Stamp, 1960a; Hodder, 1968; Chatterjee, 1968b; Mountjoy, 1969; Grigg, 1970; Clarke, J. I., 1971), while inaugural lectures and presidential addresses exhort geographers to concern themselves with these problems. Most important, an increasing number of geographers is involved in actual work in planning and advising in underdeveloped countries (Steel, 1967; Fisher, C. A., 1965; Keeble, 1967; Fisher, W. B., 1968; Hinderink, 1969; Hoy, 1968; Hunter, 1961a; Lacoste, 1962; O'Connor, 1969, 1971; Oguntoyinbo, 1968; Riabchikov, 1962; Wilmet, 1967; Bowen-Jones, Dewdney and Fisher, W. B., 1961; Chung, 1968; Chang, S. D., 1966; Chapman, 1969; Guzman, 1960; Ginsburg, 1953, 1969; Learmonth, 1964; Pico, 1968; Farmer, 1957, 1971). This article is concerned primarily with works by geographers on the problems of economic development, and in particular upon agricultural development; the literature on industrialization in the underdeveloped countries by geographers is meagre, and is only incidentally touched upon here.

THE TYPOLOGY OF ECONOMIC DEVELOPMENT

Although there is a vast literature in the field of economic development there have been few attempts to define underdevelopment or to create a typology. The most commonly used Index is *per caput* income, obtained by dividing the value of all the goods and services produced in a country in a year by the total population. There are however serious objections to this procedure (Grigg, 1970; Ginsburg, 1957, 1961, 1967; Hartshorne, 1959; Fryer, 1958). Firstly national income statistics are not available for many countries and have to be estimated: in particular, Socialist countries do not record the value of services in computing their Gross Domestic Product. Secondly, the figures have to be converted to a uniform currency for comparative purposes. The US dollar is most commonly used, but there is the difficult problem of exchange rates. Thirdly, in many underdeveloped countries many goods and services do not enter the market and are not priced and so national income figures are understated in comparison with countries which have no subsistence production. Fourthly, most underdeveloped countries have a much higher proportion of children in the total population and thus a smaller labour force (Wagner, 1960; O'Connor, 1963).

Figure 2.1 demonstrates an apparently marked difference between the advanced countries of North West Europe, North America and Australasia, and the rest of the world. However, there is no sharp gap; the countries of the world are arrayed upon a continuum (Berry, 1960, 1961a; Hustich, 1968). Most geographers have recognized an intermediate group of semi-developed nations which includes eastern and southern Europe, Russia, the Republic of South Africa, Israel, Cuba, Mexico, Venezuela, Argentina, Uruguay, Chile and Japan.

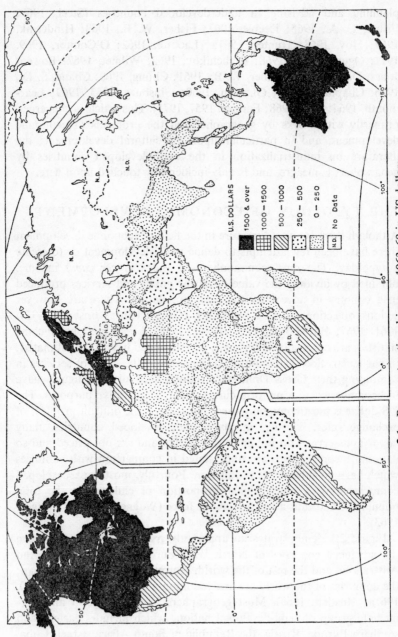

FIGURE 2.1   Per caput national income 1963–68 in US dollars

U.S. DOLLARS

1500 & over

1000 – 1500

500 – 1000

250 – 500

0 – 250

N.D.   No Data

Although *per caput* income is possibly the best single index of the level of development, there is a wide range of other criteria of underdevelopment which must be briefly noted. Underdeveloped countries are predominantly agricultural both in occupational structure and income distribution (Grigg, 1970; Fryer, 1958; Ginsburg, 1961) and thus they remain mainly rural, although their *rate* of urbanization is often high. Compared with developed countries they have high crude death rates, although these have been falling since the 1930s and especially since 1945. Infant mortality rates remain markedly higher than in the developed nations, and it has been argued that this is one of the best indicators of development (Lacoste, 1965; Mountjoy, 1969; Wrigley, 1969; Stockwell, 1960). Birth rates have remained high, thus giving a high rate of population increase. One consequence of this is that children under 15 years make up more than 40% of the population in most underdeveloped countries (Fryer, 1958; Mountjoy, 1969; Stockwell, 1966). Both young and old have inadequate diets, both in quality and quantity; one consequence of this is the prevalence of disease (see below pp. 22–9) (Lacoste, 1965; Grigg, 1970; Buchanan, 1964).

Almost by definition underdeveloped countries have a small proportion of their population engaged in manufacturing industry and little commercial energy is used *per caput* (Ginsburg, 1961; Fryer, 1958; Grigg, 1970; Guyol, 1960); indeed much production remains on a subsistence level. Thus underdeveloped nations characteristically import manufactured goods, and also because of the inefficiency of their agriculture, food grains. They export mainly primary goods, which find their markets chiefly in Western Europe or North America. In contrast the developed countries trade mainly with each other (Buchanan, 1964; Lacoste, 1965; Chatterjee, 1968a; Beguin, 1963). Criteria such as those above, and others such as literacy (Kamerschen, 1968), can be measured and thus the data may be subjected to statistical analysis (Berry, 1960, 1961a; El-Kammash, 1963; Weller and Sly, 1969; Bennett, 1951) or, equally illuminating, mapped (Leszczycki, 1968; Ginsburg, 1961). The underdeveloped countries however exhibit other criteria which can be less easily measured. It has been argued, for example, that these countries have unusually large tertiary sectors of low productivity, made up of petty traders and superfluous administrators (Lacoste, 1965). Frequently the economy is in a subordinate position to an overseas country or company, a result of colonialism or neo-imperialism (Buchanan, 1968; Lacoste, 1965). Within the underdeveloped countries the contrast between the privileged few and the impoverished majority is alarmingly large and far greater than similar contrasts in developed countries. Thus for example, the richest tenth of the population of the United States have 27% of the national wealth, but in Colombia 40% of the national wealth is held by 2·6% of the population, whilst in Gabon 56% of the national wealth is in the hands of 1% of the population (Lacoste, 1965; Buchanan, 1968). In many underdeveloped countries there is a state of chronic under-employment and unemployment both in the towns and the country, for the rate of population increase in the last thirty years has greatly exceeded the rate of increase in available jobs.

Although *most* of the underdeveloped countries exhibit *most* of the characteristics noted above, there is no simple division between developed and underdeveloped. There is indeed a great danger that it will be assumed that the underdeveloped countries make up a mono-lithic bloc, each with identical problems; and that one single ideal development policy can be devised which will solve the problems of them all. It needs to be emphasized that there are great differences between different parts of the underdeveloped world. Latin America, for example, stands above Africa and Asia on the ladder of develop-ment. Yet it is possible to construct a very convincing typology of development, for Latin America alone, which has five classes (Vekemans and Segundo, 1963), whilst Lacoste has constructed an informative five-class typology of the underdeveloped world as a whole (Lacoste, 1964).

Thus one of the most important tasks for geographers in their study of economic development is to emphasize the differences between the countries of the Third World—in cultural background, in resources, in population and in agricultural potential. In short what is needed are works of regional geography orientated to the problems of develop-ment. At a time when regional geography is in disfavour amongst geographers themselves, it is as well to emphasize that the problems of development are most likely to be solved by people in specific places devising specific plans for specific problems (Lacoste, 1965; Blaut, 1967; Moral, 1967; Monbeig, 1967; Fisher, C. A., 1959, 1965; Baker, S., 1966; Dresch, 1967).

Hunger and disease

Two of the most widely discussed characteristics of underdevelopment are hunger and disease, which are not only a result of underdevelopment but also a factor restraining growth. Nutritionists distinguish between undernutrition and malnutrition; the former leads to loss of bodyweight and a reduced capacity to work, whilst the latter, a deficiency in the quality of food intake, causes specific diseases such as beri-beri and kwashiorkor. Although hunger and malnutrition may appear obvious, it is extremely difficult to measure the amount of food available in a country and the manner in which it is distributed. Even more controversial are the minimum requirements of food necessary to avoid undernutrition and malnutrition (Sukhatme, 1961; FAO, 1963; Clark, 1970).

FAO publish annually the *per caput* daily food supplies available in a wide range of countries. These data are based on food balance sheets which compute the total output for the year, allow for imports, exports, stocks and wastage, and are converted into calories. The method for calculating these figures has been much criticized (Farmer, 1969a; Clark, 1970; Bennett, 1954, 1963). However there is little reason to doubt that there is a very marked difference between the *per caput* daily calorie supply in the developed and the underdeveloped countries (Figure 2.2). None of those countries regarded as developed or semi-developed have supplies below 2,600 calories, whereas in contrast most of the underdeveloped countries have below 2,200 calories. However, it should be noted that some underdeveloped countries—including Brazil, Jordan and Egypt—have figures of over 2,600 calories.

However, these data do not demonstrate the incidence of under-nutrition or malnutrition. To arrive at this the minimum daily requirements must be calculated. This has been done by FAO on a regional basis, taking into account variations in climate, age, sex and average bodyweight. In Figure 2.3 supplies are shown as a percentage of minimum requirements. This demonstrates that nowhere in the developed or semi-developed world do supplies fail to meet requirements. Supplies appear to be adequate—or very nearly adequate—in Brazil, Paraguay, Costa Rica, Surinam, Rhodesia, Zambia, Madagascar, Malaysia, Cambodia, Korea, Pakistan, Turkey, the countries bordering the east Mediterranean, and a few countries in West Africa. In short, food deficits are not characteristic of all under-developed countries. It should be further noted that some writers think FAO's minimum requirements are too high (Clarke, 1970).

The existence of malnutrition is even more difficult to estimate. Figure 2.4 shows the proportion of calorie intake derived from cereals, roots and sugar; the higher the figure, the lower the proportion derived from protein-rich foods such as vegetables and animal products (Bennett, 1941). Again there is a clear difference between developed

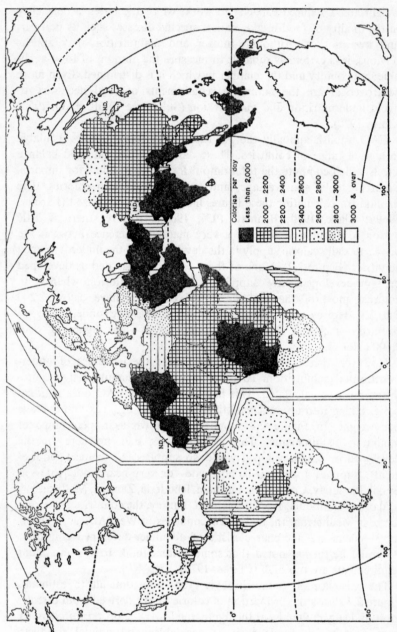

FIGURE 2.2 Daily supply of calories, per caput

Calories per day

- Less than 2,000
- 2000 – 2200
- 2200 – 2400
- 2400 – 2600
- 2600 – 2800
- 2800 – 3000
- 3000 & over

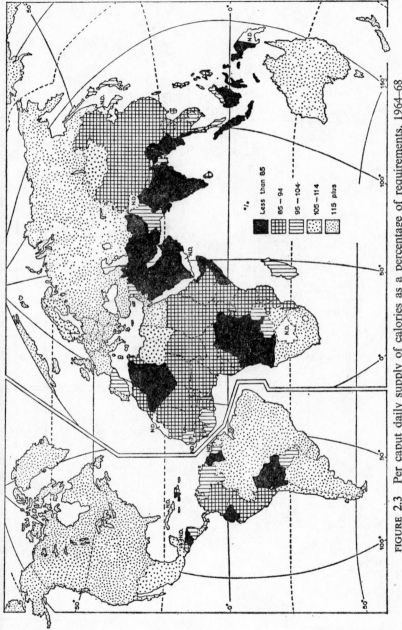

FIGURE 2.3 Per caput daily supply of calories as a percentage of requirements, 1964–68

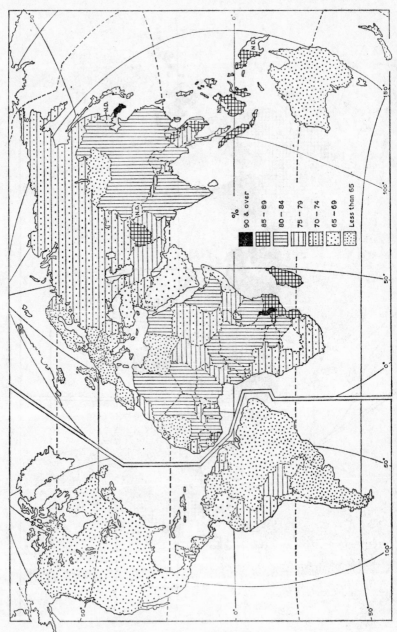

FIGURE 2.4 Calories derived from cereals, potatoes and sugar as a percentage of total calorie intake 1964-68

and underdeveloped countries. In much of Africa and Asia cereals, roots and sugar provide more than 80% of the calorie intake, a figure FAO experts regard as critical. A more direct measure of protein intake is shown in Figure 2.5. Minimum requirements have been variously put at 89 grammes per day, 65 grammes, and as low as 45 grammes (Carpenter, 1969; Clark, 1970; Stamp, 1965). It must be emphasized that the FAO data used in Figures 2.2 to 2.5 have been subject to much criticism. Although the maps show an indisputable difference in the quantity and quality of diets, it is less easy to argue, as FAO have done, that 20% of the population of the underdeveloped world suffer from undernutrition and 60% from malnutrition (FAO, 1963). The data show only whether a nation's food total balances with the estimated minimum requirements, not how many people are hungry. They do not indicate what proportion of the population is under-nourished or malnourished, or if hunger is confined to particular regions. There is, however, some local evidence on these points.

A feature of the West African savannas, and also Indonesia, is the hungry season before the harvest: food supplies are thus at their lowest at the very time when most physical effort is necessary (Hunter, 1967; Joosten, 1962). Most subsistence communities are subject to occasional harvest failure, for a variety of reasons. Thus for example harvest failures in Tanzania have been caused by drought, flood and locusts (Brooke, 1967). Where communications are poor—which is true of most of the underdeveloped world—it is possible to have food surpluses in one region and famine in another. This is particularly true of India (Chakravarti, 1970; Krishnan, 1960; Chatterjee, 1952; Kuriyan, 1952; Chaturvedi, 1962) but is also found in other countries (Gould and Sparks, 1969; Udo, 1971). Just as hunger periods are not uniformly distributed throughout the country, so different classes are subject to differential impact. The most vulnerable are the urban poor, who cannot buy food when prices rise in times of scarcity, landless labourers, and small farmers who grow no cash crops and thus cannot buy food when their harvest fails (Joosten, 1962; Schwartzberg, 1963).

The prevalence of disease

It has already been noted that malnutrition causes disease in the under-developed world. Infectious diseases are also more common in the underdeveloped countries. A poor nation cannot afford the elaborate systems of water supply, sanitation measures, hospitals, doctors and cheap drugs which have reduced the death rate in the advanced countries. Further, whilst the populations of underdeveloped countries

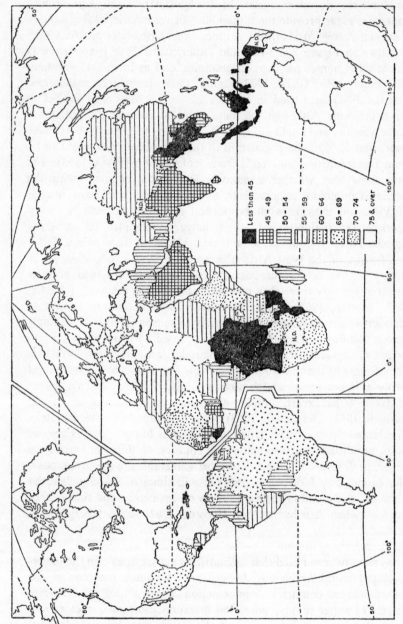

FIGURE 2.5   Daily supply of total protein (grammes)

suffer from the illnesses which are found in the developed countries, such as measles, smallpox and pneumonia, there is a number of diseases peculiar to the tropics and particularly the humid tropics (Stamp, 1964). There are, however, several diseases which are commonly thought to be tropical, such as malaria and leprosy, which formerly had a much wider range (Hutt, 1967; Prothero, 1965). Although naturally most attention has been focussed upon the diseases which kill, there are several such as malaria, ankylostomiasis (hookworm) and trachoma, which cause almost permanent debility and affect the working ability of the agricultural population (Stamp, 1965). The distribution and ecology of disease forms an interesting if neglected feature of the human geography of the Third World; the relationship of disease patterns to environments often gives an important key to the eradication of these diseases (May, 1958, 1961; Hunter, 1966; Learmonth, 1957, 1958, 1959, 1961; Prothero, 1962, 1965; Fonaroff, 1968).

REGIONAL DIFFERENCES IN ECONOMIC DEVELOPMENT WITHIN COUNTRIES

Economic development is not uniformly distributed within either developed or underdeveloped countries. On the contrary, certain regions have much of the economic activity and are growing more rapidly than the less developed and sparsely populated regions. Further, the gap between the developed *regions* and the underdeveloped is increasing, just as the gap between the developed and the underdeveloped *countries* is increasing (Myrdal, 1957; Patel, 1964). In the last two decades a number of geographers and economists have tried to delimit regions of differing levels of economic development in the advanced countries (Lewis, 1968; Logan, 1970; Thompson, Sufrin, Gould *et al.*, 1962; Hampton, 1968; Ray, 1968; Berry, 1965; Hartshorn, 1971; Megee, 1965). They have demonstrated a remarkable concentration of economic activity in limited parts of the countries concerned. Thus for example 70% of the United States manufacturing output is produced in the North East and Great Lakes region on 7% of total land area (Ullman, 1958) whilst in the Soviet Union, in spite of a policy encouraging industrial location in the east, 70% of the manufacturing employment is still in the Moscow-Ukraine-Urals triangle (Lonsdale and Thompson, 1960). The difference between the north and south of Italy is perhaps the classic case of the income inequalities which arise from such concentrations (Rodgers, 1960). Such regional income inequalities are not confined to the developed world. Indeed they are even more marked in underdeveloped countries. In Peru, Lima and Callao have a fifth of the country's population but two-thirds of its industrial employment (Smith, C. T., 1968), whilst in Brazil the South has a third of the country's population but generates half the national income (Baer, 1964). A growing number of studies is being made by geographers which demonstrates the very marked concentration of economic activity within underdeveloped countries. East Africa and India have received particular attention (Batalla, 1965; Denis, 1965; Dutt and Maikap, 1969; Fair, 1963; Hirsch, 1967; Horton, McConnell and Tirtha, 1970; O'Connor, 1963; Odell, 1967; Safier, 1969; Schwartzberg, 1962; Smith, C. T., 1968; Yadav and Prasad, 1966; Forde, 1967; Hartley and Norris, 1969).

The interest in regional income inequalities in advanced countries has arisen because certain areas have lower standards of living. In the present political climate of Western Europe this is unacceptable and the purpose of economic regionalization is to identify areas of poverty —generally old industrial regions or rural areas—so that national policy may be modified to improve their condition. In underdeveloped countries the identification of growth regions has a different purpose.

Models of regional economic development
Until recently few theories of economic development were concerned with regional differences within a state. However, since the early 1950s several economists have discussed aspects of regional development. In general they have concluded that economic growth is likely to be most rapid in one part of the country and that this will be both to the disadvantage of and at the expense of the peripheral regions beyond this core. Further, some writers have argued from this that any attempts to distribute growth more evenly over the country will hamper the national rate of growth (Myrdal, 1957; Hirschman, 1958; Perroux, 1955; Prebisch, 1959; Keeble, 1967; Friedmann, 1963; Tolosa and Reiner, 1970; Fair, 1965; Jansen, 1970).

The ideas of Myrdal, Perroux and Prebisch have a distinct family resemblance but Myrdal's arguments are perhaps the most convincing. He believed that a growth region would develop initially because it had easy access to natural resources or good transport facilities; it would grow more rapidly than the surrounding areas even after the initial location factors had become inoperative, because of internal and external economies, which would constantly attract new industries. This growth would have disadvantages for the surrounding regions which Myrdal called the 'backwash' effect. The growth region would attract migrants, who would tend to be young, progressive and skilled. The greater profitability of the growth region's industries would also attract capital, whilst free trade and improved communications within the country would allow the growth region's manufactured products to undercut established industries in the peripheral regions. All three factors would not only enhance the growth region but act to the disadvantage of the surrounding regions.

Myrdal described his hypothesis as one of 'circular and cumulative causation'; instead of an equilibrium system where the factors of production would tend towards an even distribution throughout the country, the growth region accumulates more and more advantages whilst in contrast the surrounding regions suffer from an accumulation of disadvantages. As the young and able migrate, so there is less labour to attract industrialists; the outflow of capital means less provision of education, health services, and transport facilities; and thus there is less to attract migrants or industry, and more incentive to emigrate.

Such an hypothesis helps to explain—or at least describe—why economic development is concentrated in a few regions. Myrdal also envisaged, in a later stage of economic development, what he called 'spread effects', where some of the advantages of the growth regions stimulate expansion in the lagging surrounding regions; thus for example by forming a market for agricultural produce or by encouraging industrial development around raw material sites. Growth could also get under way in the lagging regions when the growth region had grown to such a size that diseconomies of scale set in, when long established capital equipment became obsolescent and was not replaced, and when high wages in the growth region allowed peripheral industries to undercut. But for the most part Myrdal argued that once an initial advantage is established, a growth region retains its lead to the disadvantage of the peripheral regions unless the State intervenes to redistribute industry and bolster incomes; this in fact has become increasingly the policy adopted in Western Europe.

Myrdal's theory has obvious implications for policy in underdeveloped countries; if it is true that certain regions will expand at the expense of other regions then investment should be concentrated on existing growth regions rather than being dispersed throughout the country; though this may be politically difficult to implement.

URBANIZATION, MIGRATION AND
INDUSTRIALIZATION

The relationships between urbanization, industrialization and migration in the early stages of economic development in Western Europe are, in broad outline, well understood. The industrial revolution was characterized by the large scale use of coal, which was costly to move, and the introduction of the factory system; both required the concentration of the population into small areas chiefly on the coalfields. In the early nineteenth century no country had a high proportion of its population living in towns. As industrialization spread from England to Western Europe and the eastern United States there was increasing urbanization. Thus in 1801 England and Wales had between a quarter and a third of its population living in towns; by 1851 the ratio was 50%, by 1910 78%. It has not changed much since (Law, 1967). In Europe, as in England, there was an undoubted relationship between industrialization and urbanization, as town dwellers became an increasing proportion of the population, and urban populations grew more rapidly than rural populations. The latter however continued to increase until economic development was well advanced; the first absolute decline of the rural population in England and Wales came in 1861, of Belgium in 1910 and Sweden in 1920 (Davis, 1969). Although urban growth has continued in the developed countries to the present day, the rate of urbanization is now much slower (Davis, 1960).

The early stages of economic development in Western Europe were accompanied by an increase in the total population, but urban populations grew more rapidly than rural populations and it is consequently believed that migration was the main factor in accounting for urban growth. In the new industrial cities death rates were higher than in rural areas; birth rates are believed to have been somewhat lower (Smith, W., 1953). Yet in spite of these unfavourable demographic conditions the towns afforded greater economic opportunities than the country and there was a constant stream of migration from the country to the towns; the 'pull' of the cities was greater than the 'push' of the country in causing migration (Hoselitz, 1962). At first migration was predominantly short distance, and the growing cities depended upon migrants from surrounding areas, but later in the nineteenth century long-distance migration became increasingly important (Ravenstein, 1885; Smith, C. T., 1951; Darby, 1943; Osborne, 1964; Smith, W., 1953). Whilst this pattern of migration is generally accepted, some important qualifications should be made. Not all writers are convinced that migration was of greater importance than natural increase in the formation of the northern industrial cities in Britain (Deane and Cole, 1962) whilst some work on the demographic history of the Western European coalfield areas casts doubt on the validity of the assumed rural/urban differences in fertility and mortality (Wrigley, 1961).

One of the characteristic features of the nineteenth century was the more rapid growth of the larger cities compared with the smaller towns. (Table 1). This trend has continued into the twentieth century. In the 1920s, 2·8% of the world's population lived in cities of more than one million, in the 1940s 4·0% and in the early 1960s 7·0% (Linton, 1958; Mountjoy, 1968).

Until the 1920s both urban growth and urbanization were characteristic primarily of the developed world. Since then urban *growth* has progressed rapidly in the less developed world (Table 2).

TABLE 1 **The urban population of England and Wales, 1801–1911**
(% of all urban population in each size category of town)

	Over 100,000	100,000 to 50,000	50,000 to 20,000	20,000 to 10,000	10,000 to 2,500
1801	32·7	10·3	14·1	13·8	29·1
1851	46·0	10·7	13·0	11·9	18·4
1911	55·5	10·1	13·2	10·0	11·2

SOURCE: Law, 1967, p. 141

By 1960 half the world's urban population was in Africa, Asia and Latin America. Although the urban population of the developed world has continued to increase, only the Soviet Union has matched the *rate* of increase in the less developed world (Table 2). Nor are the relationships between urbanization and industrialization the same as in nineteenth-century Europe.

Thus, although there has been very rapid urban growth in the under-developed world, most of these countries still have a low level of urbanization. Despite city growth the proportion of the population in towns has not radically increased, and indeed in some countries such as Thailand and Turkey, the urban ratio has remained constant over a long period (Brice, 1954; Sternstein, 1965). This, of course, is because the rural population has continued to increase; as yet there are few signs of slackening in the rate of rural population increase, and

TABLE 2   World urban growth 1920–60
(millions)

Region	1920	1930	1940	1950	1960	% increase 1920–60
Europe	104	123	140	147	173	66
North America	43	58	64	83	112	160
Oceania	3	3	4	5	8	166
Soviet Union	16	24	47	50	78	387
Developed	166	208	255	285	371	123
East Asia	39	56	81	105	160	310
South Asia	27	34	50	77	116	329
Latin America	12	18	25	40	67	458
Africa	6	9	13	21	36	500
Less developed	84	117	169	243	379	351
World	250	325	424	528	750	200

% of world urban population

	1920	1930	1940	1950	1960
Less developed	33.6	36·0	39·8	46·1	49·4
Developed	66·4	64·0	60·2	53·9	50·5

SOURCE: United Nations, 1968, 11–12

only locally, such as in parts of Mexico, Japan and southern Brazil, is migration to the towns leading to rural depopulation (Geigner and Oxnard, 1969; Eyre, J. D., 1964; Stevens, 1968).

Although the high rate of urban growth in the underdeveloped world is undeniable, there is still some doubt about the relative contribution of migration and natural increase. It has been argued that, in contrast to the nineteenth century, urban growth has been primarily a result of natural increase, not migration from rural areas (Davis, 1969). Although migration to these cities has undoubtedly occurred, natural increase in the cities is high because there is no longer any significant difference between the death rates of town and country, nor is there any evidence to show that birth rates are falling in the cities (McGee, 1967).

However, most still believe that migration is a major contributor to urban growth in the underdeveloped world. Thus two-thirds of the increase in the urban population of Latin America between 1950 and 1960 has been attributed to immigration from rural areas, whilst in India a similar ratio has been quoted for the same period (McGee, 1964; Gosal, 1961). As a result, a large proportion of city-dwellers are recent immigrants from the country. In Cairo in 1950, one-third of the population had been born outside the city, whilst a sample survey of Baghdad in 1955–57 showed that 57% were born elsewhere. In Djakarta in 1954, 74% of the heads of households were born outside the town (McGee, 1964, 1967). Similarly in the nineteenth century industrial cities a high proportion of the population were recent immigrants: in 1851, 46% of the population of 72 cities in Britain were born elsewhere (Smith, W., 1953).

Indeed so marked has been the recent influx into Asian cities that some writers have spoken of their 'ruralization'. It is often argued that the nineteenth-century city broke down class and ethnic groupings; in contrast, so great is the influx of rural immigrants into some modern cities that rural attitudes are being perpetuated. It has been argued that this will destroy the innovating character of cities and retard economic growth (Dwyer, 1968a, 1968b; McGee, 1963). Nor is the city-size distribution of many underdeveloped countries favourable to change; innovations are frequently diffused throughout a country from the largest city, then to the medium-sized cities and so down the hierarchy (Berry, 1969; Hägerstrand, 1965; Chapman, 1969). But many underdeveloped countries, and particularly those of South East Asia, have primate distributions; thus there is a gap between the large city and the small country towns (Fryer, 1953; Berry, 1961b; Berry and Horton, 1970; Silva and Soto, 1968).

In the nineteenth century, urbanization was principally a result of industrialization; this is not so in the underdeveloped world at present, where urbanization has proceeded relatively more rapidly than industrialization. Thus, for example, in 1951 11% of India's population was urban, and 11% of the work-force was employed in manufacturing industry. In comparison, Austria had an urban ratio of 11% in 1890, but in that year no less than 30% of its work force was employed in manufacturing industry (Dwyer, 1968b). This phenomenon has occurred in other underdeveloped countries and has led some writers to describe it as 'over-urbanization' (Hoselitz, 1962; Davis and Golden, 1954). This appears to be because migration from rural areas has proceeded faster than the creation of employment opportunities in the towns. In short, the 'push' effect of poor rural conditions is now at least as important in determining rural/urban migration as the 'pull' effect of opportunity in the towns (Peach, 1968; Davis and Golden, 1954; McGee, 1967; Hoselitz, 1962). The consequences are common to cities throughout the underdeveloped world: very high densities and deplorable housing conditions; the creation of shanty towns on the edge of cities; a high rate of unemployment; and a very large tertiary sector with an excess of petty traders, rick-shaw boys, boot-blacks, and often more lawyers than clients (Clarke, C. G., 1966; Smith, C. T., 1968; Lacoste, 1965; Brisseau, 1963; Hoselitz, 1959; Orleans, 1959; Dwyer, 1968a, 1968b; Pullen, 1966; Santos, 1971).

POPULATION AND ECONOMIC DEVELOPMENT

The general features of world population growth have been frequently described (Clarke, J. I., 1965, 1968b, 1971; Trewartha, 1969; Beaujeu-Garnier, 1966; Wrigley, 1969; Stamp, 1960a; Veyret-Verner, 1965; Gonzalez, 1971; Burke, 1966; George, 1959; Mountjoy, 1969; Zelinsky, Kosinski and Prothero, 1970; Carr, 1964). Only a few points need be touched upon here. It is generally agreed that the rise in the rate of population increase in the underdeveloped world is due mainly to a decline in the death rate, as, from the 1920s 'death control' spread slowly from European settled areas to the rest of the world (Linton, 1961). But it should be noted that in many countries in the underdeveloped world there has also been an increase in the birth rate (Lacoste, 1965; Dale, 1963; Lowenthal, 1958; Dambaugh, 1959; Horst, 1967) which may have been caused in some countries partly by the eradication of malaria (Learmonth, 1966; Fisher, W. B., 1952).

Between about 1800 and 1920, the population of Europe and the European settled areas overseas increased more rapidly than that of the rest of the world (Durand, 1967); since then the population of the underdeveloped world has increased—and is likely to continue to increase—more rapidly than the developed, for a number of reasons. First, the age of marriage remains lower in much of the underdeveloped world. In India for example only 6% of the women over 15 years are

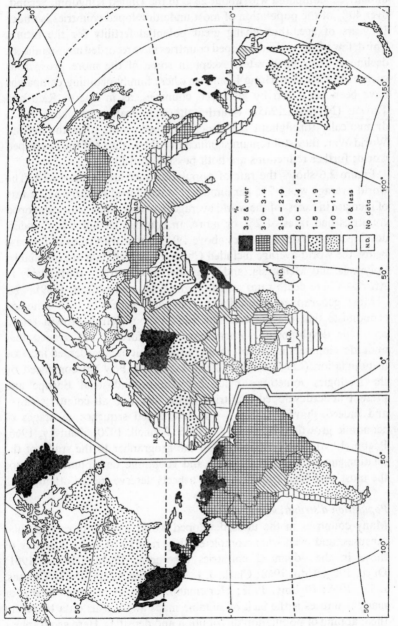

FIGURE 2.6 Average annual rate of increase in population, 1963–68

unmarried, compared with about 25% in the United Kingdom. Second, over 40% of the population of most underdeveloped countries is under 15 years of age, thus giving great potential fertility for the future. Third, few of the underdeveloped countries have recorded any significant decline in their birth rates, except in some of the more prosperous such as Malaya and Hong Kong, or where family planning campaigns have been organized by advanced countries, as in Puerto Rico and Taiwan (Niddrie, 1965). Fourth, although death rates have fallen dramatically throughout the underdeveloped world since the Second World War, they still remain significantly above those of the developed world; further reductions are both possible and likely.

Figure 2.6 shows the rate of population increase in the 1960s. The world average was 1·9% per annum. No developed country had a rate of increase in excess of the world average, and only a few semi-developed countries had rates of 2% or more. In contrast all but a few under-developed countries had rates above 1·9%; those with rates of increase below the world average included China, for which data are unreliable, Polynesia and Melanesia, and a number of countries—particularly in Africa—where death rates remain high (Ward and Moran, 1959).

Most geographers subscribe to the view generally held amongst economists that the current high rates of population growth retard economic development. Others have gone further and argued that underdevelopment is a direct result of the recent unprecedented increase in population (Lacoste, 1965; Zelinsky, 1966). Few are convinced by the analogies sometimes made between pre-industrial Europe and present underdeveloped countries, or the idea that all countries can—and indeed should—follow a pre-determined sequence of stages of economic growth (Fisher, C. A., 1965; Schnell, 1970; Zelinsky, 1966; Bacon, 1958). The contribution of the geographer to the study of the relationship between population and economic development has for the most part been empirical. Two aspects deserve special attention.

Population distribution and density
Many countries in the underdeveloped world have only recently had censuses, and even when completed they rarely attain the accuracy of those in the advanced countries (Prothero, 1961a; Hilton, 1961; Duru, 1968; Udo, 1968; Clark, J. I., 1968a; Sternstein, 1965; Thomas, I. D., 1968; Eighmy, 1968; Horstmann, 1963). A major problem for many countries is the lack of suitable maps and census data to permit the mapping of population distribution and densities. Here geographers have made important contributions, particularly in Africa (Prothero,

1959, 1961b; Hilton, 1961; Barbour, 1961; Adams, 1969; Porter, 1966; William-Olsson, 1963; Clarke, J. I., 1966). It is difficult to see how effective development planning can be undertaken without such maps.

Population density and distribution probably merit more attention in models of economic development than they have hitherto received (Hellener, 1966). Many theories of economic development are based upon the assumption that there is little cultivable land left and a dense, rapidly growing population, many of whom are unemployed or under-employed. This provides a labour surplus which can be mobilized for the construction of irrigation works, roads and other types of capital formation. These theories are based on the experience of the densely populated parts of Asia. But there are very marked differences in population density between Asia on the one hand, and Africa and Latin America on the other. Indeed the problems of *some* African states are not so much overpopulation as underpopulation. One of the more striking features of population distribution in Africa is the contrast between the large, sparsely populated areas and the 'islands' of very high density (Steel, 1955; Gleave and White, 1969). A similar pattern is to be found in southeast Asia (Withington, 1965). Although many economists are sceptical of the significance of density differences in economic development—and clearly there are underdeveloped countries with both very high and very low densities—there is no denying the importance of rapid population growth in densely populated agricultural areas.

Population growth and agriculture
The agricultural populations of developed countries have shown a characteristic sequence of change as economic development has proceeded. In the early stages they have increased rapidly, then stabil-ized as economic opportunities in the towns attract migrants; finally rural populations have diminished absolutely as agricultural pro-ductivity has risen, and the economic opportunities of the towns have progressively increased (Zelinsky, 1963). In contrast, the agricultural populations of the underdeveloped countries have increased far more rapidly in the last thirty years than European populations did at a comparable stage of development, the opportunities for industrial employment are much fewer, and only locally have improved farming methods been adopted. In spite of migration to both towns and new agricultural areas, agricultural populations in the underdeveloped countries continue to increase absolutely (Grigg, 1971).

The consequences of this have been frequently described, particularly for Africa (Gleave and White, 1969). In Africa, the evidence of population pressure was first noted in the 1930s although discounted by many, in the absence of adequate population censuses (Steel, 1955, 1970; Hance, 1970). But since the end of the Second World War the evidence of pressure upon the land has become undeniable. Most African cultivators formerly pursued some form of shifting cultivation, with a long fallow. Once numbers began to increase, a variety of consequences became apparent. The fallow was progressively reduced until, with only a short fallow, soil structure was damaged, soil humus reduced and crop yields began to fall. Responses to this have varied. In some cases there is little alteration in farming methods and soil erosion leads to severe gullying (Grove, 1951; Morgan, W. B., 1953; Aghassy, 1970; Floyd, 1965). Some livestock-keeping communities have shown little awareness of the dangers of increased human and animal numbers; overgrazing has led to the degradation of the vegetation cover, reducing the quality of the fodder and eventually causing severe soil erosion (Prescott, 1961).

In contrast, in northern Nigeria the use of manure and the adoption of mixed farming appears to be a response to high population densities (Grove, 1961; Mortimore, 1967; Mortimore and Wilson, 1968) whilst amongst the Kikuyu of Kenya terracing and manuring have become more common as population has increased (Steel, 1970). Indeed some authors have argued that increasing population pressure *necessarily* leads to the intensification of farming practices, with shifting cultivation being superseded by rotational bush fallow and eventually by permanent agriculture with manuring and legume fallows (Boserup, 1965; Gleave and White, 1969).

Not all African farming communities have responded to the increase in their populations by intensification (Hance, 1970). In some cases declining soil fertility has been countered by the adoption of crops—such as cassava—which will grow upon poorer soils. The risks of seasonal hunger become greater and the male population is forced to seek supplementary employment. At first migration only takes place in the dry season; later, migrants go away for two or three years to raise a target sum of money; finally migrants go permanently to the towns (Middleton and Greenland, 1954; Prothero, 1965, 1968; Hellen, 1962).

In Asia and parts of Latin America, agriculture had become permanent and relatively intensive long before the recent rapid population increase, and peasant agriculture was already partly commercialized.

The response to population increase has thus been different. Farms have been progressively subdivided and fragmented (Grigg, 1970) and rents have risen steeply as land has become more scarce and potential tenants more numerous (Horst, 1967; Mountjoy, 1952). Although there has been considerable emigration to the towns, this has not been sufficient to reduce pressure upon the land (Zelinsky, 1966). The creation of a large, landless population, dependent upon farm work for a living, has been one consequence of this growth (Schwartzberg, 1963; Sinha, 1962). In rural India some 7% of the population is permanently unemployed, 15% underemployed. Rural underemployment is characteristic of many other parts of the underdeveloped world (Enjalbert, 1960; Simkins and Wernstedt, 1963; Kuriyan, 1968; Ominde, 1968; Mountjoy, 1952; Grigg, 1970; Lacoste, 1965). This abundance of labour drives down wages (Mountjoy, 1952).

Population pressure often leads to attempts to colonize new areas (see below, pp. 43–5). But it also enforces the utilization of every available scrap of land in the existing areas of settlement, often to the detriment of farming standards. Woodland is cleared and steep slopes cultivated, leading to erosion and the silting of streams (Horst, 1967; Preston, 1969). It has been argued, however, that population pressure has spurred the adoption of more intensive practices in Asia, including irrigation, multiple cropping and terracing (Clark, 1967a).

PROBLEMS OF AGRICULTURAL DEVELOPMENT

Agricultural output may be increased both by expanding the area under cultivation and by increasing output per acre. Since 1945, total agricultural output in the developed countries has been increased mainly by increasing output per acre, but in the underdeveloped nations by increasing the cultivated area. In the developed countries, agricultural productivity has risen strikingly since 1945; in most of the underdeveloped countries it has, at the best, stagnated (Grigg, 1970).

There have been numerous attempts to define the world's potentially cultivable land (Fawcett, 1930; Alsberg, 1937; Pearson and Harper, 1945; Baker, 1947; Salter, 1947; Stamp, 1960a; Clark, 1967a; Grigg, 1970). They have, for the most part, been based on unreliable information and doubtful assumptions. Even the present distribution of cultivated land is only approximately known (Robertson, 1956; Cressey, 1953). Hence several types of inventory have been attempted by geographers and others, which could form the basis of agricultural planning.

The World Land Use Survey
The success of the British Land Use Survey of the 1930s (Stamp, 1948)
led to an attempt, sponsored by the International Geographical Union,
to organize a World Land Use Survey. A committee established a
classification of land use in 1950 and recommended that results be
published on maps at 1:1,000,000 scale, in a uniform colour scheme
(Anon, *Geographical Journal*, 1950; Van Valkenburg, 1950; Stamp,
1951, 1960b). There have been difficulties in adapting the scheme to
tropical territories (Wikkramatileke, 1959; Prothero, 1954; Moss,
1959; Cumberland, 1951; Ahmad, 1949; Singh, 1960; Ellefsen, 1960;
Roy, 1968; Board, 1961; Williams, 1961; Stobbs, 1968; Rao, 1957;
Lebon, 1959). Nonetheless, land use surveys have been carried out in
many countries since 1950, although the progress of the World Land
Use Survey itself (Boesch, 1968) is still slow, save for the publication of
a number of valuable monographs (Tregear, 1958; Cole, M. M., 1956;
Christodoulou, 1959; Niddrie, 1960; McMaster, 1962; Virone, 1963;
Lebon, 1965; Oluwasanmi and Dema, 1966; Janlekha, 1968; Prince,
Callender, Henshall *et al.*, 1968). The execution of land use surveys
has been speeded up by the use of air photographs and more recently
by other methods of remote sensing (Cox, 1970).

Agricultural typology and land evaluation
Many writers have argued that the improvement of peasant agriculture
requires a thorough knowledge of the existing systems. Studies of
types of farming are legion, but rarely are enquiries easily comparable.
Hence the International Geographical Union has sponsored an attempt
to define an international system of agricultural typology, the aim being
to establish a world classification of farming types together with
descriptive and analytical materials, which could serve as a basis for
planning agricultural change (Kostrowicki and Tyszkiewicz, 1970a,
1970b; Kostrowicki and Helburn, 1967; Diniz, 1969; Kostrowicki,
1968).

Although both land use surveys and agricultural typologies form a
necessary basis for agricultural planning, they only describe agriculture
as it is. A third approach is to assess the agricultural potential of unused
land. Since the disasters of the Tanganyikan groundnuts scheme it is
generally recognized that land settlement schemes should be preceded
by attempts to evaluate land potential. The value of separate soil and
vegetation surveys has long been recognized (Pullan, 1969; Moss,
1969a). More recently there have been attempts to assess the resource
potential of land systems where soils, vegetation and landforms are

regarded as a system and the totality of the landscape is assessed rather than simply its component parts (Thomas, M. F., 1969; Young, 1968, 1969; Mabbut and Stewart, 1963; Mabbutt, 1968; Wright, 1971; Vink, 1967). This approach, often referred to as integrated surveying, was developed in northern Australia and New Guinea; it has not been without its critics (Moss, 1968, 1969a, 1969b). Whatever the correct approach, the value of such evaluations can hardly be denied. As with land use surveying, the value of air photography is of increasing importance (Simonett, 1968).

Agricultural colonization

The migration of Europeans to temperate mid-latitude areas in the nineteenth century and early twentieth century led to a remarkable increase in the world's cultivated area (Robertson, 1956). Since the 1930s, however, this expansion has come to a halt, save in Australia, and the area under crops in most of the developed countries has stabilized or even declined. However, the world's total cropland has continued to expand. The area under the major crops increased by 15–17% between 1948 and 1967, and four-fifths of this expansion came in the developing countries (Grigg, 1970; FAO, 1968).

Much of the nineteenth-century expansion was undertaken by Europeans moving into new lands, for the most part unassisted by the state. The movement of this frontier has almost ended. In the post-war period it survives only in Latin America, and in particular in southern Brazil (Monbeig, 1952; Butland, 1966; Augelli, 1958a, 1958b; Waibel, 1950; Kohlepp, 1969). Increasingly, spontaneous land settlement has been replaced by government directed schemes. Whereas the nineteenth-century colonist was left to his own devices, the modern colonist often has the initial land clearance undertaken for him, roads and irrigation canals built, and credit provided on generous terms for the first few years.

Nor are the motives for land settlement quite as simple as in the past. It is true that many governments undertake colonization to increase food output; but there are other motives. Land settlement schemes are increasingly an attempt to provide land for landless labourers and to stem the rush to the towns, as well as to relieve chronic congestion in densely populated rural areas (Butland, 1966; Withington, 1967; Wernstedt and Simkins, 1965). Elsewhere military reasons have priority. In Malaya, large numbers of dispersed farmers were grouped in villages during the emergency (Sendut, 1962; Sandhu, 1964), whilst in Peru and Thailand colonists have been established in border regions for strategic reasons (Eidt, 1962; Ng, 1968). Many schemes have the dual purpose of increasing the cultivated area and improving the standard of farming. Not only is much of the settlement infrastructure provided for the settlers, but experimental farms established and the farmers' routine directly overseen (Fisk, 1952; Hance, 1954). In eastern Nigeria, farm settlements have been set up in densely populated areas with the hope that surrounding farmers will emulate the better farming methods (Floyd and Adinde, 1967).

Land settlement schemes have not been confined to one particular environment. In Latin America there has been a distinctive trend of migration from the overpopulated highland communities to the lowlands of the Pacific Coast. This has been under way since the late nineteenth century but there is also a move towards the humid tropical lowlands of the Caribbean coast and to the east of the Andes (Butland, 1966; Minkel, 1968; Stewart, N. R., 1965; Crist and Guhl, 1957; Eidt, 1962, 1964, 1967; Fifer, 1967; Stoddart and Trubshaw, 1962; James, 1968; Gonzalez, 1966; Stevens, 1967; Dozier, 1969). In south Asia the cultivation of new land has invariably depended upon the extension of irrigation. In India, the main centres of colonization have been in Rajasthan, in the *terai*, where the control of malaria has made settlement easier, and in Assam and the Dandakanya (Farmer, 1965, 1969b). In Ceylon, the dry zone has been the major area of colonization (Farmer, 1957). Throughout southeast Asia spontaneous settlement continues to be important. Thus, for example, whilst 200,000 colonists from Java have been settled in Sumatra by the government in the post-war period, over a million have migrated there of their own accord (Withington, 1967; Farmer, 1969b; Pelzer, 1945), whilst in the Philippines the island of Mindanao has received much spontaneous migration from densely populated Luzon (Krinks, 1970; Luna, 1963; Wernstedt and Simkins, 1965). The emergency resettlement schemes in Malaya have been followed, since 1956, by federal reclamation schemes mainly aimed at establishing small rubber and oil-palm holdings upon new land (Shamsul, 1969; Wikkramatileke, 1965; Ho, 1965).

Africa has been the scene of a number of land settlement schemes, many of them involving irrigation (Church, 1963). Of these perhaps the best known has been the Gezira (Hance, 1954, 1967) and, the most publicized, the High Dam at Aswan (Frood, 1967). In West Africa there have been important settlement schemes based upon irrigation (Church, 1961, 1966, 1969). In passing, it might be noted that the geographer has an important rôle to play in such integrated development schemes (White, 1963).

Land settlement schemes have had very varying degrees of success in the post-war period. There has, however, been growing criticism of the wisdom of carrying out such schemes; many governments are committed to them because of pledges to provide land for the landless. But the very low return on investment is disturbing many planners (Farmer, 1969b).

ECONOMIC PROBLEMS OF FARMERS IN THE UNDERDEVELOPED COUNTRIES

The economic problems of farming in Latin American and Afro-Asian countries are legion. Generally the farmer has a small holding—less than 4 or 5 hectares—which is worked mainly with the help of his family. His first concern is to provide food for his family; the surplus is sold for cash to pay taxes and to buy goods he cannot produce for himself. Many of the difficulties of traditional agriculture are ascribed to this predominance of a subsistence economy, although in practice this is difficult to define (Symons, 1967; Morgan, 1969). There can now be few farming communities which do not trade or use cash, although there are many which have recently emerged from pure subsistence, particularly in Southeast Asia and Polynesia (Tedder, 1966; Van Roy, 1966; Spate, 1956). Most of the agricultural populations of the underdeveloped world are in a transitional state between subsistence and fully commercialized agriculture. Subsistence and semi-subsistence farmers lack the incentives—and compulsions—that the price mechanism offers to attain higher productivity, and farming improvements are particularly difficult to introduce into such communities (Crist, 1964, 1965; Ooi Jin-bee, 1959). Farmers do not always respond to price changes in the expected manner, partly because of a high preference for leisure, and partly because of their preoccupation with providing for their family needs before the demands of the market (Morgan, 1969; Dobby, 1955; Ooi Jin-Bee, 1959).

The incomes of semi-subsistence farmers are clearly very low, and saving is thus limited. Indeed, a high proportion of the population is permanently indebted. Loans made by shopkeepers, money-lenders and landlords are commonly at very high rates of interest, and are often obtained, not for agricultural investment but to cover consumption needs. A survey made in Malacca, Malaya, showed that 83% of all farmers had to borrow money every year, that two-thirds of the loans were for consumption and that the average annual rate of interest upon loans made by shopkeepers, who provided half the credit, was

173% (Kayser, 1969; Ho, 1969; Ooi Jin-Bee, 1959; Watters, 1967).
The farmer who does not own his land—a high proportion of all
farmers—has nothing other than his harvest upon which to raise a
loan. Nor are credit institutions widely available. Although the number
of branch banks in tropical Africa nearly quadrupled between 1950
and 1964, there was still only one office to every 144,000 people, compared with one to every 4,500 people in the United Kingdom (Engberg
and Hance, 1969).

Although some writers have argued that the farming systems of many
underdeveloped countries show a careful adaptation to both the limited
needs of the farmers and to the physical environment, few traditional
systems have been able to adjust to the rapid population growth of the
last thirty years. To some extent greater productivity can be obtained
by the more efficient deployment of existing factors of production,
particularly labour, which is often under-utilized (Watters, 1967). But
in many peasant communities there are only unrewarding increases in
output for additional inputs of both labour and capital (Schultz,
1964; Lentnek, 1969).

Underdeveloped countries do not generally have one undifferentiated
and backward farming economy. More characteristically they contain
two types of economies; the stagnant peasant economy, and an export-
orientated sector, often of European origin, which is fully commercialized and relatively efficient. Such a dual economy is noticeable in
tropical Africa where little more than a tenth of the agricultural
population and cultivated area is devoted to export crops, and perhaps
a fifth of the area is for crops used for local consumption only; the rest
of the area is in a transitional stage between subsistence and commercialized agriculture (Kayser, 1969). On a map, these areas of
commercialized agriculture appear as islands in a sea of subsistence
farming (Hance, Kotschar and Peterec, 1961).

In Africa there is a very close relationship between commercial
agriculture and transport facilities. Indeed there is general agreement
amongst economists and other writers that an efficient transport system
is essential for economic development. However, whilst the first
development of a transport net will certainly spark off early economic
growth (Taafe, Morrill and Gould, 1963) later investments in elabor-
ating the network will not necessarily stimulate comparable increases
in production (Hoyle, 1970). Indeed, in some underdeveloped countries
there may have been overinvestment in transport facilities (Gauthier,
1968, 1970). Certainly it is true that the existence of railways and roads
will not automatically stimulate economic growth. In Uganda, the recent

construction of railways has had little impact upon the local economy; nor did the Bornu railway in northern Nigeria spark off growth; the provision of other factors was necessary in both cases (Barbour, 1966; O'Connor, 1965a, 1965b). But these cautionary remarks should not be taken to discount the importance of transport. In many parts of the world the provision of adequate transport has had profound effects on agricultural development.

LAND TENURE AND AGRICULTURAL DEVELOPMENT

Many authorities believe that defects in land tenure are the major obstacle to agricultural development. Unfortunately land reform does not *necessarily* lead to farming improvements, whilst some measures of land reform—such as the subdivision of plantations to provide farms for the landless—may have social and political benefits but be economically harmful.

There is, however, little doubt that the widespread occurrence of *tenancy* has adverse effects upon farming standards. In much of Latin America, southern Europe, the Middle East and Asia tenants have no security of tenure and pay exorbitantly high rents. Share-cropping, where the landlord has a fixed proportion of the produce, often in kind, is particularly iniquitous (Peruzzi, 1965). In countries where both owner-occupiers and tenants are to be found, landlords have frequently pre-empted the better land (Cutshall, 1952; Sternstein, 1967). Since the Second World War there have been frequent attempts to reform tenancy systems either by restricting rents and enforcing security of tenure, or more commonly, by converting sitting tenants into owner-occupiers (Malek, 1966; Shaw, E. B., 1954; Crossley, 1963; Crist, 1957–58; Grenier, 1964–65; Vellard, 1963; Dickinson, 1954). But the conversion, which usually requires the state to expropriate land and sell to tenants at favourable terms, has not always been successful; and the cases of marked improvement in farming as a result of such reforms are few (Trewartha, 1950).

Communal tenure has few of the social abuses of tenancy but is equally a barrier to agricultural progress. It is found among the highland Indian communities of South America (Preston, 1969; Keller, 1950, 1955; Winnie, 1965) and in the remoter parts of southeast Asia (Irwin, 1966), where it is closely associated with shifting cultivation. But it is most common in Africa south of the Sahara, where it was almost the only form of tenure until the arrival of Europeans in the nineteenth century. Since then the rise of cash cropping and the rapid growth of population has reduced the land available for bush fallows (Taylor, 1969) and given land an economic value (Benneh, 1965; Udo, 1964; Roder, 1964). Whilst communal tenure gives the occupant of land security of tenure whilst he uses the land, and rarely gives rise to the problems of indebtedness associated with tenancy, it is widely regarded as an obstacle to the introduction of new farming methods. Not the least of the tenurial problems of Africa are those in areas where Europeans have settled. In Kenya, the pre-emption of the White Highlands for European settlement has given way to schemes to settle Africans (Morgan, W. T. W., 1963; Carey-Jones, 1965; Naidu, 1967; Pollock, 1959; Shaffer, 1967) but in Rhodesia segregation of land persists (Floyd, 1962; Roder, 1964).

Throughout much of the world the ownership of land has become concentrated into a few hands, and this, coupled with the rapid growth of population and the limited amount of potential agricultural land remaining has given rise not only to the problems of tenancy but also to those of the landless labourer. Thus in the last thirty years there have been attempts to expropriate large estates and redistribute the land. In some cases this has had economic as well as social benefits. In much of Latin America, for example, latifundia have been grossly underutilized (Smole, 1963; Crist, 1942; Keller, 1950). In other parts of the world the breaking up of large units has had less happy consequences, particularly in the case of plantations, which have been prone to expropriation although they frequently provide a valuable source of export income (Robertson, 1963; Farmer, 1963; Watters, 1963; Fisher, C. A., 1964a and 1968; Koerner, 1969; Augelli, 1953; Courtenay, 1965). Indeed, there is now a tendency in some underdeveloped countries to encourage plantations under joint state and company control (Gregor, 1965).

The ideal form of ownership in most underdeveloped countries is the owner-occupier, comparable to the European peasant (Franklin, 1969) or the American family farm. But ownership of land is not in itself a guarantee of good farming; further, many family farms suffer, as do other types, from the problems of subdivision and fragmentation. Most farms in the underdeveloped world are too small, in two senses. First, they are often too small to provide the farmer with an adequate living. Thus for example, it has been calculated that a farmer needs at least 3–4 hectares of good paddy land in Malaya to make a 'reasonable living' but nine-tenths of the farmers have holdings smaller than this (Ooi Jin-Bee, 1965). The small farm predominates throughout much of the rest of Asia, Africa, and much of Latin America (Grigg, 1966). Second, large farms gain economies of scale, and they are said to find it easier to adopt new methods. It is thus argued that agricultural progress requires farm amalgamation. Such ideas are certainly applicable in Western agriculture, where increasing farm size has been associated with increased mechanization and greater productivity. It is less clear that these arguments are applicable to Asian conditions, where paddy farming requires intensive labour methods; nor is it clear how the population displaced by amalgamation would be absorbed (Farmer, 1960).

There is less contention about the disadvantages of fragmentation (Igbozurike, 1970). Throughout the underdeveloped world—and much of Europe too—farms do not consist of one single block of land but a number of scattered parcels. This wastes time in travelling, costs money to duplicate roads and boundaries, and impedes the use of machinery. There is little to be said in its favour. Unfortunately the reduction of fragmentation needs very radical changes in village life that few societies appear prepared to make (Jafri, 1953; Karan, 1957; Naidu, 1967; Lambert, 1963; Naylon, 1959, 1961: Shaw, D. J., 1963; Sinha, 1963; McGlashan, 1960; Pepelasis and Thompson, 1960).

Two other forms of tenure must be noted. In Socialist countries collective and state farms have replaced most other forms of tenure, but whilst they have undoubted theoretical advantages (Symons, 1966) they have not proved entirely successful and collectivization was halted in Yugoslavia and Poland. It would appear that some form of ownership of land is a necessary incentive to agricultural endeavour. Thus the kibbutzim of Israel and the communes of China both depend upon ideological zeal (Buchanan, 1966). The moshavim of Israel appear to offer an ideal solution; small family farms share centralized co-operative services (Blake, 1969; Tamsma, 1966).

SOCIAL FACTORS AND AGRICULTURAL DEVELOPMENT

There is now a widespread belief that economic development—and the lack of it—cannot be explained solely by the interplay of economic forces, and that social attitudes and institutions are of major significance. Thus when individual farmers' attitudes to the adoption of new farming methods are analysed it is not simply economic factors which have to be taken into consideration.

Many peasant communities are reluctant to change their ways, not surprisingly when new methods are unknown and may fail. Natural hazards and other causes of farming failure are accepted fatalistically and thought to be beyond the farmer's control (Dichter, 1967); generations of poverty have engendered an acceptance of poverty and an inability to look beyond it (Watters, 1967). A multiplicity of customs, laws and beliefs make changes in farming methods difficult. In many underdeveloped countries the extended family, with undue authority vested in the family elders, inhibits enterprise and prevents the rejection of traditional ways (Kay, 1965). Religious beliefs often have an adverse effect. Animistic ideas about crops and livestock prevent their rational use. Thus, for example, many African pastoralists still measure wealth by the number of cattle possessed rather than by their quality and output (Toupet, 1956; Onyoni, 1963; Faniran, 1968). Religious taboos also have a profound effect. Pig's meat is forbidden to Jews and Muslims, and wherever Islam has taken hold in Asia pig-keeping has declined. The effect of this is clearly seen in Malaya, where Malay and Chinese farmers follow quite different farming systems (Sopher, 1967; Wik-kramatileke, 1964). In India the Hindu belief in *ahimsa* means the maintenance of a large population of diseased and aged cows, impeding the development of an efficient cattle industry (Spate and Learmonth, 1967; Sopher, 1967). The caste system often has adverse effects; and it is in the country rather than the towns that it still persists in India. The adoption of agricultural innovations is sometimes a caste rather than an individual decision (Schwartzberg, 1965).

The adoption of innovations by farmers has been widely studied by rural sociologists. Their interest has, however, been mainly concerned with adoption over time. The spatial diffusion of innovation has been increasingly studied by geographers (Hägerstrand, 1967; Brown and Moore, 1969). Innovation theory has practical implications. Thus recently it has been argued that the most rapid way to spread new farming methods in the African countryside is to have, not a few large improvement schemes, but a large number of small centres of innovation (Siddle, 1970). The modernization of a whole state has been treated as a diffusion problem with important implications for economic policy (Soja, 1968; Riddell, 1970).

NATURAL RESOURCES AND ECONOMIC DEVELOPMENT

Early writers on economic development laid great stress upon the rôle of natural resources, and many argued that differences in natural resource endowments explained differences in the level of development (Pepelasis, Mears and Adelman, 1964). This view is no longer widely held amongst economists. Many countries which are well endowed with resources, such as Brazil, have a generally low level of development whilst others which have few are economically advanced, such as Switzerland, Israel and Holland (Mountjoy, 1969). A large literature by geographers and others has pointed out that resources are 'neutral'; they are economically useful only if demand exists, a technology is available to utilize them and they are accessible (Ginsburg, 1957; White, 1965; Zimmerman, 1933; Duncan, 1962; Zobler, 1962; Ackermann, 1959, 1967; Burton and Kates, 1965). Thus most writers now regard natural resources as playing only a secondary rôle in economic development, although such views would appear to neglect the importance, for example, of oil in Middle Eastern countries.

The significance of natural resources appears to diminish as economic development proceeds. In the early stages, the primary industries contribute a high proportion of the national income; as societies industrialize, more of the income comes from industries which are less directly dependent upon natural resources. Schultz (1965) has calculated that in 1910 income from 'All Land' in the USA contributed 36% of the national wealth, but only 17% in 1955. Similarly, the value of all raw materials consumed in 1904–13 was 23% of national wealth, by 1944–50 only 13%. It follows then that the exploitation of natural resources is of most significance in the early stages of economic development, whether in the form of mineral exports or cash crops. It is increasingly admitted by most writers on economic development that industrialization must be preceded or parallelled by an agricultural revolution (Mountjoy, 1969; Hodder, 1968). Now, whilst increases in agricultural productivity are often the result of institutional changes or new techniques, the physical environment in which these take place may be of crucial importance.

There are many different views about the importance to be attached to the rôle of the physical environment in agricultural development. At one extreme are those who largely discount its significance, see no essential difference between the tropical and temperate environments, and believe that the farming techniques developed in Western Europe and North America can be transferred unchanged to the tropics. They believe that the obstacles to the adoption of improved farming methods are essentially socio-economic. This view is still widely held, in spite of the failure of European farming methods in the tropics (Dobby, 1946). At the opposite extreme are those who believe in the inherent inferiority of the tropics. This view was widely held until the 1930s, at a time when many discussions of agricultural potential in the tropics were concerned with the settlement of Europeans. Some recent work tends to support such views (Best, 1965; Chang, J., 1968). A compromise view, widely held amongst agronomists, is that the tropics do present formidable difficulties to the farmer, and that the techniques developed in temperate areas are unlikely to work there. However, the *principles* of agronomy and soil science can be applied to the tropics and local solutions can and will be developed (Kellog, 1956, 1960).

The humid tropics
The luxuriance of the rain forest convinced many early European visitors to the humid tropics—still very variously defined (Chambers, Dalrymple and Jones, 1957; Chang, J., 1968; Tosi and Voertmen, 1964; Fosberg, Garnier and Kuchler, 1961; Blumenstock, 1958; Gaussen and Legris, 1963)—that it would have a very high agricultural potential. But the clearance of the forest, row cultivation with the plough and clean weeding led to soil erosion and declining yields (Dobby, 1946). Chang has recently demonstrated that the unvarying day-length, the lack of a cold season and, in the true humid tropics, the absence of a dry season, greatly limits the range of crops which can be grown. The net photosynthesis for the year as a whole is less than in Aw (Monsoon) and Cs (Mediterranean) climates, and not greatly in excess of other C climates. For the eight summer months, net potential photosynthesis is less than for Cs, Aw, C or D climates. It is this fact which may account for the low crop yields in the humid tropics as much as the indifferent farming methods (Chang, J., 1968; Best, 1965).

The upland humid tropical soils have an excellent physical structure but they have been leached of plant nutrients over a long period; in contrast, leaching is less effective in temperate regions, and there are more soils developed upon recent, particularly glacial, deposits. The best tropical soils are also on the more recent deposits, principally upon alluvials and volcanics (Miller, 1959; Hardy, 1954; Ooi Jin-Bee, 1959; Carter and Pendleton, 1956). But even tropical alluvial soils are generally inferior to those of temperate areas (Edelman and Voorde, 1963). On the upland latosols the removal of the forest cover exposes the soil to very high temperatures and rainfall intensities, reduces nutrients and causes soil erosion. Bush fallowing is well suited to restoring the fertility of these soils, whilst the inter-cropping of a mixture of root, tree and shrub crops protects the soil (Watters, 1960; Spencer, 1966; Pelzer, 1945; Clarke, W. C. and Street, 1967; Moss,

1969a). However, rising population densities and the introduction of cash crops have led to the reduction of forest fallows in many parts of the humid tropics and no entirely satisfactory alternative system of maintaining soil fertility has been found. Ploughing in green crops gives a limited response, and there seem to be few tropical legumes that fix nitrogen in the soil as efficiently as those in temperate areas (Ignatieff and Lemos, 1963). The separation of crop and livestock production makes the use of farm-yard manure difficult, whilst the application of artificial fertilizers is costly (Vine, 1968; Richardson, 1968; Chang, J., 1968).

Attempts to introduce mixed farming into the humid tropics have met with limited success, and the use of the plough and clean weeding have created more problems than they have solved (Stamp, 1962; Steel, 1965). Thus it has been argued that Europeans should stop trying to introduce cereals and grasses, on which their own farming systems are based, into the tropics; instead, combinations of tree and shrub crops, which simulate the rainforest, should be the basis of the agricultural economy (Tosi and Voertman, 1964). Alternatively, padi cultivation should be further encouraged. Although rice yields best in a sub-tropical climate, it is also the most satisfactory crop in the humid tropics, for it yields well on poor soils, provided water control is adequate (Goor, 1966; Chang, J., 1958). Without terracing, padi cultivation is limited to low-lying alluvial areas; even so there should be possibilities for its expansion in Africa and Latin America, where the major obstacles to its adoption seem to be cultural rather than environmental. It is significant that, although the crop has been grown since the sixteenth century in Latin America, it is still mainly a dry land crop. As an irrigated crop it has only been successful in recent major government-supported irrigation schemes, or where Asians with experience of padi farming have settled (Gourou, 1966; Leurquin, 1967).

The arid lands

The problems of the arid zone have received more attention from geographers than any other major natural region (Stamp, 1961; Hills, E. S., 1966; Walton, 1969; Meigs and Twidale, 1966). This is perhaps not surprising, for the arid zone covers at least one-third of the earth's land surface (Meigs, 1953; White, 1966; Shantz, 1956; Amiran, 1966; Thornthwaite, 1948). In a sense, much of this attention is misplaced, for only a small proportion of the arid zone is likely to be developed for agriculture in the future, given present technologies and costs. In most countries with both arid and humid regions agricultural output can be more cheaply increased by intensifying production in the humid areas than by extension into the arid zones (Davidson, 1965). Many of the occupied areas of the arid zone suffer from severe physical problems, and these merit attention.

A conventional distinction is often made between *semi-arid* areas and *arid* areas; in the former, cultivation of crops is possible without irrigation by using the special techniques of dry farming, whereas in the latter, crops can only be grown with the aid of irrigation. The semi-arid areas to some extent overlap with parts of the savanna world, which are dealt with below. Most of the problems of the semi-arid areas stem from the low annual rainfall. The distinctive features of this rainfall include a high degree of seasonal concentration which limits the range of crops which can be grown; cereals dominate most semi-arid areas, whether in developed or underdeveloped countries. The amount received varies from year to year, thus profoundly influencing crop yields (Davies, D. H., 1957; Grigg, 1970; Meigs, 1952; Bricham-baut and Wallen, 1963; Higbee, 1957; Ahmad and Khan, 1961). A major problem is to find a leguminous crop which can be put into the rotation to maintain soil fertility (FAO, 1956). In many semi-arid regions nomadic herders are encouraged to graze their stock upon the crop residues and the weed growth on the fallow, the latter being a characteristic feature of all dry-farming regions. But the high temperatures of much of the arid zone rapidly oxidizes cattle dung; similarly, the lack of soil moisture limits the usefulness of artificial fertilizers.

The soils of the arid zone vary a great deal from place to place. The *chernozems* for the most part lie on the fringe of the arid zone, and the chestnut-brown soils, on the edge of the semi-arid zone, have rainfalls so low and variable that they are risky to work (Walton, 1969). The low rainfall means that there is only an impoverished vegetation and there is thus little organic matter in the soils. Because there is little moisture in the soil, few of the minerals available in the regolith are broken down, and thus are unavailable to plants. In most arid zone soils the movement of moisture is upwards, depositing calcium carbonate, which in places forms hardpans. Evaporation on the surface gives saline crusts which inhibit, or in extreme cases prevent, plant growth (Walton, 1969; Grigg, 1970; Kellog, 1953; Aubert, 1962; Jewitt, 1966).

Dry-farming in the semi-arid regions then is faced with many problems (Kovda, 1969; Aschmann, 1963; Despois, 1961; Taylor, S. A., 1960), and it has been argued that crop production in these regions can only remain competitive with more humid areas by adopting irrigation; indeed, in most semi-arid areas the farmer is retreating (Amiran, 1965). Irrigation is of course a technique of great antiquity, and farming in the arid zones of Egypt, Iraq, West Pakistan and Soviet Central Asia has been dependent upon it for more than four millenia (Al-Khashab, 1958; Hurst, 1927; Cantor, 1967; Highsmith, 1965; Hamdan, 1961). The irrigation systems of these countries rely upon water from rivers which rise in more humid areas outside the arid zone, and it might be noted, often outside their national boundaries (Barbour, 1957). Since the Second World War there have been several major schemes to extend the irrigated areas of these countries and to introduce perennial irrigation, making double cropping possible. These schemes have somewhat distracted attention from faults in the existing systems. A huge loss of irrigation water arises from evaporation in reservoirs and canals, silting, and from seepage out of unlined canals (Baddruddin, 1961; Worrall, 1958). The lack of adequate drainage leads to a rise in the water-table, water-logging and salinity (Henderson, 1965; Davies, H. R. J., 1958; Vlugter, 1960; Ahmad, 1961). West Pakistan (now Pakistan) loses 100,000 acres of cultivable land a year from salinization (Gulik, 1963).

Nor is the provision of new irrigation systems as simple as is some-times supposed. The number of rivers in the arid zone which have adequate supplies throughout the year, flat land and suitable sites for dam construction are not particularly numerous (Ledger, 1963, 1964; Farmer, 1956; Barbour, 1959; Garnier, 1957). The real costs of building major irrigation schemes have risen steeply since the 1920s (Clark, 1967b; Hoare, 1967; Marts, 1956). It may be that the massive invest-ments in schemes such as the Aswan dam might have been more profitably employed in intensifying production in areas already ir-rigated, or in developing small-scale irrigation schemes (White, 1962; Cressey, 1958).

The savanna lands

The savannas have received less attention than either the humid tropics or the arid zone, although they occupy a large area in Africa and South America (Hills, T., 1965). Annual rainfall totals are generally higher than in the arid zone, but high temperatures and a marked seasonal concentration of precipitation mean that farmers are subject to similar problems of high rainfall variability (Kenworthy and Glover, 1958; Kenworthy, 1964; Bunting, 1961; Glover, Robinson and Henderson, 1954; Gregory, 1969). The risk of crop failure, either from low totals or the belated arrival of the wet season, is an ever-present problem.

S.H.G.—3

Rainfall intensities are very high and the risk of soil erosion great (Lawes, 1962; Floyd, 1959; Beckinsale, 1957). It is, however, the type of vegetation which principally distinguishes the savannas from the arid zone. There are great variations in savanna types, not only within Africa, where savannas vary from rainforest and grassland combinations to the meagre thorn bush of the desert fringe, but also between Africa and South America (Cole, 1963; Phillips, 1959; Cole, 1960a; Eyre, S. R., 1963). Grasses are however typical of most savanna vegetation types except in north-eastern Brazil (Cole, 1960b). They provide far less organic matter for the soil than the forest fallow of the humid tropics. The nitrogen content of savanna soils is typically low, generally less than 2%. Savannas are characteristically associated with stable plateaux areas, and thus leaching has been going on over a very long period (Cole, 1960a, 1963a and 1963b). Mineral plant nutrients are thus low, particularly phosphorus. In parts of Brazil and West Africa laterization has led to the formation of hardpans, which impede drainage and cause water-logging in the wet season and, where revealed by erosion, prevent the formation of an agricultural soil of any value. The soil structure presents problems. Savanna soils are easily compacted if heavy machinery is used in cultivation, and they are generally remarkably susceptible to erosion (Dudal and Bramâo, 1965; Maignien, 1966; FAO, 1966; Pullan, 1969). Thus, as in the humid tropics, the better soils are those which are formed upon recent deposits.

The two major areas of savanna, in Africa and Brazil, have quite different settlement histories. In Africa, much of the savanna is sparsely settled, and if used at all, is grazed by livestock. On the other hand there are locally very high population densities. In areas such as northern Nigeria and northern Ghana increasing population has compelled the reduction of the fallow period, which is in any case far less effective than the forest fallow (Moss, 1969a). There are several solutions to the problem of declining yields and severe soil erosion. In places the heavy application of farm-yard manure has given satisfactory results (Mortimore and Wilson, 1965; Prothero, 1957) but the spread of mixed farming in Africa has been inhibited by the traditional segregation of crop and livestock production. Ley farming has proved less successful, for, as noted earlier, tropical legumes seem to be less efficient than temperate legumes in restoring nitrogen (Dennison, 1959). The prevention of soil erosion has been a major aim of most Departments of Agriculture in tropical Africa, but with very mixed success (Kay, 1969). Irrigation is the obvious solution to the difficulties of rainfall variability; but there is little tradition of water conservation in

African indigenous societies and the lack of large stores of ground-water in the largely igneous and metamorphic rocks underlying the savannas, coupled with the irregular flow of rivers, has hampered irrigation development (Ledger, 1969).

In contrast to the African savannas, whose settlement dates from pre-historic times, the South American savannas were occupied late and remain largely unsettled, devoted for the most part to extensive ranching. Where crops are grown, *roca*, or land rotation, is the common method, and frequently crop cultivation is merely a preliminary to the sowing of grasses. The principal obstacle to the further settlement of the Brazilian savanna is not so much rainfall variability as the poverty of the soils, which are sandy, lack humus and have been leached of most of their mineral plant nutrients (Cole, 1960a; Crist, 1956; Vann, 1963; James, 1952, 1953; Waibel, 1948; Denevan, 1965).

Livestock production in the tropics

A very small part of the tropics is devoted to crop production; a very large proportion of the savannas and the arid zone is devoted to grazing. Yet livestock products are a small proportion of the value of agricultural output in the underdeveloped world, in contrast with the developed countries. Furthermore, crop and animal production are traditionally segregated in the tropics; in Europe and European-settled areas, farming is based on the integration of crops and livestock. The reasons for these contrasts are varied, and by no means simply a result of differences in the physical environment. Nonetheless physical difficulties do present formidable obstacles to the development of livestock industries in the tropics.

Most farmers in the tropics have a shortage of arable land and cannot afford to use it for growing fodder crops. Thus livestock depends almost entirely upon natural vegetation. This is for the most part nutritionally inferior to the grasses of temperate regions. In the humid tropics grasses only occur in places where the forest has failed to recolonize, and are generally of inferior quality. In the savannas, however, grasses are the dominant vegetation type, although, it is frequently argued, only because prolonged clearance and burning have prevented the re-establishment of forest (Morgan, W. B. and Moss, 1965; Beard, 1953; Budowski, 1956; Eyre, 1963). Although savanna grasses give a very high dry matter yield, they have serious limitations. In the long dry season they are fibrous and of little nutritional value; in the wet season the combination of high temperatures and rainfall reduces the period of high protein content. The marked phosphorous deficiency of savanna soils is reflected in the grasses; this is important, for young cattle need phosphorus in fairly large quantities. The inadequacy of the fodder supply has numerous consequences. Calving rates are low and animals put on weight very slowly. Indeed, much of the wet season is spent putting back weight lost in the long dry season. The fodder supply has been reduced in the last thirty years by overgrazing, for in many savanna areas stock numbers have increased as rapidly as human numbers. Although stocking densities are very low in the savannas compared with European areas, this increase has been enough to cause overgrazing, which leads to the degradation of the vegetation, with a decline in the more palatable species, and to soil erosion (Whyte, 1962; Prescott, 1961; Phillips, 1959; Grigg, 1970). High temperatures affect the reproductive capacity of male animals and increase the need for a large daily water intake—a serious problem in the dry season.

The improvement of savanna livestock production requires, as a first priority, the reduction of stocking densities and an improvement in the quality of the fodder supply. Only then will it be worth improving the quality of the cattle. Attempts to establish European breeds in the tropics have generally proved unsuccessful, although crosses between European breeds and indigenous varieties have been more successful. A beginning, however, has been made in the elimination of disease. In Africa the major cattle disease is trypanosmiasis, carried by the tsetse fly, which infests nearly all the African humid tropics and half the savannas (Deshler, 1960; Knight, 1971; Payne, 1962; Deshler, 1963).

SUMMARY

There are various ways in which geographers have made and can continue to make a contribution to the study of economic development. Some believe that the techniques of spatial analysis recently developed by human geographers have much to offer in the understanding of how innovations are diffused through an economy, and how regional differences in economic growth within a country come about. More traditional techniques, such as mapping and resource inventories, are also proving useful aids to economic planning. But in the overall problem of understanding economic development, and in particular agricultural development, it is not so much special techniques, but rather the traditional ways of looking at problems which may be the geographers' most useful contribution to understanding.

In the first place the traditional belief that one of the functions of the geographer is to point out differences between places would seem to be an essential corrective to the view, widely held amongst some writers, that the underdeveloped world is a monolithic bloc with much the same problems throughout. This view leads to the belief that the same development plans can be applied to any country with equal success. This is not so; each country, and each major ecological region, has a particular combination of problems; the keys to development are different and regionally unique.

In the second place geographers have been traditionally concerned with inter-relationships between environment and society. In agricultural development there is little doubt that different environments offer different opportunities to the farmer; similarly, different environments offer different problems. Solutions to these problems are most likely to be found indigenously within those environments, not by transferring the techniques of other environments. It behoves geographers to emphasize this point, however commonplace it may seem to them, or however it may smack to some of geographical determinism.

REFERENCES

Ackerman, E. A. (1959) 'Population and natural resources', in P. M. Hauser and O. D. Duncan (Eds.), *The Study of Population: an inventory and appraisal*, University of Chicago Press, 621–648.

Ackerman, E. A. (1967) 'Population, natural resources and technology', *Annals of the American Academy of Political and Social Science*, **369**, 84–97.

Adams, J. (1969) 'A population map of West Africa', *Nigerian Geographical Journal*, **12**, 87–97.

Aghassy, J. (1970) 'Population pressure and crop rotation among the Tiv of Nigeria', *Annals of the Association of American Geographers*, **60**, 299–314.

Ahmad, K. S. (1949) 'Land utilization survey in Pakistan', *Pakistan Geographical Review*, **4**, 17–21.

Ahmad, K. S. (1961) 'Reclamation of water-logged and saline land in West Pakistan', *Pakistan Geographical Review*, **16**, 1–18.

Ahmad, K. S. and Khan, M. L. (1961) 'Variability of rainfall and its bearing on agriculture in the arid and semi-arid zones of West Pakistan', *Pakistan Geographical Review*, **16**, 35–50.

Al-Khashab, Wafiq Hussain (1958) 'The water budget of the Tigris and Euphrates basin', *University of Chicago, Department of Geography Research Paper* No. 54.

Alsberg, C. (1937) 'The food supply in the migration process', in I. Bowman (Ed.) *Limits of Land Settlement*, American Geographical Society, 25–26.

Amiran, D. H. K. (1965) 'Arid zone development: a reappraisal under modern technological conditions', *Economic Geography*, **41**, 189–210.

Amiran, D. H. K. (1966) 'Man in arid lands', in E. S. Hills (Ed.), *Arid lands: a geographical reappraisal*, Methuen, 219–254.

Anon (1950) 'A world land use survey', *Geographical Journal*, **115**, 223–226.

Aschmann, H. (1963) 'Evaluations of dry land environments by societies at various levels of technical competence', in W. Thorne (Ed.), *Land and Water Use*, American Association for the Advancement of Science, Publication No. 73, 133–144.

Aubert, G. (1962) 'Arid zone soils', in *Problems of the Arid zone*, UNESCO, Arid Zone Research, 18.

Augelli, J. P. (1953) 'Patterns and problems of land tenure in the Lesser Antilles; Antigua, B.W.I', *Economic Geography*, **29**, 362–367.

Augelli, J. P. (1958a) 'The Latvians of Varpa; a foreign colony on the Brazilian frontier fringe', *Geographical Review*, **48**, 365–387.

Augelli, J. P. (1958b) 'Cultural and economic changes of Bastos, a Japanese colony on Brazil's Paulista frontier', *Annals of the Association of American Geographers*, **48**, 3–19.

Bacon, P. (1958) 'Population growth and its impact on geographic education', *Journal of Geography*, **57**, 111–118.

Baddruddin, M. (1961) 'Drainage by tube-wells in Rechna Doab, West Pakistan', *Pakistan Geographical Review*, **16**, 27–45.

Baer, W. (1964) 'Regional inequality and economic growth in Brazil', *Economic Development and Cultural Change*, **12**, 268–285.

Baker, O. E. (1947) 'The population prospect in relation to the world's agricultural resources', *Journal of Geography*, **46**, 203–230.

Baker, S. (1966) 'The utility of tropical regional studies', *The Professional Geographer*, **18**, 20–22.

Barbour, K. M. (1957) 'A new approach to the Nile waters problem', *International Affairs*, **33**, 319–330.

Barbour, K. M. (1959) 'Irrigation in the Sudan; its growth, distribution and potential extension', *Transactions of the Institute of British Geographers*, **26**, 243–263.

Barbour, K. M. (1961) 'Population mapping in the Sudan', in K. M. Barbour and R. M. Prothero (Eds.), *Essays on African Population*, Routledge and Kegan Paul, 99–114.

Barbour, K. M. (1966) 'Facility profiles as criteria for the geographical assessment of development schemes', *Nigerian Journal of Economic and Social Studies*, **8**, 455–479.

Batalla, A. B. (1965) 'A new map of economic zones and regions of Mexico', *Geographia Polonica*, **8**, 47–52.

Beard, J. S. (1953) 'The savanna vegetation of northern tropical America', *Ecological Monographs*, **23** (2), 149–215.

Beaujeu-Garnier, J. (1966) *Geography of Population*, Longmans.

Beckinsale, R. P. (1957) 'The nature of tropical rainfall', *Tropical Agriculture*, **34**, 76–87.

Beguin, H. (1963) 'Aspects structurels du commerce exterieur des pays sous-développés', *Tiers-Monde*, **4**, 81–119.

Benneh, G. (1965) 'Land tenure and farming system in Nkrankwanta', *Bulletin of the Ghana Geographical Association*, 10, 6–15.

Bennett, M. K. (1941) 'International contrasts in food consumption', *Geographical Review*, 31, 365–376.

Bennett, M. K. (1951) 'International disparities in consumption levels', *American Economic Review*, 12, 632–649.

Bennett, M. K. (1954) *The World's Food*, Harpers.

Bennett, M. K. (1963) 'Longer and shorter views of the Malthusian prospect', *Food Research Institute Studies*, 4, 3–11.

Berry, B. J. L. (1960) 'An inductive approach to the regionalization of economic development', in N. Ginsburg (Ed.), 'Essays on Geography and Economic Development', *University of Chicago, Department of Geography, Research Paper* No. 62, 78–107.

Berry, B. J. L. (1961a) 'Basic patterns of economic development', in N. Ginsburg (Ed.), 'Atlas of Economic Development', *University of Chicago, Department of Geography, Research Paper No. 68.*

Berry, B. J. L. (1961b) 'City-size distributions and economic development', *Economic Development and Cultural change*, 9, 573–587.

Berry, B. J. L. (1965) 'Identification of declining regions: an empirical study of the dimensions of rural poverty', in W. D. Wood and R. S. Thoman (Eds.), *Areas of Economic Stress in Canada*, Queen's University, Kingston, Relations Centre, 22–70.

Berry, B. J. L. (1969) 'Relationships between regional economic development and the urban system: the case of Chile', *Tidschrift voor Economische en Sociale Geographie*, 60, 283–307.

Berry, B. J. L. and Horton, F. E. (1970) *Geographic Perspectives on Urban Systems: with integrated readings*, Prentice-Hall.

Best, R. (1965) 'Production factors in the tropics', *Netherlands Journal of Agricultural Science*, 10, 347–353.

Blake, G. H. (1969) 'The origins and evolution of Israel's Moshav', *Kultur-geografi*, 109, 293–311.

Blaut, J. M. (1967) 'Geography and the development of peasant agriculture', in S. B. Cohen (Ed.), *Problems and Trends in American Geography*, Basic Books, 200–220.

Blumenstock, D. I. (1958) 'Distribution and characteristics of tropical climates', *Proceedings of the North Pacific Science Congress, 1957* (Bangkok), 20, 3–21.

Board, C. (1961) 'The world land use system and South Africa', *South African Geographical Journal*, 43, 19–32.

Boesch, H. (1968) 'The world land use survey', *International Yearbook of Cartography*, 8, 136–143.

Boserup, E. (1965) *The Conditions of Agricultural Growth*, Allen and Unwin.

Bowen-Jones, H., Dewdney, J. C. and Fisher, W. B. (1961) 'Malta: background for development', *Durham Colleges Research Series*, No. 5.

Brice, W. C. (1954) 'The population of Turkey in 1950', *Geographical Journal*, 120, 347–352.

Brichambaut, G. P. de and Wallen, C. C. (1963) *A Study of Agro-Climatology in Semi-Arid and Arid Zones of the Near East*, World Meteorological Organization, Technical Note No. 56, Geneva, 6–8.

Brisseau, J. (1963) 'Les "Barrios" de Petase: faubourgs populaires d'une banlieue de Caracas', *Les Cahiers d'outre Mer*, **16**, 5–52.

Brooke, C. (1967) 'Types of food shortages in Tanzania', *Geographical Review*, **57**, 333–357.

Brown, L. A. and Moore, G. (1969) 'Diffusion research in geography: a perspective', *Progress in Geography*, **1**, 121–157.

Buchanan, K. (1964) 'Profiles of the Third World', *Pacific Viewpoint*, **5**, 97–126.

Buchanan, K. (1966) 'The people's communes after 6 years', *Pacific Viewpoint*, **6**, 52–64.

Buchanan. K. (1968) *Out of Asia: Asian themes 1958–66*, Sydney University Press.

Buchanan, K. and Pugh, J. C. (1955) *Land and People in Nigeria*, London University Press.

Budowski, G. (1956) 'Tropical savannas; a sequence of forest felling and repeated burnings', *Turrialba*, **6**, 23–33.

Bunting, A. H. (1961) 'Some problems of agricultural climatology in tropical Africa', *Geography*, **46**, 283–294.

Burke, T. (1966) 'Food and population, time and space: formulating the problem', *Journal of Geography*, **65**, 58–66.

Burton, I. and Kates, R. W. (1965) *Readings in Resource Management and Conservation*, University of Chicago Press.

Butland, G. J. (1966) 'Frontiers of settlement in South America', *Revista Geographica*, **65**, 93–108.

Cantor, L. M. (1967) *A World Geography of Irrigation*, Oliver and Boyd.

Carey-Jones, N. S. (1965) 'The decolonization of the White Highlands of Kenya', *Geographical Journal*, **131**, 186–201.

Carpenter, K. J. (1969) 'Man's dietary needs', in Sir Joseph Hutchinson (Ed.), *Population and Food Supply*, Cambridge University Press, 61–74.

Carr, M. (1964) 'World population trends', *Pacific Viewpoint*, **5**, 211–214.

Carter, G. F. and Pendleton, R. L. (1956) 'The humid soil: process and time', *Geographical Review*, **46**, 488–507.

Chakravarti, A. K. (1970) 'Food sufficiency patterns in India', *Geographical Review*, **60**, 208–228.

Chambers, J. V., Dalrymple, P. C. and Jones, H. (1957) *Wet Tropics: limits and characteristics*, Headquarters Quartermasters Research and Engineering Command, US Army, Technical Report, EP–63.

Chang, Jen-Hu (1968) 'The agricultural potential of the humid tropics', *Geographical Review*, **58**, 333–361.

Chang, S. D. (1966) 'The rôle of the agricultural geographer in communist China', *The Professional Geographer*, **18**, 125–128.

Chapman, M. (1969) 'Geography and the study of development', *Journal of Developing Areas*, **3**, 319–338.

Chatterjee, S. P. (1952) 'India and world food supply', *Geographical Review of India*, **14**, 1–10.

Chatterjee, S. P. (1968a) 'Toward global peace and harmony: rapprochement between developing and developed countries', in S. P. Chatterjee (Ed.), *Developing Countries of the World*, International Geographical Union, Indian National Committee for Geography, 1–56.

Chatterjee, S. P. (Ed.) (1968b) *Developing Countries of the World*, International Geographical Union, Indian National Committee for Geography, Calcutta.

Chaturvedi, B. N. (1962) 'Andhra Pradesh: a food surplus state in a deficit country', *Deccan Geographer*, **1**, 54–67.

Christodoulou, D. (1959) 'The evolution of the rural land use pattern in Cyprus', *World Land Use Monograph*, **2**.

Chung, Y. P. (1968) 'Geography and agricultural development in China', *Professional Geographer*, **20**, 163–166.

Church, R. J. Harrison (1961) 'Problems and development of the dry zone of West Africa', *Geographical Journal*, **127**, 187–204.

Church, R. J. Harrison (1963) 'Observations on large scale irrigation development in Africa', *Agricultural Economics Bulletin for Africa*, **4**, 1–48.

Church, R. J. Harrison (1966) *Some Geographical Aspects of West African Development*, University of London Press.

Church, R. J. Harrison (1969) 'Some problems of regional economic development in West Africa', *Economic Geography*, **45**, 53–62.

Clark, C. (1967a) *Population Growth and Land Use*, Macmillan.

Clark, C. (1967b) *The Economics of Irrigation*, Pergamon Press.

Clark, C. (1970) *Starvation or Plenty*, Secker and Warburg.

Clarke, C. G. (1966) 'Population pressure in Kingston, Jamaica: a study of unemployment and overcrowding', *Transactions of the Institute of British Geographers*, **38**, 165–182.

Clarke, J. I. (1965) *Population Geography*, Pergamon.

Clarke, J. I. (1966) *Sierre Leone in Maps*, London University Press.

Clarke, J. I. (1968a) 'Population distribution in Sierre Leone', in J. C. Caldwell and C. Okonjo (Eds.), *The Population of Tropical Africa*, Longmans, 270–277.

Clarke, J. I. (1968b) 'World population and food resources; a critique', *Land Use and Resources: studies in applied geography*, Institute of British Geographers, Special Publication No. 1, 53–70.

Clarke, J. I. (1971) *Population Geography and the Developing Countries*, Pergamon.

Clarke, W. C. and Street, J. M. (1967) 'Soil fertility and cultivation practices in New Guinea', *Journal of Tropical Geography*, **24**, 7–11.

Cole, M. M. (1956) 'Land use studies in the Transvaal Lowveld', *World Land Use Survey. Occasional Paper* No. 1.

Cole, M. M. (1960a) 'The Brazilian Savanna', *Revista Geografica*, **52**, 5–40.

Cole, M. M. (1960b) 'Cerrado, Caatinga and Pantanal: the distribution and origin of the savanna vegetation of Brazil', *Geographical Journal*, **126**, 168–179.

Cole, M. M. (1963a) 'Vegetation and geomorphology in Northern Rhodesia: an aspect of the distribution of the savanna of Central Africa', *Geographical Journal*, **129**, 290–310.

Cole, M. M. (1963b) 'Vegetation, nomenclature and classification with particular reference to the savannas', *South African Geographical Journal*, **45**, 3–14.

Courtenay, P. *Plantation Agriculture*, Bell, 1965.

Cox, I. H. (1970) 'New possibilities and techniques for land use and related surveys with special reference to the developing countries', *World Land Use Survey. Occasional Paper*, No. 9.

Cressey, G. B. (1953) 'Land for 2·4 billion neighbours', *Economic Geography*, **29**, 1–9.

Cressey, G. B. (1958) 'Qanats, Karetz and foggaras', *Geographical Review*, **48**, 27–44.

Crist, R. E. (1942) 'Land tenure problems in Venezuela', *American Journal of Economics and Sociology*, **1**, 143–154.

Crist, R. E. (1956) 'Along the Llanos-Andes border in Venezuela: then and now', *Geographical Review*, **46**, 187–208.

Crist, R. E. (1957–58) 'Land for the fellahin', *American Journal of Economics and Sociology*, **17**, 295–306.

Crist, R. E. (1964) 'Tropical subsistence agriculture in Latin America: some neglected aspects and implications', *Annual Report of the Smithsonian Institution for 1963*, Publication 4530, 503–519.

Crist, R. E. (1965) 'Traditional agriculture: diagnosis and prognosis', *Geographical Review*, **55**, 434–438.

Crist, R. E. and Guhl, E. (1957) 'Pioneer settlement in Eastern Colombia', *Annual Report of the Smithsonian Institution for 1956*, 132–137.

Crossley, J. C. (1963) 'Agrarian reform in Latin America', *The Year Book of World Affairs, 1963*, 123–149.

Cumberland, K. B. (1951) 'Geography and land use survey in the South West Pacific: a review and suggestion', *New Zealand Geographer*, **7**, 139–155.

Cutshall, A. (1952) 'Problems of land ownership in the Philippines', *Economic Geography*, **28**, 31–36.

Dale, E. H. (1963) 'The demographic problem of the West Indies', *Scottish Geographical Magazine*, **79**, 23–31.

Dambaugh, L. N. (1959) 'Colombia's population resource', *Journal of Geography*, **58**, 174–180.

Daniel, J. B. McI. (1967) 'The Swazi rural economy: some thoughts on the problems of land tenure', *South African Geographical Society, Jubilee Conference Proceedings*, 287–296.

Darby, H. C. (1943) 'The movement of population to and from Cambridge-shire between 1851 and 1861', *Geographical Journal*, **101**, 118–124.

Davidson, B. R. (1965) *The Northern Myth; a study of the physical and economic limits to agricultural and pastoral development in tropical Australia*, Melbourne University Press.

Davies, D. H. (1957) 'Observations on land use in Iraq', *Economic Geography*, **33**, 122–134.

Davies, H. R. J. (1958) 'Irrigation in Jordan', *Economic Geography*, **34**, 264–271.

Davis, K. (1960) 'The origin and growth of urbanisation in the world', in H. M. Mayer and C. F. Kohn (Eds.), *Readings in Urban Geography*, University of Chicago Press, 59–68.

Davis, K. (1969) 'The urbanization of the human population', in Gerald Breese (Ed.), *The City in Newly Developing Countries; readings on urbanism and urbanization*, Prentice-Hall, 5–20.

Davis, K. and Golden, H. H. (1954) 'Urbanization and the development of pre-industrial areas', *Economic Development and Cultural Change*, **3**, 1–26.

Davitaya, F. F. (1964) 'Climatic resources of arid zones and their agricultural use in the USSR', in *Land Use in Semi-Arid Mediterranean Climates*, UNESCO, 1964.

Deane, P. and Cole, W. A. (1962) *British Economic Growth, 1688-1959: trends and structure*, Cambridge University Press.

Denevan, W. M. (1965) 'The campo cerrado vegetation of central Brazil', *Geographical Review*, 55, 112-115.

Denis, P. (1965) 'Une dimension nouvelle au Mexique: l'espace economique', *Revue de Géographie de Montreal*, 14, 3-42.

Dennison, E. B. (1959) 'The maintenance of soil fertility in the Southern Guinea Zone of Northern Nigeria', *Tropical Agriculture*, 36, 171-176.

Deshler, W. (1960) 'Livestock trypanosomiasis and human settlement in North-east Uganda', *Geographical Review*, 50, 541-554.

Deshler, W. (1963) 'Cattle in Africa: distribution, types and problems', *Geographical Review*, 53, 52-58.

Despois, J. (1961) 'The development of land use in North Africa (with reference to Spain)', in L. D. Stamp (Ed.), *A History of Land Use in Arid Regions*, UNESCO Arid Zone Research, 17, 245-278.

Dichter, D. (1967) *The North-West Frontier of West Pakistan: a study in regional geography*, Clarendon Press.

Dickinson, R. (1954) 'Land reform in Southern Italy', *Economic Geography*, 30, 157-176.

Diniz, J. A. F. (1969) 'I.G.U.'s suggestions and the types of agriculture: a case study', *Revista Geografica*, 70, 91-108.

Dobby, E. H. G. (1946) 'Some aspects of the human ecology of South East Asia', *Geographical Journal*, 108, 40-54.

Dobby, E. H. G. (1955) 'Padi landscapes of Malaya', *Journal of Tropical Geography*, 6, 1-95.

Dozier, C. L. (1969) *Land Development and Colonization in Latin America: case studies of Peru, Bolivia and Mexico*, Praeger.

Dresch, J. (1967) 'Géographie et sous-developpement', *Annales de Géographie*, 76, 641-643.

Dudal, R. and Bramâo, D. L. (1965) *Dark Clay Soils of Tropical and Sub-Tropical Regions*, Agricultural Development Paper, No. 83, Rome, FAO.

Duncan, C. (1962) 'Resource utilization and the conservation concept', *Economic Geography*, 38, 113-121.

Durand, J. D. (1967) 'A long-range view of world population growth', *Annals of the American Academy of Political and Social Science*, 369, 1-8.

Duru, R. C. (1968) 'Problems of data collection for population studies in Nigeria with particular reference to the 1952/53 census and the Western Region', in J. C. Caldwell and C. Okonjo (Eds.), *The Population of Tropical Africa*, Longmans, 71-77.

Dutt, A. K. and Maikap, A. K. (1969) 'Social development index for West Bengal', *Oriental Geographer*, 93-112.

Dwyer, D. J. (1968a) 'The city in the developing world and the example of South East Asia', *Geography*, 53, 353-364.

Dwyer, D. J. (1968b) 'Problems of urbanization: the example of Hong Kong', in *Land Use and Resources: studies in applied geography*, Institute of British Geographers, Special Publication No. 1, 1968, 169-186.

Edellman, C. H. and Van der Voorde, P. K. J. (1963) 'Important characteristics of alluvial soils in the tropics', *Soil Science*, **95**, 258–263.

Eidt, R. C. (1962) 'Pioneer settlement in Eastern Peru', *Annals of the
Association of American Geographers*, **52**, 255–278.

Eidt, R. C. (1964) 'Comparative problems and techniques in tropical and
semi-tropical pioneer settlements: Colombia, Peru and Argentina',
Yearbook of the Association of Pacific Coast Geographers, **26**, 37–42.

Eidt, R. C. (1967) 'Modern colonization as a facet of land development in
Colombia, South America', *Yearbook of the Association of Pacific Coast
Geographers*, **29**, 21–42.

Eighmy, T. H. (1968) 'Problems of census interpretation in developing
countries', *Svensk Geografisk Årsbok*, **44**, 151–172.

El-Kammash, M. M. (1963) 'On the measurement of economic development
using scalogram analysis', *Papers and Proceedings of the Regional Science
Association*, **11**, 309–334.

Ellefsen, R. (1960) 'Land use in Delhi state', *The Indian Geographer*, **5**,
59–68.

Engberg, H. L. and Hance, W. A. (1969) 'Growth and dispersion of branch
banking in Tropical Africa, 1950–64', *Economic Geography*, **45**, 195–208.

Enjalbert, H. (1960) 'La pression demographique au Mexique', *Les Cahiers
d'Outre-Mer*, **13**, 451–460.

Eyre, J. D. (1964) 'Regional variations in Japanese internal migration',
Papers of the Michigan Academy of Science, Arts and Letters, **49**, 271–284.

Eyre, S. R. (1963) *Vegetation and Soils: a world picture*, Arnold.

Fair, T. J. D. (1963) 'A regional approach to economic development in
Kenya', *South African Geographical Journal*, **45**, 55–57.

Fair, T. J. D. (1965) 'The core-periphery concept and population growth in
South Africa, 1911–1960', *South African Geographical Journal*, **47**, 59–71.

Faniran, A. (1968) 'Creating a commercial dairying industry in a nomadic
pastoral economy', *Australian Geographer*, **10**, 392–401.

Farmer, B. H. (1956) 'Rainfall and water-supply in the dry zone of Ceylon',
in R. W. Steel and C. A. Fisher (Eds.), *Geographical Essays on British
Tropical Lands*, Philip, 225–269.

Farmer, B. H. (1957) *Pioneer Peasant Colonization in Ceylon*, Oxford University Press.

Farmer, B. H. (1960) 'On not controlling sub-division in paddy-lands',
Transactions of the Institute of British Geographers, **28**, 225–237.

Farmer, B. H. (1963) 'Peasant and plantation in Ceylon', *Pacific Viewpoint*,
4, 9–16.

Farmer, B. H. (1965) 'The neglected plateaus of Dandakaranya', *Bombay
Geographical Magazine*, **13**, 21–39.

Farmer, B. H. (1967) 'Le paysan pionnier en Inde: eléments de comparaison
avec Ceylan', *Annales*, **22**, 1227–1244.

Farmer, B. H. (1969a) 'Available food supplies', in Sir Joseph Hutchinson
(Ed.), *Population and Food Supply*, Cambridge University Press, 75–95.

Farmer, B. H. (1969b) *Agricultural Colonization in South and South East Asia*,
University of Hull.

Farmer, B. H. (1971) 'The environmental sciences and economic development',
The Journal of Development Studies, **7**, 257–269.

Fawcett, C. B. (1930) 'The extent of the cultivable land', *Geographical Journal*, **76**, 504–509.

Fifer, J. V. (1967) 'Bolivia's pioneer fringe', *Geographical Review*, **57**, 1–23.

Fisher, C. A. (1959) *The Compleat Geographer*, University of Sheffield.

Fisher, C. A. (1964a) *South-East Asia: a social, economic and political geography*, Methuen.

Fisher, C. A. (1964b) 'Some comments on population growth in South-East Asia with special reference to the period since 1830', in C. D. Cowan (Ed.), *The Economic Development of South-East Asia*, Allen and Unwin.

Fisher, C. A. (1965) *The Reality of Place*, School of Oriental and African Studies, University of London.

Fisher, C. A. (1968) 'Social and economic consequences of western commercial agriculture in south-east Asia', in *Land Use and Resources: studies in applied geography*, IBG Special Publication No. 1, 1968, 147–154.

Fisher, C. A. (1970) 'Whither regional geography', *Geography*, **55**, 373–389.

Fisher, W. B. (1952) 'Quelques facteurs géographiques de la repartition de la malaria en Moyen-Orient', *Annales de Géographie*, **61**, 263–274.

Fisher, W. B. (1968) 'Geographical contributions to development surveys', *Advancement of Science*, **25**, 158–170.

Fisk, B. (1952) 'Dujaila—Iraq's pilot project for land settlement', *Economic Geography*, **28**, 343–354.

Floyd, B. (1959) *Changing Patterns of African Land Use in Southern Rhodesia*, Rhodes-Livingstone Institute.

Floyd, B. N. (1962) 'Land apportionment in Southern Rhodesia', *Geographical Review*, **52**, 566–582.

Floyd, B. N. (1965) 'Soil erosion and deterioration in eastern Nigeria', *Nigerian Geographical Journal*, **8**, 33–44.

Floyd, B. and Adinde, M. (1967) 'Farm settlements in Eastern Nigeria: a geographical appraisal', *Economic Geography*, **43**, 189–230.

Fonaroff, L. S. (1958) 'Man and malaria in Trinidad: ecological perspectives of a changing health hazard', *Annals of the Association of American Geographers*, **58**, 526–556.

FAO (1956) *Pastures and Fodder Crops in Rotations in the Mediterranean.*

FAO (1963) *Third World Food Survey*, Freedom From Hunger Campaign Basic Study, No. 11.

FAO (1966) *African Agricultural Development: reflections on the major lines of advance and the barriers to progress.*

FAO (1968) *Production Yearbook*, 22.

Forde, E. R. A. (1967) 'Regionalization of economic development in Sierra Leone', *Sierra Leone Geographical Journal*, **11**, 43–50.

Fosberg, F. R., Garnier, B. J. and Kuchler, A. W. (1961) 'Delimitation of the humid tropics', *Geographical Review*, **51**, 337–347.

Fournier, F. (1967) 'Research on soil erosion and soil conservation in Africa', *African Soils*, **12**, 53–96.

Franklin, S. H. (1969) *The European Peasantry: the final phase*, Methuen.

Friedmann, J. (1963) 'Regional economic policy for developing areas', *Papers and Proceedings of the Regional Science Association*, **11**, 41–61.

Frood, A. McKie (1967) 'The Aswan High Dam and the Egyptian economy', in R. W. Steel and R. Lawton (Eds.), *Liverpool Essays in Geography*, Longmans, 363–379.

Fryer, D. W. (1953) 'The "million city" in South East Asia', *Geographical Review*, **43**, 474–494.

Fryer, D. W. (1958) 'World income and types of economies', *Economic Geography*, **34**, 283–303.

Fryer, D. W. (1965) *World Economic Development*, McGraw Hill.

Fryer, D. W. (1970) *Emerging South East Asia*, Philip.

Garnier, B. J. (1957) 'The climatic aspects of irrigation development in Nigeria', *Advancement of Science*, **13**, 351–354.

Gaussen, H. and Legris, P. (1963) 'La délimitation des zones tropicales humides', *Annales de Géographie*, **72**, 313–328.

Gauthier, H. L. (1968) 'Least cost flows in a capacitated network: a Brazilian example', in F. Horton (Ed.), 'Geographical studies of urban transportation and network analysis', *North Western University Studies in Geography*, No. 16, 102–127.

Gauthier, H. L. (1970) 'Geography, transportation and regional development', *Economic Geography*, **46**, 612–619.

Geigner, Pedro S. and Oxnard, S. (1969) 'Aspects of population growth in Brazil', *Revista Geografica*, **70**, 7–28.

George, P. (1959) 'Rythme d'accroisement de la population mondiale', *Annales de Géographie*, **68**, 459–461.

Ginsburg, N. S. (1953) 'Geographic research opportunities in the field of economic development', *Professional Geographer*, 13–15.

Ginsburg, N. S. (1957) 'Natural resources and economic development', *Annals of the Association of American Geographers*, **47**, 197–212.

Ginsburg, N. S. (1961) *Atlas of Economic Development*, University of Chicago, Department of Geography Research Paper No. 68.

Ginsburg, N. S. (1967) 'On geography and economic development', in S. B. Cohen (Ed.), *Problems and Trends in American Geography*, Basic Books, 174–186.

Ginsburg, N. S. (1969) 'Tasks of geography', *Geography*, **54**, 401–409.

Gleave, M. B. and White, H. P. (1969) 'Population density and agricultural systems in West Africa', in M. F. Thomas and G. W. Whittington (Eds.), *Environment and Land Use in Africa*, Methuen, 273–300.

Glover, J., Robinson, P. and Henderson, J. P. (1954) 'Provisional maps of the reliability of annual rainfall in East Africa', *Quarterly Journal of the Royal Meteorological Society*, **80**, 602–609.

Gonzalez, A. (1966) 'Problems of agricultural development in a pioneer coastal region of southwestern coastal Mexico', *Revista Geographica*, **64**, 29–32.

Gonzalez, A. (1971) 'Population growth and socio-economic development; the Latin American experience', *Journal of Geography*, **70** (1), 36–46.

Goor, G. A. W. Van de (1966) 'Agriculture with special reference to rice cultivation in humid tropical zone deltas', in *Scientific Problems of the Humid Tropical Zone Deltas and their Implications*, UNESCO, 301–304.

Gosal, G. S. (1961) 'Internal migration in India—a regional analysis', *Indian Geographical Journal*, **36**, 106–121.

Gould, P. R. and Sparks, J. P. (1969) 'The geographical context of human diets in southern Guatemala', *Geographical Review*, **59**, 58–82.

Gourou, P. (1966) *The Tropical World: its social and economic conditions and its future status*, Longmans.

Gregor, H. F. (1965) 'The changing plantation', *Annals of the Association of American Geographers*, **55**, 221–238.

Gregory, S. (1969) 'Rainfall reliability', in M. F. Thomas and G. W. Whittington (Eds.), *Environment and Land Use in Africa*, Methuen, 57–82.

Grenier, F. (1964–65) 'Agriculture et reforme agraire en Botine', *Cahiers de Géographie de Quebec*, **7**, 26–35.

Grigg, D. (1966) 'The geography of farm-size: a preliminary survey', *Economic Geography*, **42**, 205–235.

Grigg, D. (1970) *The Harsh Lands*, Macmillan.

Grigg, D. (1971) 'Trends in the world's agricultural population', *Geography*, **56**, 320–324.

Grove, A. T. (1951) 'Soil erosion and population problems in south-east Nigeria', *Geographical Journal*, **117**, 291–306.

Grove, A. T. (1961) 'Population densities and agriculture', in K. M. Barbour and R. M. Prothero (Eds.), *Essays on African Population*, Routledge and Kegan Paul, 115–136.

Gulik, L. H. Jr. (1963) 'Irrigation systems of the former Sind Province, West Pakistan', *Geographical Review*, **53**, 79–99.

Guyol, N. B. (1960) 'Energy consumption and economic development', in N. Ginsberg (Ed.), 'Essays on Geographic and Economic Development', *University of Chicago, Department of Geography, Research Paper* No. 62, 65–77.

Guzman, L. E. (1960) 'The economic geographer in economic development', *The Professional Geographer*, **12**, 16–18.

Hägerstrand, T. (1965) 'Aspects of the spatial structure of social communication and the diffusion of information', *Papers of the Regional Science Association*, **16**, 27–42.

Hägerstrand, T. (1967) *Innovation Diffusion as a Spatial Process*, University of Chicago Press.

Hamdan, G. (1961) 'Evolution of irrigated agriculture in Egypt', in L. D. Stamp (Ed.), *A History of Land Use in Arid Regions*, UNESCO Arid Zone Research, **17**, 133–157.

Hampton, P. (1968) 'Regional economic development in New Zealand', *Journal of Regional Science*, **8**, 41–51.

Hance, W. A. (1954) 'The Gezira: an example in development', *Geographical Review*, **44**, 253–270.

Hance, W. A. (1967) *African Economic Development*, Pall Mall.

Hance, W. A. (1970) *Population, Migration and Urbanization in Africa*, Columbia University Press.

Hance, W. A., Kotshcar, V. and Peterec, R. J. (1961) 'Source areas of export production in tropical Africa', *Geographical Review*, **51**, 487–499.

Hartley, R. G. and Norris, J. M. (1969) 'Demographic regions in Libya: a principal components analysis of economic and demographic variables', *Tijdschift voor Economische en Sociale Geografie*, **60**, 221–227.

Hartshorn, T. A. (1971) 'The spatial structure of socio-economic development in the south east, 1950–1960', *Geographical Review*, **61**, 265–283.

Hartshorne, R. (1959) 'The rôle of the state in economic growth', in H. G. J. Aitken (Ed.), *The State and Economic Growth*, Committee on Economic Growth, 287–324.

Hellen, A. (1962) 'Some aspects of land use and overpopulation in the Ngoni Reserves of Northern Rhodesia', *Erdkunde*, **16**, 190–205.

Hellener, G. K. (1966) 'Typology in development theory: the land surplus economy (Nigeria)', *Food Research Institute Studies*, **6**, 181–194.

Henderson, D. A. (1965) 'Arid lands under reform in northwest Mexico', *Economic Geography*, **41**, 300–312.

Higbee, E. (1957) *The American Oasis: the land and its uses*, Knopf.

Highsmith, R. M. Jr. (1965) 'Irrigated lands of the world', *Geographical Review*, **55**, 382–389.

Hills, E. S. (1966) *Arid Lands: a geographical appraisal*, Methuen.

Hills, T. (1965) 'Savannas: a review of a major research problem in geography', *Canadian Geographer*, **9**, 216–228.

Hilton, T. E. (1960) *Ghana Population Atlas*, Nelson.

Hilton, T. E. (1961) 'Population mapping in Ghana', in K. M. Barbour and R. M. Prothero (Eds.), *Essays on African Population*, Routledge and Kegan Paul, 83–98.

Hilton, T. E. (1968) 'Population growth and distribution in the upper region of Ghana', in J. C. Caldwell and C. Okonjo (Eds.), *The Population of Tropical Africa*, Longmans, 278–290.

Hinderink, J. (1969) 'Purpose and scope of the human geography of "Non-western" countries', *Tijdschrift voor Economische en Sociale Geographie*, **59**, 289–293.

Hirsch, G. P. (1967) 'Jamaica—a regional approach', *Regional Studies*, **1**, 47–63.

Hirschman, A. O. (1958) *The Strategy of Economic Development*, Yale University Press.

Ho, R. (1965) 'Land settlement projects in Malaya: an assessment of the rôle of the federal land development authority', *Journal of Tropical Geography*, **20**, 1–15.

Ho, R. (1969) 'Rice production in Malaya: a review of problems and prospects', *Journal of Tropical Geography*, **29**, 21–32.

Hoare, E. S. (1967) 'Irrigation in semi-arid regions', *Outlook on Agriculture*, **5**, 139–143.

Hodder, B. (1968) *Economic Development in the Tropics*, Methuen.

Horst, O. (1967) 'The specter of death in a Guatemalan community', *Geographical Review*, **57**, 151–167.

Horstmann, K. (1963) 'Population census results as a basic material for the world population map', *Geografiska Annaler*, **45**, 251–261.

Horton, F. E., McConnell, H. and Tirtha, R. (1970) 'Spatial patterns of socio-economic structure in India', *Tijdschrift voor Economische en Sociale Geographie*, **61**, 101–113.

Hoselitz, B. F. (1959) 'The cities of India and their problems', *Annals of the Association of American Geographers*, **49**, 223–231.

Hoselitz, B. F. (1962) 'The rôle of urbanization in economic development:

some international comparisons', in R. Turner (Ed.), *India's Urban Future*, University of California Press, 157–181.

Hoy, D. R. (1968) 'Geography's rôle in development planning in Guatemala', *The Professional Geographer*, **20**, 336–360.

Hoyle, B. S. (1970) 'Transport and economic growth in developing countries: the case of East Africa', in R. H. Osborne, F. A. Barnes and J. C. Doornkamp (Eds.), *Geographical Essays in Honour of K. C. Edwards*, University of Nottingham, 187–196.

Hunter, J. M. (1961a) 'Geography in the service of economic development', *Bulletin of the Ghana Geographical Association*, **6** (2), 44–48.

Hunter, J. M. (1961b) 'Akotuakrom: a devastated cocoa village in Ghana', *Transactions of the Institute of British Geographers*, **29**, 161–186.

Hunter, J. M. (1966) 'River blindness in Nangodi, northern Ghana', *Geographical Review*, **56**, 398–416.

Hunter, J. M. (1967) 'Seasonal hunger in a part of the West African savanna', *Transactions of the Institute of British Geographers*, **41**, 167–186.

Hurst, H. F. (1927) 'Progress in the study of the hydrology of the Nile in the last twenty years', *Geographical Journal*, **69**, 440–463.

Hustich, I. (1968) 'Finland: a developed and an undeveloped country', *Acta Geografica*, **20**, 155–173.

Hutt, M. S. R. (1967) 'The geographical approach in medical research', *East African Geographical Review*, **5**, 1–8.

Igbozurike, M. (1970) 'Fragmentation in tropical agriculture: an over-rated phenomenon', *The Professional Geographer*, **22**, 321–325.

Ignatieff, V. and Lemos, P. (1963) 'Some management aspects of the more important tropical soils', *Soil Science*, **95**, 243–249.

Irwin, P. G. (1966) 'Land use and land tenure in the Blanche Bay District of New Britain', *Australian Geographer*, **10**, 95–104.

Jafri, A. H. (1953) 'A study of fragmentation of holdings in West Pakistan', *Pakistan Geographical Review*, **8**, 70–77.

James, P. E. (1952) 'Observations on the physical geography of north east Brazil', *Annals of the Association of American Geographers*, **42**, 153–176.

James, P. E. (1953) 'Patterns of land use in north east Brazil', *Annals of the Association of American Geographers*, **43**, 98–126.

James, P. E. (1968) 'Changing patterns of population and settlement in Latin America', in S. J. Chatterjee (Ed.), *Developing Countries of the World*, International Geographical Union, Indian National Committee for Geography.

Janlekha, K. (1968) 'Saraphi', *World Land Use Survey, Occasional Paper*, No. 8.

Jansen, A. C. M. (1970) 'The value of growth pole theory for economic geography', *Tijdschrift voor Economische en Sociale Geografie*, **61**, 67–76.

Jarret, H. R. (1956) 'Rice production in Sierra Leone', *Malayan Journal of Tropical Geography*, **8**, 74–76.

Jewitt, T. N. (1966) 'Soils of arid lands', in E. S. Hills (Ed.), *Arid Lands: a geographical appraisal*, Methuen, 103–126.

Joosten, J. H. L. (1962) 'Figures and the world's hunger', *Tijdschrift voor Economische en Sociale Geografie*, **53**, 42–46.

Jurion, F. and Henry, J. (1951) 'Cropping systems in the equatorial forest region of the Belgian Congo', *United Nations Symposium on the Conservation and Utilisation of Resources*, **6**, 563–566.

Kamerschen, D. R. (1968) 'Literacy and socio-economic development', *Rural Sociology*, **33**, 175–188.

Karan, P. P. (1957) 'Land utilization and agriculture in an Indian village', *Land Economics*, **33**, 55–64.

Kay, G. (1965) 'Changing patterns of settlement and land use in the Eastern Province of Northern Rhodesia', *Occasional Papers in Geography*, No. 2, University of Hull.

Kay, G. (1969) 'Agricultural progress in Zambia', in M. F. Thomas and G. W. Whittington (Eds.), *Environment and Land Use in Africa*, Methuen, 495–524.

Kayser, B. (1969) *L'Agriculture et la Société rurale des Régions tropicales*, Société d'Edition d'Enseignement Supérieur.

Keeble, D. A. (1967) 'Models of economic development', in R. J. Chorley and P. Haggett (Eds.) *Models in Geography*, Methuen, 243–302.

Keller, F. L. (1950) 'Finca Ingavi'—a medieval survival on the Bolivian Altiplano', *Economic Geography*, **26**, 37–50.

Keller, F. L. (1955) 'Institutional barriers to economic development—some examples from Bolivia', *Economic Geography*, **31**, 351–363.

Kellog, C. E. (1953) 'Potentialities and problems of arid soils', in *Desert Research: proceedings of an international symposium in Jerusalem*, Special Publication, No. 2, Research Council of Israel, 19–42.

Kellog, C. E. (1956) 'World food and agricultural potentialities', *American Economic Review, Papers and Proceedings*, **46**, 319–326.

Kellog, C. E. (1960) 'Transfer of basic skills of food production', *Annals of the American Academy of Political and Social Science*, **331**, 32–38.

Kellog, C. E. (1963) 'Shifting cultivation', *Soil Science*, **95**, 221–230.

Kenworthy, J. M. (1964) 'Rainfall and the water resources of East Africa', in R. W. Steel and R. M. Prothero (Eds.), *Geographers and the Tropics; Liverpool Essays*, Longmans, 111–138.

Kenworthy, J. M. and Glover, J. (1958) 'The reliability of the main rains in Kenya', *East African Agricultural Journal*, **23**, 267–272.

Knight, C. G. (1971) 'The ecology of African sleeping sickness', *Annals of the Association of American Geographers*, **61**, 23–44.

Koerner, F. (1969) 'Décolonisation et économie de plantations', *Annales de Géographie*, **78**, 654–679.

Kohlhepp, G. (1969) 'Types of agricultural colonization on subtropical Brazilian Campos Limpas', *Revista Geographica*, **70**, 131–156.

Kostrowicki, J. (1968) 'Agricultural typology. Agricultural regionalisation. Agricultural development', *Geographia Polonica*, **14**, 265–274.

Kostrowicki, J. and Helburn, N. (1967) *Agricultural Typology, Principles and Methods* (mimeographed), Boulder, Colorado.

Kostrowicki, J. and Tyszkiewicz, W. (1970a) *Agricultural Typology: selected methodological materials*, International Geographical Union Commission on Agricultural Typology, 1970.

Kostrowicki, J. and Tyszkiewicz, W. (1970b) 'Essays on agricultural typology and land utilization', *Geographia Polonica*, **19**.

Kovda, V. A. (1969) 'Land use development in the arid regions of the Russian plain, the Caucasus and Central Asia', in L. D. Stamp (Ed.),

A History of Land Use in the Arid Zone, Paris, UNESCO Arid Zone Research, **17**, 199–244.

Krinks, P. A. (1970) 'Peasant colonization in Mindanao', *Journal of Tropical Geography*, **30**, 38–47.

Krishnan, V. (1960) 'Self sufficiency of Tamilnad in foodgrains', *Indian Geographical Journal*, **35**, 37–51.

Kuriyan, G. (1952) 'Food problem in India', in G. Kuriyan (Ed.), *Indian Geographical Society Silver Jubilee Souvenir and N. Subrahmanyam Memorial Volume*, University of Madras Press, 203–216.

Kuriyan, G. (1968) 'Is India overpopulated?', *Indian Geographical Journal*, **43**, 22–28.

Lacoste, Y. (1962) 'Le sous-development: quelques ouvrages significatifs parus depuis dix ans', *Annales de Géographie*, **71**, 385–386, 247–278, 387–414.

Lacoste, Y. (1964) 'Perspectives de la géographie active en pays sous-développé', in P. George, R. Gugliolmo, B. Kayser and Y. Lacoste (Eds.), *La Géographie Active*, Presses Universitaires de France, 45–168.

Lacoste, Y. (1965) *Géographie de sous-Développment'*, Presses Universitaires de France.

Lambert, A. M. (1963) 'Farm consolidation in Europe', *Geography*, **48**, 31–48.

Law, C. M. (1967) 'The growth of urban population in England and Wales, 1801–1911', *Transactions of the Institute of British Geographers*, **41**, 125–143.

Lawes, D. A. (1962) 'The influence of rainfall conservation on the fertility of the loess plain soil of Northern Nigeria', *Nigerian Geographical Journal*, **5**, 33–38.

Learmonth, A. T. A. (1957) 'Some contrasts in the regional geography of Malaria in India and Pakistan', *Transactions of the Institute of British Geographers*, **23**, 37–60.

Learmonth, A. T. A. (1958) 'Medical geography in Indo-Pakistan', *Indian Geographical Journal*, **33**, 1–59.

Learmonth, A. T. A. (1959) 'Geography and health in the tropical forest zone', in R. Miller and J. W. Watson (Eds.) *Geographical Essays in Memory of Alan G. Ogilvie*, Nelson, 195–220.

Learmonth, A. T. A. (1961) 'Medical geography in India and Pakistan', *Geographical Journal*, **127**, 10–26.

Learmonth, A. T. A. (1964) 'Retrospect on a project in applied regional geography, Mysore State, India', in R. W. Steel and R. M. Prothero (Eds.), *Geographers and the Tropics: Liverpool Essays*, Longmans, 323–348.

Learmonth, A. T. A. (1966) 'Selected aspects of India's population geography', *Australian Journal of Politics and History*, **12**, 146–154.

Lebon, J. H. G. (1959) 'Land use mapping in Sudan', *Economic Geography*, **34**, 60–70.

Lebon, J. H. G. (1965) 'Land use in Sudan', *World Land Use Survey*, *Monograph* No. 4.

Ledger, D. C. (1963) 'The Niger dams project of Nigeria', *Tijdschrift voor Economische en Sociale Geographie*, **54**, 232–247.

Ledger, D. C. (1964) 'Some hydrological characteristics of West African rivers', *Transactions of the Institute of British Geographers*, **35**, 73–90.

Ledger, D. C. (1969) 'The dry season flow characteristics of West African rivers', in M. F. Thomas and G. W. Whittington (Eds.), *Environment and Land Use in Africa*, Methuen, 83–102.

Leighly, J. B. (1953) 'Dry climates; their nature and distribution', *Desert Research: proceedings of an international symposium held in Jerusalem*, Research Council of Israel, Special Publication No. 2, 3–18.

Lentnek, B. (1969) 'Economic transition from traditional to commercial agriculture: the case of El Llano, Mexico', *Annals of the Association of American Geographers*, **59**, 65–84.

Leszczycki, S. (1968) 'Map of economic regions of the world', *Geographia Polonica*, **14**, 231–239.

Leurquin, P. P. (1967) 'Rice in Colombia: a case study in agricultural development', *Food Research Institute Studies*, **7**, 217–303.

Lewis, G. M. (1968) 'Levels of living in the north-eastern United States, 1960: a new approach to regional geography', *Transactions of the Institute of British Geographers*, **45**, 11–38.

Linton, D. L. (1958) 'Millionaire cities to-day and yesterday', *Geography*, **43**, 253–258.

Linton, D. L. (1961) 'Population and food in the tropical world', *Advancement of Science*, **74**, 391–401.

Logan, M. I. (1970) 'The spatial dimensions of economic development: the case of the upper Midwest', *Regional Studies*, **4**, 117–125.

Lonsdale, R. E. and Thompson, J. H. (1960) 'A map of the USSR's manufacturing', *Economic Geography*, **36**, 36–52.

Lowenthal, D. (1958) 'Production and population in Jamaica', *Geographical Review*, **48**, 568–571.

Luna, T. W. (1963) 'Some aspects of agricultural development and settlement in Basilan Island, Southern Philippines', *Pacific Viewpoint*, **4**, 17–24.

McGee, T. G. (1963) 'The cultural role of cities; a case study of Kuala Lumpur', *Journal of Tropical Geography*, **17**, 178–196.

McGee, T. G. (1964) 'The rural-urban continuum debate: the pre-industrial city and rural-urban migration', *Pacific Viewpoint*, **5**, 159–181.

McGee, T. G. (1967) *The South East Asian City*, Bell.

McGlashan, N. D. (1960) 'Consolidating land holdings in Kenya', *Geography*, **45**, 105–106.

McLoughlin, P. F. M. (1966) 'Development policy-making and the geographer's regions: comments by an economist', *Land Economics*, **42**, 75–84.

McMaster, D. M. (1962) 'A subsistence crop geography of Uganda', *World Land Use Survey, Occasional Paper* No. 2.

Mabbutt, J. A. (1968) 'Review of concepts of land classification', in G. A. Stewart (Ed.), *Land Evaluation*, Macmillan of Australia, 11–28.

Mabbutt, J. A. and Stewart, G. A. (1963) 'The application of geomorphology in resources surveys in Australia and New Guinea', *Revue de Géomorphologie Dynamique*, **14**, 97–109.

Maignien, R. (1966) *Review of Research on Laterites*, UNESCO.

Malek, H. (1966) 'Après la réforme agraire iranienne', *Annales de Géographie*, **75**, 268–285.

Malin, K. M. (1967) 'Food resources of the earth', *Proceedings of the World Population Conference*, Vol. III, United Nations, Department of Economic and Social Affairs, 385–390.

Martonne, E. de (1927) 'Regions of interior basin drainage', *Geographical Review*, **17**, 397–414.

Marts, M. E. (1956) 'Use of indirect benefit analysis in establishing repayment responsibility for irrigation projects', *Economic Geography*, **32**, 132–138.

May, J. (1961) (Ed.) *Studies in Disease Ecology*, Haffner.

May, J. M. (1958) *The Ecology of Human Disease*, MD Publications.

Megee, M. (1965) 'Economic factors and economic regionalization in the United States', *Geografiska Annaler*, **47**, Ser. B, 125–137.

Meigs, P. (1952) 'Water problems in the United States', *Geographical Review*, **42**, 346–366.

Meigs, P. (1953) 'World distribution of arid and semi-arid climates', *Reviews of Research on Arid Zone Hydrology*, UNESCO, 203–209.

Meigs, P. and Twidale, C. R. (1966) *The Geography of Coastal Deserts*, UNESCO.

Middleton, J. F. M. and Greenland, D. J. (1954) 'Land and population in West Nile District Uganda,' *Geographical Journal*, **120**, 446–457.

Miller, E. V. (1959) 'Agricultural Ecuador', *Geographical Review*, **49**, 183–207.

Minkel, C. W. (1968) 'Colonisation of the Sebol region in North Central Guatemala', *Pacific Viewpoint*, **9**, 69–73.

Monbeig, P. (1952) *Pionniers et Planteurs de Sao Paulo*, Colin.

Monbeig, P. (1967) 'Point du vue géographiques sur le sous-développement en Amérique Latine', *Annales de Géographie*, **76**, 704–713.

Moral, P. (1967) 'Essai de comparaison entre L'Afrique de l'ouest aet l'Amérique Latine', *Annales de Géographie*, **76**, 681–703.

Morgan, W. B. (1953) 'The lower Shire valley of Nyasaland: a changing system of African agriculture', *Geographical Journal*, **119**, 459–469.

Morgan, W. B. (1969) 'Peasant agriculture in Tropical Africa', in M. F. Thomas and G. W. Whittington (Eds.), *Environment and Land Use in Africa*, Methuen, 241–272.

Morgan, W. B. and Moss, R. P. (1965) 'Savanna and forest in West Africa', *Africa*, **35**, 286–294.

Morgan, W. T. W. (1963) 'The White Highlands of Kenya', *Geographical Journal*, **129**, 140–155.

Mortimore, M. J. (1967) 'Land and population pressure in the Kano close-settled zone, Northern Nigeria', *Advancement of Science*, **23**, 677–686.

Mortimore, M. J. and Wilson, J. (1965) 'Land and people in the Kano close-settled zone', *Department of Geography Occasional Paper*, No. 1, Ahmadu Bello University.

Mortimore, M. J. and Wilson, J. C. (1968) 'Population distribution, settlement and soils in Kano province, northern Nigeria', in J. C. Caldwell and C. Okonjo (Eds.), *The Population of Tropical Africa*, Longmans, 298–306.

Moss, R. P. (1959) 'Land use mapping in tropical Africa', *Nigerian Geographical Journal*, **3**, 8–17.

Moss, R. P. (1968) 'Land use, vegetation and soil factors in south-west Nigeria; a new approach', *Pacific Viewpoint*, **9**, 107–127.

Moss, R. P. (1969a) 'The ecological background to land use studies in tropical Africa, with special reference to the West', in M. F. Thomas and G. W. Whittington (Eds.), *Environment and Land Use in Africa*, Methuen.

Moss, R. P. (1969b) 'The appraisal of land resources in tropical Africa', *Pacific Viewpoint*, **10**, 18–27.

Mountjoy, A. B. (1952) 'Egypt's population problem', *Transactions of the Institute of British Geographers*, **18**, 121–135.

Mountjoy, A. B. (1968) 'Million cities; urbanization and the developing countries', *Geography*, **53**, 365–374.

Mountjoy, A. B. (1969) *Industrialisation and Underdeveloped Countries*, Hutchinson.

Myrdal, G. (1957) *Economic Theory and under-Developed Regions*, Duckworth.

Naidu, N. N. (1967) 'Land tenure reform and the progress of land consolidation in the Central Province of Kenya', *Svensk Geografisk Årsbok*, **43**, 86–92.

Naylon, J. (1959) 'Land consolidation in Spain', *Annals of the Association of American Geographers*, **49**, 361–373.

Naylon, J. (1961) 'Progress in land consolidation in Spain', *Annals of the Association of American Geographers*, **51**, 335–338.

Ng, R. (1968) 'Land settlement projects in Thailand', *Geography*, **53**, 179–182.

Niddrie, D. L. (1960) 'Land use and population in Tobago', *World Land Use Survey Monograph* No. 3.

Niddrie, D. L. (1965) 'The problems of population growth in Puerto Rico', *Journal of Tropical Geography*, **20**, 26–33.

Nye, P. H. and Greenland, D. J. (1960) *The Soil under Shifting Cultivation*, Commonwealth Bureau of Soils, Technical Communication 51.

O'Connor, A. M. (1963) 'Regional contrasts in economic development in Uganda', *East African Geographical Review*, **1**, 33–43.

O'Connor, A. M. (1965a) 'Railways and development in Uganda: a study in economic geography', *East African Studies*, No. 18.

O'Connor, A. M. (1965b) 'New railway construction and the pattern of economic development in East Africa', *Transactions of the Institute of British Geographers*, **36**, 21–30.

O'Connor, A. M. (1969) 'Geographical studies of developing areas: the case of tropical Africa', in R. U. Cooke and J. H. Johnson (Eds.), *Trends in Geography: an introductory survey*, Pergamon, 275–283.

O'Connor, A. M. (1971) *The Geography of Tropical African Economic Development*, Pergamon.

Odell, P. R. (1967) 'Economic integration and spatial patterns of economic development in Latin America', *Journal of Common Market Studies*, **6**, 267–286.

Oguntoyinbo, J. S. (1968) 'The rôle of a geographer in the economic development of a nation', *Nigerian Geographical Journal*, **11**, 169–174.

Oluwasanmi, H. A. and Dema, I. S. (1966) 'Uboma. A socio-economic and nutritional survey of a rural community in Eastern Nigeria', *World Land Use Survey*, *Occasional Paper* No. 6.

Ominde, S. H. (1968) 'Some aspects of population movements in Kenya', in J. C. Caldwell and C. Okonjo (Eds.), *The Population of Tropical Africa*, Longmans, 264–269.

Onyoni, K. (1963) 'The influence of religion on livestock keeping in East Africa', *New Zealand Geographical Society Record*, **35**, 3–4.

Ooi, Jin-Bee (1959) 'Rural development in tropical areas with special reference to Malaya', *Journal of Tropical Geography*, 12, 1–222.

Ooi, Jin-Bee (1965) 'Some aspects of peasant farming in Malaya', *Tijdschrift voor Economische en Sociale Geografie*, 56, 170–185.

Orleans, L. A. (1959) 'The recent growth of China's urban population', *Geographical Review*, 49, 43–57.

Osborne, R. (1964) 'Migration trends in England and Wales, 1901–1951', *Geographia Polonica*, 3, 137–162.

Patel, S. J. (1964) 'The economic distance between nations: its origins, measurement and outlook', *Economic Journal*, 74, 119–131.

Payne, W. J. A. (1962) 'Climate and animal nutrition in the tropics', *Span*, 5, 118–121.

Peach, G. K. C. (1968) 'Urbanization in India', in R. P. Beckinsale and J. M. Houston (Eds.), *Urbanisation and its Problems*, Blackwell, 297–303.

Pelzer, K. J. (1945) *Pioneer Settlement in the Asiatic Tropics*, American Geographical Society.

Pepelasis, A. A. and Thompson, K. (1960) 'Agriculture in a restrictive environment: the case of Greece', *Economic Geography*, 36, 145–157.

Pepelasis, A. A., Mears, L. and Adelman, I. (1964) *Economic Development*, Harper and Row.

Perroux, F. (1955) 'Note sur la notion de pôle de croissance', *Economie Appliquée*, 8, 307–320.

Peruzzi, D. (1965) 'The mezzadria; a decaying system of land tenure and management in Italy', in E. S. Simpson (Ed.), *Agricultural Geography, International Geographical Union Symposium, Department of Geography, University of Liverpool Research Paper*, No. 3, 49–54.

Phillips, J. (1959) *Agriculture and Ecology in Africa*, Faber and Faber.

Pico, R. (1968) 'Notes on geography and development in the tropics', *Professional Geographer*, 20, 227–229.

Pollock, N. C. (1959) 'Agrarian revolution in Kikuyuland', *South African Geographical Journal*, 41, 53–58.

Porter, P. W. (1966) 'Map supplement No. 6, East Africa—population distribution', *Annals of the Association of American Geographers*, 56, 180–181.

Prebisch, R. (1959) 'Commercial policy in the underdeveloped countries', *American Economic Review*, 49, 251–273.

Prescott, J. R. V. (1961) 'Overpopulation and overstocking in the native areas of Matabeleland', *Geographical Journal*, 127, 212–225.

Preston, D. A. (1969) 'The revolutionary landscape of Highland Bolivia', *Geographical Journal*, 135, 1–16.

Prince, H., Callender, J. M., Henshall, J. D., Smith, C. D. and Caistor, M. E. (1968) 'Four island studies', *World Land Use Survey*, Monograph No. 5.

Prothero, R. M. (1954) 'Some problems of land use survey in Nigeria', *Economic Geography*, 30, 60–69.

Prothero, R. M. (1957) 'Land use at Soba, Zaria Province, Northern Nigeria', *Economic Geography*, 33, 72–86.

Prothero, R. M. (1959) 'Problems of population mapping in an underdeveloped territory (Northern Nigeria)', *Nigerian Geographical Journal*, 3, 1–7.

Prothero, R. M. (1961a) 'Post-war African censuses', in K. M. Barbour and R. M. Prothero (Eds.), *Essays on African Population*, Routledge and Kegan Paul, 7–15.

Prothero, R. M. (1961b) 'Population maps and mapping in Africa south of the Sahara', in K. M. Barbour and R. M. Prothero (Eds.), *Essays on African Population*, Routledge and Kegan Paul, 63–81.

Prothero, R. M. (1962) 'A geographer with the World Health Organization', *Geographical Journal*, **128**, 479–493.

Prothero, R. M. (1963) 'African population maps: problems and progress', *Geografiska Annaler*, **45**, 272–277.

Prothero, R. M. (1965) *Migrants and Malaria*, Longmans.

Prothero, R. M. (1968) 'Migration in tropical Africa', in J. C. Caldwell and C. Okonjo (Eds.), *The Population of Tropical Africa*, Longmans, 250–263.

Pullan, R. A. (1969) 'The soil resources of West Africa', in M. F. Thomas and G. W. Whittington (Eds.), *Environment and Land Use in Africa*, Methuen, 147–192.

Pullen, G. (1966) 'Some problems of rapid urbanization in Lagos, Nigeria', *Journal of Tropical Geography*, **23**, 55–61.

Rao, V. L. S. Prakasa (1957) 'Land use survey in India—its scope and some problems', *The Oriental Geographer*, July, 127–144.

Ravenstein, E. (1885) 'The laws of migration', *Journal of the Royal Statistical Society*, **48**, 167–227.

Ray, D. M. (1968) 'The spatial structure of economic and cultural differences: a factoral ecology of Canada', *Papers and Proceedings of the Regional Science Association*, **23**, 7–24.

Riabchikov, A. M. (1962) 'Geographer's rôle in the development of natural resources and national economy', *Geographical Review of India*, **24**, 52–58.

Richardson, H. L. (1968) 'The use of fertilizers" in R. P. Moss (Ed.), *The Soil Resources of Tropical Africa*, Cambridge University Press, 137–154.

Riddell, J. B. (1970) *The Spatial Dynamics of Modernization in Sierra Leone: structure, diffusion and response*, North Western University Press.

Robertson, C. J. (1956) 'The expansion of the arable area', *Scottish Geographical Magazine*, **72**, 1–20.

Robertson, C. J. (1963) 'The integration of plantation agriculture in economic planning with special reference to South East Asia', *Pacific Viewpoint*, **4**, 1–7.

Roder, W. (1964) 'The division of land resources in Southern Rhodesia', *Annals of the Association of American Geographers*, **54**, 41–58.

Rodgers, A. (1960) 'Regional industrial development with reference to Southern Italy', in N. Ginsburg (Ed.), 'Essays on geography and economic development', *University of Chicago, Department of Geography Research Paper* No. 62, 143–173.

Roy, B. K. (1968) 'The applicability of the World Land Use Survey classification in mapping land use in the arid zone of Rajastan, India', *Geographical Review of India*, **30**, 22–31.

Safier, M. (1969) 'Towards the definition of patterns in the distribution of economic development over East Africa', *East African Geographical Review*, **7**, 1–14.

Salter, R. M. (1947) 'World soil and fertiliser resources in relation to food needs', *Science*, 105, 533–538.

Sandhu, K. S. (1964) 'Emergency resettlement in Malaya', *Journal of Tropical Geography*, 18, 157–183.

Santos, M. (1971) 'L'économie pauvre des villes des pays sous-developpés', *Les Cahiers d'Outre-Mer*, 24, 8–122.

Schnell, G. A. (1970) 'Demographic transition: threat to developing nations', *Journal of Geography*, 49, 164–171.

Schultz, T. W. (1964) *Transforming Traditional Agriculture*, Yale University Press.

Schultz, T. W. (1965) 'Connections between natural resources and economic growth', in I. Burton and R. W. Kates (Eds.) *Readings in Resource Management and Conservation*, University of Chicago Press, 397–403.

Schwartzberg, J. E. (1962) 'Three approaches to the mapping of economic development in India', *Annals of the Association of American Geographers*, 52, 455–468.

Schwartzberg, J. E. (1963) 'Agricultural labour in India: a regional analysis with particular reference to population growth', *Economic Development and Cultural Change*, 11, 337–352.

Schwartzberg, J. E. (1965) 'The distribution of selected castes in the North Indian plain', *Geographical Review*, 55, 477–495.

Sendut, H. (1962) 'The resettlement villages in Malaya', *Geography*, 47, 41–46.

Shaffer, N. M. (1962) 'Land settlement in Kenya', *Yearbook of the Association of Pacific Coast Geographers*, 29, 121–139.

Shamsul, Tunku B. (1969) 'A preliminary study of the fringe alienation schemes in West Malaysia', *Journal of Tropical Geography*, 28, 75–83.

Shantz, H. L. (1956) 'History and problems of arid lands development', in G. F. White (Ed.), *The Future of Arid Lands*, American Association for the Advancement of Science, No. 43, 3–25.

Shaw, D. J. (1963) 'The problem of land fragmentation in the Mediterranean area: a case study', *Geographical Review*, 53, 40–51.

Shaw, E. B. (1954) 'Land reform in Egypt', *Journal of Geography*, 53, 229–237.

Siddle, D. J. (1970) 'Rural development in Zambia: a spatial analysis', *Journal of Modern African Studies*, 8, 271–284.

Silva, E. F. and Soto, M. V. (1968) 'Geographic considerations on underdevelopment: a Latin American viewpoint', in S. P. Chatterjee (Ed.), *Developing Countries of the World*, International Geographical Union, Indian National Committee for Geography.

Simkins, P. D. and Wernstedt, F. L. (1963) 'Growth and internal migrations of the Philippine population, 1948 to 1960', *Journal of Tropical Geography*, 17, 197–202.

Simonett, D. S. (1968) 'Land evaluation studies with remote sensors in the infra-red and radar regions', in G. A. Stewart (Ed.), *Land Evaluation*, Macmillan of Australia, 349–366.

Singh, H. S. (1960) 'Land use planning in India with special reference to agriculture', *Indian Geographer*, 5, 45–58.

Sinha, B. N. (1962) 'The bearings of population growth on the economy of Orissa', *Deccan Geographer*, 1, 1–27.

80   DAVID GRIGG

Sinha, B. N. (1963) 'Fragmentation in holdings in Orissa: a regional analysis', *Deccan Geographer*, **1**, 107–124.
Smith, C. T. (1951) 'The movement of population in England and Wales in 1851 and 1861', *Geographical Journal*, **107**, 200–210.
Smith, C. T. (1968) 'Problems of regional development in Peru', *Geography*, **53**, 260–281.
Smith, W. (1953) *An Economic Geography of Great Britain*, Methuen.
Smole, W. J. (1963) 'Owner-cultivatorship in Middle Chile', *University of Chicago, Department of Geography Research Series* No. 89.
Soja, E. (1968) 'The geography of modernization in Kenya: a spatial analysis of social, economic and political change', *Syracuse Geographical Series* No. 2.
Sopher, D. E. (1967) *Geography of Religions*, Prentice-Hall.
Spate, O. H. K. (1956) 'Problems of development in New Guinea', *Geographical Journal*, **122**, 430–440.
Spate, O. H. K. and Learmonth, A. T. A. (1967) *India and Pakistan: a general and regional geography*, Methuen.
Spencer, J. E. (1966) 'Shifting cultivation in southeastern Asia', *University of California Publications in Geography*. 19.
Stamp, L. D. (1948) *The Land of Britain—its use and misuse*, Longmans.
Stamp, L. D. (1951) 'The World Land Use Survey', *Nature*, **167**, 1010–1011.
Stamp, L. D. (1960a) *Our Developing World*, Faber and Faber.
Stamp, L. D. (1960b) 'The World Land Use Survey', *Advancement of Science*, **17**, 171–173.
Stamp, L. D. (Ed.) (1961) *A History of Land Use in the Arid Zone*, UNESCO.
Stamp, L. D. (1962) 'Climatic limitations to development in the tropics', *Proceedings of the Nutrition Society*, **21**, 84–91.
Stamp, L. D. (1964) *Some Aspects of Medical Geography*, Oxford University Press.
Stamp, L. D. (1965) *The Geography of Life and Death*, Collins.
Steel, R. W. (1955) 'Land and population in British tropical Africa', *Geography*, **40**, 1–17.
Steel, R. W. (1965) 'Problems of food and population in tropical Africa', *Kroniek van Africa*, **5**, 48–64.
Steel, R. W. (1967) 'Geography and the developing world', *Advancement of Science*, **23**, 566–582.
Steel, R. W. (1970) 'Problems of population pressure in tropical Africa', *Transactions of the Institute of British Geographers*, **49**, 1–14.
Sternstein, L. (1965) 'A critique of Thai population data', *Pacific Viewpoint*, **6**, 15–38.
Sternstein, L. (1967) 'Aspects of agricultural land tenure in Thailand', *Journal of Tropical Geography*, **24**, 22–29.
Stevens, R. L. (1967) 'European settlement ventures in the tropical lowlands of Mexico', *Erdkunde*, **21**, 258–277.
Stevens, R. L. (1968) 'Spatial aspects of internal migration in Mexico, 1950–60', *Revista Geografica*, **69**, 75–90.
Stewart, N. R. (1965) 'Migration and settlement in the Peruvian Montana: the Apurimac valley', *Geographical Review*, **55**, 143–157.

Stewart, N. R. (1968) 'Some problems in the development of agricultural colonization in the Andean Oriente', *Professional Geographer*, **20**, 33–38.

Stobbs, A. R. (1968) 'Some problems of measuring land use in underdeveloped countries: the land use survey of Malawi', *The Cartographic Journal*, **5**, 107–110.

Stockwell, E. G. (1960) 'The measurement of economic development', *Economic Development and Cultural Change*, **8**, 419–432.

Stockwell, E. G. (1966) 'Some demographic correlates of economic development', *Rural Sociology*, **31**, 216–224.

Stoddart, D. R. and Trubshaw, J. D. (1962) 'Colonization in Azhan in Eastern Columbia', *Geography*, **47**, 47–53.

Sukhatme, P. V. (1961) 'The world's hunger and future needs in food supplies', *Journal of the Royal Statistical Society* (Series A), **124**, 463–525.

Symons, L. (1966) 'Agricultural production and the changing rôles of state and collective farms in the USSR', *Pacific Viewpoint*, **7**, 54–66.

Symons, L. (1967) *Agricultural Geography*, Bell.

Taafe, E. J., Morrill, R. L. and Gould, P. R. (1963) 'Transport expansion in underdeveloped countries', *Geographical Review*, **53**, 503–529.

Tamsma, R. (1966) 'De Moshav Ovdiem', *Utrecht University Publications in Geography*, Series A, No. 23.

Taylor, D. R. F. (1969) 'Agricultural change in Kikuyuland', in M. F. Thomas and G. W. Whittington (Eds.), *Environment and Land Use in Africa*, Methuen, 463–494.

Taylor, S. A. (1960) 'Principles of dry-land crop management in arid and semi-arid zones', *Plant-Water Relationships in Arid and Semi-Arid Conditions: reviews of research*, UNESCO *Arid Zone Research*, **15**, 192–204.

Tedder, J. L. O. (1966) 'The Solomon Islands—an emerging cash economy', *Australian Geographical Studies*, **4**, 49–60.

Thomas, I. D. (1968) 'Geographical aspects of the Tanzania census of 1967', *East African Geographical Review*, **6**, 1–12.

Thomas, M. F. (1969) 'Germorphology and land classification in tropical Africa', in M. F. Thomas and G. W. Whittington (Eds.), *Environment and Land Use in Africa*, Methuen, 103–146.

Thompson, J. H., Sufrin, S. C., Gould, P. R. and Buck, M. A. (1962) 'Toward a geography of economic health: the case of New York State', *Annals of the Association of American Geographers*, **52**, 1–20.

Thornthwaite, C. W. (1948) 'An approach towards a rational classificatio n of climate', *Geographical Review*, **38**, 55–94.

Tolosa, H. and Reiner, T. A. (1970) 'the economic programming of a system of planned poles', *Economic Geography*, **46**, 449–458.

Tosi, J. A. and Voertman, R. F. (1964) 'Some environmental factors in the economic development of the tropics', *Economic Geography*, **40**, 189–205.

Toupet, C. (1956) 'Agrarian and social transformations in the Tamourt Basin, Mauritania', *Journal of Tropical Geography*, **8**, 82–86.

Tregear, T. R. (1958) 'Land use in Hong Kong and the new Territories', *World Land Use Survey Regional Monograph* No. 1, Geographical Publications Ltd.

Trewartha, G. T. (1950) 'Land reform and land reclamation in Japan', *Geographical Review*, **40**, 376–396.

Trewartha, G. T. (1969) *A Geography of Population: world patterns*, Wiley.

Udo, R. K. (1964) 'The migrant tenant farmer of Eastern Nigeria', *Africa*, **34**, 326–339.

Udo, R. K. (1968) 'Population and politics in Nigeria', in J. C. Caldwell and C. Okonjo (Eds.), *The Population of Tropical Africa*, Longmans, 97–105.

Udo, R. K. (1971) 'Food-deficit areas of Nigeria', *Geographical Review*, **61**, 415–430.

Ullman, E. L. (1958) 'Regional development and the geography of concentration', *Papers and Proceedings of the Regional Science Association*, **4**, 184–185.

United Nations (1968) 'Urbanization: development policies and planning', *International Social Development Review*, No. 1, Department of Economic and Social Affairs.

UNESCO (1962) 'Problems of the arid zone', *Arid Zone Research*, 18.

Van Roy, E. (1966) 'Economic dualism and economic change among the hill tribes of Thailand', *Pacific Viewpoint*, **7**, 151–168.

Van Valkenburg, S. (1950) 'The world land use survey', *Economic Geography*, **26**, 1–5.

Vann, J. H. (1963) 'Development processes in laterite terrain in Amapa', *Geographical Review*, **53**, 406–417.

Vekemans, R. and Segundo, J. L. (1963) 'Essay of a socio-economic typology of the Latin American countries', in E. de Vries and J. M. Echavarria (Eds.), *Social Aspects of Economic Development*, Vol. 1, UNESCO, 67–93.

Vellard, J. (1963) 'L'experience agraire de la Bolivie', *Les Cahiers d'Outre-Mer*, **16**, 201–213.

Veyret-Verner, G. (1965) 'L'acroissement de la population mondiale, 1920–1960', *Revue de Géographie Alpine*, **53**, 525–559.

Vine, H. (1968) 'Developments in the study of soils and shifting agriculture in tropical Africa', in R. P. Moss (Ed.), *The Soil Resources of Tropical Africa*, Cambridge University Press, 89–119.

Vink, A. P. A. (1967) 'Integrated surveys', *Geografisch Tijdschrift*, **1**, 253–259.

Virone, L. E. (1963) 'Borgo a Mozzano', *World Land Use Survey*, *Occasional Paper* No. 4, Geographical Publications Ltd.

Vlugter, H. (1960) 'Some aspects of water control in West Pakistan', *Pakistan Geographical Review*, **15**, 1–4.

Wagner, P. L. (1960) 'On classifying economies', in N. Ginsburg (Ed.), 'Essays on Geography and Economic Development', *University of Chicago, Department of Geography Research Paper* No. 62, 49–62.

Waibel, L. (1948) 'Vegetation and land use in the Planalto Central of Brazil', *Geographical Review*, **38**, 529–554.

Waibel, L. (1950) 'European colonization in Southern Brazil,' *Geographical Review*, **40**, 529–547.

Walton, K. (1969) *The Arid Zones*, Hutchinson.

Ward, G. R. and Moran, W. (1959) 'Recent population trends in the south west Pacific', *Tijdschrift voor Economische en Sociale Geografie*, **50**, 235–240.

Watters, R. F. (1960) 'The nature of shifting cultivation: a review of recent research', *Pacific Viewpoint*, **1**, 59–99.

Watters, R. F. (1963) 'Sugar production and culture change in Fiji', *Pacific Viewpoint*, **4**, 25–52.

Watters, R. F. (1967) 'Economic backwardness in the Venezuelan Andes: a study of the traditional sector of the dual economy', *Pacific Viewpoint*, **8**, 17–67.

Weller, R. H. and Sly, D. F. (1969) 'Modernization and demographic change; a world view', *Rural Sociology*, **34**, 313–326.

Wernstedt, F. L. and Simkins, P. D. (1965) 'Migration and the settlement of Mindanao', *Journal of Asian Studies*, **25**, 83–103.

White, G. F. (Ed.) (1956) *The Future of Arid Lands*, American Association for the Advancement of Science, Publication No. 43.

White, G. F. (1962) 'Alternative uses of limited water supplies', *Problems of the Arid Zone, UNESCO Arid Zone Research*, 18.

White, G. F. (1963) 'Contributions of geographical analysis to river basin development', *Geographical Journal*, **129**, 412–436.

White, G. F. (1965) 'The special problems of the underdeveloped countries with respect to natural resources', in I. Burton and R. W. Kates (Eds.), *Readings in Resource Management and Conservation*, University of Chicago Press, 422–426.

White, G. F. (1966) 'The world's arid areas', in E. S. Hills (Ed.), *Arid Lands: a geographical appraisal*, Methuen, 15–30.

Whyte, R. O. (1962) 'The myth of tropical grasslands', *Tropical Agriculture*, **39**, 1–12.

Wikkramatileke, R. (1959) 'Problems of land use mapping in the tropics: an example from Ceylon', *Geography*, **44**, 79–95.

Wikkramatileke, R. (1962) 'A study of planned land settlement in the Eastern marchlands of Malaya', *Economic Geography*, **38**, 330–346.

Wikkramatileke, R. (1964) 'Variable economic attributes in Malayan rural land development', *Pacific Viewpoint*, **5**, 35–50.

Wikkramatileke, R. (1965) 'State aided rural land colonization in Malaya: an appraisal of the FLDA program', *Annals of the Association of American Geographers*, **55**, 377–403.

William-Olsson, W. (1963) 'The commission on a World Population Map: history, activities and recommendations', *Geografiska Annaler*, **45**, 243–250.

Williams, O. (1961) 'Some problems of land use mapping in South Africa'. *South African Geographical Journal*, **43**, 28–32.

Wilmet, J. (1967) 'Problèmes de formation des experts—géographes pour les pays en développement', *Colloque International de Géographie Appliquée; Comptes Rendus*, Liége, 363–369.

Winnie, W. F. Jr. (1965) 'Communal land tenure in Chile', *Annals of the Association of American Geographers*, **55**, 67–86.

Withington, W. A. (1965) 'The density of population in South East Asia: problems in mapping spatial variation', *Journal of Geography*, **64**, 14–23.

Withington, W. A. (1967) 'Migration and economic development: some recent spatial changes in the population of rural Sumatra, Indonesia', *Tijdschrift voor Economische en Sociale Geografie*, **58**, 153–163.

Worrall, G. A. (1958) 'Deposition of silt by the irrigation waters of the Nile at Khartoum', *Geographical Journal*, **124**, 219–222.

Wright, R. L. (1971) 'The rôle of integrated surveys in developing countries: review and reappraisal', in R. L. Wright (Ed.), *Integrated Surveys, Rangeland Ecology and Management*, UNESCO.

Wrigley, E. A. (1961) *Industrial Growth and Population Change: a regional study of the coalfield areas of north-west Europe in the late nineteenth century*, Cambridge University Press.

Wrigley, E. A. (1969) *Population and History*, Weidenfeld and Nicolson.

Yadav, J. S. and Prasad, H. (1966) 'Spatial pattern of economic development in India', *The Deccan Geographer*, **4**, 10–42.

Young, A. (1968) 'Natural resource surveys for land development in the tropics, *Geography*, **53**, 229–248.

Young, A. (1969) 'Natural resource survey in Malawi: some considerations of the regional method in environmental description', in M. F. Thomas and G. W. Whittington (Eds.), *Environment and Land Use in Africa*, Methuen, 355–384.

Zelinsky, W. (1963) 'Rural population dynamics as an index to social and economic development', *Sociological Quarterly*, **4**, 99–124.

Zelinsky, W. (1966) 'The geographer and his crowding world: some cautionary notes toward the study of population pressure in "developing lands" ', *Revista Geografica*, **65**, 7–28.

Zelinsky, W., Kosinski, L. A. and Prothero, R. M. (Eds.) (1970) *Geography and a Crowding World*, Oxford University Press.

Zimmerman, E. W. (1933) *World Resources and Industries*, Harper and Row.

Zobler, L. (1962) 'An economic-historical view of natural resource use and conservation', *Economic Geography*, **38**, 189–194.

3 Population in movement

JOHN CLARKE

At no time in the past has mankind been so conscious of its growing numbers and movements. In many countries, elaborate statistical machinery has been devised to ascertain the state and dynamics of population, especially for purposes of planning, although over much of the world the quantity and quality of demographic data leave much to be desired, a fact affecting the accuracy of predictions of future population change. Uncertainty about future population numbers and their relationships to the environment and resources has provoked a variety of attitudes and policies concerning changes in population numbers at local, regional, national and world levels. Many of these attitudes and policies are more conditioned by factors such as religion, culture, standards of living and environmental perception than by scientific analysis; but by massive reduction in mortality and a less widespread reduction of fertility as well as by many checks upon human movement, there is no doubt that mankind is consciously affecting its numbers more than ever before.

This growing awareness of human population growth and mobility is reflected in the fact that population has become a focus of attention not only for demographers, but for biologists, anthropologists, sociologists, economists, agriculturists, planners, geneticists, medical scientists, geographers and many others. Geographers had long studied patterns of population, but it was not until the 1950s and 1960s that a considerable literature appeared, synthesized and formalized in a number of basic texts (George, 1959; Clarke, 1965; Zelinsky, 1966; Beaujeu-Garnier, 1966; Demko, Rose and Schnell, 1970). Population geography emerged as a distinctive field of geographical enquiry, focussing on population as 'the point of reference from which all other elements are observed' (Trewartha, 1953), and examining and interpreting the spatial patterns of population distribution, composition, migrations and growth in relation to human activities and the nature of places. The essence of the geographical approach to population study is that we are principally concerned in 'the spatial variations in demographic and non-demographic qualities of human populations, and the economic and social consequences stemming from the inter-action associated with a particular set of conditions existing in a given areal unit' (Demko, Rose and Schnell, 1970).

Some authors have gone so far as to claim, though without general assent, that the study of population should hold a central position within human geography; in their view, the distribution of population acts 'as a master-thread, capable of weaving into a coherent pattern the otherwise disparate strands of the subject and expressing its philos-ophical unity, particularly in the context of regional geography' (Hooson, 1960), or as a convenient nexus for geographical research 'into which all strands can be seen to lead' (Wrigley, 1965). Patterns of population have even been regarded as the touchstone of relevance for geography as a whole, and their study as being a primary focus of human geography, because they can help to explain economic activity (Wrigley, 1967).

This is a far cry from the earlier position of population in geo-graphical studies, especially regional geography, in which it was generally examined at the end of a Place-Work-People chain, on the assumption that the physical environment influenced human activities which in turn affected patterns of population. Although in agricultural societies physical influences are still strong, as they are also in industrial societies based upon mineral resources, the rôle of the physical environment diminishes with the growing mobility of population, the market-orientation of manufacturing, the increase of tertiary activities and the spread of mechanization, so that the traditional ties between man and the land are relaxed. Consequently, geographers no longer regard population merely as a response to economic processes, them-selves conditioned by the physical environment, but they examine population as a causal element. Moreover, it is no longer regarded as a rather static phenomenon, portrayed on a map as a cloud of dots or a pattern of shading of semi-immutability, but one which is extremely dynamic, involving complex patterns of natural movement (i.e. the balance of fertility and mortality), spatial mobility and changing demographic and non-demographic structures.

The approach to population geography is not everywhere the same, and to some extent one can talk of national approaches, though these are far from exclusive. In the United States, for example, cultural differentiation is stressed, perhaps as a reflection of the strong school of cultural geography; in Britain (Johnson, 1970) population geography has been closely linked with settlement analysis, sometimes under the umbrella of social geography (Houston, 1953); in France (George, 1959, 1967) it is closely linked with demography, which grew powerfully partly because of the national history of slow population growth; while the Soviet concept of population geography is as a part of economic geography, with a wider scope than is common in Western Europe or America, including the geography of urban and rural settlements as well as labour resources, and with a practical rôle in planning and development (Clarke, 1965; *Soviet Geography*, 1967). Whatever the approach, the contribution of geographers to population study has been principally in spatial analysis. Although this interest has not been exclusive to geographers, it has been largely neglected by demographers, who have concentrated on the processes of numerical population change, mainly for countries as units rather than for their component areas. Geographers must necessarily have some knowledge of these demographic processes, but much demographic analysis has little spatial significance and is of limited relevance to the geographer.

POPULATION AND AREA

Like all students of population, geographers are largely at the mercy of unreliable and insufficient population data, but in addition they are extremely dependent upon the territorial units for which most data are available. 'Population' means the number of individuals living on a given territory, and this territorial notion is very important to the geographer. The territorial units may be either administrative units or special enumeration districts, varying greatly in size and character and sometimes of little significance in terms of uniformity or coherence. Moreover, the boundaries of the reporting units may vary between censuses, making temporal comparisons difficult. Unfortunately, these areal units have had an inordinate impact upon methodology, and have considerably influenced geographical analyses of population, particularly in population mapping. In an attempt to simplify the complexities of population distributions and to relate these complexities to spatial variations in the physical and human environments, many measures of population density have been devised using different population numerators (e.g. total, urban, rural, active, agricultural or unemployed populations) and areal denominators (e.g. total, inhabited, urban, rural, cultivated, cultivable, crop or built-up areas). Yet no matter how the numerator and denominator are refined, there remains a basic dependence upon data for irregular areal units, especially administrative units, which makes most population density maps extremely crude.

Populations are rarely discrete units or isolates, except on islands, and areal units often give quite false impressions of abrupt spatial change where in fact there are gradual transitions. This is not to imply that abrupt spatial changes in population are rare; they are very common, as on the edges of moorland, valleys, cities and specific social areas, but they are not often coincident with the limits of areal units.

Simple ways of reducing the irregularity of areal units for population analysis are (a) by grouping them into fewer more regular areas, (b) by weighting them according to their size, (c) by eliminating aberrant areas, and (d) by using grid meshes to facilitate more objective analysis (Haggett, 1965a). A number of studies of computer mapping of small areas has been undertaken (e.g. Forbes and Robertson, 1967; Rosing and Wood, 1971), and no doubt the geo-coding system implemented in the British census of 1971 will encourage much more work on a national scale, as for most of the country households were referenced to 100m squares and for a selection of areas full co-ordinate referencing was undertaken for residential premises. This falls only slightly short of the optimal grid-free method in which every individual and every dwelling is allocated a unique locational reference (Robertson, 1969), from which generalized patterns of population density and other qualities might be computed.

POPULATION AND SCALE

Geographical studies of population range in scale from the parish or ward through the district, county and state to the whole earth's surface, with corresponding variations in the depth of analysis. Scale has, for example, influenced approaches to the analyses of population distribution, approaches varying from the microscopic, where there is a desire to know or depict the location of all individuals, to the macroscopic, where there is an attempt to understand the generalized spatial characteristics of populations. The common microscopic or atomic cartographic method is the dot map, of which the most detailed shows each person as a single dot, though this can be for only one moment in time and therefore gives a false impression that the population is stable. The dot map may be used in a macroscopic way by increasing the value of each dot, but other common macroscopic methods relate population either to area, as in the concept of population density, or to distance. Among the methods relating population to distance are:

(a) centrographic measures used, particularly by Russians, to describe central tendency, centrality or average position of populations by locating their mean, median or modal centres (see Figure 3.1);

(b) measures of dispersion, such as the standard distance deviation and the mean distance deviation, the latter providing an indication of aggregate travel distance, in which the value at any point represents the arithmetic mean distance in kilometres (or any other unit) required to move everyone in the population to that point by the shortest route; and

(c) population potential, which assumes that the influence of an individual in a population is inversely proportional to distance, so that the population potential of a point is a measure of the nearness of people to that point (Figure 3.1). Population potential is obtained by measuring the distance from the defined point of each population group in the territory, calculating the reciprocals of each distance and summing the reciprocals with some appropriate weighting for population sizes (Stewart, 1947; Stewart and Warntz, 1958; Warntz and Neft, 1960). This is a highly macroscopic view of population distribution, and may be used for the analysis of workplace potential, income potential and market potential, etc.

Scale is of importance not merely in the analysis of population distribution, but also of population movement, as the relative significance of net migration (the sum of in-migration and out-migration) and natural increase/decrease (the balance of births and deaths) varies according to the scale of areal units. In general, migration is more important in smaller units like parishes, towns or counties than at national or continental levels (Webb, 1963), where natural change accounts for a greater part of total population change, except in the case of small countries. The basic reason is that the volume of migration to or from a place tends to vary inversely with distance, and obviously a higher proportion of population movements is contained within larger areal units, as demonstrated by Webb in Figure 3.2.

Large units also tend to have smoothing effects, concealing considerable internal diversity. For example, although in 1968–69 Scotland as a whole experienced an increase in population through natural gain exceeding net out-migration, only one sub-region (North-East) had this pattern of population growth; in five other sub-regions there was a decrease of population through net out-migration exceeding natural gain, in one sub-region there was increase owing to net in-migration and smaller natural gain and in the final sub-region increase resulted from natural gain and smaller net in-migration. In the same way, the components of population change of some of the local

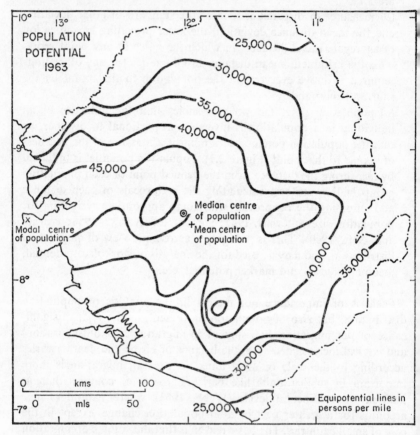

FIGURE 3.1 Population potential and central tendency in Sierra Leone, 1963

authority areas (county boroughs, municipal boroughs, urban districts and rural districts) of an English county, such as Norfolk (Figure 3.3) may have quite different weightings from those of the county as a whole. The character of natural change tends to vary with the scale of analysis, for whereas nearly all large populations experience natural increase their smaller component units exhibit a greater variety of natural change, with many units having natural decrease. For example, although the United States as a whole has always known over-all natural increase, the number of counties suffering from natural decrease has increased greatly since the Second World War, so that by 1970 about one-sixth were so affected. Similarly, although England and Wales in 1969 had a natural increase rate of 4·4 per thousand, natural decrease

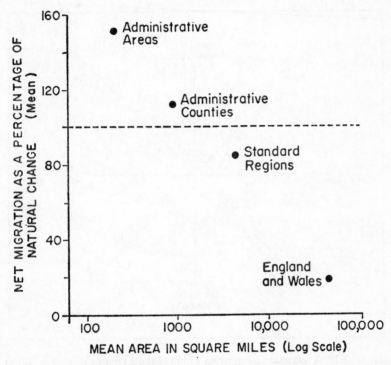

FIGURE 3.2 Net migration as a factor of population change in various sizes of areal units in England and Wales

SOURCE: Webb, 1969

occurred in five sub-regions (the rural North-East, Fylde, Lancaster, Sussex coast and north-west Wales), eight counties (East Sussex, West Sussex, Isle of Wight, Breconshire, Caernarvonshire, Cardigan-shire, Carmarthenshire and Merionethshire), and more than 200 urban areas and districts. In the county of Devon, for example, which had a 0·2 per thousand natural increase rate, 18 of the 27 urban areas and 7 of the 16 rural districts suffered natural decrease. As one might

expect, the areas of natural decrease tend to have older age structures
and unbalanced sex-ratios (e.g. seaside resorts, spas) owing to the
age-selective effects of migration.

As aspects of demographic structure like sex, age and marital status
are greatly affected by natural increase and migration, it follows that
they are also influenced by the size of areal units used in analysis

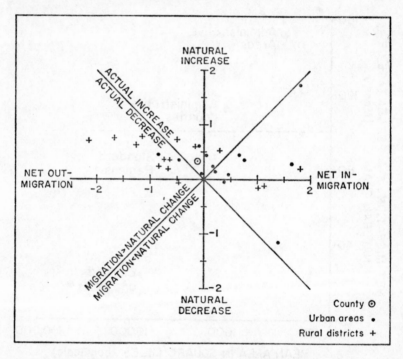

FIGURE 3.3   A Cartesian co-ordinate graph of the components of population
change in the local authority areas of Norfolk, 1951–61

(Hirst, 1971). For example, patterns of sex-ratios vary substantially
according to the size of units, and it is widely recognized that the sex-
ratios of countries vary less than those of counties, which in turn vary
less than those of local authority areas. Figure 3.4 shows the local
authority sex-ratios for one English county, Norfolk, to give some
idea of the great variation which can be concealed under a county
average. Age structures also vary considerably among local authority
areas, as revealed by Dewdney (1968) for the British Isles in Table 3:

TABLE 3 **Variation in the percentage distribution of age groups among local authorities in the British Isles, 1961**

	0–14	15–44	45–64	65+
Mean	23·7	39·4	25·2	11·7
Maximum	46·4	54·5	39·3	33·0
Minimum	8·7	24·0	10·5	0·0
Range	37·7	30·5	28·8	33·0
Inter-quartile range	3·9	4·7	3·6	4·0

The scale of demographic analysis therefore has a great influence upon results, so that conclusions derived at one scale are not necessarily applicable at another. Moreover, factors influencing population distribution, composition and movement vary with scale; for example, whereas climate has an important influence upon the migration of people to California or the south coast of England, it has less influence upon their precise location within these regions. In the same way, while migration may be the key factor in local variations in sex-ratio, in larger units the main factor may be sex-differential in mortality. Although each explanation fits into the next highest group of factors, there is obviously a scale-linkage problem which is not easily resolved (Haggett, 1965b).

Exemplifying this problem is the vast range in state populations, from six large countries each with more than 100 million inhabitants (China, India, USSR, USA, Indonesia, and Japan) containing over half the total world population, to a myriad of islands and micro-states with pocket populations. Small states like Hong Kong, Kuwait, Israel and Pacific Islands generally suffer from much greater demographic instability than larger and more populous states (Fosberg, 1965; MacArthur and Wilson, 1967), because changes in mortality, fertility and migration have more lasting results and because they are more easily effected. Restrictive regulations upon the volume of international migration are generally less applicable to small states, partly because immigrants from small states offer less threat of cultural inundation and the emergence of plural societies than do immigrants from large nations. On the other hand, small states themselves can be greatly affected in this way by large-scale immigration, as we see in Fiji and Mauritius. In addition, small states differ from large states by having simpler patterns of population distribution, largely because of less complex ecological, cultural and urban systems. For instance, many small states, especially those with a history of colonization and limited urbanization, usually have one large city, which is markedly primate and generally the capital, and which sometimes incorporates a large

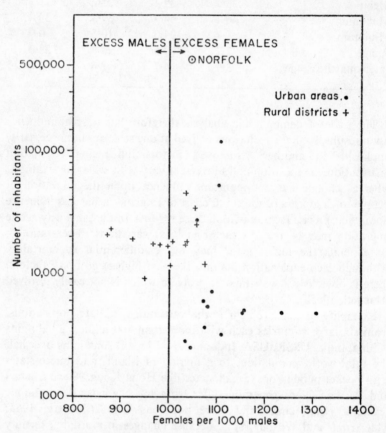

FIGURE 3.4 Semi-logarithmic dispersion graph of sex-ratios in the local authority areas of Norfolk, 1961

proportion of the total population. Montevideo, an extreme example, has nearly half the population of Uruguay (Linsky, 1965) and in Africa there are many examples of primate city-size distributions (Figure 3.5) which contrast with the log-normal distributions often found in larger countries, especially in the developed world.

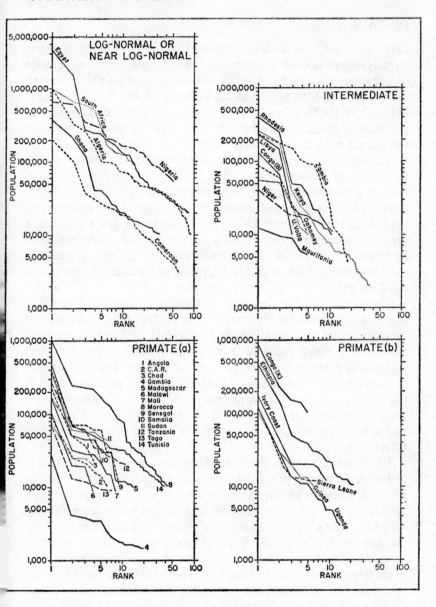

FIGURE 3.5 Types of city-size distribution in African countries

DATA AND ANALYSIS

Like many fields of human geography, population geography has recently experienced a revolution in data handling and in the application of quantitative methods, in which computers have greatly stimulated the use of statistical techniques at a variety of levels of complexity. Medvedkov (1970) refers to three levels: the first is concerned with problems of quantity, the reliability of data and its precise expression; the second with the derivation of empirical relationships and their expression as mathematical functions or formulae which allow greater precision and comparability; and the third with the construction of deductive models to explain causal relationships and the basic mechanisms of processes. Medvedkov cites an urban-shape index as an example of the first level, Clark's (1951) formula for urban population density an example of the second, and as an example of the third level he constructs models of flows of pedestrians doing their shopping on their way home from work, to determine an optimal distribution of retail outlets.

It is not relevant here to examine in detail the application of statistical techniques to population geography, but perhaps three examples will illustrate the trend. First, the analysis of spatial relationships and areal associations, which has been a continuous interest of geographers particularly through map comparisons of different distributions, has benefited greatly from the use of regression and correlation analysis (Robinson, Lindberg and Brinkman, 1961), as in Coulson's (1968) study of age structures in Kansas City, where he shows that variations of age structures are related to other attributes of the population (see Chapter 6).

The second example is the increasing use of two multivariate statistical methods, namely principal components analysis and factor analysis, both of which 'result in the collapsing of a set of intercorrelated variables on to a smaller number of basic dimensions or composite variables' (King, 1969). Multivariate analysis has been employed for instance by Ahmad (1965) in his extensive studies of Indian cities, Robson (1969) in an intensive examination of socio-economic groupings in the town of Sunderland, Henshall (1966) in her study of the influence of the demographic factor upon agriculture in Barbados, and by Moore (1969) and Hartley and Norris (1969) in their analyses of demographic regions in Ghana and Libya respectively. A fuller discussion of the factorial ecology of urban populations is to be found in Chapter 6.

A third example of statistical analysis is Compton's (1968) adoption of a Markov chain model as analogous to stable population theory and his use of it to measure the quantitative relationship between migration and population change in Hungary, excluding the effects of fertility and mortality. First he uses the technique to compute the population size implications of given unchanging migration systems. Second, he measures the time varying relationship between a given migration system and population change, on the assumption that the migration system itself is unchanging through time. Third, he calculates an equilibrium population distribution associated with an unchanging migration system, and then, by calculating the equilibrium population distributions resulting from time-consecutive migration systems, he demonstrates the changing migration tendencies of the counties and cities of Hungary. These are then classified according to the trend pattern and magnitude of their equilibrium populations, and an assessment is made of the effectiveness of the decentralization policy, which aims at slowing down migration to Budapest.

Distributional patterns

Until the 1960s, most geographical study of population was concerned with patterns of distribution and composition and especially with the statics of population rather than with the dynamics. There were some major exceptions, such as the work of Geddes (1941, 1942) on regional population change and variability in India, but in essence the objective of population geography was 'to define and to bring forth the significance of differences from place to place in the number and kind of human inhabitants'; consequently, geographers concentrated on the way in which populations established 'causal connections with the total physical, biotic and cultural environment' (James, 1954). Faced with the immense variety of areas, scales, environmental and human conditions and schooled in the philosophy of areal differentiation or in the ecological view of human geography, geographers tended to focus on the great diversity of human population distributions and compositions, a diversity which is increasing.

Whether one takes a macroscopic or microscopic view, human populations demonstrate great unevenness of spatial distribution and great variety of composition, which geographers have been at pains to explain. Not only is the distribution of population extremely uneven but there is a general tendency toward greater concentration in small areas. According to recent estimates, although the average population density of the earth's land surface is about 26 per sq.km., 64% has densities below 2 per sq.km. and about 30–40% may be regarded as uninhabited. Geographers have paid considerable attention to these uninhabited or negative areas, finding that a variety of environmental conditions hostile to man were the principal cause for their lack of population. However, the adaptation of some primitive peoples to hostile environments is evidence for the fact that there are few absolute environmental limitations to human existence; nevertheless, these environments are less attractive, and they are also more costly to develop and tend to be developed only when there is a special need. In these circumstances, it is extremely difficult to assess their environmental potential or carrying capacity, although many have endeavoured to do so with very different results. Despite such considerations and a rapid increase in technological ability to tackle harsh environments, there have been few major advances of population into the negative areas (see Chapter 2).

The immense variations in population distribution and density within the inhabited area or ecumene, and their explanation by analysis of varied physical, economic, social, political and historical influences, have been a major concern of geographers and have inspired attempts to produce a large-scale world population distribution map (William-Olsson, 1963), although with no great success. Among subsistence economies, population densities have been largely found to reflect the intensity of agriculture, which in turn is influenced by variations in the environment, but among more advanced exchange-based economies agriculture diminishes as a determinant of population density, and accordingly the influence of environmental factors is attenuated. However, the persistence of pre-industrial distribution patterns is a salient fact in relation to the three most important concentrations of humanity—in east Asia, south Asia and Europe—which together account for 58·5% of the world's population on only 8·5% of its area. There can be little doubt that continuity of human settlement and inertia in population distribution is an important explanation of patterns at the continental scale; it is estimated that Eurasia contained about 84% of the world's population in 1750, before the European expansion to the so-called 'empty continents' (Trewartha, 1969).

Marked unevenness in population distribution is also abundantly evident within countries, although there are considerable variations, as seen in Figure 3.6 which depicts Lorenz curves of population concentration for a selection of African countries, ranging from Egypt where about 99% of the total population lives on only 3% of the total area through to a fairly even distribution in Sierra Leone. The massive concentration of population in urban centres is intensifying the unevenness of population distribution in many countries; a classic example is Australia, where more than 56% of the population of this huge country with 7·7 million sq.kms. lives in only five cities. The rise in proportion of the world's population living in settlements with more than 20,000 inhabitants, from less than one in ten in 1900 to more than

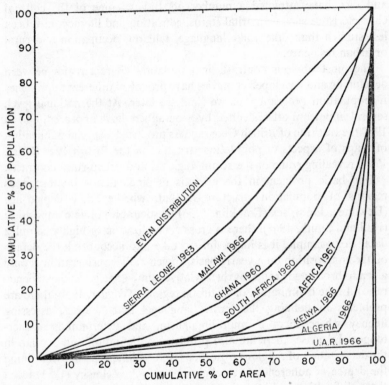

FIGURE 3.6   Lorenz curves of population densities in seven selected African countries

one in four today and probably to one in two by 2000, will of course further reduce the influence of the physical environment upon patterns of population distribution, as mankind establishes his own built environments. This strong tendency to urbanization, variable in time and place, has provoked many analyses of emerging trends through sequences of static patterns, but these have recently given way to more frequent analyses of patterns of population dynamics.

Geographers have long been interested in population composition as it varies territorially between continents, countries, regions, communities and between urban and rural areas, although they have not given equal attention to the many aspects of population composition, partly because not all population characteristics are included in census enumerations. While innate or ascribed characteristics like age, sex and race have attracted a number of studies, some of the cultural characteristics such as marital status, education and literacy have been less studied than others like language, religion, occupation and rural or urban residence.

The most obvious contrasts in population characteristics between developing and developed countries have provoked different approaches in population geography, as we shall see later. At the national level, several important atlases edited by geographers have appeared, and in 1968 the Institute of British Geographers produced a special publication of maps of aspects of population structure in the British Isles (Hunt, 1968) revealing some of the strong regional and urban-rural contrasts.

One basic problem in the analysis of single-factor homogeneous regions of population structure is that, whether they depict age (Dewdney, 1968), sex (Franklin, 1956) or socio-economic composition (Hall and Smith, 1968), there is gross generalization of highly complex data. For example, it is impossible to take into account all the details of age composition on a yearly basis, so generally consideration is only given to broad age groups or their relative numbers (e.g. the dependency ratio). In the delimitation of linguistic regions (Wagner, 1958) there are problems in defining the terms 'language' and 'dialect', assessing fluency where there is multi-lingualism, and determining mother-tongue. Likewise, there are also problems of definition and overlap in the delimitation of religious regions, as well as difficulties in ascertaining the degree of adherence to a religion or church. Zelinsky (1961) faced these difficulties in his analysis of the geography of religions in the United States. He established seven major religious regions and five sub-regions on the basis of similarity of religious composition rather than single religious denominations, because there is such a wide variety of denominations with overlapping distributions, a problem greatly exacerbated by contrasts in urban and rural patterns. Gay (1971) experienced comparable difficulties in his study of the geography of religion in England.

Of course, aspects of population structure are always interrelated, and in regional analysis of multiple factors of population the aim is to ascertain the broad characteristics of population structure. A recent

example of this sort of work is the distinction by Lewis (1968) of six
demographic regions within the north-eastern part of the United States
by establishing level-of-living indices for 397 counties and ranking them
according to 12 diverse quantitative characteristics, such as in-migration
from 1955 to 1960, persons over 25 with an inadequate formal education,
unemployed persons and housing units with a telephone.

Patterns of population composition are also very dependent upon
patterns of population dynamics, and increasing demographic diversity
partly results from the variety of stages reached in the process of
economic development. It is well known that the transition models of
fertility and mortality changes differ between developed and developing

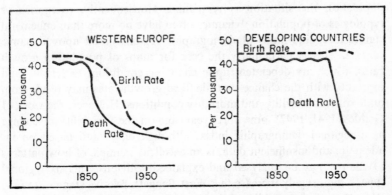

FIGURE 3.7 Models of demographic transition

countries, the abrupt decline in mortality in developing countries and
consequent rapid population growth contrasting sharply with the
more gradual changes in mortality and fertility which took place in
the demographic evolution of developed countries (Figure 3.7). But in
detail there are substantial variations in the space-time diffusion of the
transition model, especially in the initiation and duration of demographic transition, not only between countries (Chung, 1970) but also
within nations. Following the empirical and theoretical studies on
diffusion of innovations by Hägerstrand (1967), Demko and Casetti
(1970), for example, found evidence for the diffusion of fertility decline
in two regions of the USSR centred on Moscow and Leningrad, of
death rate decline in the Leningrad but not in the Moscow region and
of increase in divorce rates in the Moscow but not in the Leningrad
region.

In addition to transition in vital statistics, the modernization process also implies mobility transition, and recently Zelinsky (1971) has contributed the hypothesis that 'there are definite, patterned regularities in the growth of personal mobility through space-time during recent history, and these regularities comprise an essential component of the modernization process'. He has proposed a five phase sequence of types and volume of human mobility associated with five stages of society: pre-modern traditional, early transitional, late transitional, advanced and future superadvanced.

The demographic and mobility transitions are variable in time and space and are not always coincident, so that there is no single spectrum or cycle of population dynamics, and for any particular aspect of population the situation is very fluid. Consequently, categories or typologies of population dynamics often have no more than ephemeral significance, like maps of demographic regions based upon dynamic criteria. This is particularly the case for maps of population growth rates, which are dependent upon changing conditions of fertility and mortality with the chance that identical growth rates may result from quite different fertility and mortality conditions. However, the work of Geddes (1941, 1942) some thirty years ago on the variability of change as a regional demographic index, although dated and based on inadequate and insufficient data, is an excellent example of how patterns of change may be analysed and explained. Obviously his six regional types—high steady increase (e.g. East Bengal), relative stagnation (e.g. West Bengal), intermediate (e.g. Lee of Western Ghats), recurrent crisis (e.g. Deccan 'famine tract'), variable increase (e.g. Punjab) and colonization (e.g. Assam)—are now much less distinctive, for there are now few areas of low population increase in India, Pakistan and Bangladesh, but he inspired much other work.

Movement and interaction
Apart from distributional patterns, geographers have given increasing attention in recent years to the movements of people and ideas, the processes of interaction and diffusion. As locations are separated by distance and are specialized by function, a demand arises both for interaction with other persons and for goods and services available at other locations, and so movements occur. Obviously, in societies which are spatially confined there is only localized interaction, but as societies, economies and transport systems evolve and specialization increases, then more and longer movements take place.

Such are the complexities of human movements that many typologies have been attempted, which vary according to the criteria chosen, such as motivation, organization, duration, distance, direction, volume, consequences, population characteristics or selectivity. A typology based on the time factor (e.g. Morrill, 1970) is particularly helpful because the locational effects of movement differ in time. Temporary movements like journey to work and shopping, service, social and tourist trips are vital to the satisfaction of social needs and the efficient day-to-day functioning of society. However, such movements do not directly alter the patterns of location; in fact, temporary movements and patterns of permanent location reflect each other. On the other hand, permanent migrations, for social, economic, political or psychological reasons or for purposes of retirement, mean adjustments in location, and may be either causes or consequences of changes in the location of activities. To some extent migrations, whether rural-urban, inter-regional, intra-urban, inter-urban, international or any other category, may be looked upon as one response to opportunities and needs, and are one of the main ways in which a society may achieve equilibrium. But at the same time all societies exhibit considerable inertia or immobility, a fact abundantly evident when one examines the remarkable stability of the world population distribution. Between these temporary and permanent movements are moves which involve a temporary change of residence, and may be termed transient, such as movements of migrant labour, military personnel and students.

All these various forms of human movement have been the subject of geographical studies, as have models of migrations. Nearly all location theory assumes that spatial structure is based on the principles of minimizing distance and maximizing the utility of points and areas within the structure. The influence of distance upon movement has long been recognized (Claeson, 1968; Morrill, 1963), and the concept of least movement used as an explanatory model in the analysis of settlement, industrial and agricultural patterns. The well-known gravity model, which states that the frequency of interaction between two centres is directly proportional to the product of the two populations and inversely proportional to the distance between them, has been variously used (Hägerstrand, 1957; Olsson, 1965a and b), but it has difficulties. The movements of people are not always determined by economic cost, for some are willing to make longer trips than others because of different interpretations of opportunities. Populations differ in character and therefore necessitate different weighting; distance may be measured and perceived in different ways (Gould, 1966), and the relationships between population and distance are not normally linear

but exponential or hyperbolic—as seen in the pattern of urban population densities—possibly because people view distances and costs of travel
exponentially, strongly differentiating between local areas but regarding
remote areas as uniform. These various considerations have led to many
modifications and refinements to the gravity model.

Disillusionment with distance and the gravity model led Stouffer
(1940) to propose the intervening opportunities model which states that
the number of persons moving a distance is directly proportional to
the number of opportunities at that distance and inversely proportional
to the number of intervening opportunities. Later, Stouffer (1960)
introduced another variable, competing migrants at destination.
Intervening opportunities naturally limit interaction at greater distances,
but they are not easily defined. Moreover, like the gravity model the
intervening opportunities model has considerable predictive limitations,
resulting in the development of modifications, in particular micro-
models of migration. Hägerstrand's (1957) examination of the process
of migration through the use of a simulation model based on information flow concepts initiated much work, especially of a behavioural type,
with particular reference to the barriers and filters in the migration
process. Wolpert (1965), for example, proposes a model of migration
which incorporates three concepts of migration behaviour: (a) place
utility, in which migration is regarded as an adaptation to perceived
changes in one's surroundings (Brown and Longbrake, 1970); (b)
information field or geographical distribution (around an individual
group) of knowledge about other people or areas which is affected by
the feedback of information from previous migrants (Marble and
Nystuen, 1963); and (c) life-cycle, which visualizes individuals moving
through a series of stations in their action space (Hägerstrand, 1958).
Unfortunately, most models concerned with the movement of people
have been descriptive rather than normative, and though they have been
used to predict total movement to centres and the distribution of length
of trips, they have rarely taken into account the multi-purpose nature of
many trips.

Human movement takes place within definable fields, which have
increased in size over time as the relative cost of distance has been
reduced, so that interaction and migration fields overlap more and more,
making the problem of their definition and analysis ever more difficult.
The problem has attracted attention in recent years (Hägerstrand,
1957), as for example in the analysis of marriage-distance (e.g. Morrill
and Pitts, 1967) or internal migration regions within a country; Ng
(1969) has examined this problem with reference to Scotland. At the

national level migration has been complicated by the establishment of administrative boundaries and territories which have greatly influenced migration fields, constraining movement and interaction between some countries (e.g. the communist bloc), and even in parts of the world like tropical Africa where modern political boundaries are a recent super-imposition. On the other hand, the study of short-distance movements (Perry, 1969) may be a more profitable line of research, especially as they have been somewhat neglected for the more immediately striking long-distance movements. As short-distance moves often take place within small administrative units, they are inadequately revealed by migration statistics. Moreover, we should also remember that net migration (Johnston, R. J., 1967) may be only a small fraction of total migration (the ratio between the two is known as migration efficiency).

Movement of population within cities has become a focus of con-siderable interest to geographers, who have been concerned with the relationship of movement streams to patterns of city growth and development, the reasons for migrations, search behaviour (Silk, 1971), the characteristics of intra-urban migrants, the impact of migrations upon social areas and the problem of predicting intra-urban movement. Most intra-urban moves are short, the location of new residences being influenced particularly by the location of existing residences (Simmons, 1968), especially as city residents have only limited mental maps or images of the city (Adams, 1969). The housing needs generated by the life-cycle, particularly among people under 35 years of age, tend to be instrumental in the majority of intra-urban moves, and much urban expansion occurs without in-migration. Other models of intra-urban migration stress radial expansion from city centres and a process of filtering, especially by invasion and succession, by which properties are passed down the social scale. R. J. Johnston (1969) reviews partial models of intra-urban migration and suggests that 'in each case a separate causal mechanism produces virtually the same result', and in his analysis of population movements within Greater London he finds support for them. Brown and Moore (1970) have stressed that existing models do not possesss a high degree of predictive power and see greater benefit in acquiring an adequate understanding of the decision-making processes of the household unit. Certainly this is an area where research effort may be directed, as it would throw considerable light on latent migration potential (Johnston, J. H., 1970), a topic of considerable applied utility.

POPULATION GEOGRAPHY IN THE DEVELOPING COUNTRIES

It will be apparent that the types of analysis of population so far mentioned have not been evenly applied across the earth's surface. In particular, there has been a fairly marked contrast between geographical studies of population in developed countries and those in developing countries. The distinction between these two groups of countries is arbitrary because there is no clear-cut dichotomy, but it has some general utility in population geography (Clarke, J. I., 1971), for in general they experience different population structures and transitions, social and economic structures, literacy levels and so on, as well as substantial differences in their internal geographic patterns. Taken together, these considerations have influenced the research interests of population geographers.

Owing to the prolonged persistence of closed subsistence economies, and to the contrasts in traditional ways of life, many parts of the Third World—which today comprises nearly seven-tenths of the total world population and accounts for about four-fifths of world population growth—have long displayed considerable heterogeneity of human geography, evidenced, for example, by a plethora of peoples, languages and economic systems in tropical Africa, the Indian sub-continent and southeast Asia. Patterns of population are clearly affected by cultural groupings, so that for instance in tropical Africa the tribal framework influences not only population distribution and densities but also patterns of fertility, mortality, migration, composition, growth and population pressure. Among these peoples, mostly engaged in agriculture, population geographers have been particularly concerned with problems of pressure on the land (Prescott, 1961; Hunter, 1967) and the carrying capacity under traditional systems of agriculture such as bush fallowing (Hunter, 1966; Street, 1969). A good example of the utility of this approach is the work of Brookfield and Brown (1963) on density of occupation indices among the Chimbu of the New Guinea Highlands in order to ascertain which groups were approaching congestion and which had abundant supplies of land.

Traditional patterns of population in developing countries, which evolved rather slowly over centuries, have been greatly upset in this century by the localized development of a modern economic sector, which is found especially in towns, ports, mining regions and areas of commercialized agriculture. Developed particularly under colonial rule, these areas of modern development are often still externally orientated to former colonial powers and may also still contain a high proportion of aliens. In some smaller countries like Singapore (Neville, 1966), Malaya, Fiji and Mauritius, problems of plural societies arise (Troll, 1964) which are aggravated in South Africa by the policy of apartheid (Sabbagh, 1968). These localized areas of modernity have also become 'islandic' poles of rapid population growth (Hance, 1970) through the attraction of labour migrants as well as rapid natural increase caused by the decline of mortality brought about by improved medical facilities, sanitation, nutrition and hygiene. Although they only incorporate a small proportion of the total populations of developing countries, these poles cause great areal disparities, most evidenced by the rapidity of urban growth, which has been very great in many cities but has involved particularly large numbers in some large cities such as Kinshasa, Mexico City and Tehran. Rapid urbanization has caused acute problems of accommodation, employment and social integration, all the more serious where it is accompanied by little or no industrialization. In many developing countries it has been argued that over-urbanization occurs, but the criteria for such a view are not universally acceptable. Certainly, much urbanization responds to 'push' from rural areas rather than 'pull' from urban centres, and is characterized by the excessive growth of the tertiary sector. But not all developing countries suffer from over-urbanization—in many Latin American and especially East African countries, for example, there is a stronger case for suggesting over-concentration in primate and other cities than over-urbanization in general. Many of these problems have been looked at in detail by geographers (e.g. Clarke, C. G., 1966; Dwyer, 1964), some of whose work is summarized in the volumes edited by Zelinsky, Kosinski and Prothero (1970) and by J. I. Clarke (1971).

Population mobility in developing countries, particularly rural-urban migration, has had important effects upon traditional societies, reducing their harmony with the physical environment, a topic which was basic to the 'modes of life' approach of earlier human geographers, especially of the French school. Population mobility has brought about great changes in town and country in developing countries, the effects being extremely diverse and the problems numerous (Barbour and Prothero, 1961; Prothero, 1964, 1965; Harrison, 1966). Prothero, for example, has made many studies of specific problems arising from population mobility in Africa, and has in particular highlighted the hazard of disease transmission (Prothero, 1965). Mobility may radically alter demographic patterns even in countries where the modern sector is restricted, as seen in Figure 3.8 of Sierra Leone where the real

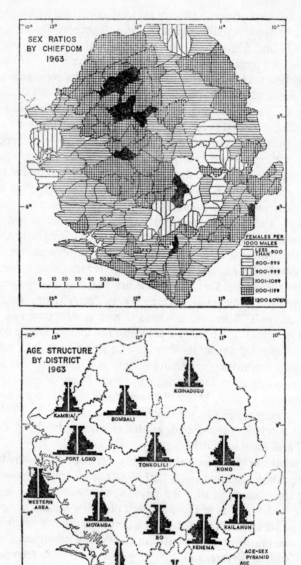

FIGURE 3.8   Patterns of age and sex structure in Sierra Leone, 1963

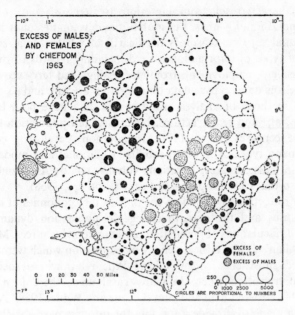

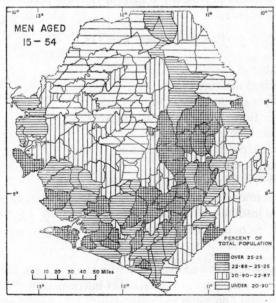

variations largely result from migrations to Freetown and to iron ore
and diamond mining areas. But mobility in developing countries is not
easy to analyse. One reason is the dearth of reliable data, so that a
variety of types of information is used including records of transport,
tax assessment, employment, frontier crossings and ferry crossings as
well as census data; census data on migration are rare and so the most
common methods of analysis using census data have been by tribal
affiliation, age and sex structures, birthplace and population totals at
successive censuses (Hirst, 1971). In addition, developing countries
exhibit many types of human mobility, traditional and modern, and
varying in cause, course, duration, volume, composition and consequences so that classification is not easy (Prothero, 1968).

The introduction of a modern sector into the economies of developing countries and the massive change in population dynamics has
bedevilled calculations of population pressure upon resources. Measures
such as Allan's (1965) critical density of population which were devised
for closed subsistence societies have little relevance to societies in
economic transition where in many rural areas there is no direct
relationship between man and land (Gleave and White, 1969). Attempts
have been made to provide a formula for resource needs, such as that
by Ackerman (1959):

$$PS = RQ(TAS_t) + E_s + T_r \pm F - W$$

where
  P = number of people
  S = standard of living
  R = amount of resources
  Q = factor for natural quality of resources
  T = physical technology factor
  A = administrative techniques factor
  S_t = resource stability factor
  W = frugality element (wastage or intensity of use)
  F = institutional advantage and 'friction' loss element consequent
        upon institutional characteristics of the society
  E_s = scale economies element (size of territory, etc.)
  T_r = resources added in trade

Since no single term can be quantified with any precision, this is hardly
a formula, but simply an identification of interactions within a system.
There have been difficulties in finding satisfactory operational indices,
and this has meant that population pressure has largely escaped
rigorous quantitative analysis (Zelinsky, Kosinski and Prothero, 1970);

it is still usually subjectively assessed by such general indicators as unemployment, underemployment, hunger, out-migration, land fragmentation and soil deterioration (Noin, 1970). The problem in finding formulae is exacerbated by the dynamism of the variables; population, resources, technology, and the economic expectations and attainments of the population. The term 'resources' for example, has been variously interpreted, but geographers and economists usually define it as substances or properties which satisfy human needs, and so resources vary with the aims, talents and efforts of peoples, with their economic and cultural attainments and their technological ability. Moreover, some resources are non-renewable and others replaceable, while some may be exploited by a foreign company or power. Consequently, for an adequate assessment of population/resource ratios, populations cannot be regarded as discrete unqualified numerical totals, and population pressure on resources is only really meaningful in the context of the cultural, political and economic organization of a society. The remedy for imbalance may also vary, in some cases being economic, social or even political, rather than demographic (Clarke, J. I., 1968). Frustrated by a fruitless search for suitable quantitative formulae of population pressure, geographers, like other social scientists, continue to use intangible terms like overpopulation and underpopulation without any generally recognized criteria of definition (Clarke, J. I., 1965); but in recent years they have paid less attention to static measures of population pressure and more to the spatial relationships between population dynamics and economic growth (Zelinsky, Kosinski and Prothero, 1970), for the essence of population problems in developing countries is that they result from change.

It may be seen that underlying much geographical work on the populations of developing countries has been a strong awareness of the relationships between population dynamics and social and economic problems in both town and country (Steel, 1970), an awareness which provoked Zelinsky (1970) in characteristic fashion, to call for 'a rationally controlled frenzy' in geographical studies of the population problems of developing countries. He is one of the geographers who have declared themselves as members of the 'alarmist' camp; many would consider that there is more value in considering the highly variable population problems of individual countries and regions than in adopting a general attitude to the population problems of the developing countries or the world as a whole. Certainly it would seem that the geographer's rôle is particularly valuable in developing countries, where spatial relationships are sometimes unrecognized and where the links between the physical environment and man are still strong.

POPULATION GEOGRAPHY IN DEVELOPED COUNTRIES

Developed countries, with much longer series of population data including pre-censal figures and records of births and deaths, have attracted rather different approaches. A variety of factors including the more advanced complex patterns of urban growth, the reduction in the importance of agriculture, the multiplicity of industrial and service functions, the great expansion of the middle classes, the ubiquity of low mortality, fertility and growth rates and the availability of modern communications systems have combined greatly to reduce areal disparities in many aspects of human geography (Lacoste, 1965). In most developed countries, between one-half and three-quarters of the population live in urban settlements, so the latter are the main bases of population distribution. People are no longer tied to their place of work and by natural resources; their land-boundedness is diminishing, and so it is no longer imperative to review population distributions and changes in the light of local environmental conditions. It is more appropriate to consider the flows and linkages that are characteristic of highly mobile modern populations, and naturally the recent revolution in techniques of geographical analysis has greatly aided this approach.

In their studies of the populations of developed countries geographers have been less motivated by desires to resolve social and economic problems than to analyse and understand processes of areal population change. Work has particularly concentrated on three evolutionary phases. First, attention has been given, though insufficiently, to the changing population patterns in pre-industrial and pre-censal times, using for example parish registers in Britain (Wrigley, 1966; Mills, 1959) or hearth rolls compiled for tax purposes in France and the Low Countries (Pounds and Roome, 1971). In this way they have made a contribution to the rapid evolution of historical demography in recent years, a field of study which has of course also become a focus of attention for economic historians, demographers, geneticists, physical anthropologists and many others. Second, work has focussed on the processes of population change and concentration (Gibbs, 1963) which took place during the early phase of industrialization and urbanization, resulting in substantial demographic differences between urban and rural populations in terms of densities, structures and dynamics. There have been many analyses of the massive redistribution of population nationally (Law, 1967; Lawton, 1958, 1967 and 1968a; Osborne, 1958 and 1964a) and internationally (Lawton, 1959a; Cousens, 1960 and 1965). Similar processes were analysed by Wrigley (1961) when he looked at the relationship between population change, economic growth and coal resources in the coalfield areas of Western Europe in the period between the nineteenth century and the First World War.

The third phase, which has attracted a great deal of research activity, is characterized by the declining influence of natural resources (especially coal) upon population patterns and consequent regional redistribution. Britain exemplifies this process very well (Osborne, 1964b), and many geographical analyses have been made of specific regional movements such as the drift from the declining coalfield of north-east England (House and Knight, 1965, 1966) and the depopulation of the Scottish highlands and islands. The third phase is also characterized by the spread of suburbanization and commuting, facilitated particularly by the development and increasing popularity of the motor car, which is blurring the distinctions between urban and rural areas (Robertson, 1961; Zelinsky, 1962), and involving much longer journeys to work. Long thought of as a phenomenon of metropolitan development, journey to work is now recognized as a very widespread feature of modern society, expressing a basic disharmony or imbalance between residential and workplace locations. Lawton (1959b, 1963, 1968b) and many other geographers have made detailed analyses of this disharmony.

Associated with population redistribution, as both cause and effect, are the striking variations in regional levels of affluence. They result primarily from variations in employment and income, as Coates and Rawstron (1971) have revealed for the United Kingdom and Lewis (1968) in the north-eastern part of the United States. The considerable changes which have taken place in the selectivity of migrations, notably age and sex selectivity, have also had an important influence upon patterns of population composition, such as of age-structures (Dewdney, 1968; Coulson, 1968), sex-ratios (Clarke, J. I., 1960), socio-economic groups (Hall and Smith, 1968), overcrowding (Lawton, 1968c), mortality (Murray, 1967; Howe, 1970) and various other population characteristics. As the forms of population mobility diversify, these patterns are becoming more complex. Certainly they are more complex than the uneven distributional patterns and sharp breaks in densities which occur among coloured and immigrant communities, as seen for example among the West Indians in Britain (Peach, 1968) and the negro ghettos of the United States (Morrill, 1965). Metropolitan cities, urbanized regions and conurbations are foci of social complexities, and their internal demographic patterns have become the subject of close scrutiny by many geographers from both descriptive and analytical viewpoints, as for example in the recent atlases of Paris (Beaujeu-Garnier and Bastié, 1967), London (Jones and Sinclair, 1968) and Birmingham (Rosing and Wood, 1971), in which analyses have been based on enumeration district data; Rosing and Wood's atlas is of particular interest as all of its maps are computer outputs in map form.

The growing distance between residence and workplace has had pronounced effects upon urban population densities in developed countries, reducing the sharp edge densities of cities as well as density gradients. Many authors (e.g. Stewart and Warntz, 1958; Berry, Simmons and Tennant, 1963) have examined these phenomena and have reviewed Clark's (1951) empirically derived expression of negative exponential decline of population density from city centre to outer suburb. Newling (1969), for example, has postulated that since both urban population densities and the growth rate are functions of distance from the city centre, then a population density-growth rule can be derived which states that urban population densities at the beginning of a given period and the associated rates of population change are inversely related. Of course, urban expansion does not necessarily imply growth of population; in some cases it has meant merely expansion of population into areas formerly considered suburban or rural.

Undoubtedly, urban populations in developed countries have attracted much more attention than rural populations, and yet the latter, increasingly heterogeneous with more service, residential, dormitory or defence elements, have changed substantially in recent decades (Robertson, 1961). Unfortunately, data are not always differentiated, and it is not always easy to distinguish the various elements, but certainly rural populations warrant much closer scrutiny.

POPULATION IMBALANCE AND PLANNING

No student of population can escape the conclusion that at all levels, from the world scale to the micro-scale, population is often inefficiently distributed and that there are innumerable examples of population imbalance. The history of demographic evolution in the world has left a situation of extreme inequalities in population pressure upon resources, which is to some extent stabilized by the establishment of political divisions preventing large-scale human migrations. In these circumstances, alleviation of population pressure is only really possible at the national level or more local level. At the national level, a variety of types of imbalance exist ranging from situations where the absolute population is too high to be supported by the available land and resources or where the rate of population increase is excessive, to situations where there are too few people to develop satisfactorily the resources or to achieve even modest economies of scale. Population imbalance is therefore a basic problem in the development of many countries, but it is one which may be solved in a variety of ways—economically, socially, politically and demographically—without there being any single universal solution. Any demographic solution is difficult because populations are not easily managed; while death control has been rapidly extended to the majority of the world's inhabitants, fertility control spreads much more slowly, and even in planned societies migrations are difficult to organize and direct. No country is able to determine or even predict its future rate of population growth with any degree of precision.

In general, populations faced with changing economic and social circumstances respond more by movement than by voluntary control of their numbers, although there is always strong population immobility. As society evolves, the nature and types of internal movements become more complex, and the rôle of government becomes increasingly important. Accordingly, there are obvious applications to planning and regional economic growth problems of the analysis of topics like inter-regional migrations (Fielding, 1966), journey to work and intra-urban migration. In Britain, much effort has been directed towards regional stabilization of population distribution through development area policy; in France there is now a deliberate attempt to counteract the excessive concentration of population and wealth on Paris through the creation of eight 'métropoles d'équilibres' and a larger number of intermediate centres; in Tanzania there is a similar effort to offset centralization on the primate city of Dar es Salaam by a policy of 'agro-industrial village-ization'; and the Chinese government has encouraged movement into the interior in order to counteract the dominance of the coastal cities, formerly so much under Western influence. In many other countries considerable efforts are made to influence the patterns and movements of population by a variety of inducements, restraints and constraints.

CONCLUSION

We live in a world where there is little stability of any sort. Change is pre-eminent and this applies particularly to populations, although the spatial patterns of today are the main determinants of the patterns of tomorrow, so that action today to influence present patterns will have long-term effects; once initiated, locational and agglomerative processes are difficult to divert or interrupt. Unfortunately, techniques for forecasting future population trends, even simple numerical totals, are exceedingly crude, and the history of population projections for countries, largely based on assumptions concerning the two variables of fertility and mortality, is dotted with major errors. At more local levels, where the less predictable variable of migration plays a more important part, the task of population forecasting is even more problematic and the likely margin of error greater. The fact that most of our data are derived from technologically obsolete decennial censuses—which are better for static situations than dynamic ones—does not help matters, nor does the fact that the data are usually for areal units which bear little resemblance to spatial patterns of population. Fortunately, however, in Britain at least the introduction of geocoded data will greatly facilitate computer mapping and more rapid analysis of trends. Despite the difficulties of forecasting, it is extremely important for geographers to use their expertise in spatial analysis in an effort to predict future spatial patterns of population, and to ask not merely where populations will be and why, but where they ought to be. They must try to forecast future patterns of distribution, structures, migration streams and pressures in a world where the rate of change is so rapid that it is difficult to envisage more than a decade ahead at macro- or micro-level, and at the same time they must endeavour to propose spatial solutions to some of our demographic problems.

For example, a great deal more research is necessary into the forces of population agglomeration and dispersion. So far this century in most parts of the world there has been increasing agglomeration of population, particularly in urban centres, and this has proceeded even more rapidly than population growth. This agglomeration has made possible increasingly centralized control over societies and their distribution, though few governments have met with great success in their policies to influence population distribution. Agglomeration is no longer necessary for central control because of the improvement in communications, and such control is now possible with a dispersed population. Responding to motor transport in particular, most cities of the developed world are experiencing local dispersion away from the central areas towards peripheral zones where there is higher residential amenity and an increasing amount of employment in secondary and tertiary activities. Consequently, areas of concentrated population are merging, spreading and infilling, leading to urbanized regions such as we see in the Midlands of England and Megalopolis in the north-eastern United States. Indeed, it is more commonly suggested that the bulk of the world's population will be living in vast interconnected urban systems roughly coincident with the ecumene, and that continuing progress in communications will help to integrate these systems, reducing the significance of relative location. The growth of communications and the spread of information and ideas are having an enormous influence upon the distribution of population. Whereas the location of population once determined the information that they received, information is now determining the places where people wish or choose to be. The choice of people is having a growing influence upon population mobility and distribution, choice which will be affected greatly by such criteria as environmental quality and amenity, because the growing numbers in tertiary sectors are not tied to fixed locations. Population growth in California and Florida exemplifies some of these tendencies, which also account for some of the drift southward in Britain. Certainly an understanding of human behaviour will be vital in the analysis of future population trends, not least to comprehend the way in which people will be affected by high population densities, and how such densities may affect physical systems without destroying them.

This will be no less important in the developing countries, where most of the above-mentioned processes are much less advanced. As the processes of information and diffusion affect most of the inhabited world, it is necessary to examine in detail how they have affected the spread of mortality decline and also migration, and how they will be likely in the future to affect the spread of fertility decline, a vital process in most of the Third World where there is excessive pressure of population growth on resources. The identification of population pressures and the means of reducing them are urgent fields for research in many developing countries, though the difficulties of finding large-scale solutions are frequently aggravated by the traditional diversity of peoples and cultures. Some of the more profitable work must be done at the local level.

Thus it is clear that there is a vast field of research to be cultivated, by geographers and others. The dynamic nature of population distributions, the evolving patterns of migration and of fertility, means perhaps an unending series of questions of high importance to mankind —an importance that at the present time is underlined by the widespread and growing concern about the impact of man upon the natural environment.

REFERENCES

Ackerman, E. A. (1959) 'Population and natural resources', in P. M. Hauser and O. D. Duncan (Eds.), *The Study of Population*, University of Chicago Press, 621–648.

Adams, J. (1969) 'Directional bias in intra-urban migration', *Economic Geography*, **45**, 302–323.

Ahmad, Q. (1965) *Indian Cities: characteristics and correlates*, University of Chicago, Department of Geography, Research Paper No. 102.

Allan, W. (1965) *The African Husbandman*, Oliver and Boyd.

Barbour, K. M. and Prothero, R. M. (Eds.) (1961) *Essays on African Population*, Routledge and Kegan Paul.

Beaujeu-Garnier, J. (1966) *Geography of Population*, Longmans.

Beaujeu-Garnier, J. and Bastié, J. (Eds.) (1967) *Atlas de Paris et de la Région Parisienne*, Berger-Levrault.

Berry, B. J. L., Simmons, J. W. and Tennant, R. J. (1963) 'Urban population densities: structure and change, *Geographical Review*, **53**, 389–405.

Brookfield, H. C. and Brown, P. (1963) *Struggle for Land*, Oxford University Press.

Brown, L. A. and Longbrake, D. B. (1970) 'Migration flows in intra-urban space: place utility considerations', *Annals of the Association American Geographers*, **60**, 368–384.

Brown, L. A. and Moore, E. G. (1970) 'The intra-urban migration process: a perspective', *Geografiska Annaler*, **52** Ser. B, 1–13.

Chung, R. (1970) 'Space-time diffusion of the transition model: the twentieth century patterns', in G. J. Demko, H. M. Rose and G. A. Schnell (Eds.), *Population Geography: a reader*, McGraw-Hill, 220–239.

Claeson, C. F. (1968) 'Distance and human interaction', *Geografiska Annaler*, **50B**, 143–169.

Clark, C. (1951) 'Urban population densities', *Journal of the Royal Statistical Society* Ser. A., **114**, 490–496.

Clarke, C. G. (1966) 'Population pressure in Kingston, Jamaica, a study of unemployment and overcrowding', *Transactions of the Institute of British Geographers*, **38**, 165–182.

Clarke, J. I. (1960) 'Rural and urban sex-ratios in England and Wales', *Tijdschrift voor Economische en Sociale Geografie*, **51**, 29–38.

Clarke, J. I. (1965) *Population Geography*, Pergamon.

Clarke, J. I. (1968) 'World population and food resources: a critique', *Institute of British Geographers Special Publication No. 1, Sir Dudley Stamp Memorial Volume*, 53–70.

Clarke, J. I. (1971) *Population Geography and the Developing Countries*, Pergamon.

Coates, B. E. and Rawstron, E. M. (1971) *Regional Variations in Britain: studies in economic and social geography*, Batsford.

Compton, P. (1968) 'A határ népesség mint vándorlási index (Stable model population as a migration index)', *Demografia*, II, 428–441.

Coulson, M. R. C. (1968) 'The distribution of population age structures in Kansas City', *Annals of the Association of American Geographers*, **58**, 155–176.

Cousens, S. H. (1960) 'The regional pattern of emigration during the Great Irish Famine, 1846–51', *Transactions of the Institute of British Geographers*, **28**, 126–129.

Cousens, S. H. (1965) 'The regional variations in emigration from Ireland between 1821 and 1841', *Transactions of the Institute of British Geographers*, **37**, 15–30.

Davis, S. G. (1962) 'The rural-urban migration in Hong Kong and its new territories', *Geographical Journal*, **128**, 328–333.

Demko, G. J. and Casetti, E. (1970) 'A diffusion model for selected demographic variables: an application to Soviet data', *Annals of the Association of American Geographers*, **60**, 533–539.

Demko, G. J., Rose, H. M. and Schnell, G. A. (Eds.) (1970) *Population Geography: a reader*, McGraw-Hill.

Dewdney, J. C. (1968) 'Age-structure maps of the British Isles', *Transactions of the Institute of British Geographers*, **43**, 9–18.

Dwyer, D. J. (1964) 'The problem of in-migration and squatter settlement in Asian cities: the two case studies, Manila and Victoria-Kowloon', *Asian Studies*, **2**, 145–169.

Fielding, A. J. (1966) 'Internal migration and regional economic growth—a case study of France', *Urban Studies*, **3**, 200–214.

Forbes, J. and Robertson, I. M. L. (1967) 'Population enumeration on a grid square basis: the census of Scotland, a test case', *Cartographic Journal*, **4**, 29–37.

Fosberg, F. A. (Ed.) (1965) *Man's Place in the Island Ecosystem*, Bishop Museum Press.

Franklin, S. H. (1956) 'The pattern of sex-ratios in New Zealand', *Economic Geography*, **32**, 162–176.

Gay, J. D. (1971) *The Geography of Religion in England*, Butterworths.

Geddes, A. (1941) 'Half a century of population trends in India: a regional study of net change and variability, 1881–1931', *Geographical Journal*, **98**, 228–252.

Geddes, A. (1942) 'The population of India: variability of change as a regional demographic index', *Geographical Review*, **32**, 562–573.

George, P. (1959) *Questions de Géographie de la Population*, Presses Universitaires de la France.

George, P. (1967) *Géographie de la Population*, Presses Universitaires de la France.

Gibbs, J. P. (1963) 'The evolution of population concentration', *Economic Geography*. **39**, 119–129.

Gould, P. R. (1966) 'On mental maps', *Michigan Inter-University Society of Mathematical Geographers*, **9**, 1–54.

Gleave, M. B. and White, H. P. (1969) 'Population density and agricultural systems in West Africa', in M. F. Thomas and G. W. Whittington (Eds.), *Environment and Land Use in Africa*, Methuen, 273–300.

Hägerstrand, T. (1957) 'Migration and area: survey of a sample of Swedish migration fields and hypothetical considerations of their genesis', *Lund Studies in Geography, Series B, Human Geography*, **13**, 27–158.

Hägerstrand, T. (1958) 'Geographical measurements of migration: Swedish data', in J. Sutter (Ed.), *Human Displacements*, Hachette, 61–84.

Hägerstrand, T. (1967) *Innovation Diffusion as a Spatial Process*, University of Chicago.

Haggett, P. (1965a) *Locational Analysis in Human Geography*, Arnold.

Haggett, P. (1965b) 'Scale components in geographical problems', in R. J. Chorley and P. Haggett (Eds.), *Frontiers in Geographical Teaching*, Methuen 164–185.

Hall, C. B. and Smith, R. A. (1968) 'Socio-economic patterns of England and Wales', *Urban Studies*, **5**, 59–66.

Hance, W. A. (1970) *Population, Migration, and Urbanization in Africa*, Columbia University Press.

Harrison, R. S. (1966) *Migration as a Factor in the Geography of Western Libya*, unpublished Ph.D. thesis, University of Cambridge.

Hartley, R. G. and Norris, J. M. (1969) 'Demographic regions in Libya: a principal components analysis of economic and demographic variables', *Tijdschrift voor Economische en Sociale Geografie*, **60**, 221–227.

Henshall, J. B. (1966) 'The demographic factor in the structure of agriculture in Barbados', *Transactions of the Institute of British Geographers*, 38, 183–195.

Hirst, M. A. (1971) *Migration and the Analysis of Census Data in Tropical Africa*, unpublished Ph.D. thesis, University of Liverpool.

Hooson, D. J. M. (1960) 'The distribution of population as the essential geographical expression', *Canadian Geographer*, **17**, 10–20.

House, J. W. and Knight, E. M. (1965) *Migrants of North-East England*, Papers on migration and mobility in North-East England, No. 2, University of Newcastle-upon-Tyne.

House, J. W. and Knight, E. M. (1966) *People on the Move*, Papers on migration and mobility in North-East England, No. 3, University of Newcastle-upon-Tyne.

Houston, J. M. (1953) *A Social Geography of Europe*, Duckworth.

Howe, G. M. (1970) *National Atlas of Disease Mortality*, Nelson, 2nd ed.

Hunt, A. J. (Ed.) (1968) 'Special number on population maps of the British Isles, 1961', *Transactions of the Institute of British Geographers*, **43**.

Hunter, J. M. (1966) 'Ascertaining population carrying capacity under traditional systems of agriculture in developing countries', *Professional Geographer*, **18**, 151–154.

Hunter, J. M. (1967) 'Population pressure in a part of the West African savanna', *Annals of the Association of American Geographers*, **42**, 101–114.

James, P. E. (1954) 'The geographic study of population', in P. E. James and C. F. Jones (Eds.), *American Geography: inventory and prospect*, Syracuse University Press, 106–122.

Johnson, J. H. (1970) 'Recent British contributions to the study of population geography', *Geographia Polonica*, **18**, 57–73.

Johnston, R. J. (1967) 'A reconnaissance study of population change in Nidderdale, 1951–61', *Transactions of the Institute of British Geographers*, **41**, 113–123.

Johnston, R. J. (1969) 'Population movements and metropolitan expansion: London, 1960–61', *Transactions of the Institute of British Geographers*, **46**, 69–91.

Johnston, R. J. (1970) 'Latent migration potential and the gravity model: a New Zealand study', *Geographical Analysis*, **2**, 387–396.

Jones, E. and Sinclair, D. J. (Eds.) (1968) *Atlas of London and the London Region*, Pergamon.

King, L. J. (1969) *Statistical Analysis in Geography*, Prentice-Hall.

Lacoste, Y. (1965) *Géographie de sous-Développement*, Presses Universitaires de France.

Law, C. M. (1967) 'The growth of urban population in England and Wales, 1801–1911', *Transactions of the Institute of British Geographers*, **41**, 125–144.

Lawton, R. (1958) 'Population movements in the West Midlands, 1841–1861', *Geography*, **43**, 164–177.

Lawton, R. (1959a) 'Irish immigration to England and Wales in the mid-nineteenth century', *Irish Geographer*, **4**, 35–54.

Lawton, R. (1959b) 'The daily journey to work in England and Wales', *Town Planning Review*, **29**, 241–257.

Lawton, R. (1963) 'The journey to work in England and Wales: forty years of change', *Tijdschrift voor Economische en Sociale Geografie*, **54**, 61–69.

Lawton, R. (1967) 'Rural depopulation in nineteenth century England', in R. W. Steel and R. Lawton (Eds.), *Liverpool Essays in Geography*, Longmans, 227–255.

Lawton, R. (1968a) 'Population changes in England and Wales in the later nineteenth century', *Transactions of the Institute of British Geographers*, **44**, 55–74.

Lawton, R. (1968b) 'The journey to work in Britain: some trends and problems', *Regional Studies*, **2**, 27–40.

Lawton, R. (1968c) 'A map of overcrowding in the British Isles', *Transactions of the Institute of British Geographers*, **43**, 19–23.

Lewis, G. M. (1968) 'Levels of living in the North-Eastern United States c. 1960: a new approach to regional geography', *Transactions of the Institute of British Geographers*, **55**, 11–37.

Linsky, A. (1965) 'Some generalisations concerning primate cities', *Annals of the Association of American Geographers*, **55**, 506–513.

MacArthur, R. H. and Wilson, E. O. (1967) *The Theory of Island Biogeography*, Princeton University Press.

Marble, D. F. (1964) 'A simple Markovian model of trip structures in a metropolitan region', in B. J. L. Berry and F. E. Horton (Eds.), *Geographic Perspectives in Urban Systems*, Prentice-Hall, 1970, 546–547.

Marble, D. F. and Nystuen, J. D. (1963) 'An approach to the direct measurement of community mean information fields', *Papers and Proceedings of the Regional Science Association*, **11**, 99–109.

Medvedkov, Y. V. (1970) 'Applications of mathematics to population geography', in G. J. Demko, H. M. Rose and G. A. Schnell (Eds.), *Population Geography: a reader*, McGraw-Hill, 144–153.

Mills, D. R. (1959) 'The poor laws and the distribution of population c. 1600–1800, with special reference to Lincolnshire', *Transactions of the Institute of British Geographers*, **28**, 185–195.

Moore, J. E. (1969) *A Population Geography of the Central Region of Ghana*, unpublished Ph.D. thesis, University of Liverpool.

Morrill, R. L. (1963) 'The distribution of migration distances', *Papers and Proceedings of the Regional Science Association*, **11**, 75–84.

Morrill, R. L. (1965) 'The negro ghetto: problems and alternatives', *Geographical Review*, **55**, 339–361.

Morrill, R. L. (1970) *The Spatial Organisation of Society*, Wadsworth.

Morrill, R. L. and Pitts, F. R. (1967) 'Marriage, migration and the mean information field', *Annals of the Association of American Geographers*, **57**, 402–422.

Murray, M. A. (1967) 'The geography of death in the United States and the United Kingdom', *Annals of the Association of American Geographers*, **57**, 301–314.

Neville, W. (1966) 'Singapore: ethnic diversity and its implications', *Annals Association of American Geographers*, **56**, 236–253.

Newling, B. E. (1969) 'The spatial variation of urban population densities', *Geographical Review*, **59**, 242–252.

Ng, R. (1969) 'Internal migration regions in Scotland', *Geografiska Annaler*, **51B**, 139–147.

Noin, D. (1970) *La Population rurale du Maroc*, Presses Universitaires de France.

Olsson, G. (1965a) *Distance and Human Interaction: a review and bibliography*, Regional Science Institute, Philadelphia.

Olsson, G. (1965b) 'Distance and human interaction, a migration study', *Geografiska Annaler*, **47B**, 3–43.

Osborne, R. H. (1958) 'The movements of people in Scotland, 1851–1951', *Scottish Studies*, **2**, 1–46.

Osborne, R. H. (1964a) 'Migration trends in England and Wales, 1901–1951', in *Problems of Applied Geography*, *Geographia Polonica*, **3**, 137–162.

Osborne, R. H. (1964b) 'Changes in the regional distribution of population in Great Britain', *Geography*, **49**, 265–273.

Peach, C. (1968) *West Indian Migration to Britain: a social geography*, Oxford University Press.

Perry, P. J. (1969) 'Working-class isolation and mobility in rural Dorset, 1837–1936: a study of marriage distances', *Transactions of the Institute of British Geographers*, **46**, 121–141.

Pounds, N. J. G. and Roome, C. G. (1971) 'Population density in fifteenth century France and the Low Countries', *Annals of the Association of American Geographers*, **59**, 116–130.

Prescott, J. R. V. (1961) 'Overpopulation and overstocking in the native areas of Matabeleland', *Geographical Journal*, **128**, 212–225.

Prothero, R. M. (1964) 'Continuity and change in African population mobility', in R. W. Steel and R. M. Prothero (Eds.), *Geographers and the Tropics: Liverpool Essays*, Longmans.

Prothero, R. M. (1965) *Migrants and Malaria*, Longmans.

Prothero, R. M. (1968) 'Migration in tropical Africa', in J. C. Caldwell and C. Okonjo (Eds.), *The Population of Tropical Africa*, Longmans.

Robertson, I. M. L. (1961) 'The occupational structure and distribution of rural population in England and Wales', *Scottish Geographical Magazine*, **77**, 165–179.

Robertson, I. M. L. (1969) 'The census and research: ideals and realities', *Transactions of the Institute of British Geographers*, **48**, 173–187.

Robinson, A. H., Lindberg, J. B. and Brinkman, L. W. (1961) 'A correlation and regression analysis applied to rural farm population densities in the great plains', *Annals of the Association of American Geographers*, **51**, 211–220.

Robson, B. T. (1969) *Urban Analysis: a study of city structure with special reference to Sunderland*, Cambridge University Press.

Rosing, K. E. and Wood, P. A. (1971) *Character of a Conurbation: a computer atlas of Birmingham and the Black Country*, University of London Press.

Sabbagh, E. (1968) 'Some geographical characteristics of a plural society: apartheid in South Africa', *Geographical Review*, **58**, 1–28.

Silk, J. A. (1971) *Search Behaviour: general characterisation and review of literature in the behavioural sciences*, University of Reading, Department of Geography, Geographical Papers No. 7.

Simmons, J. W. (1968) 'Changing residence in the city: a review of intra-urban mobility', *Geographical Review*, **58**, 622–651.

Soviet Geography: review and translation (1967) **8** (Many articles on population geography in the Soviet Union).

Steel, R. W. (1970) 'Problems of population pressure in tropical Africa', *Transactions of the Institute of British Geographers*, **49**, 1–14.

Stewart, J. Q. (1947) 'Empirical mathematical rules concerning the distribution and equilibrium of population', *Geographical Review*, **37**, 461–485.

Stewart, J. Q. and Warntz, W. (1958) 'Physics of population distribution', *Journal of Regional Science*, **1**, 99–123.

Stouffer, S. A. (1940) 'Intervening opportunities: a theory relating mobility and distance', *American Sociological Review*, **5**, 845–867.

Stouffer, S. A. (1960) 'Intervening opportunities and competing migrants', *Journal of Regional Science*, **2**, 37–64.

Street, J. M. (1969) 'An evaluation of the concept of carrying capacity', *Professional Geographer*, **21**, 104–107.

Trewartha, G. T. (1953) 'A case for population geography', *Annals of the Association of American Geographers*, **43**, 71–97.

Trewartha, G. T. (1969) *A Geography of Population: world patterns*, Wiley.

Troll, C. (1964) 'Plural societies of developing countries: aspects of social geography', *Proceedings 20th Congress International Geographic Union*, 9–33.

Wagner, P. L. (1958) 'Remarks on the geography of language', *Geographical Review*, **48**, 86–97.

Warntz, W. and Neft, D. (1960) 'Contributions to a statistical methodology for areal distributions', *Journal of Regional Science*, **2**, 47–66.

Webb, J. W. (1963) 'The natural and migrational components of population changes in England and Wales, 1921–1931', *Economic Geography*, **39**, 130–148.

Webb, J. W. (1969) 'Population geography', in R. U. Cooke and J. H. Johnson (Eds.), *Trends in Geography*, Pergamon.

William-Olsson, W. (1963) 'Report on a world population map', *Geografiska Annaler*, **45**, 243–250.

Wolpert, J. (1965) 'Behavioral aspects of the decision to migrate', *Papers and Proceedings of the Regional Science Association*, **15**, 159–169.

Wrigley, E. A. (1961) *Industrial Growth and Population Change*, Cambridge University Press.

Wrigley, E. A. (1965) 'Geography and population', in R. J. Chorley and P. Haggett (Eds.), *Frontiers in Geographical Teaching*, Methuen, 62–80.

Wrigley, E. A. (Ed.) (1966) *An Introduction to English Historical Demography from the Sixteenth to the Nineteenth Century*, Weidenfeld and Nicolson.

Wrigley, E. A. (1967) 'Demographic models and reality', in R. J. Chorley and P. Haggett (Eds.), *Models in Geography*, Methuen, 189–215.

Zelinsky, W. (1961) 'An approach to the religious geography of the United States', *Annals of the Association of American Geographers*, **51**, 139–193.

Zelinsky, W. (1962) 'Changes in the geographic patterns of rural population in the United States, 1790–1960', *Geographical Review*, **52**, 492–524.

Zelinsky, W. (1966) *A Prologue to Population Geography*, Prentice-Hall.

Zelinsky, W. (1970) 'Beyond the exponentials: the rôle of geography in the great transition', *Economic Geography*, **46**, 498–535.

Zelinsky, W. (1971) 'The hypothesis of the mobility transition', *Geographical Review*, **61**, 219–249.

Zelinsky, W., Kosinski, L. A. and Prothero, R. M. (Eds.) (1970) *Geography and a Crowding World: a symposium on population pressures upon physical and social resources in the developing lands*, Oxford University Press.

4 The location of service activities

The geography of service activities has been a strong traditional area of interest in geographical teaching and research and has consequently been treated in a variety of perspectives. In general terms, the full spectrum of service activities has been studied under the heading of the geography of tertiary activities, in contradistinction to the geography of primary activities, mainly concerned with agriculture and extractive industries, and the geography of secondary activities, mainly concerned with fabrication and manufactures. In more specialized terms, most attention has focussed on the locational characteristics of the distributive trades, traditionally constituting a major part of the field of commercial geography. It is in the particular area of marketing geography, or retailing geography, that most substantive geographic work has been done. Alternative possible fields of enquiry, such as the geography of welfare and social services, have been largely neglected, and potentially related subjects such as medical geography have been more concerned with broad areal analyses of mortality and morbidity patterns than with the locational aspects of medical services. Even distributive trades complementary to retailing, such as wholesaling and general office activities, have been relatively little investigated, although interest in the latter has recently gained considerable momentum.

Such intense pre-occupation with retail distributions is easily understood. Retail establishments are ubiquitous and conspicuous features of both urban and rural landscapes. Geography is traditionally a discipline rooted in field evidence, and shops and related shopping trips can be readily observed and measured. The widespread availability of survey data, much of it in published form (such as the Census of Distribution and the FamilyExpenditure Surveys), provides considerable material for numerical analyses. For this reason, there is also a strong association between the progress of retail studies and the so-called 'quantitative revolution' in geography. In the USA in particular, impetus for the quantitative revolution was provided by Berry and

Garrison and their students from studies of retail activities in the late 1950s (Garrison *et al.*, 1959); in Britain, the roots of a quantitative approach to geography are perhaps more firmly embedded in physical geography, although innovative work was prompted by retailing specialists, such as Diamond and Garner in the early 1960s following on from their Chicago experience (Diamond and Gibb, 1962; Garner, 1966). In addition to this broad methodological relationship, the study of retailing in particular and of service activities more generally has been strongly identified with the development of theory and a systems approach to geography. In these respects, the most influential single body of theory to emerge inside the entire discipline, central place theory, refers directly to the locational provision of services and related movement flows.

Although most theoretical approaches to the geography of retail activities relate to a spatial supply and demand system, the bulk of the literature concerned with empirical case studies deals with the structural aspects of the supply side rather than with the nature of consumer demands. There is a rich heritage particularly in descriptions and classifications of shopping centres, both at the regional and urban scales. For the most part, these studies concentrate on distinguishing between size levels, functional characteristics and the physical layouts of different retailing configurations. Such studies have been significant in the evolution of planning concepts and policies towards retail activities, especially in Britain. The structural composition and locational patterns of shopping centres are continually changing, however, and dramatically so in the USA; increasingly, geographers have been concerned with monitoring the nature and effects of these changes. In this respect, geographers have also contributed to the development of a set of forecasting techniques for estimating the growth potentials of new or existing retail outlets. Recent work in these techniques has in turn emphasized the need for greater understanding about the complexity of consumer behaviour, and it is in this area of enquiry that most constructive research is currently being pursued.

There are five major areas of study reviewed in this essay:

1. Developments in alternative methodological viewpoints and theoretical avenues of enquiry about retail activities.
2. Descriptions of regional systems of shopping centres, mainly for Britain and the USA.
3. Descriptions of intra-urban systems of shopping centres, mainly for Britain and the USA and with special reference to central areas.

4. Studies of processes of change and of various methods for forecasting requirements in retail activities.

5. Studies of consumer movements and individual preferences in shopping behaviour.

ALTERNATIVE METHODOLOGICAL FRAMEWORKS

Central place theory (Christaller, 1933; Lösch, 1954; Berry, 1967) is but the most conspicuous of a number of theoretical frameworks and different methodological viewpoints from which the location of service activities has been studied. A more recent pre-occupation of geographers has been with general interaction theory (Olsson, 1965; Carrothers, 1956) within which service facilities may be theoretically distributed in the landscape through a series of gravity models. In this case, an essentially interdisciplinary body of theory composed of models which relate to many different kinds of activity has been applied specifically to retailing and allied business land uses (Cordey-Hayes, 1968; Lanchester Polytechnic, 1969). In addition, certain other more particularistic avenues have been explored by geographers, namely a more empirical, micro-approach to the analysis of individual store locations by a school of 'marketing geographers' (Applebaum, 1954; Murphy, 1961). A further approach attempts to utilize the foundations of economic rent theory as a basis for understanding the small-scale interlinkages existing inside shopping centres (Scott, 1970; Garner, 1966).

Central place theory

Central place theory is a comprehensive theory to explain the location and inter-relationships of settlements seen as 'central-places'. It was also conceived (Christaller, 1933) as a theory of urban trades and institutions to be set alongside von Thünen's theory of agricultural activity and Weber's theory of industrial location. Since there are always certain kinds of services to be found in every urban settlement, the theory becomes appropriate for explaining the size and spacing of settlements themselves. Central place theory, therefore, seeks to explain both the centralization of service activities and the locational characteristics of the places in which these are found. Whereas service provision has generally grown up in response to similar kinds of locational processes, however, many urban places are less of a response to market forces operating in the service sector than to the special resource influences found in unique situations. Central place theory as a general theory of urbanism is therefore only strictly applicable to one category

S.H.G.—5*

of urban places, those market or service centres in which service functions are the major determinants both of their existence and their size. Other categories of urban places, such as manufacturing towns and mining centres, will be seen as anomalies in a service-oriented urban framework.

In its basic postulates, the theory is relatively simple. A class of central places exists primarily to provide goods and services to surrounding rural areas. Under isotropic conditions, a first level of smallest urban places will become located at uniformly spaced positions according to a maximum limit on travel which consumers will be prepared to undertake. Such places will provide the everyday conveniences of life, the lowest level of centralized activities. In order to allow for equal accessibility to all centres on the part of rural consumers, and to assure an equilibrium situation where no excess profits are earned by any particular centre, the trade-area boundaries which define the catchment area of support for each centre will be of equal size and hexagonally shaped. Certain of the places will grow in business importance, however, as demand for more specialized goods and services increases by consumers willing to travel greater distances on fewer occasions to less numerous service outlets. The locations of larger centres will then again be optimized at equally distant, but more widely spaced positions: they will be central to greater, but still hexagonally shaped trade areas. Since the larger centres grow up out of former small centres, they continue to distribute lower levels of centralized goods and services also. Given sufficient variation in demand for different activities, a hierarchy of tiered size-orders of centres will emerge within the theoretically ideal landscape, and trade areas for varying levels of activity will be seen to nest within each other in a regular way (Figure 4.1).

The theory becomes more complex, especially in geometric terms, when distortions to the nature of the hierarchy and the pattern of trade areas are introduced. Such distortions may arise from varying initial assumptions about the uniformity of purchasing power amongst rural consumers, or by introducing special influences on travel behaviour, such as a transport network or a framework of administrative boundaries. Christaller suggested three main basic kinds of central place system, which respectively accord to an optimum marketing situation, a situation constrained by optimum transportation linkages, and a situation of optimum administrative spheres of influence (Figure 4.2). The fundamental way in which these systems differ lies in the varying proportional support given to larger centres and trade areas by smaller

centres and trade areas. In the 'perfect' marketing case, frequencies of
occurrence follow a rule of three, where for each larger trade area
there will be three trade areas at the next lower size order, then
successively 9, 27 and so on. In the transportation-constrained case,
frequencies follow a rule of four, in the administrative-constrained case,
a rule of seven. Lösch (1954) subsequently suggested a whole series of
possible central place systems which could be geometrically derived by
varying such proportionality factors. The basic mechanism involved
in this was both to rotate the locations and enlarge the trade areas of
central places to meet any desired equilibrium situation. Such a variety

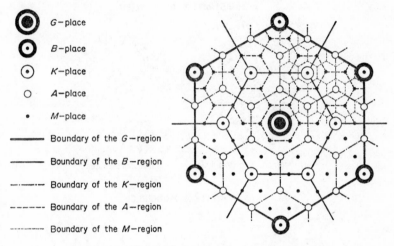

FIGURE 4.1   The nesting arrangements of trade areas

of trade-area arrangements and resulting hierarchical structures then
better approximates to the real world variability in levels of importance
for different centralized activities. Lösch attempted to represent the
full complexity of real world activities by superimposing all possible
variant geometries on top of each other and rotating these to positions
of most duplication. The resultant form is a theoretical landscape which
more nearly resembles real cases, and suggests that certain areas are
more densely served by centres than others (Figure 4.3). A particularly
important implication from this is that when the size orders for all
centres are plotted on a graph, the distinct hierarchical tier-structure
advanced by Christaller is not met and centres are instead distributed

MARKETING PRINCIPLE

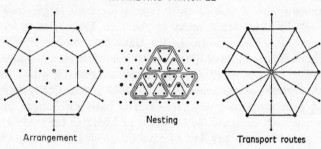

Arrangement   Nesting   Transport routes

ADMINISTRATIVE PRINCIPLE

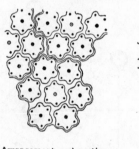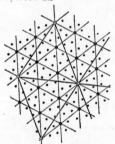

Arrangement and nesting   Transport routes

TRANSPORTATION PRINCIPLE

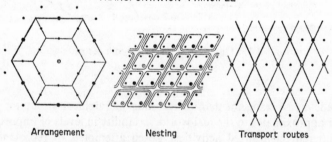

Arrangement   Nesting   Transport routes

FIGURE 4.2   Christaller's alternative central place systems

as a size continuum. This discrepancy has constituted a major focus of
enquiry in central place research.

Most attention in recent years has been given to the empirical
evaluation of the hierarchy concept in the real world rather than to the
validity of precise, orderly trade-area arrangements. This is particularly
true of the work concerned with service activities, in the strict sense,

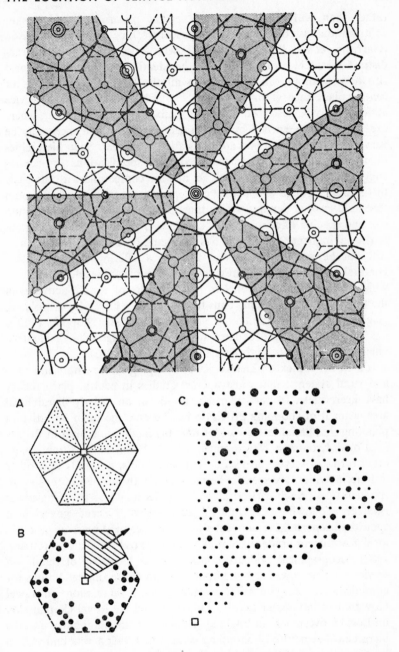

FIGURE 4.3   The Löschian complex landscape

rather than with the form of settlement patterns. The dominant contribution has come from the empirical work of Berry and Garrison (Garrison, *et al.*, 1959; Berry, 1967) who have sought to show that distinct hierarchies of centres may be identified in many real world situations without full reference to all the limiting assumptions of central place theory. In particular, hierarchies of centralized service activities may be described for areas of mixed purchasing power, where excess profits are earned by certain centres, and where there may be varying transportation and administrative influences. Such hierarchies then inevitably lack the formal frequency specifications for centres suggested by Christaller and Lösch, and are compatible with the basic theory only through two general concepts: that there is some minimum threshold level of demand which must be met to establish a minimum size and spacing of centres; and that there is some maximum range of territorial influence which facilities command beyond which consumers will not be prepared to travel to centres offering those facilities. Hierarchies of shopping centres may also be perceived inside urban areas which have a general parallel to the hierarchy of service activities in the total settlement system. Thus for the USA, a hierarchy of isolated, neighbourhood, community, regional and central area shopping centres has been identified and equated with the functional rôles of hamlets, villages, towns, cities, and the metropolis (Berry, 1963).

It is in the context of hierarchies of shopping centres, both in urban and rural systems, that most applied studies in central place theory have been made. In particular, the notion of an orderly hierarchical arrangement of shopping provision has become the main objective in planning the spatial framework of retailing facilities, at least in Britain (National Economic Development Office, 1970). In addition, many other forms of service provision, such as schools, hospitals and other welfare activities, are seen to be most efficiently located according to the hierarchy principle (Berry, 1967). In Germany, perhaps somewhat belatedly following Christaller's early work, recent government sponsored reports have advocated an entire regional reorganization in local government practice according to the central-place model (Isbary, 1967). Geographical evidence concerning the hierarchy of retail and service provisions was also incorporated into the recommendations for administrative reorganization by the Royal Commission on Local Government in Greater London (1957–60) and the Royal Commission on Local Government in England (1966–69). A special inquiry into the hierarchical structure of shopping centres in London was undertaken by Carruthers for the Herbert Commission; in the Redcliffe-Maud

Commission, the separate minority report of Senior stressed particularly the desirability of relating welfare provisions to the existing hierarchy of major service centres in England.

General interaction theory

General interaction theory differs from central place theory in being more concerned with an evaluation of existing locational attributes of service activity, especially in terms of consumer use, than with the derivation of an optimum arrangement of centres. As a theory, it is also less formally constituted in abstract terms and mainly comprises a series of empirically derived structural equations linked together by the single concept of gravity. The basic premise is that movement or exchange between an area of demand and one of supply will take place in direct proportion to the strength and attractiveness of competing centres providing goods and services and in inverse proportion to the distances or perceptual barriers between them. The theory is essentially analogous to Newton's law of physical gravitation. There are two particularly important features in the geographical context. Firstly, no rigid and fixed assumptions are made about the nature of the trade-areas of centres, which can be treated as varying in size and shape, and as overlapping one another rather than being discrete and juxtaposed. Secondly, the underlying mathematical relationship can be easily manipulated, expanded and modified to suit a variety of unique situations: these may include specification of certain threshold levels of consumer demand, the effect of new or potential centres in given locations, and description of the distribution of trip movements. Because of this seemingly greater real-world relevance and thus the availability of more 'operational' models, general interaction theory has become widely accepted as a framework for the prediction of likely states of future service activity, whereas central place theory has been used for description of past states and desirable goals. For these reasons, too, a greater contribution to the development of these alternative models has been made by geographers working outside the profession in a narrow sense, especially in marketing and planning, than within the academic discipline itself.

Two core formulas have been historically important. Reilly (1931) first proposed a 'law of retail gravitation' in direct analogy to Newton's law, where the frequency with which residents in an area trade with two competing towns is proportional to the population sizes of the two towns and inversely proportional to the square of the distances that separate consumers from each of the two towns.

$$\frac{T_a}{T_b} = \frac{P_a}{P_b} \left[\frac{d_b}{d_a}\right]^2$$

where

T_a, T_b = proportion of trade drawn to towns a and b
P_a, P_b = population sizes of towns a and b
d_a, d_b = distances from residential area to towns a and b

This may then become the basis for demarcating trade-area boundaries around towns, in a so-called 'break-point' model (Converse, Huegy and Mitchell, 1930), where the computed boundary lines indicate the proportional division of consumers in an area, in accordance with the relative gravitational 'pulls' of the two towns.

$$D_b = \frac{d_{ab}}{1 + \sqrt{\frac{P_a}{P_b}}}$$

where

D_b = the breakpoint distance of trade to town b
d_{ab} = the distance between towns a and b

The second general interaction model is the potential model, extensively developed by geographers in demographic studies (Stewart, 1948), but which has also been used to assess market potentials over large areas as a guide to the evaluation of the locations of firms and service centres (Dunn, 1956). Alternatively, this may indicate the relative accessibility of firms or centres to surrounding trade areas, giving some weight, if necessary, to population characteristics.

$$V_j = \Sigma \frac{P_i}{d_{ij}^{\,2}}$$

where

V_j = potential or accessibility of a centre j
P_i = a series of population or consumer areas i = 1 to n
d_{ij} = distance between i and j

Development of these two approaches with specific application to retailing studies has followed lines familiar in transportation research (Casey, 1955). In particular, the notion that the number of trips generated by any centre declines with increasing distance away according to a squared exponential value has been relaxed; instead, varying parameters are fitted to find that which best approximates the 'distance-decay' function in actual survey findings. The models have been expanded to consider the case of several competing centres serving consumers in a variety of contrasting residential areas. The attraction and distance variables involved have been more precisely defined in terms of shopping attractiveness, such as the range of shops provided or floorspace size, and various deterrence factors on travel behaviour, such as the time involved in journeys or the cost of transportation. A common root formula for a general retailing trip-distribution model is given in these terms:

$$S_{ij} = K_i E_i A_j F(d_{ij})$$

subject to constraints

$$\Sigma S_{ij} = S_j$$

$$\Sigma S_{ij} = E_i$$

K_i is a constant of proportionality $\dfrac{1}{\Sigma A_j} F(d_{ij})$

where
$\quad S_{ij} \quad$ = expenditures in centre j by consumers in area i
$\quad E_i \quad$ = expenditure available in area i
$\quad A_j \quad$ = a measure of shopping attractiveness at j
$\quad S_j \quad$ = sales generated at j
$\quad F(d_{ij}) \quad$ = deterrence on travel from i to j

Adaptation of these developments to the classic problems of trade area delimitation and the assessment of growth potential at shopping centres may be illustrated in the work of Huff (1963) and Lakshmanan and Hansen (1965). Huff considered the problems that arise when consumers make varying trips for different goods and services to a series of competing centres. To establish the choice in actual centres visited, he suggested that a utility function (U_j) would need to be satisfied which would be inversely proportional to the utilities emerging from going elsewhere. Thus the probability of any centre being visited (P_j) for a particular purpose would be

$$P_j = \frac{U_j}{\Sigma U_j}$$

where
$\quad \Sigma P_j = 1 \cdot 0$

In practical terms, the utility function becomes interpreted as the combination of an attraction level at any centre and the distance deterrence function involved in serving particular groups of consumers. Operationally, the model then takes the form

$$P_{ij} = \frac{F_j/d_{ij}^{\alpha}}{\Sigma(F_j/d_{ij}^{\alpha})}$$

where

P_{ij} = probability of any specific trip going to a centre j, from areas i=1 to n

F_j = attractiveness of centres (i.e. floorspace) in a series j=1 to m

d_{ij} = the deterrence function (i.e. travel time)

a = an exponent calibrated for different trip purposes, which may also be entered on F_j

The probability values which may be computed for different consumers for different trip purposes may then be interpolated by contour lines (Figure 4.4). Where similar contour values become tangential (for example 0·5 and 0·33) these represent the equivalence in choice between different centres in like manner to the break-point model, or the point of consumer indifference.

Lakshmanan and Hansen proposed a similar methodological procedure for estimating the impact on existing retail systems of new, planned shopping centres. The specific problem they treated concerned an evaluation of strategies for locating 'satellite' shopping centres in metropolitan Baltimore and forecasting sales capacities of such centres if arranged in different positions. The model they used took the form:

$$S_{ij} = E_i \frac{F_j/d_{ij}^{\alpha}}{\Sigma(F_j/d_{ij}^{\alpha})}$$

subject to the constraint

$$\Sigma S_j = \Sigma E_i$$

where

S_{ij} = sales at any centre j in series j=1 to n

E_i = consumer expenditure from areas i=1 to n

other variables interpreted as above

This model has subsequently become the most common reference model used in British planning research into shopping systems

(Manchester University, 1966; Rhodes and Whitaker, 1967). In addition, this type of model is commonly integrated into the wider comprehensive sub-regional land use planning models currently being experimented with in this country (Cripps and Foot, 1969; Batty, 1970).

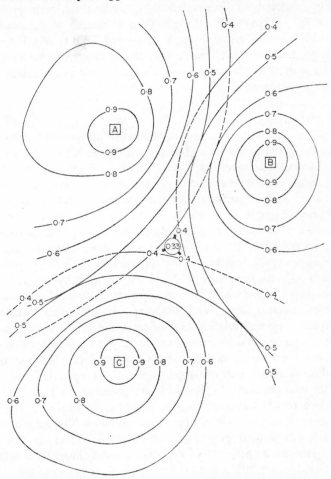

FIGURE 4.4 Probability contours for consumers shopping in three centres

Further models have been developed which differ mainly in terms of the variables utilized. Increasingly, attempts have been made (Harris, 1964) to interpret the deterrence function as a series of intervening opportunities rather than as some variant of distance. There has been much pre-occupation with alternative indices of the attractiveness of

centres (Clarke and Bolwell, 1968), which provides a parallel problem
to the definition and measurement of centrality in functional terms in
descriptive studies of the hierarchy of centres (Davies, W. K. D., 1966).
Related to these concerns is the desirability of disaggregating the
variable constructs of gravity models to make them more generally
suitable for approximating the greater individuality of behaviour at
small scale levels of enquiry (Parry Lewis and Trail, 1968). However,
gravity models are seen to 'work' best at a broader regional and sub-
regional scale, and the problems of data assembly at the urban scale
are particularly acute.

Other approaches
During the last two decades, a somewhat independent school of
'marketing geographers' has emerged within the USA with its own
distinctive methodological approach. This was initiated by Applebaum
(1954) who defined marketing geography 'as concerned with the
delimitation and measurement of markets and with the channels of
distribution through which goods move from producer to consumer'.
Despite the availability of central place theory and general interaction
theory as frameworks within which such studies could be pursued,
Applebaum singularly avoided any reference to them. The particular
emphasis of this approach to marketing geography centres on a
decision-making procedure for assessing the individual site requirements of separate stores and shopping centres, rather than upon
the broader regional relationships of an entire retailing system. The
movement gained notable momentum during the supermarket revolution following the post-war years in the USA and the emergence of the
'out-of-town' centre, and many geographers took up consultancy rôles
as store location analysts. Applebaum stipulated, in fact, that 'the
best place to develop marketing geography is in business, using the
laboratory of actual business operations'. Subsequently, he evolved an
academic educational programme at Harvard University based on
teaching marketing geography by actual case-study histories of retailing
firms (Applebaum, 1961). For the most part, these laid emphasis on the
importance of field surveys to assess site locations and trade area
characteristics, rather than using model simulations. A similar type of
approach, based mainly on empirical observation rather than any
general theory of consumer behaviour, is epitomized in Britain by the
work of Thorpe and his associates at the Manchester Business
School (for example, Thorpe and Kivell, 1971).

A further methodological development in marketing geography, though so far with less impact, concerns the attempt to use economic rent theory as a framework within which to study especially the internal locational structure of shopping centres. The relevance of this is quite obvious and rent theory underlies many broader urban land use models, of which retailing systems form one component (Hoyt, 1933; Alonso, 1964; Wingo, 1961). Scott (1970) and Hoyt (1968) have examined the nature of various rent gradients inside shopping centres in relation to the locations of different retail activities. Garner (1966) has proposed a spatial model which systematizes retail activities in terms of similar threshold levels[1] of functions, which are then seen to be arranged spatially to command alternative sites of varying rent levels. In the larger shopping centres, 'convenience' functions with low threshold levels tend to concentrate in peripheral positions where rent levels are low, more specialized functions with higher threshold levels tend to occupy a middle belt of positions with medium levels of rent; the most specialized of all functions, requiring the most centralized sites, tend to congregate at the peak nodal positions found within centres where rent levels are consequently highest. This model is particularly important since it attempts to link rent theory not only to shopping-centre land use structures, but also to the basic premises of central place theory. Thus Garner equates successive belts of functional differentiation inside the larger shopping centres with the structural orders of a hierarchy of shopping centres. Scott (1970) has noted that, apart from this extension, central place theory, unlike von Thünen's theory and Weber's theory, has never been properly allied to economic rent theory.

STRUCTURAL MODELS OF REGIONAL SYSTEMS

The bulk of the work concerned with the spatial provision of services at the regional and also national scale has focussed on the size relationships of centres performing particular complexes of functions and hence the classification of these centres into hierarchical size orders. There have been two separate kinds of concern, however. Most studies have utilized some form of service criterion, particularly retailing, to establish the degree of importance (and so centrality) of urban centres as a whole as central places to surrounding areas. A second group of studies has sought to discriminate between the sizes of service com-

---

[1] The threshold value accorded to a shop represents the minimum amount of purchasing power (or size of trade area) necessary to support its existence.

ponents themselves, especially retailing again, and to describe the nature
of activity systems, rather than total urban systems. There are several
extensive bibliographies which summarize these studies (Berry and
Pred, 1965; Andrews, 1970).

Regularities in sizes of centres

Following the early work by Christaller in southern Germany, many of
the classic descriptions of urban hierarchies have emanated from
Britain. Dickinson (1947) initiated this involvement with studies of
small settlements in East Anglia, and the tradition is represented in
many later studies, for example by Bracey (1953), W. K. D. Davies
(1967) and Tarrant (1967), treating respectively the South West, part
of south Wales, and east Yorkshire. Smailes (1944), Carter (1965) and
Fleming (1954) have been more ambitious in assessing the hierarchical
nature of entire national systems of urban centres, for England, Wales
and Scotland, though in these cases the descriptions relate to larger
places for which there are more published statistics. The criteria
utilized for measuring centrality have differed considerably (Davies,
W. K. D., 1966), from numerical counts of establishments to selected
indices, such as the incidence of department stores, banks and schools,
with the result that comparative assessments are difficult to effect from
one study to another.

Considerable research has also been made into the structural orders
of urban centres in the USA, especially in the Mid-West where the
isotropic conditions inherently assumed in central place theory are
more realistically approximated. Brush (1953), Berry and Mayer (1962)
and Borchert and Adams (1963) have all described hierarchies for
different parts of the region though again with little consistency in
approach. An interesting national hierarchy of urban centres has been
provided by Taaffe (1962), based on air passenger traffic, but a more
comprehensive study is that by Forstall (1965), for the Rand McNally
Company, utilizing a composite index of centrality made up of several
criteria of retailing, wholesaling and business service activities.

Many more such classifications have been made in other parts of
the world, for example by Mayfield for India (1967), Scott for Tasmania
(1964), and Abiodun for Nigeria (1967). Most of these hierarchy studies
have been primarily descriptive, for the limited purpose of classification,
but recurring and related issues in all of them concern the testing of
certain aspects of central place theory, the development and application
of statistical techniques for analysis of the hierarchy, and the improvement of field work procedures. Much contention remains over the

validity of distinct tier-structures in the size orders of centres, as opposed to a continuous distribution of sizes which is only arbitrarily capable of categorization. Some recent studies suggest that both forms may be identified (Berry and Barnum, 1962; Berry and Mayer, 1962) according to the classificatory methods employed. There appears to be less certainty about discrete size clusterings for settlements when the criteria indexing centrality are treated in broad, aggregative terms (O'Farrell, 1969). Certain studies (Thomas, 1962; Smith, 1965) have also considered the nature of change in size and urban rank relationships over time: in general, these have concluded that the main structural levels remain relatively stable, although there may be temporal differences in the functional provisions found (Parr and Denike, 1970) and in the number of centres at any one level; and exceptions occur particularly in metropolitan vicinities (Berry, 1960). In addition, forecasts of future hierarchical size relationships have been used as regional planning frameworks for settlement control, and in one or two cases as design formats for *ab initio* development of new urban centres, such as on the Dutch polders (Christaller, 1966).

Hierarchies of shopping centres, as distinct from towns in their full service rôles, have also been considered extensively by British geographers. Two outstanding contributions are by Carruthers (1967) and Thorpe (1968), both of whom have described the national system of retailing. Carruthers' hierarchical classification is derived from a composite index of shopping importance based on a points system for three sets of criteria: total sales in a centre and the proportion in non-food goods; the difference between actual sales in a local authority area and an expected average regional sales figure; and the relative provision of six retail classes handling durable goods. Thorpe's index was more simply based on the total volume of sales and not unexpectedly there are classificatory discrepancies with Carruthers. A major problem which has confronted both these and other researchers is the lack of detailed information contained in the Census of Distribution for small towns and also central area coverage. Other significant regional descriptions of shopping centres are those by Lomas (1964) for the West Midlands, and Thorpe and Rhodes (1966) for the North East. Further hierarchical descriptions have been used as a framework within which gravity models have then been applied to test the effects of a change or addition within the hierarchy (Manchester University, 1966; Royal Town Planning Institute, 1967). In such cases, the rank order importance of centres is equated with the attraction variable in the gravity model formulae.

Criteria for defining centrality and shopping attractiveness

The notion of centrality refers to the full complex of activities provided by any centre for its surrounding trade area, and the diversity of this can normally only be represented by a proxy variable or some compound index of certain activity systems. Because of the need to select simple criteria to represent centrality, much debate has been engendered in the literature as to the best criteria to use (Marshall, 1969). Thorpe and Rhodes (1966) have criticized the use of numbers of shops and decide in favour of a sales turnover figure; W. K. D. Davies (1967) has criticized the use of numbers of service employees in favour of a composite index, a ratio derived from the varying frequencies of functional types of stores; Carter (1965) has criticized the use of retailing statistics altogether in favour of an index of wholesaling. McEvoy (1968) recently compared the rank placements of shopping centres around Manchester using different indices advocated by various other workers and found little substantial difference in effectiveness between them. In broader studies of urban systems at the national and regional scales, R. L. Davies (1970) likewise concluded that no single index was particularly superior to all others. In this case, rank correlations were made between a series of general variables of retailing and the more specific indices developed by previous workers and also with detailed census figures giving the sales performance of central area activities. Some examples of the coefficients derived are given in Table 4.

Similar kinds of personal preference for certain indices or variables now characterize the gravity model literature, where shopping attractiveness has alternatively been defined by varying numbers of establishments, sales figures, selected ranges of services and retail floorspace. In many of these studies, however, there is a conflict between the need to disaggregate the models when applied to localized circumstances and the ease with which different parameters can be manipulated to compensate for the inadequacies of generalized variables. Given, particularly, the limitations of data availability for small areas and the greater relevance of gravity models, methodologically, as broad guide-lines for development, it would seem preferable to structure the models in terms of general indices and improve the basis for parameter estimation. The use of numbers of service employees, for example, in a retail potential model also integrates quite readily into the overall design of comprehensive sub-regional planning models, based on the Lowry (1964) mode of approach.

Two further issues emerge from these considerations. Firstly, it has

TABLE 4 Rank correlation coefficients for various indices of centrality in the North West

Example (a) for 21 most important places

	Haydock	Carruthers	7-fold	City pop.	Hint. pop.	Tot. ests	Tot. sales	Employ.	C.A. ests	C.A. sales	C.A.D. ests	C.A.D. sales
Haydock method	1·00	0·93	0·84	0·78	0·71	0·81	0·92	0·92	0·77	0·84	0·85	0·88
Carruthers' method		1·00	0·84	0·80	0·79	0·78	0·96	0·97	0·81	0·96	0·87	0·95
7-fold method			1·00	0·93	0·73	0·99	0·90	0·89	0·62	0·73	0·76	0·75
Population size				1·00	0·67	0·93	0·89	0·88	0·59	0·73	0·67	0·69
Hinterland population					1·00	0·67	0·80	0·79	0·60	0·71	0·72	0·65
Total establishments						1·00	0·85	0·84	0·61	0·67	0·74	0·70
Total sales							1·00	0·99	0·75	0·90	0·82	0·88
Full employment								1·00	0·78	0·92	0·83	0·90
Central area establishments									1·00	0·87	0·94	0·85
Central area sales										1·00	0·87	0·94
C.A. durable establishments											1·00	0·88
C.A. durable sales												1·00

Example (b) for 44 most important places

	Haydock	City pop.	Hint. pop.	Tot. ests	Tot. sales	Employ.
Haydock method	1·00	0·81	0·87	0·89	0·91	0·91
Population size		1·00	0·83	0·90	0·92	0·90
Hinterland population			1·00	0·85	0·90	0·90
Total establishments				1·00	0·93	0·93
Total sales					1·00	0·99
Full employment						1·00

Note: Hanley, Stoke and Accrington are omitted because of census limitations.

SOURCE: Davies, R. L., 1970

recently been questioned (Davies, R. L., 1971) whether service indices—whether they refer to central area activities or total urban activities—really discriminate between those functions drawing consumers in from outside as opposed to those which serve the local urban populations. Selected functional criteria may be seen to distinguish between convenience and specialized (or comparison) trade, but not between the local clientele and visiting consumers from other places. It is not surprising that since retailing and service activities cannot be distinguished in this way, the literature on regularities in size distributions of centres exhibits conflicting findings. Secondly, it is precisely because this discrimination is not made that the classical equation relating level of centrality of a centre to a certain trade-area population size is not always realized in many case studies. There is much support in the literature for an exceedingly close relationship between centres ranked in terms of total business importance and their local urban, rather than trade area, population sizes (Haggett and Gunawardena, 1964; Berry and Garrison, 1958; Davies, R. L., 1969). As a further example, Table 4 indicates that there are higher rank correlation coefficients between urban population sizes for cities in the North West and several widely-used indices of centrality, than occurs between these same indices and computed trade-area population sizes (derived by Manchester University, 1964, utilizing a break-point model). The relationships in this particular case, of course, may be affected by imprecise measurements of trade-area population sizes, which are usually extremely difficult to determine.

STRUCTURAL MODELS OF URBAN SYSTEMS

The distribution of retailing and service activities internally in towns and cities has been treated like that at the regional scale, essentially through a series of static, deterministic, conceptual models. The notion of a hierarchical structure of urban shopping centres has been viewed in two different perspectives. On the one hand, several geographers (notably British) have described an orderly sequence of size-orders for all centres, according to some general index of shopping importance; on the other hand, other geographers (mainly American) have differentiated between alternative typologies of centres (in analogous ways to distinctions in settlement types) and they have described an hierarchical system for one class of centres only. The largest of all urban retail configurations, the central business area, has naturally been the subject of many special studies, amounting to a separate body of work.

Patterns of retail and service distribution

The most comprehensive classification of shopping centres (or more broadly commercial centres) has been undertaken by Berry (1963) and several of his students in Chicago. Berry differentiates between contrasting classes of compact retail nucleations, linear dispersal in ribbon developments and specialized functional areas of the type of 'automobile row' (Table 5). The retail nucleations, alone, parallel the

TABLE 5 **Berry's classification of business service configurations**

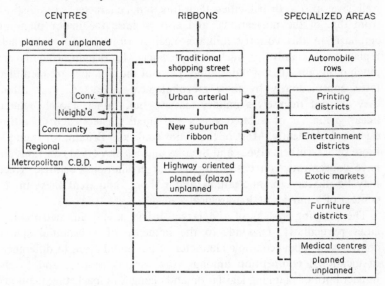

SOURCE: Berry, 1963

classification of central places in settlement descriptions, and for these an orderly hierarchical structure may be identified. Ribbon developments are distinguished in terms of differences in functional character and age (Berry, 1959), though attempts to differentiate between discrete size levels have also been made (Simmons, 1966). Specialized functional areas, including services such as medical complexes and transportation facilities, are concentrated near the central area, from which they are excluded mainly by high rent levels. The essential distinctions between the three types are seen by Berry to stem from their relative accessibility to consumer patronage. Nucleations serve predominantly localized, nearby trade areas; ribbons cater much more to the needs of people travelling along major thoroughfares; and specialized functional areas attract a select group of special-purpose motivated consumers who will seek them out in whatever location to achieve the maximum advantage of comparative shopping or to benefit from the increased range of services which large-scale aggregation produces.

Recognition of these separate classes of retail configuration has generally been ignored in British studies, though there are exceptions in the work of the economist Parker (1962) and in some current research in hand. The neglect of serious attention to ribbon developments in particular is partly explained by the fact that these are relatively less well developed in British cities, their functional character is less distinct from that of the nucleations, and also because the major planning emphasis in this country militates against ribbons and seeks their replacement mainly by nucleated precincts. In Britain, ribbons are much more a feature of older, inner parts of the city, and are identified most conspicuously by their morphological character. Very often, they are not themselves unitary features but, rather, loosely related linear groupings of isolated stores and small clusters each operating quasi-independently. Most of the major studies in Britain, for example those by Carruthers (1962) and Smailes and Hartley (1961) on London, have concentrated on describing the larger shopping centres, which may be mixtures of nucleations and ribbons, and treat these in the context of a univariate hierarchical scheme.

The retailing system of the larger urban areas, in metropolitan cities particularly, responds to the influence of substantial spatial contrasts in socio-economic character of the population, to differences in locational competition amongst the various centres, and to the impact both of planning legislation and changes in marketing methods. Such influences have been treated in detail in several specific studies, including the effects of racial differences on shopping structures by Pred (1963) and historical building facilities on modes of retail operation by Leeming (1959). The effects of socio-economic and locational conditions have also been assessed in terms of their distortion of the hierarchy. Distortive influences may be seen both horizontally, in the detailed functional composition of centres at any one level in the hierarchy, or vertically, through the promotion of different size-order relationships. The former influence has been traced by R. L. Davies (1968) in comparative assessments of small shopping centres in high and low income areas of Leeds, where the functional rôles of seemingly similar-sized centres were found to be quite different. The latter influence has been identified by Berry (1963) and Garner (1966) in studies of Chicago, where altogether different functional sub-systems of an hierarchical nature could be related to high and low income areas. The low income hierarchy differs mainly in terms of having a better-developed set of neighbourhood and community level centres, and a weaker set of regional-level centres. This is because lower income consumers generally live nearer the central area of the city, which captures much of the specialized shopping activity which otherwise might be diverted to the support of strong but non-central business areas. In addition, higher income consumers are more freely mobile to utilize various components of the overall shopping system.

Clear differences in the spacing of shopping centres also exist inside large cities, particularly between the high density of retailing activity in the older, inner areas compared to the relatively low density of developments in the suburbs. Such differences are partly explained by historical growth processes and partly by the effect of both planning and marketing influences on outlying facilities, which are considered in a later section. Several geographers, however, have sought to generalize about the overall pattern of centres especially in seeking to make comparisons with certain theoretical statistical distributions, in an attempt to determine the degree to which there are spatial regularities. Thus Garner (1966) perceives a general resemblance between the spacing of nucleated retail centres in Chicago with Christaller's $K=4$ network for central place patterns. W. A. V. Clark (1969), on the other hand, having compared the overall pattern of all types of shopping centres in Christchurch, New Zealand, with Poisson distributions, concludes that centres are generally randomly spaced, though with some tendency to concentration in particular parts of the city. Curry (1962) has likewise referred to Poisson distributions, though in this case incorporated in a time-series model to postulate how random locations for centres may be generated at any single stage in time. In addition, Rogers (1969) has recently compared the binomial, Poisson, negative binomial and Neyman Type A distributions with quadrat frequencies of individual shops in Lubljana, Yugoslavia and San Francisco, California, suggesting that the negative binomial distribution provides the best overall fit.

Studies of the central area
There have been numerous case studies of central areas, commonly referred to as central business districts (the CBD) in geography. Primarily, these studies are concerned with the description of major land use arrangements (Diamond, 1962; Carter and Rowley, 1966) and with the problem of delimiting boundaries (Murphy and Vance,

1954a; Davies, D. H., 1959). Murphy and Vance have been especially influential on subsequent researchers in their attempts to find a suitable technique for defining the spatial extent of the CBD to facilitate comparative studies (Murphy and Vance, 1954b). They have suggested two rules of thumb: in the calculation of a central business height index (CBHI), which is the total floor area of central business use in a street block divided by the ground-floor area of the block; and a central business intensity index (CBII), which is the percentage of all floorspace in a block accounted for by central business use. Although these have been found generally practical for defining the CBD in many American cities, the use of blocks as the unit of measurement renders the technique less satisfactory for assessments of the CBD in other parts of the world (Scott, 1959).

Many studies attest to the extreme variability in the locational structure of service activities within the city centre and perhaps it is for this reason alone that there has been relatively little spatial theory developed about underlying regularities. The major summary conceptual model available is that by Horwood and Boyce (1959), which is represented in the schematic diagram, Figure 4.5. A fundamental distinction is made between a 'core' nucleus of retail and office activities in the central area, and a surrounding 'frame' of mixed but highly segregated land uses, especially wholesaling, transportation facilities, and light industrial activities. The boundaries between the core and frame are not always easy to demarcate since they are essentially gradational, but the core and frame are usually conspicuous by various features: these include a greater vertical height to buildings in the core compared to more horizontal development in the frame; greater pedestrian traffic in the core compared to more motorized traffic in the frame; the dominance of intra-urban linkages in transport connections inside the core, while inter-urban linkages (transport termini) characterize the frame. Significantly, what is basically a 'free-market' model developed to symbolize central area characteristics of American cities has remarkable similarities and relevance to the current planning design models in operation in Britain.

The core-frame concept, however, reveals little about the complex locational relationships of retailing and allied business services inside the core area. Getis (1968) has investigated the nature of frequencies in spatial affinities existing between store types within thirteen American core areas. Using a technique called sequence analysis, he compared the actual incidence in occurrence of certain groups of store types locating next to each other with a theoretically expected number of affinities that would arise given random circumstances. It was only for the category of clothing activities that he found any significant amount of retail association, although his samples of establishments were limited

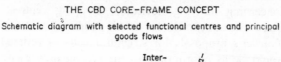

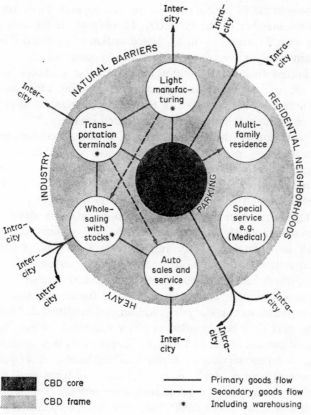

FIGURE 4.5   The central business district core-frame concept

to stores immediately around the peak land-value nodes of central areas. Other kinds of retail affinities may well be apparent in more peripheral locations. Stronger spatial linkages have been identified amongst the variety of office activities in London (Goddard, 1968), using multivariate statistical procedures. In this case, more precise definition has been possible for demarcating the various financial, legal and publishing quarters of the City.

A potential avenue for further conceptual formulation about core area retailing characteristics may be found in an extension of Garner's model concerning outlying nucleated shopping centres. Since the central area is the apex to the hierarchic system of nucleated shopping centres, Garner's proposals for structural belts of ordered threshold values should be as appropriate to the central area as to any other constituent member of the hierarchy. In addition, if the central area exhibits spatial features of the nucleated system of shopping it is likely to contain embryonic vestiges of the ribbon system, too, and tendencies to specialized functional groupings of particular activities. In other words, the underlying spatial structure of retailing activities in the central area may be conceived in terms of a microcosm of the three variant city-wide retailing systems established by Berry.

The reduction of the complex mix of retailing activities to three component parts, each with its own locational attributes, is indicated in Figure 4.6. In this schematic diagram, nucleated facilities are structured within the core area along lines suggested by Garner, representing gradations in intensity of activity from highly specialized shops to lower order convenience functions. Ribbon developments begin to emanate only from peripheral positions within the core area, but may be differentiated according to the degree of emphasis on traditional street functions to more strongly automobile-oriented facilities, which become larger space users. Such ribbon developments are often conspicuous in extending into the frame area and creating serious problems in boundary delimitation. Special functional groupings of stores may then be identified as either nucleated facilities (such as clusters of clothes shops or furniture shops) or ribbon developments (such as business services or repair establishments) or as particular mixed activity areas, such as entertainment districts and markets. In the frame area, such mixed activity areas become comparable with those already identified as medical complexes, transportation terminals and other 'segregated service' land uses. In addition, special areal groupings of shops may be identified in terms of like-levels of the quality image generated. In this case, a belt of medium quality shops is generally equated with the more specialized functions occupying the peak nodal positions within the central area and catering to the bulk consumer demand; a belt of lower quality shops is found tangential to the core, mainly in the frame, and related to the convenience and ribbon functions serving generally lower income patronage; and a relatively

THE COMPLEX MODEL

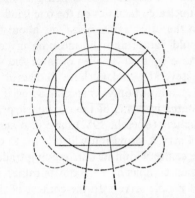

NUCLEATED CHARACTERISTICS

Shop types	Example clusters
1 Central area	A Apparel shops
2 Regional centres	B Variety shops
3 Community centres	C Gift shops
4 Neighbourhood centres	D Food shops

RIBBON CHARACTERISTICS

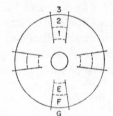

Shop types	Example clusters
1 Traditional street	E Banking
2 Arterial ribbon	F Cafes
3 Suburban ribbon	G Garages

SPECIAL AREA CHARACTERISTICS

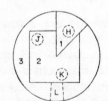

Shop types	Example clusters
1 High quality	H Entertainments
2 Medium quality	J Market
3 Low quality	K Furniture
	L Appliances

FIGURE 4.6 The internal structure of central area core retailing facilities

freely located section of higher quality shops, usually strategically found near to the peak nodal positions but not necessarily within them, determines its own special resource factors in site conditions by generating a prestige image for a limited but widely dispersed high income clientele.

S.H G.—6

The specific locational distinctions which this model then makes between groups of nucleated facilities on the one hand and segregations of quality levels on the other raises questions about the proper interpretation of threshold values and the meaning of centrality. So far, most geographers have equated the idea of threshold values with types of functions, but several scholars have indicated that trade-area drawing capacity depends not only on specific associations of activities, but also on their status in terms of the quality of provision (Garner, 1967). Such geographers (Boesch, 1952) have also suggested that it is really the quality of service provision which helps to define the degree of centrality of any centre within its surrounding trade area, while the quantity or functional complexity of shops is rather an expression of the total number of people served. In the context of the above model, threshold values which might then be assigned to shops according to their quality status relate much more specifically to the territorial extent or the sphere of influence commanded by shops; whereas threshold values assigned to the functional differentiations of nucleated facilities refer merely to the total volume of consumers served (irrespective of whether these are made up by people coming in from outside the city or are derived from the local urban population alone). It is the 'quality' aspect of retailing which then epitomizes most completely the postulates of central place theory in relation to trade area support. There is the further implication that indices of centrality discussed in a previous section relate much more to the volumetric size of consumer support for centres than to the territorial spheres of influence which such centres may command.

STUDIES OF LOCATIONAL CHANGE

In many ways, the structural models of retail location determined mainly in the USA are becoming less relevant to that country, particularly in the urban context, because of rapid and extensive decentralization of service activities related to increased metropolitan sprawl. Interestingly, the basic notions inherent in these models remain more tenable for the British situation, since strong planning control maintains a rigid spatial organization of retailing over more limited areas of urban expansion. In the USA the supermarket revolution had a dramatic effect in promoting new sites for retail centres, especially in the suburbs, whereas in Britain, though there have been substantial marketing changes, supermarkets have been mainly constrained to the existing pattern of retail provision, chiefly in town centres. At the present time, however, there are strong pressures to relax the traditional forms of location constraint in Britain, with the planning applications now lodged for the development of so-called 'hypermarkets', which are envisaged as free-standing, suburban facilities of a much larger store capacity size than has hitherto been seen. A slight trend towards decentralization is also to be seen in various 'Woolco' developments on the outskirts of large towns (Jones, 1969). It is likely, nevertheless, that the central areas of large British cities will remain much more viable and subject to less serious deterioration and decline than is now found in much of the USA, if only because of the enormous capital investments recently injected into redevelopment schemes (National Economic Development Office, 1971).

The impact of population change

The fate of the central area of large American cities has been well documented by economists (Hoyt, 1966) and planners (Sternlieb, 1963) who forecast a continuing decline in the proportionate amount of urban retailing sales as well as in numbers of establishments in central areas. Many of the essential, highly specialized and attractive facilities like department stores have now migrated to large out-of-town regional centres which command greater accessibility to the higher-income, more mobile and rapidly growing suburban populations. The central area of many cities is thus becoming an outworn shopping centre, catering increasingly to a consumer body made up of office workers, the poorer sections of an inner city population and a generally older age structure (Vance, 1962). In the rest of the city, too, the exodus to the suburbs has left a legacy of unplanned, heavily duplicated, and mainly outdated 'convenience' sets of functions which are now rapidly decaying.

Contrasts in these overall trends in retailing between the older and newer parts of the metropolis have been considered in detail in their impact on the hierarchical structure. Berry (1963) perceives a four-tier structure of new planned centres in suburban Chicago, identified as neighbourhood, community, smaller shopping goods, and major regional centres. Such levels may in fact be more sharply defined than the hierarchy in the older city (Simmons, 1964), since property developers and planners alike have adopted standard sizes of floorspace and ground acreage for specifically designated centres. The functional differentiation of these centres may be more difficult to discern, however, since with increases in individual store size and large-scale merchandizing of products, traditional distinctions between convenience and speciality types of activities have become confused, as customer trade-areas have greatly expanded and shopping trips are increasingly multiple-purpose in nature (Cohen and Lewis, 1967). One of the main differences between the old and the new hierarchies has also resulted from enlarged trade areas, and this implies the weakening of the smaller centres at the expense of the large ones, particularly in regard to local isolated store clusters. This is seen in terms of the relatively low density of isolated store clusters in the suburbs and also in urban redevelopment schemes within the old city, where numerous small independent businesses have been forced out of the retailing system to be replaced by fewer, larger chain operations (Berry, Parsons, and Platt, 1968). A similar trend is found to apply to central places in an entire settlement pattern. Smaller centres suffer not only as a result of increased consumer accessibility to larger centres through increased car ownership (Hodge, 1965; Stiglbauer, 1967) but also because of the encroachment of metropolitan areas into rural domains (Berry, 1960). The effect of increased accessibility generated by new highway developments on both urban and regional service provisions has also been considered in depth (Garrison, et al., 1959).

Many other kinds of service activity which are heavily concentrated in central areas, however, such as business services and offices, have not yet become decentralized to the same extent as retailing. Indeed, recent government attempts in Britain through the Location of Offices Bureau to induce decentralization have met with little success. This is mainly due to the fact that business services and offices depend on close interlinkages with each other, which only highly central locations provide: they are concerned essentially with an exchange of information between the working populations rather than the distribution of goods to a resident consumer body (Cowan, 1968). Continued concentration of business services and offices in a few highly central locations, however, leads both to local problems in traffic congestion and to imbalance in the distribution of service employment in both regional and national economies. Since service employment has become the chief growth sector in most advanced economies, many governments have tried to force decentralization, from the congested areas of primate cities into provincial locations; and the British government has encouraged dispersal to depressed areas. Whilst some nationalized services and headquarters offices in Britain have exhibited some locational change (Hammond, 1967), the majority of businesses have remained in their old positions. There has been more movement within London itself than away from the metropolis. Goddard (1967), however, has shown

that where small locational changes may be perceived, this is largely
the result of the birth and death process among business firms rather
than many conscious decisions to move.

Forecasting and allocation models
The methodology involved in forecasting the future growth of any
individual centre or particular activity has developed from assessments
of present and future trade-area characteristics. There is a rich, traditional geographical literature concerned with trade-area delimitation,
involving both a wide range of survey techniques about consumer
travel behaviour and estimates of the effective range of centralized
goods and services. Survey methods of the 'pavement' and 'home
interview' kind have been extensively used by store location researchers
in the USA (Applebaum, 1966), where appraisal of income levels,
propensity to spend, and consumer buying habits may need to be
considered in detail in determining the potential of a new or expanded
shopping centre site. The use of broader indicators of trade areas
(such as the network of public transport linkages, volumes of news-
paper circulations, and deliveries of various goods and services) has
been mainly in descriptions of retail systems at a national or regional
scale (Green, 1951; Godlund, 1956). In the shopping centre case, where
forecasts of future size capacity for an individual centre are made,
the size-factor predicted is usually floorspace, which is determined
from projected increases of population and therefore consumption in
the trade area assessed. This may involve only a simple set of calculations or become a complex structure of linear equations. Essentially,
the procedure represents a step-by-step approach to forecasting, based
on initial work by Nelson (1958). The steps involved in Diamond and
Gibbs' (1962) forecasts for the shopping capacities of new towns in
Scotland are outlined in Table 6.

The step-by-step approach to forecasting becomes more involved
as predictions for several competing centres are made, rather than for
a single centre in isolation. Usually, in this case, reference to the
hierarchy of centres is invoked (Manchester University, 1964) and
trade-areas are worked out initially in relation to the existing structural
size-orders of centres. Likely population changes within these trade-
areas and their impact on a future hierarchy are then determined in a
variety of ways. Berry (1963 and 1965) has provided a complex procedure based on his factor analysis classifications of various hierarchies
of nucleations and ribbon centres in Chicago. A series of regression
equations is computed for different time periods for number of

TABLE 6   **A step-by-step approach to retail forecasting for one town**

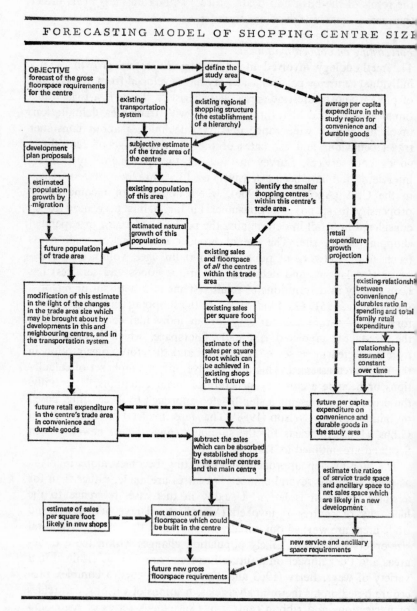

FORECASTING MODEL OF SHOPPING CENTRE SIZE

SOURCE: National Economic Development Office, 1970

establishments as a function of various trade-area population characteristics (particularly income levels), and these are then transposed to floorspace and other retailing criteria through further linear models. The procedure requires considerable refinement in the data utilized, and hence whilst detailed field inventories can be made for a past or present time period, the essential business of forecasting future states is more difficult to pursue.

The use of gravity (potential) models in forecasting represents a fundamental departure, in that trade areas as such are not worked out, but potential consumer movement to any centre is determined in accordance with the attractiveness of that centre and the relative distance that needs to be travelled. Very often in such models, however, the variable used to represent attraction is the same attribute of size for which a model is trying to predict, so that floorspace may be used as the attraction variable if it is floorspace that needs to be determined. Linear projections of floorspace are thus first made before the model can be calibrated, to see how the projected figure becomes affected by competing centres. The gravity model thus really redistributes within a system of centres the projected figure for the size capacities of centres which may have been arrived at by other (mainly trade area based) methods. In this way, the model becomes an allocative model rather than strictly a projection technique (Cordey-Hayes, 1968). The full allocation function is seen when the model is used to determine new potential source locations for centres and to evaluate the possible repercussions of these on an existing system of centres (as for example in Lakshmanan and Hansen, 1965). Consideration of the repercussive effects of new developments would seem to be crucial, especially since piece-meal forecasting for individual centres has tended to lead to over-estimation of viable capacity and thus to problems of store letting in many British cities. In operational terms, most potential (gravity) models are first calibrated on past data, and the parameters estimated (either by trial-and-error iterative procedures or through regression techniques) are assumed to remain constant through time. There are clearly problems, therefore, regarding assumptions about normative behaviour: for this reason as well as the basic limitation of the gravity notion, that it characterizes only aggregate behaviour, the models do not readily simulate shopping trips for small areas.

Gravity models are also being experimented with in seeking new locations for other service provisions, namely hospital facilities and physician centres (Morrill and Earickson, 1969), and possible source areas for office growth (Daniels, 1970). In these cases, the models are used to determine areas of greatest accessibility to recent population movements and related functional activities. Alternative optimising procedures, such as linear programming formulations, have mainly been used to test the efficiency of existing systems, such as the accessibility of physicians to patients (Morrill, 1967) and of school districts to residential areas (Yeates, 1963). Linear programming solutions have also been applied to retailing activities, though these lie largely outside the field of geography.

STUDIES OF CONSUMER BEHAVIOUR

Since assessments of the future locational characteristics of service facilities depend on knowledge of the nature of consumer demand, considerable attention has been given to understanding in more detail the structure of consumer behaviour. Geographical investigations of consumer behaviour have followed two main lines of approach. There has been considerable testing of the notions inherent in central place theory and general interaction theory regarding the aggregate nature of trip movements. Alternatively, there has been much criticism that the essentially economic base to these theories is inappropriate as a framework within which to characterize the full complexity of reference group or individual travel behaviour. Increasingly, a series of more flexible behavioural models has been put forward to simulate the decision making procedure by which consumers evaluate shopping centres, given their imperfect states of knowledge.

Empirical validity of the structural models

There are numerous studies which have tested the degree to which consumers in either rural or urban situations functionally identify the notion of a hierarchy of central places or shopping centres. Most of these depend on questionnaire surveys assessing the aggregate frequency and direction of shopping trips undertaken, or of visits to doctors, solicitors or hospitals (for example, Bracey, 1953; Tarrant, 1967). Other studies, however, refer to published statistics of traffic flow, public transport connections, school enrolments and the like. For the most part, such studies confirm the broad validity of the concept of the hierarchy to the extent that small centres are used for convenience functions and larger centres are visited for more specialized needs on more infrequent occasions (Berry, Barnum and Tennant, 1962). In certain specific aspects of central place theory, however, conflicting findings have been reported. The theoretical postulate that consumers will always visit the nearest centre offering a required good or service has been largely discredited, both for urban areas (Clark, 1968) and rural areas (Golledge, Rushton, and Clark, 1966); consumers do not usually utilize all the structural levels of a hierarchy for different trip purposes (Johnston and Rimmer, 1967); trade areas do not consequently nest within each other in distinct, orderly ways.

Discrepancies between actual travel behaviour and the theoretical desiderata are usually explained in terms of increased mobility levels and changes in marketing methods. Alternatively, Marble and Nystuen (in Garrison *et al.*, 1959) have implied that the structural characteristics of retail centres are not always clearly identified by consumer use because shopping often forms only a part of a more complex set of multi-purpose trips. Thus many shopping activities are part of the journey to work, visits to the hospital, or trips to collect children from school. So, too, shopping often becomes a leisure occupation (Ambrose, 1968), particularly for some age groups of women, from the teenage ritual of Saturday's visit to the central area, to the young mothers' meetings in the local neighbourhood parades.

Certain features of general interaction theory have been tested by geographers, alongside the work of transportation specialists and planners. Some doubt has been thrown on the validity of the distance-decay function of gravity models in different situations, especially in terms of trip frequencies declining with distance from centres (Garrison, 1956; Carrothers, 1956). This has led to many different interpretations of the distance variable itself, such that it is seen as a general deterrence on travel, and this has also led to experimentation with different statistical transformations of raw data. In Britain, shopping trips remain heavily dependent on public transportation systems and where city-based services terminate at urban boundaries, the theoretical log-normal distance-decay function in trip frequencies often becomes seriously interrupted. There are, too, psychological affinities between consumer groups and their home territories which distort the general rule that distances travelled relate to size of centre visited (an adhesive effect which Stewart and Warntz, 1958, have pointed to in a wider territorial setting). Certain critics of gravity models contest whether consumers really evaluate in 'pay-off' terms between the relative attractions of centres versus the distance deterrence involved (Andrews, 1967).

Space preferences in consumer movements
Increasingly, the diversity of shopping behaviour is being considered
S.H.G.—6*

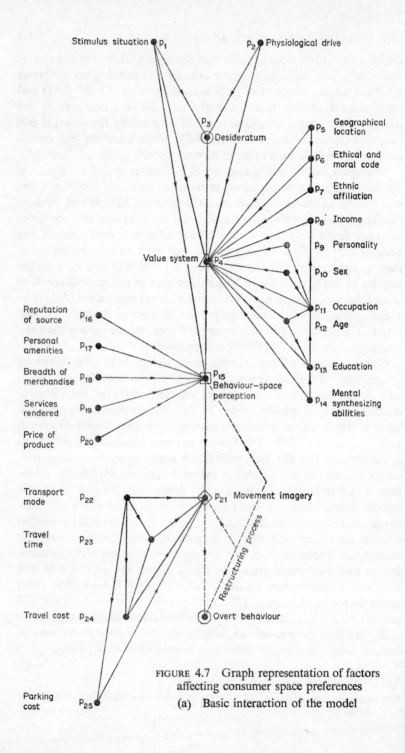

Stimulus situation p_1

p_2 Physiological drive

p_3 Desideratum

p_5 Geographical location

p_6 Ethical and moral code

p_7 Ethnic affiliation

p_8 Income

p_9 Personality

Value system p_4

p_{10} Sex

p_{11} Occupation

p_{12} Age

Reputation of source p_{16}

Personal amenities p_{17}

Breadth of merchandise p_{18}

p_{15} Behaviour-space perception

p_{13} Education

Services rendered p_{19}

p_{14} Mental synthesizing abilities

Price of product p_{20}

Transport mode p_{22}

p_{21} Movement imagery

Travel time p_{23}

Restructuring process

Travel cost p_{24}

Overt behaviour

Parking cost p_{25}

FIGURE 4.7 Graph representation of factors affecting consumer space preferences

(a) Basic interaction of the model

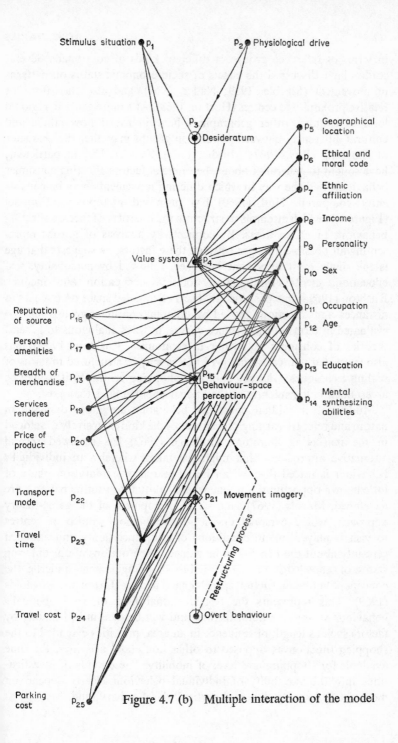

Figure 4.7 (b) Multiple interaction of the model

in terms of reference groups of different kinds of consumers. Several studies have discussed the effects of socio-economic status on patterns of movement (Marble, 1959; Nader, 1969), and also the effects of relative proximity to centres (Horton, 1968). At a more general, regional level of enquiry, other geographers have indicated how ethnic and cultural differences between population groups may alter the character of shopping (Ray, 1967; Murdie, 1965). Two studies, in particular, have sought to generalize about the range of factors affecting consumer behaviour, and the way in which differing movements may be consistently compared. Huff (1960) has proposed a topological model (Figure 4.7) which attempts to structure the interplay of factors affecting behaviour in urban areas. By connectivity analysis of graphs representing all possible linkages between these factors, he suggests that age is the single most important influence, followed by personality, sex, education, mental synthesizing abilities, occupation and income. Rushton (1969a) has proposed that sets of revealed space preferences in distances and directions moved by different consumer groups may be evaluated in terms of indifference curves, in ways analogous to general theories of consumer behaviour in economics. Rushton (1969b) has also suggested that consumer preferences may be structured in terms of scaling techniques, whereby choice in shopping centres visited may be ascertained independently of the known opportunities that exist.

Models of individual consumer behaviour are more dynamic in nature and refer to learning procedures of the kind extensively developed in the marketing literature. Golledge (1969) has reviewed several alternative approaches that might be taken whereby an individual's behaviour is traced through an initial search or exploration phase of little known opportunities to one where habitual or routine patterns are developed. Marble (1967) suggests a development of the game-theory approach, where personal decision-making about choice of centres to visit is played out in conditions of risk, uncertainty and assumed certainty about the benefits to be gained. Such notions about differing states of knowledge of the available shopping system underlie the concept of 'individual action space' formulated by Horton and Reynolds (1969). This represents the organizational field of an individual's behaviour at any one point in time and will be determined mainly by factors such as length of residence in an area, priorities extended to the shopping function as opposed to other household activities, the time available for shopping and level of mobility. These kinds of investigations into the variability of individual behaviour clearly depend on more detailed survey data and particularly of a diary kind.

SUMMARY

Geographical studies of the location and use of service facilities have mainly related to two broad theories, central place theory and general interaction theory, which in turn refer to an essentially economic system of supply and demand. Most of the empirical work has been concerned with description of the supply structure, which is seen to reflect in itself the broader characteristics of demand. In particular, the notion of a hierarchy of shopping provision has been intensively examined in various regional and urban situations. Considerable applications of this and other related constructs about retailing activity have been made in policy-oriented research, so that a close liaison exists with studies in the planning and marketing professions.

Increasingly, however, interest in these conceptual frameworks is being diverted to new avenues of enquiry. A general dissatisfaction is expressed that the static, deterministic nature of central place theory and general interaction theory is not sufficient for characterizing the full processes of structural change. It is felt that assumptions are too readily made that the retailing structure of supply provides a mirror image of demand expressed through aggregate, normative consumer behaviour. So too, the theories are seen to be macro-theories in approach and do not accommodate the peculiarities of individual actions. For these reasons, a series of more dynamic simulation and behavioural models, often referring to individual performances, is currently being widely experimented with.

The area of consumer behaviour, particularly, is becoming the most important frontier in geographical research into service activities (Thompson, 1966). Much attention has already focussed on the attitudes and perceptions of consumers to different shopping opportunities, especially to evaluate the precise influence of economic constraints. There is considerable exploration of the marketing literature on purchasing behaviour by consumers, in order to derive analogous concepts and hypotheses about the broader patterns of movement behaviour. This will inevitably entail a greater understanding of the psychological and personality factors behind the decision-making process involved in shopping. In short, rather than viewing consumer behaviour as a conditional response to existing retail supply facilities, the emerging trend is to treat shopping as a search procedure on the part of people. This trend is commensurate with a general shift in emphasis within geography as a whole to 'behavioural' studies.

Throughout the development of the field of retailing geography, however, there has been some divergence in the emphasis given to certain topics by researchers in different countries, especially between the USA and Britain. This naturally relates to differences in the societal habits and customs of the countries concerned, the nature of their organizational methods of retail supply and the historical legacies with which they may be faced. In general, geographers in the USA have tended to specialize in the formulation and testing of theoretical constructs about retailing activity to a greater degree than in Britain. Associated with this has been a greater development and application of a wide range of statistical techniques of analysis. Where empirical case studies have been undertaken for their own sake, they often relate to changes in the locational structure of shopping centres or the identification of potential sites for growth. U.S. geographers have been much more active as marketing consultants to property developers and speculators than their European counterparts. In Britain, conversely, there has tended to be much more emphasis given to descriptions of the historical evolution of retail distributions, the morphology of particular centres, and subjective appraisals of the relative importance of towns as service providers. There has also traditionally been a closer liaison with the planning profession than with private retail enterprises, with most contributions coming from geographers working inside the profession itself rather than from outside.

These differences in perspective should not be exaggerated, however. There has been much cross-fertilization of ideas and considerable duplication of methods of approach, particularly in central place research and the use of gravity models in forecasting. The same kind of hierarchical structure has been referred to by the marketing consultant in the USA as by the city planner in Britain. Techniques used to estimate size capacities of suburban regional shopping centres in the American city have often been identical to those employed in predicting the retail requirements of British towns.

In the future, certain major societal problems about service provision are likely to dominate the thinking of applied geographers. In Britain, the fundamental issue confronting the planning profession is the degree to which there should be continued concentration of services within the central area; and if there is to be substantial decentralization of facilities, what are the most suitable forms in which this might take place? The rôle of the geographer in such appraisals will be concerned with assessments of consumer attitudes and perceptions towards the alternatives that could be made available. It is unlikely, however, that there will be rapid and serious erosion of the existing system of retail supply and considerable attention will still be given to examining the efficiency of traditional centres in satisfying consumer demands. In the USA, the greatest impact of decentralization of the retail system has already taken place, and consumers, especially in the suburbs, are now faced with a wide variety of choices for shopping. In the short term, much geographic research in that country will undoubtedly focus on the ways in which consumers adjust to their changing circumstances. In the longer term, concern is likely to crystallize on the problems created by the older, decaying shopping centres and the rôle to be played by the central area in a social as well as an economic context.

REFERENCES

Abiodun, J. O. (1967) 'Urban hierarchy in a developing country', *Economic Geography*, **43**, 347–367.

Alonso, W. (1964) *Location and Land Use: Toward a General Theory of Land Rent*, Harvard University.

Ambrose, P. (1968) 'An analysis of intra-urban shopping patterns', *Town Planning Review*, **39**, 327–334.

Andrews, H. F. (1967) 'A note on forecasting shopping demand', *Journal of the Royal Town Planning Institute*, **53**, 352–354.

Andrews, H. F. (1970) 'Working notes and bibliography on central place studies', *University of Toronto, Department of Geography, Discussion Paper 8*.

Applebaum, W. (1954) 'Marketing geography', in C. Jones and P. James (Eds.), *American Geography—Inventory and Prospect*, Syracuse University.

Applebaum, W. (1961) 'Teaching marketing geography by the case method', *Economic Geography*, **37**, 48–60.

Applebaum, W. (1966) 'Methods for determining store trade areas, market penetration, and potential sales', *Journal of Marketing Research*, **3**, 127–141.

Batty, M. (1970) 'An activity allocation model for the Nottinghamshire–Derbyshire subregion', *Regional Studies*, **4**, 307–332.

Berry, B. J. L. (1959) 'Ribbon developments in the urban business pattern', *Annals of the Association of American Geographers*, **49**, 145–155.

Berry, B. J. L. (1960) 'The impact of expanding metropolitan communities upon the central place hierarchy', *Annals of the Association of American Geographers*, **50**, 112–116.

Berry, B. J. L. (1963) 'Commercial structure and commercial blight', *University of Chicago, Department of Geography, Research Paper 85*.

Berry, B. J. L. (1965) 'The retail component of the urban model', *Journal of the American Institute of Planners*, **31**, 150–155.

Berry, B. J. L. (1967) *Geography of Market Centers and Retail Distribution*, Prentice-Hall.

Berry, B. J. L. and Barnum, H. G. (1962) 'Aggregate relations and elemental components of central place systems', *Journal of Regional Science*, **4**, 35–68.

Berry, B. J. L., Barnum, H. G. and Tennant, R. J. (1962) 'Retail location and consumer behaviour', *Papers of the Regional Science Association*, **9**, 65–106.

Berry, B. J. L. and Garrison, W. L. (1958) 'Functional bases of the central place hierarchy', *Economic Geography*, **34**, 145–154.

Berry, B. J. L. and Mayer, H. M. (1962) *Comparative Studies of Central Place Systems*, US Office of Naval Research, Washington.

Berry, B. J. L., Parsons, S. J. and Platt, R. H. (1968) *The Impact of Urban Renewal on Small Business: The Hyde Park–Kenwood Case*, University of Chicago.

Berry, B. J. L. and Pred, A. (1965) *Central Place Studies: A Bibliography of Theory and Applications*, Regional Science Research Institute.

Boesch, H. (1952) 'Central functions as a basis for a systematic grouping of localities', *International Geographical Union, Abstract of Papers, 17th International Congress*.

Borchert, J. R. and Adams, R. B. (1963) 'Trade centers and trade areas of the upper midwest', *Upper Midwest Economic Study Urban* Report 3, University of Minnesota.

Bracey, H. E. (1953) 'Towns as rural service centres', *Transactions of the Institute of British Geographers*, **19**, 95–105.

Brush, J. E. (1953) 'The hierarchy of central places in Southwestern Wisconsin', *Geographical Review*, **43**, 380–402.

Carrothers, G. A. P. (1956) 'An historical review of the gravity and potential concepts of human interaction', *Journal of the American Institute of Planners*, **22**, 94–102.

Carruthers, W. I. (1962) 'Service centres in Greater London', *Town Planning Review*, **33**, 5–31.

Carruthers, W. I. (1967) 'Major shopping centres in England and Wales, 1961', *Regional Studies*, **1**, 65–81.

Carter, H. (1965) *The Towns of Wales*, University of Wales.

Carter, H. and Rowley, G. (1966) 'The morphology of the central business district of Cardiff', *Transactions of the Institute of British Geographers*, **38**, 119–134.

Casey, H. J. (1955) 'Applications to traffic engineering of the law of retail gravitation', *Traffic Quarterly*, **9**, 313–321.

Christaller, W. (1933) *Die zentralen Orte in Suddeutschland*, Verlag. Translated by C. Baskin (1966), *Central Places in Southern Germany*, Prentice-Hall.

Christaller, W. (1966) 'Applied geography—spatial models', *Nürnberger Wirtschafts und Sozial Geographische Arbuten*, **5**, 35–38.

Clark, W. A. V. (1968) 'Consumer travel patterns and the concept of range', *Annals of the Association of American Geographers*, **58**, 386–396.

Clark, W. A. V. (1969) 'Applications of spacing models in intra-city studies', *Geographical Analysis*, **1**, 391–399.

Clarke, B. and Bolwell, L. (1968) 'Attractiveness as part of retail potential models', *Journal of the Royal Town Planning Institute*, **54**, 477–479.

Cohen, S. B. and Lewis, G. K. (1967) 'Form and function in the geography of retailing', *Economic Geography*, **53**, 1–42.

Converse, P. D., Huegy, H. W. and Mitchell, R. V. (1930) *Elements of Marketing*, Prentice-Hall.

Cordey-Hayes, M. (1968) 'Retail location models', *Centre for Environmental Studies, Working Paper 16*.

Cowan, P. (1968) *The Office: a facet of urban growth*, University of London.

Cripps, E. L. and Foot, D. H. S. (1969) 'A land use model for sub-regional planning', *Regional Studies*, **3**, 243–268.

Curry, L. (1962) 'The geography of service centers within towns: the elements of an operational approach', *Lund Symposium on Urban Geography*, University of Lund.

Daniels, P. W. (1970) 'Offices in the suburbs', *University College, London University, Department of Geography, Occasional Paper 7*.

Davies, D. H. (1959) 'Boundary study as a tool in C.B.D. analysis', *Economic Geography*, **35**, 322–345.

Davies, R. L. (1968) 'Effects of Consumer Income Differences on the Business Provisions of Small Shopping Centres', *Urban Studies*, **5**, 144–164.

Davies, R. L. (1969) 'A note on centrality and population size', *Professional Geographer*, **21**, 108–112.

Davies, R. L. (1970) 'Variable relationships in central place and retail potential models', *Regional Studies*, **4**, 49–61.

Davies, R. L. (1971) 'Structural models of retail distribution: analogies with settlement and urban land use theories', paper presented to the Institute of British Geographers, Annual Conference. Forthcoming in *Transactions*, **58**, 1972.

Davies, W. K. D. (1966) 'The ranking of service centres: a critical review', *Transactions of the Institute of British Geographers*, **40**, 51–56.

Davies, W. K. D. (1967) 'Centrality and the central place hierarchy', *Urban Studies*, **4**, 61–79.

Diamond, D. (1962) 'The central business district of Glasgow', *Lund Symposium in Urban Geography*, University of Lund.

Diamond, D. and Gibb, E. B. (1962) 'Development of new shopping centres: area estimation', *Scottish Journal of Political Economy*, **9**, 130–146.

Dickinson, R. E. (1947) *City, Region and Regionalism*, Kegan Paul.

Dunn, E. S. (1956) 'The market potential concept and the analysis of location', *Papers of the Regional Science Association*, **2**, 183–194.

Fleming, J. B. (1954) 'The analysis of shops and service trades in Scottish towns', *Scottish Geographical Magazine*, **70**, 97–106.

Forstall, R. (1965) *City Rating Guide: the nation's markets at a glance*, Rand McNally.

Garner, B. J. (1966) 'The internal structure of retail nucleations', *Northwestern University, Department of Geography, Research Studies*, **12**.

Garner, B. J. (1967) 'Some reflections on the notion of threshold in central place studies', *Annals of the Association of American Geographers*, **57**, 788.

Garrison, W. L. (1956) 'Estimates of the parameters of spatial interaction', *Papers of the Regional Science Association*, **2**, 280–288.

Garrison, W. L. *et al.* (1959) *Studies in Highway Development and Geographic Change*, University of Washington.

Getis, A. and Getis, J. M. (1968) 'Retail store spatial affinities', *Urban Studies*, **5**, 317–332.

Goddard, J. (1967) 'Changing office location patterns in the City of London', *Urban Studies*, **4**, 276–286.

Goddard, J. (1968) 'Multivariate analysis of office location patterns in the city centre: a London example', *Regional Studies*, **2**, 69–85.

Godlund, S. (1956) 'The function and growth of bus traffic within the sphere of urban influence', *Lund Studies in Geography, Series 6, Human Geography*, 18.

Golledge, R. G. (1969) 'The geographical relevance of some learning theories', in K. Cox and R. G. Golledge (Eds.), 'Problems of behavioral geography', *Northwestern University, Department of Geography, Research Studies 17.*

Golledge, R. G., Rushton, G. and Clark, W. A. V. (1966) 'Some spatial characteristics of Iowa's dispersed farm population and their implications for the grouping of central place functions', *Economic Geography*, **52**, 261–272.

Green, F. H. W. (1951) 'Bus services as an index to changing urban hinterlands', *Town Planning Review*, **22**, 345–356.

Haggett, P. and Gunarwadena, K. (1964) 'Determination of population thresholds for settlement functions by the Reed-Muench method', *Professional Geographer*, **16**, 6–9.

Hammond, E. (1967) 'Dispersal of government offices: a survey', *Urban Studies*, **4**, 258–276.

Harris, B. (1964) 'A model of locational equilibrium for retail trade', *Penn–Jersey Transportation Study*, Philadelphia. (mimeo).

Hodge, G. (1965) 'The prediction of trade centre viability in the Great Plains', *Papers of the Regional Science Association*, **15**, 87–115.

Horton, F. E. (1968) 'Location factors as determinants of consumer attraction to retail firms', *Annals of the Association of American Geographers*, **58**, 787–807.

Horton, R. E. and Reynolds, R. D. (1969) 'An investigation of individual action spaces', *Proceedings of the American Association of Geographers*, **1**, 70–75.

Horwood, E. M. and Boyce, R. R. (1959) *Studies of the Central Business District and Urban Freeway Development*, University of Washington.

Hoyt, H. (1933) *One Hundred Years of Land Values in Chicago*, University of Chicago.

Hoyt, H. (1966) 'US metropolitan area retail shopping patterns', *Urban Land*, **25**, No. 3, 3–15; No. 4, 3–16.

Hoyt, H. (1968) 'Land values in shopping centres', *Traffic Quarterly*, **22**, 315–328.

Huff, D. L. (1960) 'A topographical model of consumer space preferences', *Papers of the Regional Science Association*, **6**, 159–174.

Huff, D. L. (1963) 'A probability analysis of shopping centre trading areas', *Land Economics*, **53**, 81–89.

Isard, W. (1956) *Location and Space Economy*, Wiley.

Isbary, G. (1967) 'Zentrale Orte und Versorgungsnahbereiche', *Mitteilungen Nr. 56, Institut fur Raumforschung*. Translated by H. Ellen Dietrichs as

Central Places and Local Service Areas, Federal Ministry of the Interior, West Germany.

Johnston, R. J. and Rimmer, P. J. (1967) 'A note on consumer behavior in an urban hierarchy', *Journal of Regional Science*, 7, 161–166.

Jones, C. S. (1969) *Regional Shopping Centres: their location, planning and design*, Business Books.

Lakshmanan, T. R. and Hansen, W. C. (1965) 'A retail market potential model', *Journal of the American Institute of Planners*, 31, 134–143.

Lanchester Polytechnic, Department of Town Planning (1969) *Gravity Models in Town Planning*, Lanchester Polytechnic.

Leeming, F. A. (1959) 'An experimental survey of retail shopping and service facilities in a part of north Leeds', *Transactions of the Institute of British Geographers*, 26, 133–152.

Lomas, G. M. (1964) 'Retail trading centres in the Midlands', *Journal of the Royal Town Planning Institute*, 50, 104–119.

Lösch, A. (1954) *Die Raumliche Ordnung der Wirtschaft*. Translated by W. Woglam and W. Stopler as *The Economics of Location*, Yale University.

Lowry, I. (1964) *A Model of Metropolis*, Rand Corporation.

Manchester University, Department of Town Planning (1964 and 1966) *Regional Shopping Centres in North West England, Parts I and II*, Manchester University.

Marble, D. F. (1959) 'Transport inputs at urban residential sites', *Papers of the Regional Science Association*, 5, 253–266.

Marble, D. F. (1967) 'A theoretical exploration of individual travel behavior', in W. L. Garrison and D. F. Marble (Eds.), 'Quantitative Geography, Part I', *Northwestern University, Department of Geography, Research Studies 13*.

Marshall, J. U. (1969) 'The location of service centres', *University of Toronto, Department of Geography, Research Publication 3*.

Mayfield, R. C. (1967) 'A central place hierarchy in Northern India', in W. L. Garrison and D. F. Marble (Eds.), 'Quantitative Geography, Part I', *Northwestern University, Department of Geography, Research Studies 13*.

McEvoy, D. (1968) 'Alternative methods of ranking shopping centres', *Tijdschrift voor Economische en Sociale Geografie*, 59, 211–217.

Morrill, R. L. (1967) 'The movement of persons and the transportation problem', in W. L. Garrison and D. F. Marble (Eds.), 'Quantitative Geography, Part I', *Northwestern University, Department of Geography, Research Studies 13*.

Morrill, R. L. and Earickson, R. J. (1969) 'Problems in modelling inter- action: the case of hospital care', in K. R. Cox and R. G. Golledge (Eds.), 'Behavioral problems in geography', *Northwestern University, Depart- ment of Geography, Research Studies 17*.

Murdie, R. (1965) 'Cultural differences in consumer travel', *Economic Geography*, 41, 211–233.

Murphy, R. E. (Ed.) (1961) Special Issue of *Economic Geography* on Market- ing Geography, 37.

Murphy, R. E. and Vance, J. E. (1954a) 'Delimiting the central business district', *Economic Geography*, 30, 197–223.

Murphy, R. E. and Vance, J. E. (1954b) 'A comparative study of nine central business districts', *Economic Geography*, **30**, 301–336.

Nader, G. A. (1969) 'Socio-economic status and consumer behaviour', *Urban Studies*, **6**, 235–245.

National Economic Development Office, Committee for the Distributive Trades (1970) *Urban Models in Shopping Studies*, NEDO.

National Economic Development Office, Committee for the Distributive Trades (1971) *The Future Pattern of Shopping*, NEDO.

Nelson, R. (1958) *The Selection of Retail Locations*, Dodge.

O'Farrell, P. (1969) 'Continuous regularities and discontinuities in the central place system', *Geografiska Annaler*, **52**, 104–114.

Olsson, G. (1965) *Distance and Human Interaction—a review and bibliography*, Regional Science Research Institute.

Parker, H. (1962) 'Suburban shopping facilities in Liverpool', *Town Planning Review*, **33**, 197–223.

Parr, J. B. and Denike, K. G. (1970) 'Theoretical problems in central place analysis', *Economic Geography*, **46**, 568–587.

Pred, A. (1963) 'Business thoroughfares as expressions of urban negro culture', *Economic Geography*, **39**, 217–233.

Parry Lewis, J. and Trail, A. J. (1968) 'The assessment of shopping potential and the demand for shops', *Town Planning Review*, **38**, 317–326.

Ray, D. M. (1967) 'Cultural differences in consumer travel behavior in Eastern Ontario', *Canadian Geographer*, **11**, 143–156.

Reilly, W. J. (1931) *The Law of Retail Gravitation*, Knickerbocker.

Rhodes, T. and Whitaker, R. (1967) 'Forecasting shopping demand', *Journal of the Royal Town Planning Institute*, **53**, 188–192.

Rogers, A. (1969) 'Quadrat analysis of urban dispersion, Part 2: case studies of urban retail systems', *Environment and Planning*, **1**, 155–173.

Royal Commission on Local Government in England (1966–69) Vol. 1, Report, Cmnd 4040; Vol. 2, Memorandum of Dissent, Cmnd 4040—I, H.M.S.O.

Royal Commission on Local Government in Greater London (1957–60) Cmnd 1164, H.M.S.O.

Royal Town Planning Institute, West Midlands Branch (1967) *Predicting Shopping Requirements*, Royal Town Planning Institute.

Rushton, G. (1969a) 'Analysis of spatial behavior by revealed space preference', *Annals of the Association of American Geographers*, **59**, 391–401.

Rushton, G. (1969b) 'The scaling of locational preferences', in K. Cox and R. G. Golledge, (Eds.), 'Problems of behavioral geography', *Northwestern University, Department of Geography, Research Studies 17*.

Scott, P. (1959) 'The Australian C.B.D.', *Economic Geography*, **35**, 290–312.

Scott, P. (1964) 'The hierarchy of central places in tasmania', *The Australian Geographer*, **9**, 134–147.

Scott, P. (1970) *Geography and Retailing*, Hutchinson.

Simmons, J. W. (1964) 'The changing pattern of retail location', *University of Chicago, Department of Geography, Research Paper 92*.

Simmons, J. W. (1966) 'Toronto's changing retail complex: a study in growth and blight', *University of Chicago, Department of Geography, Research Paper 104*.

Smailes, A. E. (1944) 'The urban hierarchy in England and Wales', *Geography*, **29**, 41–51.

Smailes, A. E. and Hartley, G. (1961) 'Shopping centres in the Greater London area', *Transactions of the Institute of British Geographers*, **29**, 201–213.

Smith, R. D. P. (1965) 'The changing urban hierarchy', *Regional Studies*, **2**, 1–19.

Sternlieb, G. (1963) 'The future of retailing in the downtown core', *Journal of the American Institute of Planners*, **29**, 102–112.

Stewart, J. Q. (1948) 'Demographic gravitation: evidence and applications', *Sociometry*, **11**, 31–58.

Stewart, J. Q. and Warntz, W. (1958) 'Physics of population distribution', *Journal of Regional Science*, **1**, 99–123.

Stiglbauer, K. (1967) 'Some problems of central places at the lowest level in Austria', *Papers of the Regional Science Association*, **18**, 47–65.

Taaffe, E. J. (1962) 'The urban hierarchy: an air passenger definition', *Economic Geography*, **38**, 1–14.

Tarrant, J. R. (1967) 'Retail distribution in Eastern Yorkshire in relation to central place theory', *University of Hull, Occasional Papers in Geography 8*.

Thomas, E. N. (1962) 'The stability of distance–population size relationships for Iowa towns from 1900 to 1950', *Lund Studies in Geography, Series B, Human Geography*, **24**, 13–30.

Thompson, D. L. (1966) 'Future directions in retail area research', *Economic Geography*, **42**, 1–19.

Thorpe, D. (1968) 'The main shopping centres of Great Britain in 1961: their locational and structural characteristics', *Urban Studies*, **5**, 165–206.

Thorpe, D. and Kivell, P. T. (1971) *Study of an Out-of-Town Shopping Centre: Woolco, Thornaby*, Manchester University, Retail Outlets Research Unit, Report 3.

Thorpe, D. and Rhodes, T. C. (1966) 'The shopping centres of the Tyneside region and large scale grocery retailing', *Economic Geography*, **42**, 53–73.

Vance, J. E. (1962) 'Emerging patterns of commercial structure in American cities', *Lund Symposium on Urban Geography, 1960*, University of Lund.

Wingo, L. (1961) *Transportation and Urban Land Use*, Resources for the Future.

Yeates, M. (1963) 'Hinterland delimitation: a distance minimizing approach', *Professional Geographer*, **15**, 7–10.

5 Structure and scale in the city system

HAROLD CARTER

The idea that the urban settlements of a country or region fall into characteristic size groups, so that they can be best comprehended within the context of a distinctive structuring by size and associated functional attributes, long pre-dates the development of classical Central Place Theory and the enquiries of academic geographers. Such a structuring was inherent in descriptive terminology even in Roman Britain: 'Towns were graded in privilege—colonies of Roman citizens at the top, then *municipia* of Roman citizens, the communities of Latin status . . . and finally communities of peregrine status' (Reynolds, 1966). Later descriptions were in the less formalized terms of hamlet, village, town and city. Dawson has reviewed early speculation concerning structuring of this sort and has shown that as early as 1755 Cantillon 'presented the first attempt to view settlements as groups similar in size and function' (Dawson, 1969). In effect Cantillon demonstrated the existence of a settlement hierarchy in France by showing that in size and function those settlements which were called 'villages' were clearly differentiated from the 'bourgs' which were in turn distinct from the 'villes'. Again Dawson demonstrated that Lalanne in 1863, even at that date making the assumption of a plain homogeneous as to topography and resources, together with an even distribution of population, deduced the emergence of an hierarchy of places—villages, bourgades, villes, cités—with places of equal status being located at equal distances from each other. From early times, therefore, some form of ordered progression in settlement size has been implicit and academic geography appropriately has found a major area of concern in seeking for adequate criteria by which to measure size relations, to identify any regularities which might exist in these relations, to examine the functional correlates of size groups and to establish in theoretical terms the forces which operate in producing a tendency to regularity.

From the outset the idea of some structuring in the urban scale revolved about the concept of 'the market town' as a central and ideal construct, one indeed which is still apparent in the contemporary notion of 'the fully fledged town' (see p. 177). Such a town acted as the focus for a tributary area, or dominated a sphere of influence, which included lower order settlements, to which names such as village and hamlet were applied and of which the lowest rank was the isolated individual farmstead. But after the mid-eighteenth century, extractive and manufacturing industries became much the most potent forces in the growth of towns and the creation of size variation. Indeed so significant to the character and scale of urbanization has been the onset of industrialization that it has been taken as a major conceptual break. Thus Sjoberg develops the study of *The Preindustrial City* (Sjoberg, 1960), and Lampard contrasts 'classic urbanization' with 'industrial urbanization', for in the latter 'prevailing constraints and conditions are relaxed through the final achievement of technological and organizational capacities for unprecedented population concentration' (Lampard, 1965). Again Reissmann in his study of *The Urban Process* subtitles his book 'Cities in Industrial Society', for he considers that earlier cities were 'quite different social phenomena' (Reissman, 1964).

The changes brought about in the nature of urban development by industrialization have been briefly pursued because they carry the implication that a change took place in the balance of forces operating. These operative forces can be designated as 'central place' and 'agglomerative'. Before industrialization, the wealth derived from the agriculture of the surrounding countryside was critical to the well-being of the central town, which acted as the exchange point to which local produce was brought for redistribution and export and from which imported products were distributed, The chief rôle of a town was 'to be the centre of its rural surroundings and mediator of local commerce with the outside world' (Gradmann, 1916). After the middle of the eighteenth century the wealth of the rural countryside became of secondary importance for the growth of towns into conurbations, brought about by manufacturing. It is partly due to this most recent historical sequence, and partly due to the precedence of Central Place Theory in urban geographical literature, that the received academic convention is to assume a basic regularity, which is consequent upon the operation of central place influences, and to look upon industrialization as producing distortions of this regularity due to the vagaries of resource location and the development of agglomeration tendencies.

This introduces one further problem, since most studies, both theoretical and empirical, are set in a static context. As a result, there has been little attempt to derive size groupings from a long growth process and to accept a contemporary state of flux. Indeed, it could be argued that towns owe their origins mainly to very specialized rôles and that central place tendencies act upon very irregular 'original' networks. To some extent this difficulty can be subsumed under the heading of 'distortions' by entitling it 'distortions due to time lag' or some such equivalent term.

This chapter attempts to consider the theoretical underpinnings for the suggested regularity in town size and location patterns and subsequently to note some of the empirical studies which have sought to test such theoretical speculation. The distortions that are related to dynamic growth are introduced, followed by those consequent upon agglomeration tendencies, and, finally, the nature of the largest scale urban agglomerations is briefly considered.

THEORETICAL CONSIDERATIONS

It is implicit that there are two associated concepts which lie behind the conviction that towns can be thought of as forming a structured size sequence. There can be no attempt to deal with either of these in depth in this essay but some brief notice is essential in order to put empirical studies in their proper context.

The first of these concepts is that towns must be considered as forming part of an urban system. There is no need to pursue the more recondite aspects of general systems theory (Bertalanffy, 1950) to put forward what is essentially a simple notion, for geographers have long thought implicitly in such a way (Chisholm, 1967). A system has been defined as 'a set of objects together with relations between the objects and their attributes' (Hall and Fagen, 1956), or as 'arbitrarily demarcated sections of the real world which have some common functional connections' (Haggett, 1965). The major feature is that the objects, in this case the towns, are seen not as existing *in vacuo* with unique reasons for their sizes, but as interacting with each other through functional connections within the system. In this system an energy input is derived from the needs and demands of the population for goods and services. This is realized as the movement of people, freight and information which in turn is channelled into distinct networks by the physical lines of communication, road, rail, telephone, and the whole complex of linkages. Within this network there is a series of nodes which constitute the focal points at which flows converge. These nodes, or central places, are the towns and it is worth adding that the old and traditional geographic idea of nodality and the later concept of an urban hierarchy are conceptually as one, so long as nodality is thought of in terms of movement and interaction. A system of cities constitutes an interacting whole, even if it is arbitrarily demarcated and never closed, and any change in the nature of demand, the energy input, in the channels or the nodes has repercussions throughout the system. Central place theory must be set in the context of such a system.

This theory is the second concept which needs comment and explanation. This is described in Chapter 4 by Ross Davies and does not require repetition here. A point made there, however, does need to be taken up, for as Davies shows once the rigid restrictions imposed by Christaller are relaxed an hierarchical structuring becomes less tenable, and, indeed, a continuum is produced rather than characteristic size classes. 'Whilst the functional array of services does fall into distinct groupings in all cases, it is only when a fixed **k** is assumed that a strict hierarchy in the Christaller sense is obtained' (Davies, W. K. D., 1964).

Moreover, in purely empirical terms Zipf developed the so-called Rank-Size Rule for cities (Zipf, 1949) which is usually given the form

$$P_r = P_1/rq$$

where Pr is the population of a city of rank r and P_1 is the population of the largest city. If the constant q is unity, then the rule proposes that the population of any city can be found by dividing its rank into the population of the largest city. But this implies a continuous and not a stepped or hierarchical relation between city sizes for the logarithmic form

$$\log P_r = \log P_1 - q \log r$$

which gives a straight line plot (Figure 5.1). This continuous relation is apparently at variance with an hierarchical structuring.

Even if this is accepted as a valid empirical finding however, for there have been studies which do not accept it (Rosing, 1966), the discrepancy is not as disconcerting as at first appears. It is worth noting at the outset that hierarchical studies aim to measure centrality by the total functions of a settlement while the Rank-Size Rule measures importance by total population. But more fundamentally the discrepancy can be explained in terms of differences of scale. In the large scale

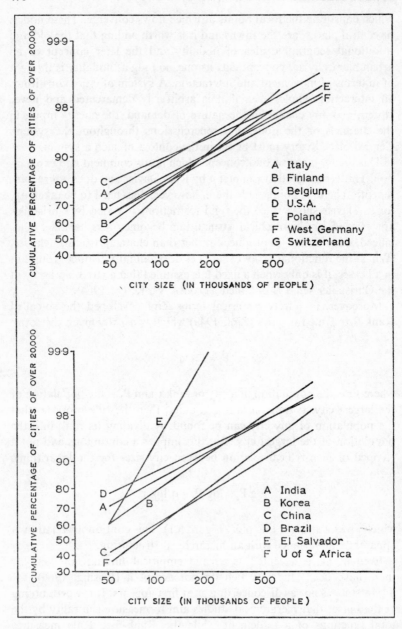

FIGURE 5.1   The rank-size rule

context of a country, or indeed a continent, the mixing of areas of different economic bases and population densities means a compounding of hierarchies of differing characteristics into an approximation to a rank-size situation (Berry and Garrison, 1958a). Moreover, in theoretical terms, Beckmann has demonstrated that if populations are allowed to vary about the mean size for a given class, as if a random disturbing factor were operating, then a rank-size situation will appear even given a fixed k, that is a Christaller type model rather than the Lösch type (Beckmann, 1958).

These theoretical considerations have been introduced in a very brief fashion because they are necessarily reflected in the empirical attempts to demonstrate a structuring in urban scale by the identification of hierarchies.

EMPIRICAL STUDIES OF STRUCTURING

To a large extent the first attempts at providing an urban structuring took the notion of the urban hierarchy quite uncritically from the theoretical literature and proceeded to the identification of ranks by the means of arbitrary criteria. Indeed, the earliest attempt in Britain predates Christaller and was presented with reference to the ideas of Kolb (Kolb, 1925). This was an examination of settlements in East Anglia (Dickinson, 1932). Dickinson argued that 'urban status' varied according to the number and variety of functions and went on to grade towns according to a check-list of functions and to correlate grade with population. The study was set in an historical context of growing and declining towns. Four grades were recognized, the first of which was called 'fully fledged' towns and a fifth was suggested which was to be called the 'urban village'.

The succeeding work in this line of development was that of Smailes, who extended the approach to the whole of England and Wales (Smailes, 1944). Smailes' critical issue was the identification of the 'fully fledged town', a rank which was subjectively perceived as distinctive in the British hierarchy. 'Any grading', he wrote, 'must in some measure be arbitrary, since the urban scale is as continuous as the social scale. Yet the indefiniteness of boundaries in neither case warrants denial of the reality of stratification'. In this context 'a minimum endowment of key services which indicates full urban status' was sought and resolved by the selection of a bundle of functions which, the author maintained, tended to occur together as a *trait complex*.

These were

	A	Branches of three of the five major banks together with a Woolworth's store
diminishing to	A'	Three branch banks
	A"	Two branch banks
	B	Grammar school and Hospital
diminishing to	B'	Only one of above
	C	Cinemas
diminishing to	C'	Only one cinema
	D	Publication of a local newspaper

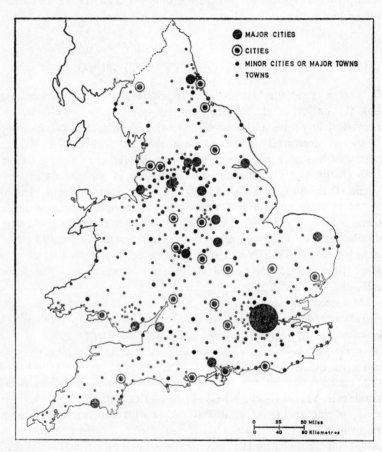

FIGURE 5.2 The urban hierarchy in England and Wales

From this array A'B'C' D or A' BC were accepted as the minimum qualification for a settlement to be regarded as a town. Below that level sub-towns were identified, and above superior grades were identified, although without the clear use of *trait complexes*. The result was a proposed structure (Figure 5.2) which was:

Metropolis	London only
Major City	e.g. Liverpool, Birmingham, Bristol, Southampton
City	e.g. Preston, Wolverhampton, Swansea, Oxford, Brighton, Ipswich
Minor City/Major Town	e.g. Shrewsbury, Chester
Town	e.g. Barnstaple, Margate, Caernarvon
Sub Town	

There are clear drawbacks to this sixfold structure. The criteria were arbitrarily chosen and the ranks arbitrarily defined, for in spite of the use of data it is a subjectively derived sequence. The problems of an hierarchical as against a continuous distribution are summarily dismissed, and apart from the presentation of an hierarchical array there is no point at which the empirical study is related to theory.

To a large extent work in Britain continued on the lines established by Smailes and although criteria were varied the outcome was the production of structures generally similar and only differing in detail. Characteristic is the work of Carruthers (Carruthers, 1957) developed from that of Green (Green, 1950). At the outset five orders were proposed:

First Order	London
Second Order	e.g. Bristol, Newcastle
Third Order	e.g. Chelmsford, Worcester
Fourth Order	e.g. Bridgwater, Ely, Ripon
Fifth Order	Local village centres

These were to be identified by plotting each settlement on a graph of the total number of bus journeys to a centre on market days and Saturdays against the proportion which served smaller places exclusively. The first axis measured total services, the second relative dominance. So complex were the results, particularly because of the physical proximity of centres in Britain, that all the intermediate orders

were divided into three sub-orders so that the scheme eventually
appears as:

Order 1		London only
2	A	Birmingham, Bristol, Cardiff, Leeds, Manchester, Newcastle, Nottingham
	B	Liverpool, Norwich, Plymouth
3	A	Above average for the Group. e.g. Coventry, Derby, Leicester, Salisbury, Bradford, Sheffield, Sunderland
	B	Average. e.g. Maidstone, Guildford, Bedford, Darlington, Wolverhampton, Wrexham
	C	Losing ground to 3A centres. e.g. Durham, Hartlepool, Harrogate, Merthyr Tydfil, Aldershot, Barnstaple
4	A	Above average. e.g. Neath, Castleford, Penrith, Dartford, Maidenhead, Dover, Ely
	B	Average. e.g. Stalybridge, Pudsey, Whitby, Ross, Wellington, Bude, Harwich
	C	Transitional
5		Not examined. Local village centres

The schemes of Smailes and Carruthers can be compared in the most
general terms, with Smailes' 'City to Major Town' group, equivalent to
the 'Third Order' of Carruthers. But it is quite clear that the division is
arbitrary and almost without meaning in theoretical terms, though
possibly of use for the pragmatic needs of the planner.

This contrast of method and purpose is one which few of those
engaged in empirical work were prepared to recognize. It is possible
to conceive of town-ranking as an arbitrary classification process. In
this sense the orders recognized provide a useful basis for considering
the growth and decay of centres and to describe regional situations. It
is also possible to look upon the ranking of towns as part of the empirical investigation of the postulates of central place theory. But this
creates a situation where the ranking process demands precision,
statistical justification and complete objectivity.

The confusion that existed between these two approaches was made
worse by attempts at international comparability. Early attempts by
Brush and Bracey (Brush and Bracey, 1955) were followed by Philbrick
and Carol (Philbrick, 1957; Carol, 1960) to produce the idea of a
seven-fold universal structuring of urban scale:

TABLE 7 **An hierarchy of central places**

General hierarchy	Special hierarchies for the highest level of central function		
	Entire settlements		
	Christaller (Germany)	Great Britain	Switzerland
First Lowest		Roadside hamlet	Dorf
Second Low order	Marktort	Village (Old Buckenham)	Marktort
Third Middle order	Amtsort Kreisort Bezirksort	Town (Thetford)	Stadt
Fourth High order	Gauort Provinzhauptort	City (Norwich)	Grossstadt
Fifth Higher order	Landstadt	Metropolis (Bristol)	Metropole
Sixth Highest order	Reichsteile	Super Metropolis (Manchester)	
Seventh World wide order	Reichstadt	World Metropolitan centre (London)	

SOURCE: Everson and Fitzgerald, 1969, p. 92.

It would be mistaken, however, to regard this structuring as anything more than a useful and suggestive tabulation which ignores most of the problems and much of the complexity.

Dissatisfaction with the geographer's limited ability to develop an acceptable methodology for the ranking of towns (Berry and Garrison,

1958b; Davies, W. K. D., 1966) has led to the emergence of two basic procedures which are now widely used, the one using a multivariate approach, the other relying on the simpler basis of the location quotient. Perhaps the most widely quoted work using a multivariate approach is that by Abiodun in her study of Ijabu province in Nigeria (Abiodun, 1967). The procedure is that selected functions of settlements, twenty-eight functions in this case, are identified in relation to all settlements and a correlation matrix of each function against all others is constructed. Two problems intrude at this stage. The first is that an arbitrary selection of functions was employed since the field work in accumulating data relating to all functions was not possible. The second is that in order to maintain some relation between the various functions an arbitrary weighting was adopted. The correlation matrix is now subject to principal components analysis with the purpose of abstracting 'new variables with zero intercorrelation which must be mutually independent'. Sixteen components were abstracted but the first four accounted for 82·2% of the total variance. These four were used to define the hierarchy. The four components were interpreted as: a measure of overall importance, a measure of economic and administrative functions and two measures of social services. But the interpretation of the components, often one of the difficulties in these analyses, is not important since their basic use is in a standard grouping procedure to give orders of towns. Such a procedure progressively associates settlements by minimum functional distance, measured in four dimensions by the components. Maximum generalization, that is where all the settlements formed one group, was achieved at the seventy-third step but, writes Abiodun, 'a close examination of the grouping steps before this stage is reached enables distinct groups to be identified. A good knowledge of the area under study greatly facilitates such an identification' (Abiodun, 1967). Again it would appear that a subjective decision is made as to the vital point of how many groups are to be identified. Abiodun identifies five orders of town and is one of the few workers who goes on to demonstrate that there is close agreement in her area with a $k=3$ system, probably because of its 'undeveloped' and rural character. But so many subjective elements underlie this apparently complex statistical analysis that in the end it is nearer a classificatory device controlled by the author than a ranking emerging inevitably from a real world situation.

W. K. D. Davies, working on the Rhondda valleys of South Wales in a cultural situation as different from Nigeria as one could wish, devised a method which has not only the advantage of being rather more objective, but also simpler (Davies, 1967). A location quotient for every functional type in the area (e.g. grocers and chemists) was calculated:

$$C = \frac{t}{T} \cdot 100$$

where C is the coefficient of function t, t is one outlet of function t and T is the total number of outlets of type t in the whole system. If the number of outlets in any one settlement is multiplied by the coefficient then the degree of centrality (the centrality value) imparted to each settlement for each function will be given. Davies then weighted these by the number of shop assistants to offset differences in size of outlets. The total of these centrality values will give a Functional Index which is the measure of the town's participation in all central place activities within the area. These Indexes were used to identify a five-group hierarchy by minimizing in-group and maximizing between-group differences. Davies' method is not without its problems, in particular it presupposes a closed system, that is, that there are no external forces operating in the area and that nothing is bought outside it. This is manifestly not so and a major weakness of the method. It is also significant that Davies was examining a relatively small area using a complete data set which he himself gathered in the field. Davies concludes by arguing that although his results do not bear any relevance to the theoretical formulations in the context of numbers of settlements in each size group, he is satisfied that the operation of threshold and range even in such a highly urbanized area has produced distinctive bundles of functions at recognizable levels, that is, an hierarchical structure emerges (Figure 5.3).

The argument so far implies that given relatively small areas, or larger areas homogeneous as to economy and terrain, it is possible to substantiate the operation of the ideas implicit in central place theory. Under the controls outlined in theory, a distinctive structuring appears. All the most convincing studies have concentrated on limited areas. As soon as the extension is made to larger areas where there are disparities in the economic base and great variations in the density and distribution of population, then local or sub-regional hierarchies are fused and any clear ranking in meaningful central place terms is lost. Nevertheless, it is still possible, using concepts derived from central place theory, to produce a ranking in descriptive terms which has both its academic and its practical uses.

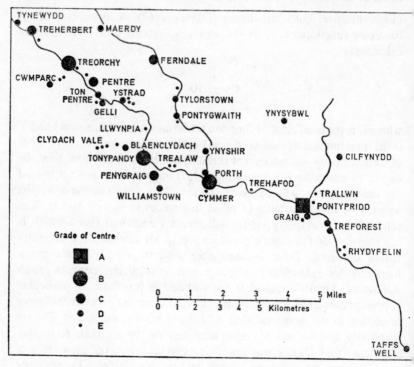

FIGURE 5.3 The urban hierarchy in the Rhondda valleys

URBAN GROWTH AND URBAN SCALE

At this stage it is necessary to introduce the problem of the dynamic growth or decline of towns into the concept of their static organization into defined orders, for if an ordering is identifiable then it poses the question of how it has come into being. Recent work by R. D. P. Smith (Smith, 1968 and 1970) has attempted to isolate secular changes in the hierarchy of English and Welsh towns over the short term. Smith uses a range of some 35 selected functions to establish a five-class hierarchy which is then compared with the schemes of Smailes and Carruthers. In general, Smith notes the association of population decline with the down-grading of towns. It is here that the lack of precision in early schemes is most clearly seen, apart from the changes in the particular criteria selected, such as the rôle of cinemas. Smith's attempt is interesting but the classes of towns are so inadequately defined that it is difficult to accept conclusions when the changes themselves are on a fine scale.

Longer term and cruder changes have been considered by Carter, who attempted to show the nature of change in south-west Wales over some eight hundred years and has attempted to generalize the processes

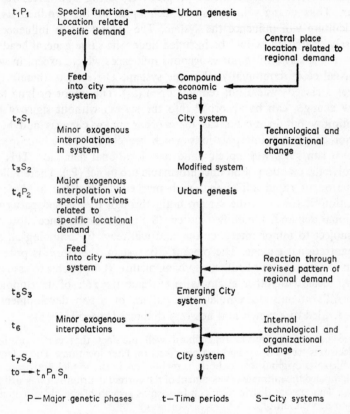

t_1P_1 Special functions- ◄────► Urban genesis
Location related
specific demand

Central place
location related to
regional demand

Feed
into city ───────► Compound
system   economic ◄────
base

t_2S_1 City system

Minor exogenous
interpolations   Technological and
in system   organizational
change

t_3S_2 Modified system

t_4P_2 Major exogenous
interpolation via   Urban genesis
special functions
related to
specific locational
demand

Feed
into city ───────►
system

Reaction through
◄──── revised pattern of
regional demand

t_5S_3 Emerging City
system

t_6 Minor exogenous
interpolations ───────►

Internal
◄──── technological and
organizational
change

t_7S_4 City system
to ─► $t_nP_nS_n$

P—Major genetic phases   t—Time periods   S—City systems

FIGURE 5.4   The growth of a system of cities

at work on a larger, Welsh scale (Carter, 1955 and 1969). This is illustrated in Figure 5.4, which attempts to portray a conceptual framework which summarizes the various influences on the hierarchy of towns. The urban system (S) is conceived as being created at time t_1 through a phase of genesis (P_1). The system itself becomes rapidly composed of two elements, one a set of towns owing their origin to special functions with peculiar locational demands, the other a set of towns owing their growth to central place functions derived from general regional demand. These are intimately related, for their complex interaction produces an urban net (S_1). This net is then itself subject to the continuing modification brought about by two sets of influences. The first of these is the economic, technological and organizational changes which progressively bring new pressures to bear. Thus changes in transport techniques or the productivity of agriculture will influence the system. The second set of influences is closely related and could be included under the same general heading. This is the series of minor exogenous influences which, except in very unusual cases, continually affect the system. The system, therefore, is never a closed system but remains open (S_2). The minor or long term slow changes can be absorbed into the system without signs of discontinuity but in most areas there occur major changes and hence major exogenous interpolations which are clearly related to specific new urban rôles with specific and new locational demands. This can involve the creation of an unconformable urban net (P_2). There follows a period of rapid adjustment with marked fluctuations in the rank position of towns in the system until, through the revised pattern of regional demand, a modified system (S_3) is produced. Once more this is subject to minor interpolations and will react to technological and organizational change. The present city system, therefore, is properly seen as a momentary 'still' in a moving picture. It is possible to associate these ideas with other attempts to evaluate the rôle of development. Morrill's attempt to simulate the pattern of urban development in Sweden led to a conclusion not very different (Morrill, 1966):

> the simulation process reproduced well the fact that early locational decisions have strong and lasting effects on later locations. The extent to which the original towns, both in reality and in the model, restricted and channeled the ultimate development of the current distribution was striking. . . . The present distribution can be seen as growth of the old distribution into new conditions.

Madden's work on the growth of the US cities leads in a similar direction (Madden, 1956):

> we can see how the different growth rate of the cities may be interpreted as depicting the degree of success with which they each compete for influence or proportion of total economic activity.

There are other theoretical formulations which can be linked with the scheme outlined. The whole process of town founding can be conceived as an innovation and the subsequent development as a diffusion process. Hägerstrand's three stages in the process (Hägerstrand, 1952) are very similar to the stages of 'town genesis', 'transition and sorting' and 'climax' that Carter has outlined for the Welsh system (Carter, 1969), and indicated in a generalized form on Figure 5.4. Each major phase has many analogies with the way in which the available space and economic potential are eventually taken into the urban service network and the way in which this network increases in density. Again the patterns of urban-industrial growth in a cumulative fashion set out by Pred (Pred, 1966) can be associated with the way in which the initial creations of a genetic phase can effectively remain the major foci by the positive influence of self-sustaining growth rather than by the sole operation of external circulation. Lampard (Lampard, 1968) in considering urban systems introduces the two notions of morphostasis and morphogenesis. Morphostasis represents the result of 'deviation-counteracting feedback networks' or 'a most probable state under constraint'. Morphogenesis is a deviation-amplifying process, giving an open-ended development with no evident tendency to entropy. Lampard quotes Maruyama (Maruyama, 1963) as concluding that every system, including city systems, is made up of sub-systems variously manifesting deviation-correcting or amplifying processes whose prevalent effect will either tend to return the whole to morphostatis or transform it by morphogenesis. To some extent, the genetic phase or the major exogenous interpolations envisaged in Figure 5.4, represent transformation by morphogenesis; the emerging city systems within phases of transition represent morphostasis. Generalizations which argue for increasing entropy in a city system— that is the movement of the system to a more ordered and less random form—are only acceptable for certain selected phases or periods; no universal process can be isolated (Semple and Golledge, 1970).

GROWTH, STRUCTURE AND DISTORTION

In the earlier parts of this essay, where central place theory was under discussion, it was expedient to ignore the distorting features brought about by resource location and agglomeration tendencies. In the course of the review it has become clear that on the closely associated grounds of substantial areal variations in population densities and distribution patterns and of the characteristics of town growth, some attempt has to be made to reconcile these disparate approaches.

At this point, therefore, it is necessary to reinforce the notion of the influence of specialized functions on urban growth and to demonstrate them as something more than a mere distortion of a basic regularity. Perhaps the simplest model of these influences has been put forward by Pred (Pred, 1966), although his work owes something to the earlier schemes of 'cumulative causation' put forward by Myrdal (Myrdal, 1956) in his studies of economic growth on a regional basis. Pred concerns himself more directly with the growth of American cities between 1860 and 1910 and proposes a model of 'the circular and cumulative process of industrialization and urban-size growth'. If the introduction of factory industries into a mercantile city is envisaged, then the chains of reaction illustrated in Figure 5.5 are initiated. 'New manufacturing functions, whether or not they primarily serve local markets, will have an initial multiplier effect' (Pred, 1966); that is, new services will be demanded, while linked industries will be encouraged. The result will be 'an alteration of the city's occupational structure (with a more even balance struck between the industrial sector and the wholesaling-trading complex), an increase in population, or growth in urban size, and the probable attainment of one or more new local or regional industrial thresholds'. This attainment of new thresholds will, in turn, support new manufacturing functions and encourage invention and innovation, and so the whole circular and cumulative process continues, until interrupted or impeded by diseconomies or by competition from other growing centres. To some extent, Pred's work is a more sophisticated interpretation of the old elementary notion of 'geographical inertia', for which he provides a convincing rationale. Nor has Pred been alone in attempting to suggest generalizations of this sort. Smolensky and Ratajczak have proposed a sequence of three stages which they call 'elemental settlement', 'conforming city' and 'urban agglomerate'. The 'elemental settlement . . . originates because of economies of specialization in performing what would otherwise be ubiquitous economic activities'. This explanation is directly in line with central place theories. Such a settlement 'becomes a "conforming city" when a factor specific to that site, giving an absolute cost advantage to entrepreneurs locating in that town, becomes economically relevant to profit-maximizing entrepreneurs' (Smolensky and Ratajczak, 1965). This implies the sort of transformation suggested by Pred which initiates cumulative growth. Thompson has also proposed what he calls 'stages of urban growth' beginning with the 'stage of export specialization', where the local economy is dominated by a single industry or even a single firm (Thompson, 1965). Presumably one could envisage this as equivalent to the town in former times, when it was dominantly a defensive, military strongpoint. This is followed by a

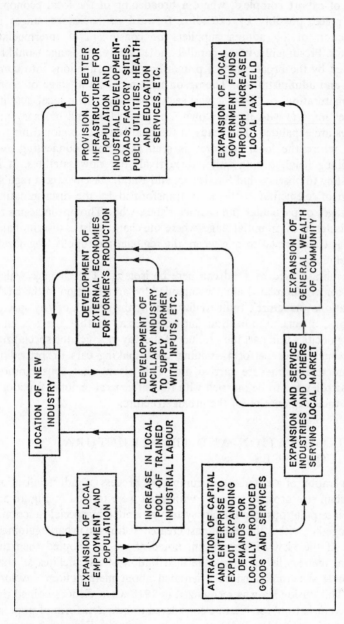

FIGURE 5.5 The process of cumulative causation at the root of agglomeration trends

'stage of export complex', where a broadening of the local economy takes place, possibly by extending forward or backward stages in production or by adding suppliers or consumers of intermediate products. Presumably, in the parallel quoted above, this stage would be achieved by the broadening of primarily military functions into commerce and administration. Thompson next proposes a 'stage of economic maturation' or 'local service sector puberty' where local activity replaces imports with its new 'own use' production and business and services are expanded. This leads to the final 'stage of regional metropolis', where the local economy is seen as a node connecting and controlling neighbouring cities, once rivals but now satellites. It is interesting to observe that Smolensky and Ratajczak envisage a regular pattern of 'elemental' settlements transformed by the discriminating advantages of particular site characteristics, while Thompson seems to think in terms of an initial stage, where site characteristics discriminate, which is transformed to one where the regional metropolis 'organizes' its satellites.

One phrase used by Pred can here be isolated. The changes which have been contemplated are accompanied by 'an alteration in the city's occupational structure'. Industrialization, or the growth of any special functions, affects urbanization and vice versa, so that the size and spacing of cities is in part the product of the way in which the specialized tasks which cities perform—mining coal, making cars or providing rest and relaxation—are carried out. This means that consideration of these rôles has to be married with that of general regional functions in any total explanation of the urban structure.

AGGLOMERATION AND ITS STRUCTURAL CONSEQUENCES

The operation of a circular and cumulative process of industrialization and urban size growth, together with what were termed in Figure 5.3 major interpolations into the city system generated by special functions, have together within the recent past created distinctive urban agglomerations. If the view of Thompson, noted above, is adopted then the regional metropolis organizes the distribution of its satellites so that the whole structure must be orientated about metropolitan development. This basic idea was recognized in 1915 when Geddes coined the word 'conurbation' for what he considered to be a new form of population grouping (Geddes, 1915). In the inter-war years Fawcett developed the concept of the 'conurbation' and provided the first definition: 'A conurbation is an area occupied by a continuous series of dwellings, factories and other buildings, harbour and docks, urban parks and playing fields, etc., which are not separated from each other by rural land' (Fawcett, 1932). Whereas this implicitly included the basic idea of urban areas growing into each other, it was meaningless as a definition unless given a minimum value for geographical extent or population. It was in general also considered to put too great an emphasis on bricks and mortar rather than on economic and social structure and so when the 1951 census *Report on Greater London and Five other Conurbations* was published the definition used was much broader (General Register Office, 1956). Even so no precise formula was presented and the six major conurbations were arbitrarily identified and arbitrarily defined. These were Greater London, Greater Manchester, which was renamed South East Lancashire, Greater Birmingham, renamed The West Midlands, Tyneside, West Yorkshire and Glasgow. The criteria that were employed were stated to be: that the conurbation should consist of an aggregation of local authorities; that it should be a continuously built-up area though allowing for rural enclaves and excluding ribbon extensions; that it should take in those areas which were tied to the core by movements to work, shopping, higher education, sport and entertainment; that population density should be considered.

The lack of any clear notion of what constituted a 'conurbation' was clearly illustrated in the major study of the phenomenon made by Freeman (Freeman, 1959, 1966). Adopting Fawcett's bricks and mortar basis, Freeman added a minimum population of 50,000, so that his book became a descriptive study of the urban pattern of Britain rather than of a distinctive feature in the structuring of settlement. Alongside this may be placed the American Standard Metropolitan Statistical Area (SMSA) although in this case a complex but specific formula is provided for definition (Linge, 1965; Hall, 1971). To a large extent the structure of the conurbation could be treated by the approaches already noted, as for example in Davies' study of central place functions in the Rhondda. But this introduces a further problem in that it is possible to consider these larger-scale elements in the urban hierarchy in a number of different ways. In the first instance they can be viewed as discrete 'cities' in the way in which they were introduced into early rankings. More recent work by Kearsley has attempted to continue this approach (Kearsley, 1971). Two studies were carried out. The first was an assessment of a mass of data relating to high order functions which included retail, financial, social and administrative and professional services and entertainment. The second was a component analysis of thirty

S.H.G.—7*

variables, including such measures as numbers of department stores, chain jewellers, insurance companies and chartered accountants, followed by a linkage study to produce a grading. The two studies produced similar results, an hierarchical array in which the A centres were Birmingham, Manchester, Liverpool, Leeds, Newcastle, Notting-ham, Bristol, Sheffield and Cardiff. The B grade included centres such as Leicester, Southampton and Coventry whilst amongst those at the

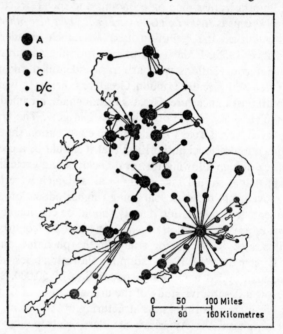

FIGURE 5.6   The upper ranks of the urban hierarchy in England and Wales and the linkages with London and A-ranked centres

C level were Exeter, Sunderland and Cambridge. The full scheme is shown in Figure 5.6. This map shows the B and C centres linked to their regionally associated A level superiors. This outlines the structure of the British city system at a gross level of generality.

It is evident that from Figure 5.6 the accepted notion emerges of a south-east dominated by London and a north and west with a poly-nuclear structure dependent upon the large-scale urban creations of industrialism. The word 'dominated' recalls the notions of Thompson already introduced, where a regional metropolis organizes its satellites. Again this concept can be approached in a number of different ways.

In the first instance, as in the Rhondda study, the city region can be considered as made up of a number of subsidiary business districts of different ranks, a view which is developed by Davies in Chapter 4. It can also be viewed as made up of an internal land-use pattern, based on a structuring into social areas, as treated by Robson in Chapter 6. Yet again it can be viewed in the context of distance decay characteristics. These have generally been associated with population densities and several studies have considered the relationship between distance from the city centre and urban population densities (Clark, 1951, 1958; Berry, Simmons and Tennant, 1963; Newling, 1966; Gurevich and Saushkin, 1966; Cassetti, 1971). In terms of the general patterns of land-use and organization of space, however, the earlier work was by Bogue, who attempted to characterize the structural pattern within the 'metropolitan community' (Bogue, 1950). Figure 5.7 is one of his charts which indicates the decline in specialization with distance from the metropolitan centre. Retail trades show only a very gentle decline due to their intimate association with population, whereas the more centrally orientated services and, above all, wholesaling show rapid declines with distance. Manufacturing differs in that it seems essentially metropolitan but not characteristic of the central city itself. Thus the metropolitan community is seen as engendering its own organization, both of settlements and land-uses, within the context of the larger scale national structuring at a grosser level.

But even this scale is being replaced as the palaeotechnic phase is succeeded by the neotechnic and strong forces working for population dispersal mean that not only central cities but also the conurbations lose population. These new processes are best considered in relation to the concept of Megalopolis, a term which was coined by Gottmann for his study of the northeastern seaboard of the USA (Gottmann, 1961). An extended quotation will clarify his ideas (Gottmann, 1961, 776–7).

The larger metropolitan areas are attracting the larger part of population growth. Cities are expanding one toward the other. The nebulous structure of urbanized regions is becoming frequent and hints at a new redistribution of functions within such regions. Residential land use is gaining in all directions around the congested older nuclei. The more densely agglomerated nuclei no longer specialize in manufacturing and administration as they used to. Production industries often move out to the periphery of the city and beyond into spaces that were until recently considered rural or interurban. The functions that continue to gather in what may be called central districts or hubs of the urban nebulae are offices, laboratories, and all the activities related to the various forms of entertainment. As in Roman

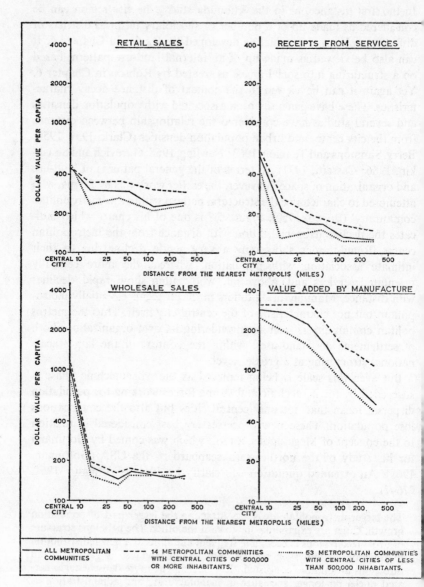

FIGURE 5.7 Indexes of specialization by distance from the nearest metropolis

times, the arena and the forum, in their modern versions, occupy an increasing share of the hubs. Entertainment and offices are related one to another, thriving on proximity. They create a large market for white-collar labor. All these trends started at an earlier time and they have already developed on a great scale in Megalopolis. The forces bringing about this evolution are rooted in a deep transformation of modern modes of life and habitat.

Hall in his study of *The World Cities* has extended this kind of treatment to seven World Cities created under the three forces of population growth, a shift of populations from country to town and a progressive concentration of urban growth in the largest cities (Hall, 1966). From Hall's work three trends can be separated which can transform the settlement patterns so far examined. These are, first, attempts at dispersal by the establishment of new towns and centres for overspill, second the progressive expansion of the city margins in a rural-urban fringe and third, and in consequence, a new distribution of functions.

There is no space within the limited context of this essay to review the development of overspill schemes and new towns. The critical issue is that in the context of increasing suburban extension they represent attempts to coagulate population about well defined centres endowed with appropriate bundles of functions. Although, therefore, they are interpolations into the system of cities and as difficult to reconcile with central place theory as the creations of industry, they operate within the context of creating set thresholds and provide no necessity for any departure from the conventional analyses described in this essay. But the growth at the margins of the metropoles and the development of extensive areas of so-called rural-urban fringe introduces more difficult problems. Pahl has argued that the characteristics of such fringe areas can be summed under four headings (Pahl, 1965). The first two, segregation and selective immigration, are not vital here but the second two are. The first of these is commuting and this stresses the extreme mobility of these populations, able to move about the metropolis with ever increasing ease. Finally, the last characteristic is the collapse of geographical and social hierarchies for the residential groups of population. Mobility means that people can turn towards other parts of the city for certain services. The result is that the service content of the fringe becomes modified and indeed it is possible that the conventional *trait complexes*, the bundles of functions, can become separated and arranged in a different fashion. To some extent this sort of organization has been outlined in the context of 'the dispersed city'

(Stafford, 1962; Burton, 1963), where in an area dominated by several closely adjacent centres the various functions, instead of being horizontally sorted and hierarchically distributed in all of the centres, are distributed between them; that is, the functions are located by kind of centre rather than by hierarchical rank. It is possible that as the urban complex both grows and becomes denser this sort of arrangement, dependent above all else on the mobility of the population, will become characteristic. An extreme view has been presented by Foley (1966, 11):

> Urban regions, as they are emerging, are neither separate nor clearly definable, for they, in turn, are interlocked in an even larger urban system of amazing complexity. In the United States, at least, it no longer makes sense to try to ascertain exactly how many urban regions we have or exactly what hierarchial position each region's centre holds with respect to the larger system. . . . With the revolutionary strides in communication and transportation, with industrialisation trends sweeping all activities including agriculture, with the pervasive impact of mass education and mass culture, we are becoming an urban society and our citizens are no longer simply members of this or that local community. Mobility, fluidity, interconnectedness and interpenetration, pluralistic organisational arrangements defying local or regional limits, non-stop automobility via smoothly engineered freeways [motorways], long-distance commuting (including intermetropolitan commuting by air), toll-free telephone rate structures, long-distance and frequent week ending, periodic retreats to one's second domicile—these and many other characteristics are coming to supplant traditional characterisations of community life.

Such a sketch is essentially one of Megalopolis where the old hierarchical structure, which was a product of limited movement, has broken down. Webber has also stressed the same type of idea,

> To date, very few observers have gone so far as to predict that the nodally concentric form, that has marked every spatial city throughout history, could give way to nearly homogeneous dispersion of the nation's population across the continent; but the hesitancy may stem mainly from the fact that a non-nodal city of this sort would represent such a huge break with the past. Yet, . . . never has intimacy been so independent of spatial propinquity. Never before has it seemed possible to build an array of specialized transportation equipment that would permit speed of travel to increase directly with mileage length of trip, thus having the capability of uniting all places within a continent with almost-equal time distance. And never before has it seemed economically feasible for the nodally cohesive spatial form that marks the contemporary large settlement to be replaced by drastically different forms, while the pattern of internal centering itself changes or, perhaps, dissolves. (Webber, 1963, 43.)

In a similar way Hall at the conclusion of his study of World Cities looks 'Towards a new metropolitan structure' and considers that present polycentric metropolitan regions, such as Randstad, Holland, have advantages over the single-centred giant cities.

> They achieve success by concentrating specialised types of activity, or systems of urban linkage, into partly specialised centres. In a different way it is claimed that Los Angeles and other cities of the western United States achieve equal success by pure dispersion of activities and by a transportation system which makes for equal accessibility over the whole of the metropolitan area. (Hall, 1966, 242.)

It is apparent that there are two notions which Hall clarifies, the one to which Foley and Webber look with a maximum dispersion and the one which Hall notes which represents a polycentric situation marked by specialization, a development of the dispersed city. Either way, the conventional hierarchical situation would be greatly changed.

To some extent this discussion has moved into a consideration of trends and of the future but even so these must be the prevalent concerns in the consideration of those settlement structures which characterize the large urban regions.

CONCLUSION

At the outset of this essay it was demonstrated that the size relations between settlements have been a core interest of human geographers and indeed of social scientists long before the emergence of modern human geography. In this interest, Central Place Theory has been predominant, partly as an explicand of observed settlement structuring, partly as the leader in the growth of theory and model building in geography. As a result, all considerations of scaling in the urban system have grown about central place ideas as the central theme. Other postulates have been of a more empirical character and have always been immediately reconcilable. Thus the early principle of Jefferson outlined as the Law of the Primate City suggested a situation where one outstanding city dominates an undifferentiated array of smaller cities (Jefferson, 1939). To a limited extent only has this been identified as a possible primitive situation before the economic competition associated with a developed region generates differentiation and initiates a sorting out process from which a hierarchical structure emerges (Berry, 1961; Linsky, 1965). This sorting process, in representing an interaction of those forces favouring dispersal and those favouring concentration, was seen as producing a rank-size situation. But here, too, a reconciliation with hierarchical structuring has been developed.

The main factor which has undermined central place influences has been the distortions introduced by unequal resource locations, the growth of industry and the influence of other specialized activities, such as resort functions. But even given such distortions it can be held that the twin controls of threshold population required and the maximum range which can be tolerated will operate within the given population distribution, however uneven, to segregate centres into distinctive ranks and produce a clear structuring. But it has been emphasized that such structuring applies only within a clearly defined system of cities.

> In analysing central places to determine whether they are hierarchically structured, the identification of a central place system is only the first step. It is a vital step, because it ensures that subsequent stages of the analysis deal with an array of centres known to form a meaningful functional whole. (Marshall, 1969, 79.) ,

If this condition is relaxed, then the 'mixing' that ensues will cloud any clear appreciation of a central place ranking, and

> the concept of a hierarchy of urban places functions as an exceedingly useful, though somewhat arbitrary, analytical tool. In this respect the use of a system of types, or classes, or levels, of urban places is not unlike the regional concept as promulgated by geographers. . . . Neither the regions nor the urban classes do, in fact, exist in other than arbitrary form. . . . Even the use of impersonal statistical mechanisms does not divorce the resultant classification, or areal differentiation, from the initial assumptions of the statistical manipulator. (Snyder, 1962, 29–30.)

The real problem is that most geographers wish to identify structuring on a large-scale regional or national basis where those associations which have been called conurbations or metropolitan areas dominate and organize. Even so, and if only at a classificatory level, the concept of ranking provides real insight into the structuring of these agglomerations. Figure 5.4 attempts to epitomize the various influences on the growth of the city system, but the diagram operates only within certain scale limitations. For what are termed exogenous interpolations, or the growth of the massive conurbations initially based on point resources, have in part taken over as the organizers of population and of urban location. The total national pattern in Britain, for example, can be seen as the product of both a long historical evolution and of more recent agglomeration tendencies, but with central place restraints exerting a consistent and discriminating influence. To some extent this reverses the notion of a basic central place system distorted by a variety of other factors. Even so, the whole system is the product of limited mobility, or the friction of space. The more mobile becomes the population the fewer the constraints exercised by the existing system of settlements. Many studies of consumer behaviour reflect this growing footloose characteristic. It is, therefore, possible to consider that the system, as it has operated, is being transformed. With absolute mobility it would be absolutely changed.

REFERENCES

Abiodun, J. C. (1967) 'The urban hierarchy in a developing country', *Economic Geography*, **43**, 347–367.

Beckmann, M. J. (1958) 'City hierarchies and the distribution of city size', *Economic Development and Cultural Change*, **6**, 243–248.

Berry, B. J. L. (1961) 'City size distribution and economic development', *Economic Development and Cultural Change*, **9**, 573–588.

Berry, B. J. L. and Garrison, W. L. (1958a) 'Alternate explanations of the urban rank-size relationships', *Annals of the Association of American Geographers*, **48**, 83–91.

Berry, B. J. L. and Garrison, W. L. (1958b) 'The functional bases of the central place hierarchy', *Economic Geography*, **34**, 145–154.

Berry, B. J. L. and Garrison, W. L. (1958c) 'A note on central place theory and the range of a good', *Economic Geography*, **34**, 304–311.

Berry, B. J. L., Simmons, J. W. and Tennant, R. J. (1963) 'Urban population densities: structure and change', *Geographical Review*, **53**, 389–405.

Bertalanffy, L. von (1950) 'An outline of general systems theory', *British Journal of the Philosophy of Science*, **1**, 134–165.

Bogue, D. J. (1950) *The Structure of the Metropolitan Community*, University of Michigan.

Brush, J. E. and Bracey, H. E. (1955) 'Rural service centres in southwestern Wisconsin and southern England', *Geographical Review*, **45**, 559–569.

Burton, I. (1963) 'A restatement of the dispersed city hypothesis', *Annals of the Association of American Geographers*, **53**, 285–289.

Carol, H. (1960) 'The hierarchy of central functions within the city', *Annals of the Association of American Geographers*, **50**, 419–438.

Carruthers, I. (1957) 'A classification of service centres in England and Wales', *Geographical Journal*, **123**, 371–385.

Carter, H. (1955) 'Urban grades and spheres of influence in south west Wales', *Scottish Geographical Magazine*, **71**, 43–58.

Carter, H. (1969) *The Growth of the Welsh City System*, University of Wales Press.

Cassetti, E. (1971) 'Alternate urban population density models: an analytical comparison of their validity range', in A. G. Wilson (Ed.), *Urban and Regional Planning*, Pion.

Chisholm, M. (1967) 'General systems theory and geography', *Transactions of the Institute of British Geographers*, **42**, 45–52.

Christaller, W. (1966) *The Central Places of Southern Germany*. Translated by W. Baskin, Prentice-Hall.

Clark, C. (1951) 'Urban population densities', *Journal of the Royal Statistical Society*, Ser. A, **114**, 490–496.

Clark, C. (1958) 'Urban population densities', *Bulletin de l'Institute Internationale de Statistique*, **36**, 60–68.

Davis, K. *et al.* (1959) *The World's Metropolitan Areas*, International Urban Research, University of California Press.

Davies, W. K. D. (1964) *The Hierarchy of Commercial Centres; a case study in South Wales*, unpublished Ph.D. thesis, University of Wales.

Davies, W. K. D. (1966) 'The ranking of service centres: a critical review', *Transactions of the Institute of British Geographers*, **40**, 51–65.

Davies, W. K. D. (1967) 'Centrality and the central place hierarchy', *Urban Studies*, **4**, 61–79.

Dawson, J. (1969) 'Some early theories of settlement location and size', *Journal of the Royal Town Planning Institute*, **55**, 444–448.

Dickinson, R. E. (1932) 'The distribution of functions of the smaller urban settlements of East Anglia', *Geography*, **17**, 19–31.

Everson, J. A. and Fitzgerald, B. P. (1969) *Settlement Patterns*, Longmans.

Fawcett, C. B. (1932) 'The distribution of the urban population in Great Britain', *Geographical Journal*, **129**, 100–116.

Foley, D. (1966) 'The structure', in D. Senior (Ed.), *The Regional City*, Longmans.

Freeman, T. W. (1959, 2nd edition 1966) *The Conurbations of Great Britain*, Manchester University Press.

Geddes, P. (1915) *Cities in Evolution*. New and revised edition, Williams and Northgate, 1949.

General Register Office (1956) *Report on Greater London and Five Other Conurbations*, HMSO.

Gottmann, J. (1961) *Megalopolis: the urbanized seaboard of the United States*, M.I.T. Press.

Gradmann, N. R. (1916) 'Schwäbische Städte', *Zeitschrift der Gesellschaft für Erdkunde zu Berlin*, 427–460.

Green, F. H. W. (1950) 'Urban hinterlands in England and Wales: an analysis of bus services', *Geographical Journal*, **116**, 65–88.

Gurevich, B. L, and Saushkin, Y. G. (1966) 'The mathematical method in geography', *Soviet Geography: reviews and translations*, **7**, 3–34.

Hägerstrand, T. (1952) 'The Propagation of Innovation Waves', *Lund Studies in Geography*, Ser. B, *Human Geography*, **4**.

Haggett, P. (1965) *Locational Analysis in Human Geography*, Arnold.

Hall, A. D. and Fagen, R. E. (1956) 'Definition of a system', *General Systems Yearbook*, **1**.

Hall, P. (1966) *The World Cities*, Weidenfeld and Nicolson.

Hall, P. (1971) 'Spatial structure of metropolitan England and Wales', in M. Chisholm and G. Manners (Eds.), *Spatial Policy Problems of the British Economy*, Cambridge University Press, 96–125.

Jefferson, M. (1939) 'The law of the primate city', *Geographical Review*, **29**, 226–232.

Kearsley, G. W. (1971) *The Upper Ranks of the Urban Hierarchy in England and Wales*, unpublished Ph.D., University of London.

Kolb, J. H. (1925) *Service Institutions for Town and Country*, Agricultural Experimental Station, University of Wisconsin, Research Bulletin 66.

Lampard, E. E. (1965) 'Historical aspects of urbanization', in P. M. Hauser and L. F. Schnore, *The Study of Urbanization*, John Wiley.

Lampard, E. E. (1968) 'The evolving system of cities in the United States', in H. S. Perloff and L. Wingo (Eds.), *Issues in Urban Economics*, Johns Hopkins Press.

Linge, G. J. R. (1965) *The Delimitation of Urban Boundaries*, Australian National University Department of Geography, Publication G/2.

Linsky, A. S. (1965) 'Some generalizations concerning primate cities', *Annals of the Association of American Geographers*, **55**, 506–513.

Madden, C. H. (1956) 'Some spatial aspects of urban growth in the United States', *Economic Development and Cultural Change*, **4**, 371–387.

Marshall, J. U. (1969) *The Location of Service Towns*, University of Toronto Press.

Maruyama, M. (1963) 'The second cybernetics: deviation amplifying mutual causal processes', *General Systems Yearbook*, **8**, 233–241.

Morrill, R. L. (1966) *Migration and the Spread and Growth of Urban Settlement*, Lund Studies in Geography, Ser. B, Human Geography, No. 26, Lund.

Myrdal, G. M. (1957) *Economic Theory and under-Developed Regions*, Duckworth.

Newling, B. E. (1966) 'Urban growth and spatial structure: mathematical models and empirical evidence', *Geographical Review*, **56**, 213–225.

Pahl, R. E. (1965) *Urbs in Rure. The Metropolitan Fringe in Hertfordshire*, London School of Economics, Geographical Papers, No. 2.

Philbrick, A. K. (1957) 'Principles of areal functional organization in regional human geography', *Economic Geography*, **33**, 299–336.

Pred, A. R. (1966) *The Spatial Dynamics of U.S. Urban Industrial Growth 1900–1914: interpretive and theoretical essays*, M.I.T. Press.

Reissman, L. (1964) *The Urban Process*, Collier-Macmillan.

Reynolds, J. M. (1966) 'Legal and constitutional problems', in J. S. Wacher (Ed.), *The Civitas Capitals of Roman Britain*, University of Leicester Press.

Rosing, K. (1966) 'A rejection of the Zipf model (rank-size rule) in relation to city size', *Professional Geographer*, **18**, 75–82.

Semple, R. K. and Golledge, R. G. (1970) 'An analysis of entropy changes in a settlement pattern over time', *Economic Geography*, **46**, 157–160.

Schnore, L. F. (1962) 'Metropolitan development in the United Kingdom', *Economic Geography*, **38**, 215–233.

Sjoberg, H. (1960) *The Preindustrial City*, Collier-Macmillan.

Smailes, A. E. (1944) 'The urban hierarchy in England and Wales', *Geography*, **29**, 41–51.

Smith, R. D. P. (1968) 'The changing urban hierarchy', *Regional Studies*, **2**, 1–19.

Smith, R. D. P. (1970) 'The changing urban hierarchy in Wales', *Regional Studies*, **4**, 85–96.

Smolensky, E. and Ratajczak, P. (1965) 'The conception of cities', *Explorations in Entreprenurial History*, Second Series, **2**, 90–131.

Snyder, D. E. (1962) 'Urban places in Uruguay, and the concept of a hierarchy', in H. C. Prunty (Ed.), *Festschrift: Clarence F. Jones*, Northwestern Studies in Geography, No. 6.

Stafford, H. A. Jnr. (1962) 'The dispersed city', *Professional Geographer*, **14**, 8–10.

Thompson, W. R. (1965) *A Preface to Urban Economics*, Johns Hopkins Press.

Webber, M. M. (1963) 'Order in diversity: community without propinquity', in L. Wingo (Ed.), *Cities and Space. The future use of urban land*, Johns Hopkins Press.

Zipf, G. K. (1949) *Human Behavior and the Principles of Least Effort*, Addison-Wesley.

6 A view on the urban scene

BRIAN ROBSON

Like the jungle, with which it has so often been compared, the city offers many and varied species for the academic explorer. Since almost any discipline in the social sciences can be prefixed by the term 'urban', economists, geographers, historians, lawyers, political scientists and sociologists have each contributed to urban studies. The realm of urban studies is, however, distinctly multi-disciplinary rather than inter-disciplinary since the contributing disciplines have continued to be characterized by rather different modes of explanation: the function-alist paradigm of some sociologists for instance, contrasts with the environmentalist paradigm of some ecologists and the two lead to very different interpretations of such urban phenomena as crime or poverty. Likewise, and only to some extent springing from these different perspectives, the various disciplines have looked at very different objects within the city: at houses, street plans, social groups, sub-areas, individual households, organizations. The city may have acted as a backcloth, but the dramas have often been radically dissimilar since the variety of viewpoints, while doing some justice to the complexity of the subject, has so far proved irreconcilable.

Geographers have tended to adopt a rather eclectic rôle amongst this varied flora and fauna; collecting bits from urban history, from urban economics, from urban sociology and from planning. Their over-riding concern, however, has been with form and with pattern. An early and continuing focus has been on urban morphology and on the patterns of overall land use, but a more recent and rapidly growing interest has focussed on social rather than physical phenomena by turning to the study of urban social structure. To this now-burgeoning literature is given the name 'urban ecology'. Unlike the functionalist in sociology, the urban ecologist has defined social structure in terms of the socio-economic attributes of residential sub-areas; arguing, more implicitly than explicitly, that any structural or spatial regularities which emerge are reflections of the way in which social relationships and social and economic value systems are played out in space. The questions which urban ecologists have therefore posed are basically these: are there discernible dimensions which underlie the complexity of residential differentation; are there spatial patterns in the distribution of the variables or dimensions which measure this differentiation; and do the social dimensions and the spatial areas in any way map into one another? The number of possible measures of this differentiation of residential areas is obviously enormous and hence these questions have progressively been tackled by examining more and more variables as the necessary computational hardware and software have grown more sophisticated. Concern has therefore moved from the uni-dimensional notions of the early ecologists to the more recent multi-dimensional ecological studies which have used factor analysis to isolate the dimensions of social structure.

Given its initially strong dependence on analogy, it would not seem inappropriate to review the work in urban ecology within the framework of a monumental tree: a tree with its roots in the classical ecology of the Chicago School of the 1920s and the Social Area Analysis of the west coast of America; its trunk in the proliferating factorial ecologies of city structure; its sustaining sap in the evolving models of residential household mobility which give life to the system; and its branches in the use of an ecological methodology in studying the distribution of types of social pathologies. Whether the tree be a fully-grown American redwood, an English oak or merely an ornamental monkey puzzle, it is undeniably large and undoubtedly still growing, and to its growth geographers and sociologists have contributed in roughly equal proportions.

THE ROOTS: EARLY ECOLOGIES

The best collection of the work of the classical Chicago ecologists is still that by Theodorson (1961), but there are also useful accounts by Burgess and Bogue (1964), Hatt and Reiss (1957) and Faris (1970). Critiques are provided by Beshers (1962) and Reissman (1964), and, from a geographical view, by Robson (1969). To geographers, the particular fascination of their work lies in its spatial bias. Park's derivation of a theory of urban social structure, which distinguished a biotic level of human activity based on competition from a cultural level based on consensus, relied heavily on the notion of territoriality and so it translated readily into the spatial model of urban growth which Burgess suggested in 1924. While derived from a theory of social change, the Burgess model of the city is essentially static. He saw the

city as being divided into a series of concentric zones with increasing
social status and declining social disorganization as one moved into
rings further from the city centre; thus emphasizing the same components of distance and density as did von Thünen's land-use theory
which has played so large a part in geographical work. Early criticism
of this ecological analogue focussed both on its theoretical (Alihan,
1938; Firey, 1947) and empirical aspects and it was the latter which gave
rise to a second urban model, the sectoral model of the land economist
Hoyt (1939), which emphasizes a directional component in the patterning of differentiated areas within a city through the channelling of
different rental areas outward along existing lines of travel. A third
pattern, proposed by the geographers Harris and Ullman (1945),
suggested a grouped or neighbourhood pattern with different types of
land use clustering in discrete nodes to form multiple nuclei.

To the classical ecologists, physical space was synonymous with
social space: the friction of distance reinforced the symbiotic processes
of competitive-co-operation and so produced 'natural areas' within
the city. Their analysis of social structure was therefore set within the
context of an 'organic solidarity' in which social patterning was determined by primary social relationships within inclusive locality-based
social groups. 'Human ecology, as sociologists view it, seeks to
emphasize not so much geography as space. In society we not only live
together, but at the same time we live apart, and human relations can
always be recognized, with more or less accuracy, in terms of distance.
Insofar as social structure can be defined in terms of position, social
change can be defined in terms of movement' (Park, 1926). This
emphasis on primary, space-dominated relationships derived essentially
from Park's romantic attachment to the pre-industrial community. His
distaste for what he saw as the weakening effect which urbanization
had on community ties was a potent stimulus to his emphasis on pathological aspects of urban life.

By contrast, as Orleans (1966) suggests, the Social Area analysts
(Shevky and Williams, 1949; Shevky and Bell, 1955) who introduced an
alternative view of urban structure, concentrated not on spatial
contiguity, but on the 'mechanical solidarity' of the community of
interest. Their 'social areas' were defined, not in physical space, but in
social space and can be seen simply as groupings of people with similar
structural sets of social and economic characteristics. This distinction
between physical and social space rapidly attracted criticism (Duncan,
O. D. and Duncan, B., 1955), since, of the Social Area analysts, only
Greer (1962) formally considers physical space. Unlike Park, Shevky

and Bell stressed the organized rather than the unorganized aspects of urban society and emphasized, either implicitly or explicitly (as in Bell and Force, 1956; or Greer, 1956), the secondary exclusive membership groups which laid the basis for non-territorial organization. It is not surprising that classical ecology grew out of the dense industrial streets of early twentieth-century Chicago, whereas Social Area Analysis was spawned from the low-density far-flung mass of post-industrial San Francisco and Los Angeles.

The aim of Social Area analysts was to isolate basic underlying dimensions by which one could find order in the differentiation of residential sub-areas. Their suggestion was that three dimensions, each conceptually and measurably separate from one another, could 'explain' the complexity of urban society. These three dimensions were the product of the increasing 'scale' which characterized the total society of which the cities were an integral part. Social rank (or, as Bell termed it, economic status) derived from changes in the occupational mix of an industrial society and measured by occupation, income and education. Urbanization (or family status) derived from the changing economic activities of society. It reflected the varying strength of the family as a social and economic unit and was measured by fertility, women in the labour force and single family dwellings. Segregation (or ethnic status) derived from the changing composition of a population through increasing mobility and was measured by the degree of segregation of racial or national groups.

While subject to continuing controversy about the derivation of the three dimensions, Social Area Analysis has been widely applied to cities in America and, to a lesser extent, to cities in other parts of the world. Timms (1970) provides a useful and careful review of many of the recent applications, but with few exceptions (Herbert, 1967), geographers have largely bypassed the technique in favour of the more objective and pragmatic use of multivariate analysis.

THE TRUNK: FACTORIAL ECOLOGIES

Structural dimensions

It was from these roots that current factorial ecologies stem. The widespread use of factor analysis since the early 1960s has enabled the handling of very large numbers of variables, by reducing them, through linear combinations, to a smaller number of independent or orthogonal axes or dimensions which statistically explain a large proportion of the initial variance of the input data. A comprehensive discussion of the application of factor analysis to urban ecology is given by Janson (1969).

It might appear that factor analysis, ideally suited in many ways to tackle the problems of urban ecology, should have solved many of the questions posed by Social Area Analysis by providing clear indications of whether or not there are universal dimensions of urban social structure and, if there are, how these are distributed in space. The fact that the use of the technique seems not to have resolved such questions may be related both to the problems of making comparisons between cities and to certain technical and operational uncertainties of the method itself. Leaving aside the lively debate on the appropriateness of factor analysis as either a theory testing or a classificatory device (see for example, Eysenck, 1952; Ehrenberg, 1962; Armstrong, 1967; King, 1969; Davies, W. K. D., 1971), the problems of comparison are twofold: the difficulty of deriving comparable sets of variables; and the lack of precision with which factor axes have been interpreted.

The variety of data available for intra-urban sub-areas varies widely from one country to another (Dogan and Rokkan, 1969; Robson, 1969) as well as from one date to another in a single country. Income data are available in the United States, but not in Britain; data on ethnic groups or on mobility are available in some countries, but not in others. As a consequence, the basic input data used in factorial ecologies have inevitably differed substantially between countries and the pleas for more truly cross-cultural ecological studies (Sirjamaki, 1964; Sjoberg, 1959) have thus been somewhat frustrated. But there has also been little standardization of input variables even within single countries and, given the dependence of factor output on data input, the composition and ordering of axes is difficult to compare as between independent studies. Paradoxically, in one case where an attempt was made to use a list of standard variables suggested by the Centre for Urban Studies (Herbert, 1970; Norman, 1969) it was found that many of the variables which had been derived for London were highly inappropriate in the two towns of Swansea and Cardiff to which they were applied.

There have also been technical problems associated with comparison of factors. Different operational techniques have tended to distinguish American from British studies: American workers incline to use factor analysis (with communality estimates in the diagonal and a mathematical basis to the method), usually allied with some form of rotation of the axes; while in Britain component analysis has been more usual (with diagonal entries of unity and a purely statistical theory underlying the method), and axes have not been rotated. As Berry (1971) has suggested, these are but two of a whole family of factorial models. Moreover, there have been many technical problems found with the comparisons themselves. Within a single study, where comparisons are made between factors from more than one town or between factors at different times in a single town, such comparisons are usually made on an essentially qualitative assessment of 'similarity', which sits oddly with the effort expended on the technical elegance of the initial derivation of the factors themselves. Having got the axes ground, there seems little to cut with them. More refined comparative methods have been used, such as coefficients of congruence (Sweetser, 1965a; Murdie, 1969; Pinnaeu and Newhouse, 1964; Veldman, 1967), but such comparisons obviously rely on there being a common set of input variables in the first instance and so are inappropriate for the great bulk of studies. More usually one is left with the vaguest of verbal comparisons and a welter of factors designated by names which are often at once mysterious, pretentious, infelicitous, and occasionally downright dishonest.

However, this is not to decry the interest of the results suggested by factorial ecologies. To date there have been studies made of cities in various parts of the world: in North America, of Chicago (Rees, 1970), Boston (Sweetser, 1965a), Newark (Janson, 1968), New York (Carey et al., 1968), Seattle (Schmid, 1960; Schmid and Tagashira, 1964), Washington, D.C. (Carey et al., 1968), Montreal (Greer-Wootten, 1968), Toronto (Murdie, 1969; Goheen, 1970); in Britain, of Birmingham (Rosing and Wood, 1971), London (Norman, 1969), Merseyside (Gittus, 1964), Sunderland (Robson, 1969), Swansea and Cardiff (Herbert, 1970); in Australia, of Canberra (Jones, F. L., 1965), Melbourne (Jones, F. L., 1969), Brisbane and Adelaide (Timms, 1970); in Europe, of Copenhagen (Pederson, 1967), and Helsinki (Sweetser, 1965a and b); and in the developing world, of Cairo (Abu-Lughod, 1969) and of Calcutta (Berry and Rees, 1969). In very general terms, the results have suggested a good deal of similarity within each of the culture areas concerned, but some notable differences between them.

The North American studies, for example, have tended to emphasize the recurrence, in one form or another, of three general factors: one associated with aspects of socio-economic status; a second with differences in life style, seen particularly in terms of age-structures and the life-cycle; a third associated with ethnic segregation of minority groups. To these three main factors, a fourth might be added, namely 'mobility' or 'urbanism' (Sweetser, 1965b; McElrath, 1968; Timms, 1970) which has been isolated with less frequency and whose composition has been identified with much less certainty, but which has been interpreted as measuring areas of a transient population which is largely unmarried or divorced. Many, such as Berry (1965), have taken these findings to indicate support for the earlier ideas of Social Area Analysis. Of the three main factors, the least clearly independent appears to be the third. Rees (1970), for example, discusses the various possible combinations of the three factors, indicating the conditions necessary for their independence and the types of society in which various of the combinations may be expected to occur. He finds in his own study of Chicago that the ethnic dimension, while not merging with socio-economic status completely, as it may tend to do in southern cities in the United States, does show a strong relationship with variables measuring access to and possession of economic resources, and consequently he names the dimension 'race and resources'. This tends to parallel the earlier studies of Social Area Analysis which suggested that the segregation dimension was the least independent of the three (Bell, 1955).

Australian students have tended to place somewhat similar weight on two of these same three factors—socio-economic status and the life cycle—with much less certainty as regards the ethnic dimension. Timms (1970) in particular suggests not only the close comparability of the factor structures of Brisbane, Adelaide, Melbourne and Canberra, but also the close approximation of the factorial results with the ideas of Social Area Analysis.

British studies have been notably less confident in drawing general conclusions. Gittus, Robson and Herbert all found that persons per room was a variable of recurring importance in the composition of one of their urban dimensions, but their results have not been interpreted in terms of any universal factorial 'principles' even though there is evidence from Sunderland, Birmingham, Swansea and Cardiff that social status, age structure and housing conditions tend to fall into separate dimensions. The study of London suggested the importance there of a transient high status dimension which has not appeared in other British towns, but this is largely a reflection of the importance of this type of life style within a metropolitan context as against the smaller provincial towns elsewhere studied.

From these studies have come, too, some interesting findings regarding the stability of ecological factors. Stability refers to three separate aspects. First is the technical stability or invariance of factors where different sets of variables are used as input data. Schmid and Tagashira (1964), for example, show that matrices based on different sub-sets of variables produce the same three basic dimensions, whether a full set of 42 variables or (by progressively reducing the variables) as few as 10 are used. Sweetser (1965b) finds the same for Helsinki, and these findings have been used by others, such as Rees (1970), to reduce their input data. Second is the question of the invariance of factors where different areal definitions of the towns are used. Here there is much less agreement and it would appear that different boundaries can greatly affect the results which emerge. Sweetser (1969) considers that there are three spatial levels at which different *modes* of ecological differentiation appear: an inner-city or urban level; an urban-suburban or metropolitan level; and a rural-urban or regional level. He suggests that greatest differentiation is found at the urban level, and that it is to the metropolitan level that ecologists should address themselves. Timms (1970) suggests results rather different from this, but certainly it is clear that great care needs to be exercised in delimiting the boundaries of areas which are studied, although it is by no means clear how one effectively defines an appropriate unit (Gibbs, 1961).

The evidence on the effect of the varying size of the sub-areas used for collecting the original observations is even less clear. Not only do the units vary within single study areas, but equally the sizes of enumeration districts, census tracts and collectors' districts—the most common units in Britain, America and Australia respectively—vary widely and, although there are suggestions that broadly similar factors emerge whether one uses individuals or aggregates of individuals (Goheen, 1970) or census tracts as against the much larger community areas and municipalities (Rees, 1970), the size and variability of sizes of observational units is a largely unexplored problem whose potential dangers have been spelled out by Duncan, Cuzzort and Duncan (1961), Gelkhe and Biehl (1934), A. H. Robinson (1956) and Thomas and Anderson (1965).

Substantively, the third aspect of stability—that of stability over time—is of far greater interest since it broaches the whole topic of temporal changes in the dimensions of urban society. A great many of the early factorial studies looked simply at cross-sections at one point in time. This was the case with the British studies, since small-area data only became available in 1961. Some of the American studies, however, have been able to look at the changes in urban ecologies over time, with interesting results.

Two strategies have been adopted: either the comparison of factors from a single place at different times; or alternatively, the use of factor analysis to analyse matrices of the changes in variables between two dates. As examples of the first, Goheen (1970) and Murdie (1969) have provided sets of factors for Toronto for dates as far apart as 1870 and 1961, drawing the overall conclusion that the ecological factors have shown remarkable stability. Goheen's study of the nineteenth century suggests to him that from 1880 onwards the city was essentially 'modern' in that the distribution of groups can be seen in terms of economic status, family status and religious segregation. Obviously limited in the sources of data, however, this conclusion is drawn less from a detailed comparison of factor structures than from the results of multiple regressions studying the various elements by which the town's population was spatially segregated. His factorial dimensions for the successive decades show no very clear consistency over time—and are obviously difficult to compare because of the inevitable change in input data—but nevertheless do show a well-developed age-related dimension throughout the whole period, even though an economic status dimension is often much less unambiguously apparent. Murdie is on much surer ground in making comparisons between 1951 and 1961 and discovers that the two sets of dimensions are remarkably similar: social status and family status appear in both years and together explain approximately half of the total variance; recent growth likewise appears as a dimension at both dates; and Italian and Jewish segregation and a mixture of occupational and household characteristics both appear, each either loading on one or two dimensions. Murdie also illustrates the second strategy by deriving a simple matrix of the changes in each variable over the ten-year period and extracting the dimensions of change which suggest rather weakly a number of factors, such as suburbanization, ethnic and occupational change, change in the levels of 'urbanization' and in residential stability. Brown and Horton (1970a) have produced a rather similar analysis for Chicago. As a method, however, the approach suffers markedly from its dependence on the initial characteristics of the set of areas.

While one could not claim that these studies, using either strategy, have revealed the nature of longitudinal change in factorial ecologies, they do at least hint that, over short periods of time, and where sufficient data are available, factors which are broadly comparable would appear to emerge. 'Change, at least as inferred in the cross-sectional analyses, indicates that the ecological *structure* of metropolitan Toronto remained relatively stable during the decade, but that the *spatial patterns* of the cross-sectional dimensions changed considerably' (Murdie, 1969).

Most of the ecological argument about changes over time has, however, been concerned with much longer sweeps of time and to this end has contrasted cities at different stages of some hypothesized span of urbanization/modernization. Here the studies of pre-industrial or early-industrial cities have been invaluable, even though a little thin on the ground. Both in Calcutta (Berry and Rees, 1969) and in Cairo (Abu-Lughod, 1969) the clear emergence of a trio of factors, of economic status, family status and segregation factors failed to materialize. In Calcutta, a rather confused set of factors appears, with age-related variables being found associated both with land-use characteristics and with the 'substantial residential areas' dimension which Berry and Rees see as a proxy for social status. More clearly in Cairo, Abu-Lughod suggests that her inability to separate out a social status and a family status dimension is related to the absence in pre-industrial society of the 'necessary conditions' for the emergence of such orthogonal factors which are found in industrial societies. These conditions she sees in terms of residential segregation according to 'modern ranking systems' based on definitions of social status, relatively low correlations between social status and differences in fertility and family size and high differentiation of residential sub-areas by house type.

Whether or not these striking differences between the factorial ecologies of a small sample of 'modern' cities and an even smaller sample of developing cities is sufficient to support an hypothesis of increasing differentiation of social and family status dimensions over time, it certainly accords with the early Social Area Analysis view that urban differentiation is related to the 'scale' of a society, and Timms (1970) has begun to fill in some of the argument along such lines, drawing both on the factorial and Social Area literature. McElrath (1968) provides the most convincing evolutionary argument relating the four ecological dimensions to the process of urbanization/modernization when he posits: that economic and family status are related to industrialization through, on the one hand, technical skills replacing skills ascribed to age and, on the other, to the diminished relevance of sex as a distinguisher of rôles; and that ethnic status and migration status are the products of modernization through the increased rates of physical mobility which introduce people of visible differences on the one hand and which force people through such sharp social and cultural divides as the rural/urban dichotomy on the other. Timms (1970) has attempted to relate different types of city to various combinations of these four 'basic' dimensions, suggesting under what circumstances one might expect to find one or other of them emerging as separate. It would, however, be difficult to see his city categories (such as modern, feudal, immigrant, colonial) in terms of an unambiguous linear process through time.

The argument that one might relate structural urban dimensions to the effects of changes associated with urbanization and modernization as a process through time is certainly appealing and holds out the prospect of a truly dynamic cross-cultural ecological theory, but as yet the details of the argument linking a macro-social scale to a micro-urban scale are still insufficiently spelled out for the concept to be more than a tentative hypothesis.

Spatial dimensions
The second question to which urban ecologists have addressed themselves is whether or not there are distinctive patterns in the spatial distribution of factor scores or of variables measuring residential differentiation. The three spatial models of rings, sectors and nuclei have long offered tempting sails for budding ecological Quixotes and geographers have not been slow in tilting at them. The majority of studies have favoured the sector concept (for example, Pownall, 1957; Smith, 1962; Morgan, 1971), but others have compromised by pointing to both sectors and rings (Jones, E., 1960; Smailes, 1964; Robson, 1966; Johnston, 1966). The apparent 'state of cognitive dissonance' (Simmons, 1965) which three simultaneous models might be expected to engender, is somewhat resolved, however, when one considers that Burgess derived his rings from an interest in family disorganization, that Hoyt's sectors were the result of a study of land and house rental values (Robson, 1970), and that Harris and Ullman's nuclei related to land uses. Thus, depending on the particular variable under study, a single city might validly be expected to show any or all of the three patterns simultaneously. Anderson and Egeland's (1961) finding that the Social Area dimension of economic status was distributed sectorally whereas family status was distributed zonally helps to reinforce this interpretation. To this suggested pattern one might add (Berry, 1965; Salins, 1971) the expectation that segregation should be found clustered in distinctive neighbourhoods, in other words in nuclei. There is thus the suggestion of a happy isomorphism between the early ecological spatial patterns on the one hand and the three suggested urban dimensions on the other.

More recent empirical evidence on this point, however, is far from uniform. Whereas, like Anderson and Egeland, Murdie (1969) concludes that Toronto does show economic and family status distributed sectorally and zonally respectively, other studies, which likewise use analysis of variance to test such patterns, have suggested a much less certain correspondence. McElrath (1962) in Rome, Rees (1970) in Chicago, Johnston (1969a) in Melbourne and Timms (1970) in Brisbane find that economic status and family status varied both sectorally *and* zonally. In addition they note a good deal of zone-sector interaction, suggesting a tendency for clustering within individual cells of the spider's web of zone and sectors, a point which is reinforced by the findings of Haynes (1971) who looks more explicitly at the existence of nuclear patterns. Nevertheless, the ratios of F-values for sectors and zones in these various studies do suggest that social status varies *predominantly* by sectors and family status *predominantly* by zones (Timms, 1970), with greater spatial complexity tending to be found in large cities because of the presence within them of sizeable minority groups clustered in space.

The spatial patterns of change over time have also been seen in terms of zones and sectors (Murdie, 1969; Brown and Horton, 1970a). Murdie suggests, for Toronto, that economic status is not only distributed sectorally but also moves sectorally over time; that family status is distributed zonally and changes by zones; and that ethnic status is distributed sectorally and moves sectorally (Murdie, 1969). This conclusion, however, seems only very loosely supported by his data except in the case of his ethnic dimension. Indeed the economic status dimension fails to emerge as a dimension of change.

There is, therefore, some suggestion of regularity in the spatial patterning of sets of variables in the present-day city, even though the sectoral and zonal concepts appear to be poor *general* models of the variety of data involved. There is also, much more strongly, evidence that over longer spans of time certain generalizations appear in the spatial patterning of urban ecologies. Studies of pre-industrial cities (Sjoberg, 1960 and 1965) have repeatedly demonstrated a reversal of Burgess' social gradient, since pre-industrial cities have the rich living at the core and the poor at the periphery. Such a pattern bears a strong resemblance to the ideas of the nineteenth-century geographer Kohl (Peucker, 1968). While to the myopic eyes of the Chicago ecologists this was seen as an aberration from the 'normal', it is now fairly confidently established as a general characteristic of early cities. Subsequent changes to an 'American' pattern, with the poor living at the centre, appear to be linked to the technological, political, social and economic changes associated with the industrial city (Schnore, 1965). Wheatley, for example, stresses that the earliest urban forms were 'the preconceived undertakings of sacerdotal élites rather than haphazard aggregations of people responding to a human desire for economic gain' (Wheatley, 1967) and that the ceremonial nature of such places had a strong centralizing effect and made central locations attractive to the rich and influential. Butlin (1965) shows the concentration of the wealthy in the central areas of intra-mural Dublin in the seventeenth century and notes that by the end of the century a process of centrifugal movement of the wealthy to peripheral locations had only just begun. And, of course, early American towns themselves were equally characterized by the pre-industrial pattern of the wealthy living at the centre: Warner (1968), for example, points to the central location of the more affluent population in colonial Philadelphia. Indeed, through time it would appear that, not only are there changes in such aggregate spatial patterns, but also that at a more detailed scale a progression is found from the 'walking city' of pre-industrial societies to the industrial and post-industrial cities of today. The pre-industrial city tends to consist of separate cells (somewhat akin to the industrial cells of nineteenth-century British towns (Marshall, 1968)) and to show much less residential segregation of population types. In America, Warner (1968) shows the continuing intermixture of population in mid-nineteenth century Philadelphia, and Goheen (1970) pinpoints a significant change for Toronto between 1870 and 1880 with a marked increase in social segregation by the latter date. Such progressive changes in the internal patterning of cities appear to be linked most convincingly to changes in transportation technologies which act as enabling factors in permitting the development of different life styles encouraged by industrial and social change. The relative ease of inter- as against intra-urban mobility has tended, with the advent of electric tramcars or street railway cars (Ward, 1964), the gradual introduction of cheap railway fares (Dyos, 1955; Pollins, 1964), and the coming of the motor lorry (Moses and Williamson, 1967), to change in favour of the latter. Such enabling changes not only affect the overall shape of a town's morphology (Boal, 1968; Adams, 1970), but also the internal ecology of the patterning of social and economic characteristics so as to create separate genuses of pre-industrial, industrial and post-industrial cities (Friedman and Miller, 1965).

THE SAP: RESIDENTIAL MOBILITY

From the review of factorial studies, it is evident that the two factors which emerge most clearly as descriptions of urban social structure are those relating to social status variables and to age-related variables. If such independent aggregate dimensions do exist, the literature suggests

S.H.G.—8

that they reflect, at the level of the individual, processes of residential mobility which are both theoretically and empirically well supported. The classical ecologists never studied the process of the movement of households in any depth, but assumed a regular outward process of invasion and succession as pressure from new immigrants built up at the city centre. To this notion, the economists added the concept of filtering as houses progressively grew older, physically less desirable and hence attracted to them successively lower income groups. While each notion appears to have a good deal of qualified support at an aggregate level (see, for example, Johnston, 1969d), at the level of the individual household recent research has suggested new concepts which add considerable theoretical rationale to the importance of the two ecological factors which we have isolated.

Segregation by social class or by occupation (Duncan and Duncan, 1955; Davies, 1964) can be seen as reflecting, at an individual level, not only the income restraints which are important considerations at a late stage in the sequential decision of where to move (Rossi, 1955), but also the individual's aspiration to achieve in residential terms a location which will reinforce his self-evaluation of his social status or his social aspirations. As Beshers (1962) argues, spatial distance underlies and underlines social distance by decreasing the probability of contact with those with whom individuals may not wish to associate. The various studies showing decreasing rates of marriages with greater distances between prospective partners (Bossard, 1932; Ramsøy, 1966; Morrill and Pitts, 1967; Perry, 1969) suggest that this is highly plausible. Furthermore, sociological studies of the thesis of *embourgeoisement* suggest that, while recent income changes may have blurred the economic difference between manual and non-manual groups, there are still marked differences between social classes in terms of their relational and normative aspects (Goldthorpe and Lockwood, 1969). The aggregate ecological dimension of socio-economic status would thus appear to find substantial support at the level of the individual.

Likewise, with the age-related dimension, the growing literature on residential mobility (Simmons, 1968) consistently suggests the importance of the stage in the family life cycle as a determinant both of when and to where individual households are likely to move. Rossi (1955) suggested that residential mobility was a process by which families fitted their housing accommodation to fluctuations in family size. He laid great emphasis, at least for short-distance moves within the city (which tend to be prompted by family rather than economic considerations), on the importance of the household's stage in the life cycle.

Foote *et al.* (1960) suggest a simple model of the life cycle, based on empirical data from America, which links changes in family size and income to the age of the household head. They suggest that high rates of mobility are found in the early family-forming and child-rearing stages and that each move at a given stage in the life cycle tends to be to a particular type of area within the city through the constraints of the type and density of housing found in the area.

Most of the studies of intra-urban mobility have, therefore, added considerable validity to the aggregate ecological studies by hinting at the similarity between the key dimensions of social class and of stage in the life cycle which appear to be crucial at both the macro- and micro-scales of study. In so far as residential mobility is the lynch pin in the creation, maintenance or change of ecological patterns, the development of increasingly sophisticated ideas contributing to a theory of individual household mobility lends vital perspective to the factorial ecologies. Both Chapin (1968) and Brown and Moore (1970) suggest a similar framework within which one might best conceptualize residential mobility. Its complexity might be seen in two stages; a decision to move, and the choice of a new location. The first of these is the outcome of stress factors (Wolpert, 1965 and 1966) which reflect a growing discordance between the set of housing and environmental factors desired by the household and those provided by their present house and location. At a particular critical level of stress the household will seek to resolve such discordance by revising its aspirations or by restructuring its environment or by seeking to move. If the latter course is chosen, the second stage of the model applies and one can conceptualize the household's search for new housing in terms of its attempts to seek, through those channels which are available to it (the concept of an action space documented by Marble and Nystuen (1963), Wolpert (1965), Moore and Brown (1969), Cox (1969), and Moore (1970) amongst others), to match its aspirations with an available vacancy. If the search is frustrated the household will revert to one of the alternative strategies by lowering its aspirations or by making alterations to its present house or environment. If the search is successful, the household will move. Moore (1969) has suggested that more attention might be paid to those who do not move as well as to those who do. If there is a mobile élite (Goldstein, 1958) which contributes a large proportion of the total flux of intra-urban mobility, there is a need to consider the ratio of movers to stayers in any area in attempts to explain the process of household moves (Goodman, 1961; Johnston, 1969b).

While much of such a conceptual scheme has not as yet been

made operational, its importance to urban ecology lies not only in the insight which it gives to the process of residential differentiation at an individual level, but also to the fact that the mobility literature clearly suggests that social class and stage in the life cycle are vital components of the aspiration sets by which households match their locational desires to their actual circumstances. This certainly suggests valuable theoretical support for the validity of the two factorial dimensions related to socio-economic status and age-related variables. The prospect for a more convincing link between the individual and aggregate ecological concepts appears within sight if not within grasp.

THE BRANCHES: STUDY OF SOCIAL PHENOMENA

While the main thrust of urban ecology has been towards isolating and mapping the dimensions of urban social structure, it has also branched into the study of more strictly social phenomena either by adopting an ecological approach to the examination of pathological traits or social attitudes, or by using the output of factorial studies as a spatial framework for such study.

Studies of social pathologies follow very much the precedents of the roots of classical ecology from which a torrent of individual studies cascaded out of Chicago. Whereas many of these early writings were concerned with particular social groups (hobos, taxi dance-hall men, Chinese laundrymen) within particular neighbourhoods (the gold coast, the slum, the ghetto), others looked at general social problems such as drug addiction, juvenile delinquency, crime, and family disorganization (Burgess and Bogue, 1964). It is in the latter direction that recent geographical work has tended. Timms' (1970) study of crime and mental health in Luton and Derby, and Griffiths' (1971) study of mortality in Exeter are instances. As a general example, Giggs' (1970) study of social disorganization in Barry illustrates the complexity of ecological patterning which real world data frequently suggest. Unlike Schmid (1960), who found a regular outward gradient in his factorial study of crime rates, Giggs' use of a linkage tree grouping of the factor scores of variables measuring health and crime rates shows that high levels of 'disorganization' occur both in the centre and in outlying suburbs and that low levels are found in some areas close to the centre. Nor does he find a tendency for rates of mobility and of social disorganization to change in concert away from the city centre. With high scores found in areas of commercial and industrial land use, in areas of substandard housing in both central and peripheral locations, and in peripheral post-war council estates, he has to turn to the details of the historical process of urban growth rather than to Burgess' notions of gradients to provide an explanation of the pattern.

A second stream of geographical ecology has looked at non-pathological social phenomena. Robson's (1969) study of attitudes to education is an example of the use of factor scores to provide a sampling framework within which to test the effects of contextual rather than individual characteristics on attitudes. Cox's (1968) work on political voting patterns is again an example of the use of an ecological methodology. He tests the effects of suburbanism on voting behaviour using both factor analysis and Blalock's method of causal inference to demonstrate that suburbanism affects voting indirectly through its influence on social class, age structure and commuting patterns, but that it also has its own independent effects in addition. These may be attributed to either of two explanations: a conversion theory which would hold that, on moving to the suburbs, the individual is subjected to relatively new sets of stimuli which may lead him to change his party identification; or a transplantation theory which would argue that migration to the suburbs is a selective process differentially weighted in favour of people with a particular political attitude. In the context of his ecological research design, Cox is unable to say which may be the more likely.

This indeed is a good instance of a basic problem common to ecological work. Using data aggregated within areal units the ecologist is faced not only with the operational problems of ecological correlation (Robinson, W. S., 1950; Menzel, 1950; Duncan and Davis, 1953; Goodman, 1953) and the influence of variation in the size of those units (see p. 210 above), but also the problem of drawing causal inferences from his results. If the schizophrenic is found concentrated in transient rooming-house districts in central areas, can one establish whether his location is the result or the cause of his condition? While the difficulty has led many to suggest that only individual longitudinal case studies provides a valid approach, this is to ignore the well-demonstrated influences of contextual variables which suggest that either the individual or the ecological approach used independently may contain their own fallacies (Allardt, 1969; Valkonen, 1969). 'In ordinary survey research the individual is usually treated, albeit by implication, as an atom. Just adding atoms does not of course make for molecules' (Scheuch, 1969). It is this belief which has sustained the best of ecological work.

DISCUSSION

If one were to draw up a bold summary of urban ecology from what has so far been said, the generalizations would take something of the following form (Figure 6.1). Urban society is differentiated in terms of the three basic dimensions of economic status, family status and ethnic status with a possible fourth dimension related to mobility. Other factors unique to particular cities, but of little general interest, would also exist. Such differentiation is the product, at an individual level, of the process of residential mobility by which households seek to match physical distance with social distance and to match family size with housing space: at a societal level, it reflects scale changes associated with increasing urbanization and modernization, with the axes of the dimensions becoming more separate and distinguishable as the process proceeds. Spatially, modern cities show these three dimensions distributed in sectors, zones and nuclei respectively and through time the spatial pattern of the variables comprising these dimensions would show increasing segregation as the city progressed through stages of the pre-industrial and post-industrial span. Given this residential differentiation, the mosaic of social worlds produces social spaces which map into physical spaces and provide a framework within which the distribution and aetiology of social phenomena can profitably be viewed.

Such a summary would certainly be justified from a reading of the sweeping conclusions of many writers, particularly of American geographers and sociologists. Yet one feels profoundly uneasy in the face of such apparent sureness. Urban society is an infinitely complex maze and a number of factors tend too readily to be glossed over in much of the ecological literature. One is the argument from a society-wide to an individual city scale, a concern to which sociologists rather than geographers have addressed themselves. A second is the question of the very interpretation of the factor results and the tendency to generalize uncertain factor dimensions. Factorial output is so strongly

---

FIGURE 6.1   Social areas in Chicago

The city can be seen in terms of the three dimensions of socio-economic status (A), life cycle (B) and ethnicity (C). The real-world pattern (I) is the product of these three elements transformed in space by: the concentric life cycle pattern of ethnic areas, parallel to the city as a whole (E); the shape of the physical growth of the city (F); and the existence of peripheral work-place nuclei (H). (Redrawn from Berry and Rees, 1969).

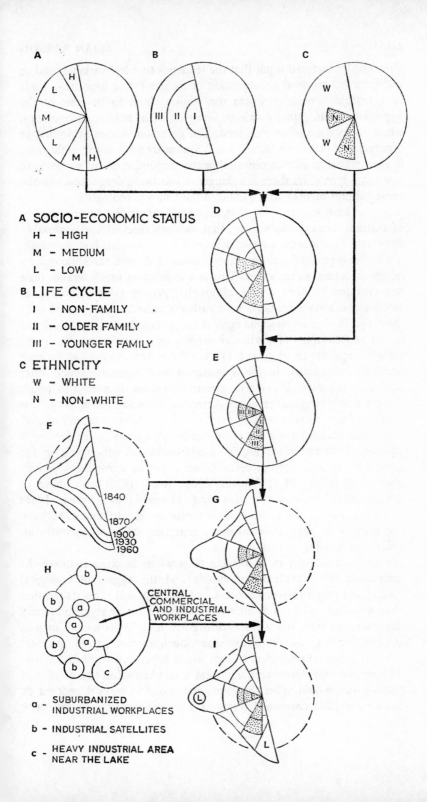

A SOCIO-ECONOMIC STATUS
  H – HIGH
  M – MEDIUM
  L – LOW

B LIFE CYCLE
  I – NON-FAMILY
  II – OLDER FAMILY
  III – YOUNGER FAMILY

C ETHNICITY
  W – WHITE
  N – NON-WHITE

CENTRAL
COMMERCIAL
AND INDUSTRIAL
WORKPLACES

a – SUBURBANIZED
    INDUSTRIAL WORKPLACES
b – INDUSTRIAL SATELLITES
c – HEAVY INDUSTRIAL AREA
    NEAR THE LAKE

governed by factorial input that the tendency to select variables and to
interpret factors on the assumption of a three-factor hypothesis leads
to a certain circularity where the studies claim to be tests of the
hypothesis itself. Equally serious, however, is the bold confidence with
which factors are often identified. The grandiose names attributed to
separate axes often hide factors which appear by no means unambiguous
in their meaning. Furthermore, since the preponderance of studies is of
American-type cities there is a danger of our being dragooned into the
same cultural myopia which afflicted the Chicago ecologists.

At the best, one can say that the results of studies from a variety
of cultural contexts do suggest that modern cities almost invariably
show two dimensions, somewhat variously composed, but essentially
measuring aspects of socio-economic status on the one hand and aspects
of age structure on the other. This is a conclusion much weaker than
has customarily been drawn although Sweetser (1969), looking at
Boston and Helsinki, comes to a rather similar conclusion and calls
these two factors *universal* as against the *special* dimensions which are
found as reflections of particular aspects of a specific culture. There
certainly appears to be great scope for the cultural variations between
areas to be reflected in the appearance of dimensions which differ
markedly (Landay, 1971). The ethnic dimension is a case in point.
Rather than being universal, as American literature might suggest, it
is absent from many areas and this is not simply because (as in Finland)
substantial minorities do not exist, but because many areas, even with
substantial ethnic minorities, have not developed sub-groups in the
same way as in American cities. Comparison of work on American
ghettoes (Frazier, 1937; Morrill, 1965; Rose, 1970) with those of
British black populations (Rex and Moore, 1967; Peach, 1968;
Doherty, 1969; Jones, P. N., 1970) suggests marked differences between
the degrees of such concentration, reflecting different institutional,
social and housing constraints.

Perhaps a useful way of viewing the ecology of cities is to see the
interaction of individual households and the aggregate ecological
pattern as being a two-way process. A household will select its location
in terms of its social self-awareness and income, its life style and family
size characteristics, but will be constrained both by its mental map of
the city's ecology and its action space. Such a process would produce
the two universal ecological factors which have been suggested above.
At the same time, however, the process would be subject to a number of
filters which would affect the locational choice in ways dependent on
the type of filter concerned. Figure 6.2 indicates such a notion, with

the universal filters of social status and the life cycle determining the basic matching of the individual/aggregate inter-relationship, but with special filters, where they exist, constraining the choices and perceptions of appropriate sub-groups of the population and hence affecting both individual locational choices and the aggregate ecology.

Examples of such special potential filters, whose effects are particular to each given culture, but, where they operate, produce sub-strata which are reflected in the factorial ecologies of the city concerned,

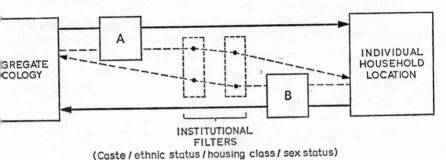

FIGURE 6.2 The inter-relationship of aggregate and individual scales

The aggregate pattern is produced by the locational decisions of individual households, but in turn the individual household selects its location with reference to its perception of the aggregate ecology (solid lines). Isomorphism between the two scales might be expected to depend on the similarity of the two filters A and B: if the universal aggregate dimensions of socio-economic status and life cycle (A) are similar to the factors influencing individual household locations (B), one might claim that the ecological dimensions are interpretable in terms of individual processes. The effect of specific institutional filters—where they are present—is to constrain the locational decisions and the locational perceptions of the affected subgroups (dotted lines) along dimensions additional to those of the universal filters.

would include the following: institutionalized discrimination as with the Indian caste system producing factors of Bengali and non-Bengali commercial caste factors in Calcutta (Berry and Rees, 1969); the somewhat less institutionalized racial discrimination producing ethnic factors, and particularly black ethnic factors, in American cities; religious filters such as those noted for early nineteenth-century Toronto (Goheen, 1970); sexual filters such as that producing Sweetser's (1965b) 'career women' factor in Helsinki, which he sees as the product of Finnish attitudes to the definition of rôles for females, there being a

S.H.G.—8*

generally higher proportion of women working, with such jobs as dentist and barber being largely the preserve of females; the housing filters such as apply most noticeably in Britain to produce a marked dimension associated with council-house tenancy (Robson, 1969; Herbert, 1970). Such filters are by no means universal: a given society may show none or may show many. But where they do operate, their effect is to produce elements of social structure articulated along dimensions other than the factors of social class and age characteristics which seem basic to modern societies.

Reservations such as these suggest that many urban ecologists have been too readily prone to draw general conclusions from complex data on urban structure. There is still a large number of gaps and inadequacies in the existing literature and from them the following four points have been isolated for discussion: the rôle of housing, which takes up the general point about institutional filters as well as emphasizing the importance of housing as a general intervening variable; age structure, which, as a basic element in one of the two universal factors, is suggested to be a much more complex phenomenon than urban ecologists might suggest; the notion of social space which, as writers such as Chombart de Lauwe (1952) have shown so well, is an intricate concept only crudely represented by existing spatial techniques; and the question of time and the importance of the persistence of past urban forms in the development of urban ecologies.

Housing

The rôle of local authority housing in Britain is only the most striking of a whole set of more subtle effects which housing has as an intervening variable in the process of residential differentiation. There is nothing comparable in the structure of the American housing market to the massive build-up, in twentieth-century Britain, of a 'council' housing sector which now provides more than 40% of dwellings in England and Wales. This fact has undoubtedly been responsible for some of the more marked differences between the results of British and American factorial ecologies, since the effects of such housing are not only to introduce novel combinations of physically good housing with relatively low social status, but also to alter many of the relationships between sets of purely social characteristics through their selective effects in terms of age and family size characteristics (Robson, 1969; Mabry, 1968) and in terms of relatively low physical mobility (Brooks, 1967). Patterns of social segregation in British new towns (Heraud, 1966) reinforce some of the same points and the conclusion must be that local authority housing in Britain has altered both the structural dimensions as well as the spatial pattern of urban areas.

Geographers, in many ways, are well placed to consider the relations of house type to social structure. There is an impressive body of morphological literature (Smailes, 1955; Conzen, 1960; Carter, 1965) some of which has applied rather sophisticated classificatory techniques (Forster, 1968; Grimshaw et al., 1970). However, there have been few signs of the emergence of morphological laws or theories (Garrison, 1962) and a more useful approach in the context of urban ecology may well be the more conscious recognition of the importance of government housing policies which, in Britain, have been sensitively explored in a large number of studies by Cullingworth (see, for example, Cullingworth, 1960 and 1966). An especially valuable concept is that of 'housing classes' which Rex sees, comparing it to the Marxist definition of social classes, in terms of groups being categorized by differential access to a limited but desired housing stock through their ability to raise mortgages or to qualify for local authority tenancy (Rex and Moore, 1967; Rex, 1968). The definition of appropriate housing categories depends, of course, both on what housing characteristics are considered desirable (Wilson, R. L., 1962; Peterson, 1967; Sommer, 1969) as well as on the institutionalized policies which create and maintain or alter the financial and social implications of each type. Changes in policy such as that recently proposed in *Fair Deal for Housing*, whereby all tenancy categories, except for furnished lettings, would be treated on the same basis, could obviously have marked effects in the long term on the ecology of British towns (Secretary of State for the Environment, 1971).

It may well be that a more valid strategy for incorporating the stock of housing into factorial models is not, as has been the practice especially in British studies, simply to add variables measuring housing characteristics to the list of input data, but rather, as Openshaw (1969) does, to treat social characteristics and housing characteristics as two separate sets whose factor dimensions can then be matched by cannonical correlation. Likewise, one of the points of interest in the work of Echenique et al. (1969) in building a gravity-based urban model akin to the work of Lowry (1964) and A. G. Wilson (1969), has been their use of two sub-models, one of which provides an output of housing stock which then feeds in as a constraint to the second sub-model which allocates land uses to sub-areas.

Such considerations lead back to the wider field of the residential location decision, which much of the literature has treated from a

purely demand side even though evidence suggests that in a country
such as Britain one is dealing with a seller's market. Greater emphasis
on the intervening rôle of housing would add greater realism by adding
the supply element which provides the opportunities surface formed by
the supply of houses potentially available to the would-be mover. This
can be seen as a function of the vacancy chains, initiated by new construction or by a household's death or by outmigration, and terminated
by demolition and the filling of vacancies by incoming migrants or by
newly-created households (Donnison, 1961; Lansing et al., 1969). But
it is a process whose operation is constrained and effected by a complex
of decision-makers running from landowners through financiers,
developers, builders and planning officials to the household as only
the final element. There is now an accumulating body of evidence
pertaining to the impact of each of these separate supply elements, all
of which will be needed in the development of more refined families of
linked mobility models (Kaiser, 1969) or of Markov chain models
(Harvey, 1967; Drewett, 1969). On the landowner, for example, Fellman
(1957), Ward (1962) and Mortimore (1969) have each shown the
effects of patterns of land ownership on the type and location of
residential development; local authority building in England, for
example, being largely restricted to areas held in large compact
holdings. As Ward shows, the consequent effect in Leeds is the differentiation between housing developments in the north and south of the
town. Carter (1970) has stressed the scale of the decision-maker on the
subsequent urban patterns which emerge, examining Llandudno as an
example. On the developer side, both Kaiser (1968) and Craven (1969)
have noted the interrelationships between the size of the developer firm,
the characteristics of potential sites and the types and prices of houses
which are built. Craven shows that for private development in Kent,
housing is increasingly being built by large, non-local developers. The
standardized medium-density, three-bedroom housing which results
is built largely in the Outer Metropolitan area, rather than more
centrally, through the influences of land price, planning constraints
and availability of land. Lower income households must perforce
follow the locational patterns which such developments suggest.
Rather than being a simple supplier of needs, he argues that the developer
is an *independent* element in urban growth, 'a catalyst who interprets,
albeit inaccurately, major forces in the urban environment; an initiator
of action based on this interpretation and a challenger of public policies
which obstruct such actions' (Craven, 1969). Such a rôle is equally
demonstrated by the builder's and developer's ability to place income

restraints on potential residents, as Gans (1967) reports for Levittown in America. Just as such supply decisions loom large in the development process, so too do they in the redevelopment process where, for example, Bourne (1967) shows that the spatial clustering of private redevelopments in Toronto is the product of a chain reaction produced by the mechanics of the real estate market rather than by any intrinsically greater attractiveness of one potential area over another.

The important points for urban ecology arising from this discussion would seem to be: that housing classes such as local authority tenants in Britain must be seen as one of a class of institutional filters complicating the two basic dimensions of urban social structure; and that housing itself and the manner by which housing opportunity surfaces emerge need to be given greater weight in the process of residential mobility by which urban ecological structure is created and altered or maintained.

Life cycle
The evidence of factorial studies strongly suggests the importance, not of an unambiguous linear dimension of familism, but rather that age-related variables are an important element in residential differentiation. Again, this is a much less forthright conclusion than has commonly been drawn, but, if it is true, it suggests the need for considerably more refined work on the classification of age structure. The likelihood of its truth is certainly suggested by some of the factorial results since there is a wide variety of age-related factors which have been extracted, even though they are usually subsumed under a blanket title of 'life-cycle'. Sweetser (1965b), for example, found no fewer than three age dimensions in Helsinki which he called 'progeniture', 'established familism' and 'postgeniture'; Janson (1968) found both 'old age' and 'familism' in Newark; and the fourth factor suggested by Timms and McElrath—'mobility'—tends also to be a strongly age-related dimension since, in the areas which it describes, the five types of central city dweller which Gans (1962) identifies contain at least three which are typically of certain age groups. Were familism or the life cycle a clear linear dimension, a single factor would doubtless emerge consistently, but the evidence suggests that as more age variables are included a multiplicity of age factors emerges.

The problem is basically that, while for the individual, age *is* a continuous linear phenomenon, areal or aggregate age structure is *not* linear or continuous. Before one can convincingly match together studies of individual mobility (which in itself usually involves an aggregate, the household), with the aggregate ecological patterns, one needs to be able to classify and understand such areal age structures. The studies of spatial age structures have shown both the wide variation between (Franklin, 1958) and within (Jones, E., 1960) communities. Such studies have used either graphic presentation of age-sex pyramids or summary indices such as the dependency ratio (Browning, 1961). But classification has inevitably proved harder than description. Coulson (1968) has suggested the fitting of regression lines to age distributions as a basis for classification, but this proves to be a relatively crude attempt to enforce linearity on what is a non-linear fact. Goldsmith *et al.* (1970) have proposed an interesting four-digit classification scheme based on the dominant adult age category, the family life-cycle stage, the proportion of dependent children and the degree of selectivity for the dominant adult age group. Its complexity is an interesting reflection of the difficulty of dealing with areal age character-istics.

Both the studies of household mobility and the interpretation of factorial ecologies would benefit from a clearer notion of idealized household age structures as well as the empirical combinations of such idealized profiles which might be expected to characterize areas at different stages of an *areal* life-cycle progression. Foote *et al.* (1960, see above, p. 217) have suggested one rather simplified suggestion of stages in the family life-cycle. One might, however, characterize the combinations in a slightly more complex form (Figure 6.3) by allowing for a greater variety of routes from birth to death. This could provide the basis for the derivation of idealized combinations of ages and so produce curves against which the various components found in particular sub-areas might be matched. Thus, for example, an area undergoing invasion, in which young married couples with growing families are moving into housing vacated either by the death of old households or by the movement of households whose grown children leave home, might be characterized by the superimposition of two idealized household life-cycle profiles. This could in turn form the basis for the characterization of an *area's* life cycle progression and help to map individual mobility into the patterns of areal change or stability.

Certainly the scope for clarifying our ideas about areal and household age structures is considerable. The value of a sharper set of notions on age characteristics to the output of urban ecologies is very clear.

Social space and physical space
The format in which most ecological research is conducted has pro-

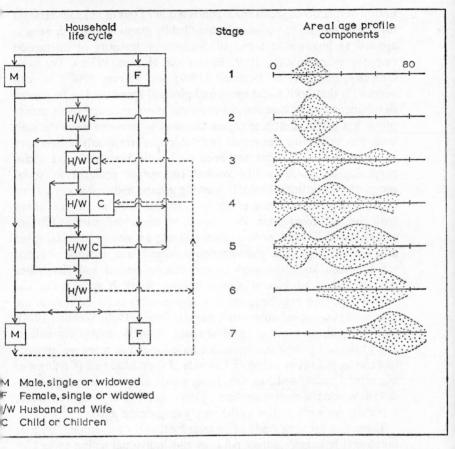

FIGURE 6.3   Household life cycles and the age profiles of areas
The left-hand side represents alternative routes through a household life cycle.
Dotted lines indicate the possibility of households in the later stages of this
cycle moving to join the households formed by their offspring. The right-
hand side shows schematic profiles of the age structures corresponding with
each major life cycle stage. The actual age profile of any given area might
best be measured against one, or combinations of more than one, of these
basic curves.

duced the tacit assumption that social and physical space are synonymous or at least isomorphic. That this is not so is clearly apparent and
the conceptual and operational problems which this implies raise
difficulties of considerable magnitude. Geographers have traditionally
been well equipped to handle space viewed in a Euclidean sense and the

notion of functional social space conceived of as sets of linkages between functional entities can equally be handled by graph theory with weights applied to linkages in terms of distance or intensity of interaction (see, for example, Cox, 1969; Brown and Horton, 1970b). The basic difficulty, however, as Buttimer (1969) and Harvey (1969) so well suggest, is that both social space and physical space need to be treated simultaneously and here our conventional geometries and mathematics prove less useful. Buttimer argues the need to consider what she calls both the 'subjective' (internal) and 'objective' (external) perspectives of social space and that the need to handle both real and socio-psychological space is 'the central conceptual problem in social geography' (Buttimer, 1968). In viewing groups and environments one can consider social space either in a formal way, as do the urban ecologists by considering the mosaic of areas defined by different complexes of life style, or in a functional way by looking at social space as a nodally organized phenomenon arranged in a network of social spaces which are articulated around certain centres and channelled through certain arteries of communication. While it appears that the second approach may be growing in importance, as the decriers of the notion of place-based community suggest (Stein, 1960; Webber, 1964), the first, with its basis in physical space, is by no means redundant. The evidence of those studies which have looked at marriage patterns (see above, p. 216) or the spatial aspects of friendship nets (Festinger *et al.*, 1950; Caplow and Forman, 1950) would certainly lend support to this; as would the evident continuing importance of the neighbourhood, especially for such groups as the very young or the aged.

There is a growing body of geographical literature looking both at functional linkages, contact patterns and individual action space (for example, see Bullock *et al.*, 1970; Goddard, 1970; and the literature cited above, p. 217), as well as at perceptions of space in a socio-psychological sense (for a review, see Downs, 1970). Most of these studies inevitably approach empirical work through studies of individual behaviour and consequently pose the, as yet, intractible problem of how one builds up from individual to aggregate concepts, as well as how one simultaneously incorporates continuous and discontinuous spatial notions. Such questions of scale shifts and of concepts of distance are clearly crucial weaknesses at the core of geographical methodology. Not only would it seem that urban ecological studies need to inject greater sociological sophistication into the use of concepts such as 'social structure' or 'social class', but their assumption of a one-to-one correspondence between social and physical space needs radical modification by utilizing as yet undeveloped approaches which take cognizance of what Webber (1963) calls 'community without propinquity'.

Time and persistence
A final aspect of urban ecology, which bears on what has been said about housing as an intervening variable, is the question of the rôle of time in models of urban structure. Abu-Lughod (1968) has suggested that a curious fact about theories of the city is that they have tended always to be developed about city structures which are on the point of disappearing or which no longer exist. Many of the early sociological dichotomies, such as gemeinschaft/gesellschaft or organic/mechanical, were introduced at a time when the distinction between urban and rural ways of life was becoming virtually non-existent: the Chicago ecologists developed their urban theory in terms of a city which was essentially an atavistic throwback to the nineteenth century and soon proved remarkably transient; today, physical space and distance friction are still used as important components of the evolving urban theory despite the advent of what Berry (1970) calles 'telemobility' and despite the decline of core domination in cities. Megalopolis and the multicentred regional city make it difficult even to define a city as a functional entity. Are the models towards which urban ecology has been working going to be out of date even before they are achieved?

The reason why one need not take too gloomy a view relates very largely to the persistence of the urban fabric. The life expectancy of buildings is usually considerably longer than the pace of technological, political and social changes which activate the city and its inhabitants. And the basic morphological skeleton, which partly determines the spatial pattern and functional linkages of built forms, of channels, of activities and hence of many aspects of the spatial patterns of social characteristics, is even harder to alter (Duncan, B., *et al.*, 1962; Winsborough, 1962). Beverley Duncan (1964) has outlined a scheme of critical variables in urban morphology—GASP—in which the 'P' stood for persistence and her emphasis is borne out not only by the evident fact of the longevity of buildings, but also in numerous studies from the classic work of Firey (1947) to the more recent works of Johnston (1966, 1969c) and Davis (1965) which illustrate the persistence of high-status residential areas over long periods of time.

It may indeed be true that many of the spatial patterns which emerge from ecological theories are reflections less of current processes and more of the historical residues of earlier types, densities and dispositions of housing, but this makes the patterns no less valid and no less interesting since they are the facts of life with which planners as well as theoreticians are faced. The 'tyranny of space' (Warntz, 1967) may today be less tyrannical, but it is nevertheless often validly incorporated into theories precisely because the built forms which reflect past responses to distance, among other things, are still very much with us. This is not to argue a neglect for the development of new methodologies which might handle the more refined notions of social and socio-psychological space, but simply to stress the need to consider the palimpsest nature of the city. It is for this reason that such studies as Adams' (1970) work on urban morphology and its connections with past cycles of building activity throw interesting light on current urban patterns and for the same reason that there are valuable lessons to be learned from the growing body of urban historical studies which are now being produced by geographers (Ward, 1971) as well as economic historians (Dyos, 1968; Thernstrom and Sennett, 1969).

CONCLUSION

Harvey (1971) suggests that we know next to nothing about urban spatial structure and social processes. But it is clear that urban ecology, while far from providing a theory of urban residential differentiation, has already provided the intimations of certain regularities in urban society which are both tantalizing and exciting. The cautionary points raised in discussion of the gaps and shortcomings of the existing literature may suggest certain lacunae in the skeleton of an ecological theory which might profitably be fleshed out. The fact that geographers have begun to tackle some of these tasks offers hopes for a more tightly bound set of notions which might begin to tie together the decisions and behaviour of the individual household with the aggregate ecological structure of cities.

REFERENCES

Abu-Lughod, J. (1968) 'The city is dead—long live the city: some thoughts on urbanity', in S. F. Flava (Ed.), *Urbanism in World Perspective*, Cromwell, 254–265.
Abu-Lughod, J. (1969) 'Testing the theory of Social Area Analysis: the ecology of Cairo', *American Sociological Review*, 34, 198–212.

Adams, J. S. (1970) 'Residential structure of mid-western cities', *Annals of the Association of American Geographers*, **60**, 37–62.

Alihan, M. A. (1938) *Social Ecology: a critical analysis*, Columbia University Press.

Allardt, E. (1969) 'Aggregate analysis: the problem of its informative value', in M. Dogan, and S. Rokkan (Eds.), *Quantitative Ecological Analysis in the Social Sciences*, MIT Press, 41–51.

Anderson, T. R. and Egeland, J. A. (1961) 'Spatial aspects of Social Area Analysis', *American Sociological Review*, **26**, 392–398.

Armstrong, J. S. (1967) 'Derivation of theory by factor analysis or Tom Swift and his electric factor analysis machine', *American Statistician*, **21**, 17–21.

Bell, W. (1955) 'Economic, family and ethnic status: an empirical test', *American Sociological Review*, **20**, 45–52.

Bell, W. and Force, M. T. (1956) 'Urban neighborhood types and participation in formal associations', *American Sociological Review*, **21**, 25–34.

Berry, B. J. L. (1965) 'Internal structure of the city', *Law and Contemporary Problems*, **30**, 111–119.

Berry, B. J. L. (1970) 'The geography of the United States in the year 2000', *Transactions of the Institute of British Geographers*, **51**, 21–53.

Berry, B. J. L. (Ed.) (1971) 'Comparative factorial ecology', *Economic Geography*, **47** (Supplement), 209–367.

Berry, B. J. L. and Rees, P. (1969) 'The factorial ecology of Calcutta', *American Journal of Sociology*, **74**, 445–491.

Beshers, J. M. (1962) *Urban Social Structure*, The Free Press.

Boal, F. L. (1968) 'Technology and urban form', *Journal of Geography*, **67**, 229–236.

Bossard, J. H. S. (1932) 'Residential propinquity as a factor in marriage selection', *American Journal of Sociology*, **38**, 219–224.

Bourne, L. S. (1967) 'Private redevelopment in the centre of the city: spatial processes of structural change in the City of Toronto', *Research Paper No. 112*, Department of Geography, University of Chicago.

Brooks, E. (1967) 'Public housing and labour mobility in Britain', in 'Aspects of central place theory and the city in developing countries', *Urban Study Group, Institute of British Geographers* (mimeographed).

Brown, L. A. and Horton, F. E. (1970a) 'Social area change: an empirical analysis', *Urban Studies*, **7**, 271–288.

Brown, L. A. and Horton, F. E. (1970b) 'Functional distance: an operational approach', *Geographical Analysis*, **2**, 76–83.

Brown, L. A. and Moore, E. G. (1970) 'The intra-urban migration process: a perspective', *Geografiska Annaler, Series B*, **52**, 1–13.

Browning, H. L. (1961) 'Methods for describing the age-sex structure of cities', in J. Gibbs (Ed.), *Urban Research Methods*, Van Nostrand, 129–139.

Bullock, N., Dickens, P. and Steadman, P. (1970) 'Activities, space and location', *Architectural Review*, **147**, 299–306.

Burgess, E. W. and Bogue, D. J. (Eds.) (1964) *Contributions to Urban Sociology*, University of Chicago Press.

Butlin, R. A. (1965) 'The population of Dublin in the late seventeenth century', *Irish Geographer*, **5**, 51–66.

234   BRIAN ROBSON

Buttimer, A. (1968) 'Social geography', in D. L. Sills (Ed.), *International Encyclopedia for the Social Sciences*, Macmillan and The Free Press, 6, 134–145.
Buttimer, A. (1969) 'Social space in interdisciplinary perspective', *Geographical Review*, 59, 417–426.
Caplow, T. and Forman, R. (1950) 'Neighborhood interaction in a homogeneous community', *American Sociological Review*, 15, 357–367.
Carey, G. W. (1966) 'The regional interpretation of Manhattan population and housing patterns through factor analysis', *Geographical Review*, 56, 551–569.
Carey, G. W., Macomber, L. and Greenburg, M. (1968) 'Education and demographic factors in the urban geography of Washington, D.C.', *Geographical Review*, 58, 515–537.
Carter, H. (1965) *The Towns of Wales: a study in urban geography*, University of Wales Press.
Carter, H. (1970) 'A decision-making approach to town plan analysis: a case study of Llandudno', in H. Carter and W. K. D. Davies (Eds.), *Urban Essays: studies in the geography of Wales*, Longmans, 66–78.
Chapin, F. S. Jr. (1968) 'Activity systems and urban structure: a working schema', *Journal of the American Institute of Planners*, 11–18.
Chombart de Lauwe, P.-H., *et al.* (1952) *Paris et l'agglomeration Parisienne*, 2 vols., Presses Universitaires de France.
Conzen, M. R. G. (1960) 'Alnwick, Northumberland: a study in town plan analysis', *Institute of British Geographers*, Special Publication No. 27.
Coulson, M. R. C. (1968) 'The distribution of age structures in Kansas City', *Annals of the Association of American Geographers*, 58, 155–176.
Cox, K. R. (1968) 'Suburbia and voting behaviour in the London Metropolitan Area', *Annals of the Association of American Geographers*, 58, 111–127.
Cox, K. R. (1969) 'The genesis of acquaintance field spatial structures: a conceptual model and empirical tests', in K. R. Cox and R. Golledge (Eds.), 'Behavioural geography', *North Western University Studies in Geography*, No. 17, 146–168.
Craven, E. A. (1969) 'Private residential expansion in Kent', *Urban Studies*, 6, 1–16.
Cullingworth, J. B. (1960) *Housing Needs and Planning Policy*, Routledge and Kegan Paul.
Cullingworth, J. B. (1966) *Housing and Local Government*, Allen and Unwin.
Davies, R. J. (1964) 'Social distance and the distribution of occupational categories in Johannesburg and Pretoria', *South African Geographical Journal*, 46, 24–39.
Davies, W. K. D. (1971) 'Varimax and the destruction of generality: a methodological note', *Area*, 3, 112–118.
Davis, J. T. (1965) 'Middle class housing in the central city', *Economic Geography*, 41, 238–251.
Dogan, M. and Rokkan, S. (Eds.) (1969) *Quantitative Ecological Analysis in the Social Sciences*, MIT Press.
Doherty, J. (1969) 'The distribution of concentrations of immigrants in London', *Race Today*, 1, 227–231.

Donnison, D. V. (1961) 'The movement of households in England', *Journal of the Royal Statistical Society*, Series A, **124**, 60–80.

Downs, R. M. (1970) 'Geographic space perception', in C. Board *et al.* (Eds.), *Progress in Geography*, Arnold, **2**, 65–108.

Drewett, J. R. (1969) 'A stochastic model of the land conversion process: an interim report', *Regional Studies*, **3**, 269–280.

Duncan, B. (1964) 'Variables in urban morphology', in E. W. Burgess and D. J. Bogue (Eds.), *Contributions to Urban Sociology*, University of Chicago Press, 17–30.

Duncan, B., Sabagh, G. and van Arsdol, M. D. (1962) 'Patterns of city growth', *American Journal of Sociology*, **67**, 418–429.

Duncan, O. D. (1955) 'Review of Shevky and Bell, 1955', *American Journal of Sociology*, **56**, 84–85.

Duncan, O. D., Cuzzort, R. P. and Duncan, B. (1961) *Statistical Geography: problems in analyzing areal data*, The Free Press.

Duncan, O. D. and Davis, B. (1953) 'An alternative to ecological correlations', *American Sociological Review*, **18**, 665–666.

Duncan, O. D. and Duncan, B. (1955) 'Residential distribution and occupational stratification', *American Journal of Sociology*, **60**, 493–506.

Dyos, H. J. (1955) 'Railways and housing in Victorian London', *Journal of Transport History*, **2**, 11–21 and 90–100.

Dyos, H. J. (Ed.) (1968) *The Study of Urban History*, Arnold.

Echenique, M., Crowther, D. and Lindsay, W. (1969) 'A spatial model of urban stock and activity', *Regional Studies*, **3**, 281–312.

Ehrenberg, A. S. C. (1962) 'Some questions about factor analysis', *Statistician*, **12**, 191–208.

Eysenck, H. J. (1952) 'Uses and abuses of factor analysis', *Applied Statistics*, **1**, 45–49.

Faris, R. E. L. (1970) *Chicago Sociology: 1920–1932*, Chandler Publishing Co.

Fellman, J. D. (1957) 'Pre-building growth patterns in Chicago', *Annals of the Association of American Geographers*, **47**, 59–82.

Festinger, L., Schachter, S. and Back, K. (1950) *Social Pressures in Informal Groups*, Harper and Row.

Firey, W. (1947) *Land Use in Central Boston*, Harvard University Press.

Foote, N. N., Abu-Lughod, J., Foley, M. and Winnick, L. (1960) *Housing Choices and Housing Constraints*, McGraw-Hill.

Forster, C. A. (1968) 'The development of bye-law housing in Kingston-upon-Hull: an example of multivariate morphological analysis', in 'Techniques in urban geography', *Urban Study Group, Institute of British Geographers* (mimeographed).

Franklin, S. H. (1958) 'The age structure of New Zealand's North Island communities', *Economic Geography*, **34**, 64–79.

Frazier, E. F. (1937) 'Negro Harlem: an ecological study', *American Journal of Sociology*, **43**, 72–88.

Friedmann, J. and Miller, J. (1965) 'The urban field', *Journal of the American Institute of Planners*, **31**, 312–320.

Gans, H. J. (1962) 'Urbanism and suburbanism as ways of life: a re-evaluation of definitions', in A. Rose (Ed.), *Human Behavior and Social Processes*, Houghton Miflin and Co, 625–648.

Gans, H. J. (1967) *The Levittowners*, Allen Lane, The Penguin Press.

Garrison, W. L. (1962) 'Comments on urban morphology', in K. Norborg (Ed.), *IGU Symposium in Urban Geography*, Gleerups, 463–464.

Gelkhe, C. E. and Biehl, K. (1934) 'Certain effects of grouping upon the size of the correlation coefficient in census tract material', *Journal of the American Statistical Association*, **29**, 169–170.

Gibbs, J. P. (1961) 'Methods and problems in the delineation of urban units', in J. P. Gibbs (Ed.), *Urban Research Methods*, Van Nostrand, 57–77.

Giggs, J. A. (1970) 'Socially disorganised areas in Barry: a multivariate analysis', in H. Carter and W. K. D. Davies (Eds.), *Urban Essays: studies in the geography of Wales*, Longmans, 101–143.

Gittus, E. (1964) 'An experiment in the definition of urban sub-areas', *Transactions of the Bartlett Society*, **2**, 109–135.

Goddard, J. B. (1970) 'Functional regions within the city centre: a study by factor analysis of taxi flows in central London', *Transactions of the Institute of British Geographers*, **49**, 161–182.

Goheen, P. (1970) 'Victorian Toronto, 1850–1900: pattern and process of growth', *Research Paper*, No. 127, Department of Geography, University of Chicago.

Goldsmith, H. F., Stockwell, E. G. and Unger, E. (1970) 'A technique for classifying population age profiles', *Laboratory Paper*, No. 33, Mental Health Study Center, National Institute of Mental Health.

Goldstein, S. (1958) *Patterns of Mobility, 1910–1950: the Norristown Study*, University of Pennsylvania Press.

Goldthorpe, J. H., Lockwood, D., *et al.* (1969) *The Affluent Worker in the Class Structure*, Cambridge University Press.

Goodman, L. A. (1953) 'Ecological regressions and the behaviour of individuals', *American Sociological Review*, **18**, 663–664.

Goodman, L. A. (1961) 'Statistical methods for the mover-stayer model', *Journal of the American Statistical Association*, **56**, 841–868.

Greer, S. (1956) 'Urbanism reconsidered: a comparative study of local areas in a metropolis', *American Sociological Review*, **21**, 19–25.

Greer, S. (1962) *The Emerging City*, The Free Press.

Greer-Wootten B. (1968) 'Cross-sectional social area analysis: Montreal, 1951–1961', Department of Geography, McGill University (mimeographed).

Griffiths, M. (1971) 'A geographical study of mortality in an urban area', *Urban Studies*, **8**, 111–120.

Grimshaw, P. N., Shepherd, M. J. and Willmott, A. J. (1970) 'An application of cluster analysis by computer to the study of urban morphology', *Transactions of the Institute of British Geographers*, **51**, 143–161.

Harman, H. H. (1960) *Modern Factor Analysis*, University of Chicago Press.

Harris, C. D. and Ullman, E. L. (1945) 'The nature of cities', *Annals of the Academy of Political and Social Sciences*, **242**, 7–17.

Harvey, D. (1967) 'Models of the evolution of spatial patterns in human geography', in R. J. Chorley and P. Haggett (Eds.), *Models in Geography*, Methuen, 549–608.

Harvey, D. (1969) *Explanation in Geography*, Arnold.

Harvey, D. (1971) 'Social processes, spatial form and the redistribution of real income in an urban system', in M. Chisholm, *et al.* (Eds.), *Regional Forecasting*, Butterworths, 267–300.

Hatt, P. K. and Reiss, A. J. (Eds.) (1957) *Cities and Society: the revised reader in urban society*, 2nd ed., The Free Press.

Haynes, K. E. (1971) 'Spatial change in urban structure: alternative approaches to ecological dynamics', *Economic Geography*, **47** (Supplement), 324–335.

Heraud, B. J. (1966) 'The new towns and London's housing problem', *Urban Studies*, **3**, 8–21.

Herbert, D. T. (1967) 'Social area analysis: a British study', *Urban Studies*, **4**, 41–60.

Herbert, D. T. (1970) 'Principal components analysis and urban social structure: a study of Cardiff and Swansea', in H. Carter and W. K. D. Davies (Eds.), *Urban Essays: studies in the geography of Wales*, Longmans, 79–100.

Hoyt, H. (1939) *The Structure and Growth of Residential Neighborhoods in American cities*, Federal Housing Administration, Washington, D.C.

Janson, C.-G. (1968) 'The spatial structure of Newark, New Jersey', *Acta Sociologica*, **11**, 144–169.

Janson, C.-G. (1969) 'Some problems of ecological factor analysis', in M. Dogan and S. Rokkan (Eds.), *Quantitative Ecological Analysis in the Social Sciences*, MIT Press, 301–41.

Johnston, R. J. (1966) 'The location of high status residential areas', *Geografiska Annaler, Series B*, **48**, 23–35.

Johnston, R. J. (1969a) 'Zonal and sectoral patterns in Melbourne's residential structure', *Land Economics*, **45**, 463–467.

Johnston, R. J. (1969b) 'Some tests of a model of intra-urban population mobility: Melbourne, Australia', *Urban Studies*, **6**, 34–57.

Johnston, R. J. (1969c) 'Processes of change in the high status residential areas of Christchurch, 1951–64', *New Zealand Geographer*, **25**, 1–15.

Johnston, R. J. (1969d) 'Population movements and metropolitan expansion: London 1960–61', *Transactions of the Institute of British Geographers*, **46**, 69–91.

Jones, E. (1960) *A Social Geography of Belfast*, Oxford University Press.

Jones, F. L. (1965) 'A social profile of Canberra, 1961', *Australian and New Zealand Journal of Sociology*, **1**, 107–120.

Jones, F. L. (1969) *Dimensions of Urban Social Structure: the social areas of Melbourne, Australia*, Australian National University Press.

Jones, P. N. (1970) 'Some aspects of the changing distribution of coloured immigrants in Birmingham, 1961–66', *Transactions of the Institute of British Geographers*, **50**, 199–219.

Kaiser, E. J. (1968) 'Locational decision factors in a producer model of residential development', *Land Economics*, **44**, 351–362.

Kaiser, E. J. (1969) 'Some components of a linked model for the residential development decision process', *Proceedings of the Association of American Geographers*, **1**, 75–79.

King, L. J. (1969) *Statistical Analysis in Geography*, Prentice-Hall.

Landay, S. (1971) 'The ecology of Islamic cities: the case for the ethnocity', *Economic Geography* **47** (Supplement), 303–313.

Lansing, J. B., Clifton, C. W. and Morgan, J. N. (1969) *New Houses and Poor People: a study of chains of moves*, University of Michigan, Institute for Social Research.

Lowry, I. S. (1964) *A Model of Metropolis*, The Rand Corporation.

Mabry, J. H. (1968) 'Public housing as an ecological influence in three English cities', *Land Economics*, 44, 393–398.

McElrath, D. C. (1962) 'The social area of Rome: a comparative analysis', *American Sociological Review*, 27, 376–391.

McElrath, D. C. (1968) 'Societal scale and social differentiation: Accra, Ghana', in S. Greer *et al.* (Eds.), *The New Urbanization*, St Martin's Press, 33–52.

Marble, D. F. and Nystuen, J. D. (1963) 'An approach to the direct measurement of community mean information fields', *Papers of the Regional Science Association*, 11, 99–109.

Marshall, J. D. (1968) 'Colonisation as a factor in the planning of towns in north-west England', in H. J. Dyos (Ed.), *The Study of Urban History*, Arnold, 215–230.

Menzel, H. (1950) 'Comment on Robinson's "Ecological correlation and the behavior of individuals" ', *American Sociological Review*, 15, 674.

Moore, E. G. (1969) 'The structure of intra-urban movement rates: an ecological model', *Urban Studies*, 6, 17–33.

Moore, E. G. (1970) 'Some spatial properties of urban contact fields', *Geographical Analysis*, 2, 376–386.

Moore, E. G. and Brown, L. A. (1969) 'Spatial properties of urban contact fields: an empirical analysis', *Research Paper*, No. 52, Department of Geography, Northwestern University.

Morgan, B. S. (1971) 'The residential structure of Exeter', in K. J. Gregory and W. Ravenhill (Eds.), *Exeter Essays in Geography*, University of Exeter, 219–236.

Morrill, R. L. (1965) 'The negro ghetto: problems and alternatives', *Geographical Review*, 55, 339–361.

Morrill, R. L. and Pitts, F. R. (1967) 'Marriage, migration and the mean information field: a study in uniqueness and generality', *Annals of the Association of American Geographers*, 57, 401–422.

Mortimore, M. J. (1969) 'Landownership and urban growth in Bradford and its environs in the West Riding conurbation', *Transactions of the Institute of British Geographers*, 46, 99–113.

Moses, L. and Williamson, H. F. (1967) 'The location of economic activity in cities', *American Economic Review*, 57, 211–222.

Murdie, R. A. (1969) 'Factorial ecology of Metropolitan Toronto, 1951–61: an essay in the social geography of the city', *Research Paper*, No. 116, Department of Geography, University of Chicago.

Norman, P. (1969) 'Third survey of London life and labour: a new typology of London districts', in M. Dogan and S. Rokkan (Eds.), *Quantitative Ecological Analysis in the Social Sciences*, MIT Press, 371–396.

Openshaw, S. (1969) 'Cannonical correlates of social structure and urban building fabric: an exploratory study', *Seminar Paper*, No. 12, Department of Geography, University of Newcastle.

Orleans, P. (1966) 'Robert Park and Social Area Analysis: a convergence of traditions in urban sociology', *Urban Affairs*, **1**, 5–19.

Park, R. E. (1926) 'The urban community as a spatial pattern and a moral order', in E. W. Burgess (Ed.), *The Urban Community*, University of Chicago Press, 3–18.

Peach, C. (1968) *West Indian Migration to London*, Oxford University Press.

Pederson, P. O. (1967) 'An empirical model of urban population structure: a factor analytic study of the urban population structure in Copenhagen', in *Proceedings of the First Scandinavian-Polish Regional Science Seminar*, Polish Scientific Publishers.

Perry, P. J. (1969) 'Working class isolation and mobility in rural Dorset, 1837–1936: a study of marriage distances', *Transactions of the Institute of British Geographers*, **46**, 115–135.

Peterson, G. L. (1967) 'A model of preference: quantitative analysis of the perception of the visual appearance of residential neighborhoods', *Journal of Regional Science*, **7**, 19–31.

Peucker, T. K. (1968) 'Johann Georg Kohl, a theoretical geographer of the nineteenth century', *Professional Geographer*, **20**, 247–250.

Pinnaeu, S. R. and Newhouse, A. (1964), 'Measures of invariance and comparability in factor analysis for fixed variables', *Psychometrika*, **29**, 271–281.

Pollins, H. (1964) 'Transport lines and social divisions', in Centre for Urban Studies, *London: aspects of change*, MacGibbon and Kee.

Pownall, L. L. (1957) 'Surface growth of New Zealand towns', *New Zealand Geographer*, **13**, 99–116.

Ramsøy, N. R. (1966) 'Assortive mating and the structure of cities', *American Sociological Review*, **31**, 773–786.

Rees, P. (1970) 'Concepts of social space: toward an urban social geography', in B. J. L. Berry and F. E. Horton, *Geographic Perspectives on Urban Systems*, Prentice-Hall, 306–394.

Reissman, L. (1964) *The Urban Process: cities in industrial society*, The Free Press.

Rex, J. (1968) 'The sociology of a zone in transition', in R. E. Pahl (Ed.), *Readings in Urban Sociology*, Pergamon, 211–231.

Rex, J. and Moore, R. (1967) *Race, Community and Conflict: a study of Sparkbrook*, Oxford University Press.

Robinson, A. H. (1956) 'The necessity of weighting values in correlation analysis of areal data', *Annals of the Association of American Geographers*, **46**, 233–236.

Robinson, W. S. (1950) 'Ecological correlation and the behavior of individuals', *American Sociological Review*, **15**, 351–357.

Robson, B. T. (1966) 'An ecological analysis of the evolution of residential areas in Sunderland', *Urban Studies*, **3**, 120–142.

Robson, B. T. (1969) *Urban Analysis: a study of city structure with special reference to Sunderland*, Cambridge University Press.

Robson, B. T. (1970) 'Review of Hoyt, 1939', *Urban Studies*, **7**, 217–218.

Rose, H. M. (1970) 'The development of an urban subsystem: the case of the negro ghetto', *Annals of the Association of American Geographers*, **60**, 1–17.

Rosing, K. E. and Wood, P. A. (1971) *Character of a Conurbation: a computer atlas of Birmingham and the Black Country*, London University Press.

Rossi, P. H. (1955) *Why Families Move: a study in the social psychology of urban residential mobility*, The Free Press.

Salins, P. D. (1971) 'Household location patterns in American metropolitan areas', *Economic Geography*, **47** (Supplement), 234–248.

Scheuch, E. K. (1969) 'Social context and individual behavior', in M. Dogan and S. Rokkan (Eds.), *Quantitative Ecological Analysis in the Social Sciences*, MIT Press, 133–155.

Schmid, C. F. (1960) 'Urban crime areas', *American Sociological Review*, **25**, 527–542 and 655–678.

Schmid, C. F. and Tagashira, K. (1964) 'Ecological and demographic indices: a methodological analysis', *Demography*, **1**, 194–211.

Schnore, L. F. (1965) 'On the spatial structure of cities in the two Americas', in P. M. Hauser and L. F. Schnore (Eds.), *The Study of Urbanization*, Wiley, 347–398.

Secretary of State for the Environment (1971), *Fair Deal for Housing*, Cmnd. 4728, HMSO.

Shevky, E. and Bell, W. (1955) *Social Area Analysis: theory, illustrative application and computational procedure*, Stanford University Press.

Shevky, E. and Williams, M. (1949) *The Social Areas of Los Angeles: analysis and typology*, University of California Press.

Simmons, J. W. (1965) 'Descriptive models of urban land use', *Canadian Geographer*, **9**, 170–174.

Simmons, J. W. (1968) 'Changing residence in the city: a review of intra-urban mobility', *Geographical Review*, **58**, 622–651.

Sirjamaki, J. (1964) *The Sociology of Cities*, Random House.

Sjoberg, G. (1959) 'Comparative urban sociology', in R. K. Merton *et al.* (Eds.), *Sociology Today: problems and prospects*, Basic Books Inc., 334–359.

Sjoberg, G. (1960) *The Preindustrial City: past and present*, The Free Press.

Sjoberg, G. (1965) 'Cities in developing and in industrial societies: a cross-cultural analysis', in P. M. Hauser and L. F. Schnore (Eds.), *The Study of Urbanization*, Wiley, 213–263.

Smailes, A. E. (1955) 'Some reflections on the geographical description and analysis of townscapes', *Transactions of the Institute of British Geographers*, **21**, 99–115.

Smailes, A. E. (1964) 'Greater London: the structure of a metropolis', *Geographische Zeitschrift*, **52**, 163–189.

Smith, P. J. (1962) 'Calgary: a study in urban pattern', *Economic Geography*, **38**, 315–329.

Sommer, R. (1969) *Personal Space: the behavioural basis of design*, Prentice-Hall.

Stein, M. R. (1960) *The Eclipse of Community: an interpretation of American studies*, Princeton University Press.

Sweetser, F. L. (1965a) 'Factor structure as ecological structure in Helsinki and Boston', *Acta Sociologica*, **8**, 205–225.

Sweetser, F. L. (1965b) 'Factorial ecology, Helsinki, 1960', *Demography*, **2**, 372–385.

Sweetser, F. L. (1969) 'Ecological factors in metropolitan zones and sectors', in M. Dogan and S. Rokkan (Eds.), *Quantitative Ecological Analysis in the Social Sciences*, MIT Press, 413–456.

Theodorson, G. A. (Ed.) (1961) *Studies in Human Ecology*, Row, Peterson and Co.

Thernstrom, S. and Sennett, R. (Eds.) (1969) *Nineteenth Century Cities: essays in the new urban history*, Yale University Press.

Thomas, E. N. and Anderson, D. L. (1965) 'Additional comments on weighting values in correlation analysis of areal data', *Annals of the Association of American Geographers*, **55**, 492–505.

Timms, D. W. G. (1970) *The Urban Mosaic: towards a theory of residential differentiation*, Cambridge University Press.

Valkonen, T. (1969) 'Individual and structural effects in ecological research', in M. Dogan and S. Rokkan (Eds.), *Quantitative Ecological Analysis in the Social Sciences*, MIT Press, 53–68.

Veldman, D. J. (1967), *Fortran Programs for the Behavioral Sciences*, Holt, Rinehart and Winston.

Ward, D. (1962) 'The pre-urban cadaster and the urban pattern of Leeds', *Annals of the Association of American Geographers*, **52**, 150–166.

Ward, D. (1964) 'A comparative historical geography of streetcar suburbs in Boston, Massachusetts and Leeds, England, 1850–1920', *Annals of the Association of American Geographers*, **54**, 477–489.

Ward, D. (1971) *Cities and Immigrants: a geography of change in nineteenth century America*, Oxford University Press.

Warner, S. B. Jr. (1968) *The Private City*, University of Pennsylvania Press.

Warntz, W. (1967) 'Global science and the tyranny of space', *Papers of the Regional Science Association*, **19**, 7–19.

Webber, M. M. (1963) 'Order in diversity: community without propinquity', in L. Wingo (Ed.), *Cities and Space: the future use of urban land*, Johns Hopkins, 23–54.

Webber, M. M. (1964) 'The urban place and the nonplace urban realm', in M. M. Webber *et al.* (Eds.), *Explorations into Urban Structure*, University of Pennsylvania Press, 79–153.

Wheatley, P. W. (1967) 'Proleptic observations on the origins of urbanism', in R. W. Steel and R. Lawton (Eds.), *Liverpool Essays in Geography*, Longmans Green, 315–345.

Wilson, A. G. (1969) 'Disaggregating elementary residential location models', *Working Paper*, No. 37, Centre for Environmental Studies, London.

Wilson, R. L. (1962) 'Livability in the city: attitudes and urban development', in F. S. Chapin and S. F. Weiss (Eds.), *Urban Growth Dynamics in a Regional Cluster of Cities*, Wiley, 359 399.

Winsborough, H. H. (1962) 'City growth and city structure', *Journal of Regional Science*, **4**, 35–49.

Wolpert, J. (1965) 'Behavioral aspects of the decision to migrate', *Papers of the Regional Science Association*, **15**, 159–169.

Wolpert, J. (1966) 'Migration as an adjustment to environmental stress', *Journal of Social Issues*, **22**, 92–102.

7 Regional development,
with particular reference to Britain

GERALD MANNERS

There is widespread and growing awareness amongst students of contemporary affairs that many of the problems posed by changes in Britain's economic geography will not yield to ready solutions. Some places suffer from too little development. Others experience (what is judged by some to be) too much. On one side of the spatial development coin there is, for example, the worsening unemployment crisis on Clydeside, the prospect of a further contraction of jobs in the textile mills, steelworks and coal mines of Lancashire, and the fears of the Greater London Council that the economic base of the Metropolis is being eroded too rapidly partly as a result of long-standing public policies to decentralize employment. On the other side can be seen the recent success of powerful pressure groups in the Home Counties, combining to persuade the Secretary of State for the Environment to locate the third London airport and its associated developments on a coastal site and thus, in the eyes of some observers, to 'shift an unwelcome guest into someone else's house' (CTLA, 1970, 445); similarly, a major common denominator of public planning enquiries in Southern England—be they for motorways or hypermarkets, power stations or new towns—is a deep-rooted suspicion of substantial local change, both environmental and economic. The conflicts are not new. The problems facing many communities in the older industrial areas of northern England and the industrial zones of Scotland and Wales have been recognized for more than a generation. Indeed, ever since the First World War, the traditional livelihoods of many of the people in these regions have been threatened as industries have contracted on account of changing technology and shifting comparative advantage; and the national community has taken on the responsibility of trying to help them to adjust to present-day economic circumstances. Likewise, contemporary local objections to motorway construction or large scale urban development had their nineteenth-century counterparts in the powerful resistance to the routes of many railways and the frequent opposition to the building of company towns.

The questions concerning regional development in Britain fall into two broad groups. The first is both factual and analytical. What changes are taking place in the spatial patterns of economic activity and job opportunities throughout the country and can they be readily explained? Do the factors that principally determine the location of manufacturing and service industries yield to accurate definition, and are they tending to change? Can the problems associated with local and regional economic development be so specified that meaningful distinctions can be drawn between the difficulties of places with superficially similar symptoms of distress—areas such as south Wales and northeast England, the West Riding and east Lancastria, inner London and inner Birmingham?

The second set of questions is more normative. In what ways can private initiatives and public policies ameliorate the deteriorating situation of such regions and localities? Should a new development— be it a motorway or an aluminium smelter, an international airport or a large decentralized government office—be located to influence the evolution of economic events in its immediate hinterland and sub-region, and to what extent (and with what accuracy) can its effects be predicted? How can one reconcile the desire for personal mobility with local objections to transport investments? Assuming that several policy options are open to both local and central governments, which are the more easily espoused and which are the more cost-effective? And in which spatial context should public policies be framed—within a preserved Edwardian geography of British settlement, or within some notions of a new European suburban form?

For more than a generation, in fact, successive governments have addressed themselves to these and related geographical questions. Since the Special Areas (Development and Improvement) Act of 1934, there has been persistent, deliberate and growing public intervention in the evolution of the British space economy. Under various Distribution of Industry and Local Employment Acts, the New Towns legislation, a forest of Town and Country Planning regulations, and special provisions in successive Finance Acts, government has provided itself with an ever more comprehensive set of tools for handling regional and sub-regional problems. The money committed to spatial planning has steadily increased. The number of public servants in central and local government actively engaged in the formulation and administration of these policies has been similarly multiplied, and a very expensive and complex planning machine has been set in motion. Many of its achievements command widespread admiration: the restructuring of Merseyside industry (Rodgers, 1972) and the preservation of the London Green Belt (Thomas, 1970), the run-down in the coal industry's workforce (Manners, 1971a) and the pioneering success of the new and expanded town overspill programmes (Thomas, 1969), all stand to its substantial credit. The fact remains, however, that many of the fundamental dilemmas of regional policy persist and, in the opinion of many observers, the search for solutions has become more urgent with the passage of time.

Questions about regional development have professionally interested a small but now increasing number of geographers since the 1930s, when the Royal Geographical Society was asked to submit evidence to the Royal Commission on the Distribution of the Industrial Population (E. G. R. Taylor et al., 1938; Willatts, 1971). Their interest has been shared with workers in several other social sciences, and the growing convergence of inter-disciplinary research interests (by economists, political scientists, planners and sociologists as well as geographers) upon the uncertainties and problems of spatial economic change and resource allocation has produced a body of literature and an emerging understanding that it would be improper to associate solely with a single discipline (Brown, 1969; Mackintosh, 1968; CES, 1970). Indeed, many of the more recent insights into regional economic and social change at a variety of scales have in fact followed especially from those studies that have eschewed the traditional boundaries of the individual social sciences. The appearance and the growing importance of such journals as *Urban Studies*, first published in 1964, and *Regional Studies*, which appeared initially in 1967, are distinctive symbols of this evolution.

In his 1969 essay, Brown reviewed the work of economists on questions of regional change in this country and, taking his brief literally, virtually ignored the work done in other disciplines. One purpose of the present essay, therefore, is to redress the balance somewhat by discussing the contributions of geographers. Since no one discipline has a monopoly of work on regional development, however, to exclude consideration of contributions from workers in disciplines other than geography would give an unbalanced picture. Consequently, though pride of place is given here to work done by geographers, an attempt is made to set this in a context both of the activities of other disciplines and of government itself.

The essay elaborates three principal areas of current interest in a rapidly growing literature: (i) the monitoring of interregional and intraregional change; (ii) the search for higher levels of generalization and the modelling of spatial development processes; and (iii) the exploration of the dynamic elements in regional growth. The essay concludes with some suggestions for the likely direction of future research. The emphasis of the discussion is placed upon industrial and urban development in Britain. Geographical contributions to developmental problems in rural areas (Economic Associates, 1966; Turnock, 1970) are therefore neglected, as are some of the more recent distinguished contributions to the study of recreational land use (Patmore, 1970; Rodgers, 1967 and 1969). Throughout the essay there runs an important theme. It will be noted that the greater part of geographical research into regional development in the past has been concerned with the crucially important task of laying a solid descriptive foundation for spatial analysis and understanding. More recently, however, the discipline has come to be characterized by research which adopts a more problem-oriented stance. In part, this mirrors a shift in the interests of the majority of students and of society at large. It also reflects the slow but crucial intellectual rapprochement between geography and economics in particular. The contemporary cross-fertilization of geographical enquiries with the notions and techniques of other problem-conscious and prediction-oriented disciplines appears likely to accelerate this trend.

MONITORING INTERREGIONAL AND INTRAREGIONAL CHANGE

The long-standing interest of geographers in the spatial variations in economic life has expressed itself over the years in a wealth of books, essays, surveys and reports (Daysh and Symonds, 1953; Mitchell, 1962; Smith, W., 1949; Stamp, 1948; Stamp and Beaver, 1933). From the local scale (Daysh, 1958) to the regional scale (Freeman et al., 1966; Smailes, 1960) and the national scale (Best and Coppock, 1962; Watson and Sissons, 1964), detailed expression has been given to the infinite variety of the features to be found in the British economic landscape and to some of the human and natural forces that shape its evolution. In the process, much emphasis has been placed upon the unique attributes of site and locality. Studies of land and natural resource use (Beaver, 1944; Simpson, 1966; Stamp, 1948) have been paralleled by enquiries into the changing spatial characteristics of particular industries and activities in both the manufacturing and service sectors of the economy (Appleton, 1962; Fullerton, 1963; Rawstron, 1957); and once again the distinctive nature of many local and regional economic developments, and their associated geographical attributes, has been persistently stressed.

This ideographic concern with the uniqueness of places militated against the formulation of general statements and hypotheses, especially when the detailed information about localities could only be obtained by laborious field investigation which tended to become an end in itself. However, the considerable literature amassed in the inter-war and early post-war years showed just how striking are the interregional and intra-regional socio-economic contrasts in Britain and materially helped to generate a climate of opinion which was concerned by the lack of spatially disaggregated data. This concern was espoused in the 1960s by first the National Economic Development Council (established in 1962) and then the short-lived Department of Economic Affairs (1964–70) which generated a demand from within the machinery of government for more detailed and geographically comparable data sets. In its earlier reports, and in its search for a faster rate of national economic growth (NEDC, 1963a, 1963b), the Council laid great stress upon the need to harness as quickly as possible the country's under-employed regional resources, especially labour. This view was officially espoused by the government two years later in its ill-fated *National Plan* (First Secretary of State, 1965). Yet such an objective could only be fully attained if substantial advances were made in the understanding of regional growth processes; and a more immediate requirement was the availability of certain key economic indicators disaggregated on a regional and sub-regional basis. Simultaneously, the newly created Regional Planning Boards and Regional Economic Councils became aware of the woefully inadequate nature of existing statistics for the examination of the characteristics and the problems of their regions. All these developments, therefore, prompted not only a wider accept-ance by government departments of the ten new Standard Regions for purposes of data collection and interpretation, but also in some instances they encouraged the disaggregation of those data into one of two very similar sets of official subdivisions (based upon local authority areas and employment exchange areas respectively) for descriptive and analytical purposes.

With the much enhanced supply of spatially disaggregated data, particularly at the interregional scale (CSO, 1965), the geographer's traditional concern with variations in phenomena from place to place can be married with the economist's attempts to build robust descriptive and explanatory models. Geographers and others have been quick to seize the opportunities thus presented. Besides probing more vigorously into census data on population and social conditions (Hunt, 1968), students of late have been able to explore with a new thoroughness the changing interregional geography of personal income (Coates and Rawstron, 1966, 1971), contrasts in the size and structure of regional employment (Humphrys, 1962; Stilwell, 1969, 1970) and differences in the activity or participation rates of the working-age population in different parts of the country (Gordon, 1970). The spatial characteristics of unemployment (Salt, 1969; Sant, 1967), of productivity (Parsons, 1971), of interregional net migration (Department of the Environment, 1971; Hart, R. A., 1970; Lawton, 1968) and of industrial and commercial building activity (Secretary of State for Economic Affairs, 1969) have also been examined. Many of the broad changes in the use of land that have been associated with these indices of economic and social change have also received considerable attention, as well as those land-use changes which have followed from the shifting political economy of agriculture (Best, 1959; Best and Coppock, 1962). Intraregional studies have similarly recorded change in much the same range of economic and social phenomena, occasionally complementing official published and unpublished statistics with information derived from special local and regional surveys. The monitoring of economic developments in northeast England has been outstanding in this respect (House, 1969), although our knowledge and understanding of other regions have also been substantially advanced by work in local departments of geography (Edwards, 1949; Lawton and Cunningham, 1970; Lewis and Jones, 1970; Manners, 1964; Martin, 1966). More often than not, it has been geography departments that have been entrusted with the preparation of the interdisciplinary local handbooks which are published on the occasion of the British Association's peripatetic annual conference (e.g. Balchin, 1971).

Predictably, at both the interregional and intraregional scales, these studies have revealed a great diversity of regional and sub-regional socio-economic character and change. To this extent they endorsed the validity of the traditional descriptive approach of much geographical enquiry. Simultaneously, however, research has repeatedly confirmed the persistence of 'the two Britains'. The contrast between the rapidly expanding and relatively prosperous communities of southern and central England on the one hand, and the slowly growing and relatively poorer regions of the north and the west of the country on the other, is a basic reality of British economic geography. The five southern and midland regions of England, for example, with 57·7% of the national employment in 1959, captured 87·5% of the net growth of jobs in the subsequent eight years (Stilwell, 1969). During those same years, the country's five other northern and 'Celtic' regions (neglecting for the moment Northern Ireland, which is a special case) experienced in general a sluggish rate of growth, and even in some localities a decline in their employment opportunities. These same regions also witnessed a slower net addition to both industrial and commercial premises, significantly higher rates of unemployment than in the country as a whole, and a low or declining proportion of their womenfolk at work. Combined, these characteristics expressed themselves in the steady out-migration of people from the poorer counties of the north and the west. These tendencies in the less prosperous regions were reinforced by the relatively poor intraregional and interregional transport and communication facilities available to industry there, and also by the undoubted effects of their considerable share of the country's outdated built environment which they inherit from the hey-day of Victorian and Edwardian urban expansion. All these and other indices of economic and social well-being were the 'causes for concern' that were noted by the Hunt Committee on *The Intermediate Areas* in its final report (Secretary of State for Economic Affairs, 1969), a document which pointed to important geographical contrasts within the less prosperous regions and which also underlined the urgent need for an improvement in our understanding of both the processes of spatial economic development and the appropriate responses of the community to their associated problems (Manners, 1970).

Geographical studies designed to monitor socio-economic change have generally been inspired by empirical questions, and for the most part they have employed essentially descriptive tools. The value and the achievements of such a research style are not in doubt. Nevertheless, it frequently lacks the clear sense of direction that characterizes enquiries centred upon a problem-probing hypothesis; and its findings often exhibit a remoteness from the generalizations espoused by theory. In turn, this has meant that many of the more fundamental questions raised by even a cursory examination of the changing patterns of regional development as yet remain unanswered, and the development of spatial theory has been relatively slow. For example, the suggestion was made by Williamson in 1965 that in an industrially and socially advanced economy a natural convergence tends to occur in interregional levels of income and economic opportunity; yet by 1972 his thesis had still to be tested rigorously in the British context. The bold contrasts between the economic fortunes of the regions of Britain in the inter-war years on the one hand, and the much narrower range of the disparities that have existed since the Second World War on the other, might intuitively suggest that the thesis holds true in the British case. Although interregional disparities remain and continue to be worthy of political attention, they are obviously narrower today than they were 25 or 35 years ago. However, recent studies of employment statistics by Stilwell (1969) tentatively suggest that the 1960s was a decade of increasing regional employment imbalance, even though the industrial mix of the less prosperous regions was simultaneously being substantially improved. Thus the Williamson hypothesis remains open to doubt. Only following a much closer study of the various indices of regional prosperity and health in a framework designed to test the hypothesis will it be possible to judge its validity.

In the past, the quest for theories of interregional economic growth and intraregional development has been largely eschewed by British geographers. It is nevertheless important to recognize that a substantial body of spatial theory, developed by economists (Hoover, 1948; Ohlin, 1933), regional scientists (Isard, 1956; Isard *et al.*, 1960, 1969), planners (Friedman and Alonso, 1964) and geographers in the United States (Berry, 1967; Warntz, 1959), has provided an influential context within which a small but increasing volume of empirical monitoring work has been either explicitly or implicity placed. At the intraregional scale, for example, the notions of Myrdal (1957) and Hirschman (1958) especially have served as theoretical reference points in geographical investigations, and the concepts of 'circular causation', 'spread effects', 'backwash' and 'trickle-down' effects have intermittently found a place in studies concerned with monitoring and interpreting spatial developments (Manners, 1964; Spooner, 1971). Again, the idea of a 'growth pole' (Perroux, 1955) has from time to time been (somewhat uncritically) embraced as a vehicle suitable for the explanation of particular events and phenomena—although once again its validity has never been rigorously tested (Cameron, 1971; Darwent, 1969; Lasuen, 1969). At the interregional scale, theoretical writings have laid great stress upon the interdependence of phenomena through space, and the theme of systems and sub-systems has been repeatedly stressed in theories of regional economic structure such as interregional input-output, in central place theory and in notions of accessibility as interpreted in gravity and potential models (Isard *et al.*, 1960). In turn, these theories have shaped the concepts underlying a number of studies monitoring and interpreting national patterns of economic development (Caesar, 1964), urbanization (Hall, 1972) and freight flows (Chisholm and O'Sullivan, forthcoming). Few in number, and generally structured to lean on but not necessarily to test theory, such studies have generated only limited feedback for the improvement of that theory.

In the absence of better-tested hypotheses and theories, it is inevitable that many of the problems involved in formulating precise goals in spatial planning, and of selecting criteria for interregional and regional resource allocation, should remain generally neglected (Foster and Smith, 1969). Clearly, much will be gained from a more determined attempt to associate spatial monitoring studies more closely with the testing of hypotheses and theory. Especially if approached from an interdisciplinary rather than simply a geographical base, such research will afford new insights into the processes of spatial development and also into the opportunities for constructive public intervention therein. There is evidence to suggest that this much-needed change of emphasis in geographical research has already begun.

THE SEARCH FOR HIGHER LEVELS OF GENERALIZATION AND THE MODELLING OF SPATIAL DEVELOPMENT PROCESSES

Besides permitting and encouraging a more comprehensive examination of the country's socio-economic geography, the greater availability of spatially disaggregated data has had a further important effect upon the style of geographical research. The new statistical series have permitted the adoption and the refinement of new modes of statistical description, new types of spatial analysis and new accounting frameworks which were previously denied to the British researcher. An example of the newer style of geographical description and analysis—in this case at the intraregional scale—is the use by D. M. Smith (1968) of factor analysis and related grouping procedures to define with a new comprehensiveness those localities suffering from economic distress. His work underlined the need to supplement or even to replace the local level of unemployment as the principal criterion for making government assistance available to the Development Areas (for many years a level of 4% was taken as the threshold above which assistance was assured from the Board of Trade, now the Department of Trade and Industry). Examining the case of north-west England in some detail, Smith demonstrated how local levels of unemployment in fact correlate weakly with the many other possible indices of local industrial and socio-economic ill-health, indices such as the rate of change in the employment structure, the construction of new industrial floorspace or the local level of household rateable values. He also showed how the degree of socio-economic distress, as measured by these and similar criteria, is frequently considerably greater outside the Development Areas, defined conventionally on the basis of their unemployment records, than inside them.

Amongst the techniques recently employed for the first time by geographers to explore the structure and economic relationships within a local economy is input-output analysis. Modifying the static and open Leontief (1966) model, and using extensive local surveys, Morrison (1971) has demonstrated for the first time the feasibility of constructing a detailed (45 × 42 matrix) input-output table for a British sub-region without resorting to the use of non-survey coefficients derived from the national table. He was thus able not only to throw new light upon the existing pattern of internal and external financial transactions within the Peterborough economy, and so to demonstrate those sectors which are more 'open' or 'closed'; he was also able to speculate more confidently about the future economy of the region and in particular about some of the implications of the plans to double the size of the city. Further studies of this type will make it possible to gain additional insights into variations in intraregional trade coefficients for different regions and the characteristics of interregional trade relationships with different types and sizes of regional economy. In the process, impact and multiplier analysis will be placed upon a much firmer foundation.

The full implications of new investments and employment creation in a local or regional economy hitherto have been measured by means of either crude multipliers (Allen, 1969) or variations of the simple economic base model such as the 'minimum requirements' approach (Klassen, 1965). Economic Associates Ltd. estimated that, in the case of the prospective third London airport, each basic employment would generate a further 2·2 jobs; and each basic and non-basic job in turn would add 2·5 people to the airport urbanization (CTLA, 1970, Appendix B). Crude though these figures might have been, they served well enough in the context of forecasts which looked to the end of the present century. However, in future the use of the more detailed accounting framework afforded by a reasonably accurate regional or local input-output table will provide opportunities to clarify the nature of the multiplier process. With additional data inputs, it will also provide a much sounder basis for analysing and forecasting the implications of either new investments or the withdrawal of major employment oportunities in a region, especially in the short term when greater accuracy is required.

With the adoption and development of such new quantitative techniques and accounting frameworks, a growing body of geographical research has thus moved away from detailed local (and primarily literary) descriptions and has embarked upon a search for new and higher levels of generalization. One product of this development has been the emergence of a fresh and more scientific approach towards regionalization. Spence (1968; Spence and Taylor, 1971), for example, used component analysis to isolate the basic spatial variations in the geography of employment on a county basis and then applied grouping techniques to produce a typology of county employment structures and a definition of uniform employment regions. On the other hand, in the Political and Economic Planning study of British urbanization (Hall, 1971, 1972), new Standard Metropolitan Labour Areas were defined comprising an urban core with a high density of workers plus a surrounding ring of communities sending at least 15% of their resident employed populations into the core on a regular daily basis; in consequence, new light could be thrown upon the principal population and employment changes within urban and suburban England in recent years, and an important set of public policy conclusions emerged. A more generalized yet deeper understanding of the geography of employment has been obtained from the use of such measures as the location and diversification quotient to measure the degree to which particular activities are tending to concentrate in particular places, and the Lorenz curve to explore the relative level of regional and sub-regional job specialization (Britton, 1967; Conkling, 1964). The complexities of central city communication patterns have been disentangled by Goddard (1971) into a highly generalized set of relationships by latent profile analysis; by this means, he was able to produce typologies of associated communication activities among offices in central London.

At the interregional scale, a particularly vivid example of this search for higher levels of generalization is the application of the concept of gravity fields to the measurement of access to markets. Using the concept of economic potential, previously developed by geographers in America, Clark (1966; Clark et al., 1969) has produced maps for both Britain alone and for Western Europe including Britain showing the geographical variation in potential access to national and European markets. Geographers have also sought to discover whether, as is to be expected from the logic of external economies and Myrdal's concept of cumulative causation, the more accessible areas of the country do in fact exhibit relatively high rates of industrial growth (Norcliffe, 1970) and economies in freight transport costs compared with the peripheral areas (Chisholm and O'Sullivan, forthcoming). Both of these studies indicate that while economic potential is an explanatory factor, it does not account for a very large proportion of the variance in the relevant dependent variables.

A significant product of this search for more generalized levels of spatial economic description and understanding has been the awakening of an interest amongst geographers in mathematical modelling and forecasting. As yet, only a few scholars are active in this field. Nevertheless, there can be few doubts concerning its prospective importance and, once again, its essentially inter-disciplinary nature (Chisholm *et al.*, 1971). The relevant literature is burgeoning. Details of some regional models, their theoretical basis, their design and calibration, and their practical value have been extensively explored by Wilson (1968, 1971). At the interregional scale, models have been developed for replicating population migration (Hart, 1970), the movement of manufacturing activity (Keeble, 1971), and interregional freight flows (Chisholm and O'Sullivan, forthcoming) and all have been successfully calibrated with recent empirical data. It has, however, been on an intraregional scale that the most vigorous modelling activity has been taking place. It can be interpreted as a search for an improved and tested body of spatial theory, the absence of which in the past has been a serious restraint upon the understanding of regional development. Traffic and shopping models (Hall, P., 1967a; Kantorowich, 1964; Wilson *et al.*, 1969), urban growth and land use models (Drewett, 1969; Hall, 1967b), housing and population mobility models (Pilgrim, 1969) have all been formulated and tested with varying degrees of success at a number of regional and sub-regional scales. Many of these models have in common some variant of the simple gravity model as a basis for understanding the nature of spatial interaction; a large number of them have been designed specifically to aid in the planning and decision-making process, more especially in so far as they permit the evaluation of alternative development strategies (Lichfield, 1970).

To the extent that the assumptions underlying such studies are specific, well-founded and likely to remain valid in the future, these models can play a useful rôle in forecasting. However, such stringent conditions are only occasionally fulfilled, with the result that the application of interaction models for planning purposes has to be handled with particular care. Ideally, spatial models should be made dynamic for forecasting purposes. This means that, in the case of input-output models, evidence is required on temporal changes in both average and

marginal trade coefficients and on changing sectoral capital requirements; and, in the case of a gravity model, modifications to the distance
exponent, with the growth of and changes in the interacting system
through time, have to be ascertained. Alternatively, spatial models can
be used to arrange sets of 'fixes' or constraints for the variables under
public control and then used to generate associated forecasts of all the
other variables in the system; in this way, the impact of various
geographical possibilities can be better evaluated and the public policy
options more explicitly defined. In their studies of land use in Bedford-
shire, for example, Cripps and Foot (1969) 'fixed' the location of employment, and then endogenously estimated the geography of the household
and service sectors within the county economy. This type of study,
whose inspiration stems from the work of Lowry (1964) in the United
States, represents an important new departure in sub-regional land use
planning studies (Drewett, 1969).

Interaction models in particular assume some knowledge of causal
relationships between the elements in the model. Where regularities in
the geography of regional development are noted without the ready
availability of an explanatory hypothesis, however, simulation models
are sometimes developed to afford a better basis on which to postulate
future states of the system, or even to hold together a loose set of
forecasting tools in the context of a regional or sub-regional planning
exercise (McLoughlin, 1969). Invaluable though they may be in this
rôle, simulation models are basically a stop-gap until advances are
made in our understanding of the processes and the dynamic elements
in regional development. It is to work in this area that this essay now
turns.

EXPLORING THE DYNAMIC ELEMENTS IN REGIONAL DEVELOPMENT

Industrial location studies

The main driving force in regional socio-economic change is, of course,
the locational behaviour of productive activities within both the manufacturing and service sectors of the economy. Most geographical
studies of industrial location have been of an essentially empirical
nature, reaching for generalizations within relatively simple conceptual
frameworks. However, the existence of a body of partial location
theory (Weber, 1929; Isard, 1956) has provided an opportunity for
some research to be shaped by the formulation and testing of theoretically derived hypotheses. The contributions of geographers to the

refinement of classical location theory—which places relative transport costs as central to an industry's spatial efficiency and discounts the importance of labour and agglomeration economies in a firm's costs— has been somewhat limited. The valuable papers by Rawstron (1958) and D. M. Smith (1966) stand as exceptions rather than the rule. A great deal of geographical thinking and teaching has nevertheless taken full note of this literature, and the most recent full summary of this tradition has been provided by D. M. Smith (1971). One branch of location theory has, however, been advanced primarily as a result of geographical scholarship. This has been the development of a more articulate be- havioural theory of location in which the imperfections of entre- preneurial and managerial knowledge and competence are more openly recognized (Pred, 1967 and 1969; Townroe, 1971). A fundamental assumption of this theory is that every locational decision should be viewed as occurring under conditions of varying information and entrepreneurial ability, ranging, at least theoretically, from null to perfect knowledge of all possibilities, and as being governed by the varying abilities (as well as the objectives) of the decision-maker(s) (Pred, 1967). Wood (1969) has pressed for a more formal adoption of the behavioural theory of the firm (Cyert and Marsh, 1963), stressing that the location decisions of an enterprise must be seen as a by-product of the general process of choosing desirable strategies for the firm's survival and expansion. The gap between the classical and behavioural theories of location, with the latter's new emphasis upon the various modes of investment decision-making in different firms, is both wide and as yet largely unbridged. It could well be, as Chisholm (1971) has recently argued, that notions and insights derived from welfare econo- mics will serve in time to provide some substantial middle ground.

The mounting volume of empirical geographical work on the location of industry has forcefully demonstrated the considerable diversity of influences that bear upon the evolution of employment patterns and hence the nature of regional development. The work of Warren (1970) on the British iron and steel industry, for example, is a classic exposure of both plant and management inertia in an activity which *par excellence* might have been thought likely to respond strongly to the Weberian imperatives of minimizing transport costs with successive investment opportunities. Likewise, empirical research on the geography of the chemical industry (Warren, 1971) has underlined the locational inertia of sunk costs and existing production facilities in an expanding industry, especially when there is an understandable tendency of management to discount longer term costs in favour of short and medium term benefits. The importance of changing production and transport technology and their costs was noted in studies of the gas industry by Manners (1959; 1971b). The attractions of unemployed labour in the movement of lighter manufacturing industries to the Development Areas has been emphasized by Keeble (1971). And the nature of an industry's structure and institutional framework—with the consequential implications for the priorities and the location of new investments—have been repeatedly emphasized by Odell (1965; 1970); clearly, the internationally owned and multicorporate oil industry in Britain has produced a geography of refinery operations and product hauls that would not have been the choice of a single nationalized concern responsible for the performance of the whole industry.

The dependence of many firms upon easy access to and efficient communications with other firms in the same or related industries has occasioned a number of detailed studies of linkages between sets of manufacturing concerns in different parts of the country (Keeble, 1969; Lomas and Wood, 1969; Taylor, M. J., 1969) and between offices in London (Goddard, 1970, 1971). This work has pointed to the external economies being derived from these associations, although their importance obviously varies with particular firms and industries. Wood (1969) has attempted to develop a typology of linkages between firms that recognizes the existence between them of simple and complex, weak and strong, material and informational connections, all of which combine to make up a firm's 'total operational linkages'. To the extent that these economies cannot be foregone lightly in planned industrial developments, the research has obvious normative implications. Nor was it without its influence upon the 1970 *Strategic Plan for the South East* (SEJPT, 1970, 1971). However, although many of these studies demonstrate the possibility of stretching links over increasing distances—for this is what has been happening in the past as, for example, firms in the outer GLC suburbs shift to the Outer Metropolitan Area and still maintain many of their close connections with inner London—no clear evidence is available on the distances over which particular links can be stretched without a loss in efficiency. Moreover, it is not at all clear that existing and recorded links are in any way optimal. They change in size, nature and direction as firms grow and internalize many activities which formerly were purchased locally; they also shift as firms seek out new locations and in the process re-examine their traditional patterns of behaviour.

The growing interest in the close relationships which exist between firms within a particular industry, or between firms in different industries, has demonstrated the need increasingly to interpret locational economics not so much in terms of a single plant or office or facility operating as an independent unit, but rather as a spatial system of interrelated investments within which any change will inevitably have widespread impact. Such a change of emphasis in location studies is well illustrated by the interpretative literature on the electricity generating industry which at one time was studied in an essentially Weberian framework; location decisions, in other words, appeared to hinge largely upon the alternative costs of different modes of raw material (fuel) and product (energy) transport (Rawstron, 1955; Manners, 1971b). More recent work, however, and particularly that of Hauser (1971), has demonstrated the need to understand the geography of new generation investment within the context of the total production-transmission system, bearing in mind the fact that the addition of a new facility inevitably affects the rôle and the costs of all other power stations in the rest of the system. For example, in deciding between a new atomic power station in south-east England, an oil-fired station on lower Thamesside and a coal-fired unit in the east Midlands to serve an increment to the base load demand of London and the Home Counties, the Generating Board have to consider not only the construction and operating costs of the three plants in their respective locations, but also the fact that they will differentially affect other power station operations and costs throughout the country; this is because the working costs of nuclear, oil and coal generation are sufficiently different to place each hypothetical plant at a different place in the station 'merit order' and so to affect in contrasting ways the output and rôle of most other plants in the grid-linked, production-supply system (Manners, 1971b). This shifting emphasis of location studies away from discrete production units and towards system economics follows quite naturally from the increasing scale of industrial organization and the growing importance of the multi-plant firm, the international corporation and the development of new techniques of investment appraisal and corporate planning.

Of the many economies to be obtained by large scale organizations (economies such as specialized management, large scale and carefully planned sales promotion, the bulk purchase of raw materials and components, and in certain instances a lower real cost of capital) a number have been seen to have important geographical implications. Apart from the ability to concentrate its production processes in fewer locations and to exploit scale economies, one of the more common is the opportunity to locate certain of its internalized service functions, such as the advertising section, sales departments, accounts, research and

transport divisions, in a head office sited away from the main production units. Many of these services, which were characteristically
purchased locally by many smaller and scattered firms during an
earlier phase of industrial organization, have come not only to be
internalized within the larger corporation but also strongly localized
in the south of the country. In so far as many of these specialized head
office services find certain external economies available in locations
where similar and related service activities are to be found—the
advertising section of a large corporation finds it advantageous to be
near agencies, specialist advertising services, the relevant professional
institutes and even other head office advertising sections—the attractions
of London in particular and the south-east in general have been over-
whelming. A survey by Parsons (1970) has revealed the very powerful
forces for regional inequality inherent in the growing concentration
of corporate control units in south-east England, and the apparent
incompatibility between central government policies in the fields of
industrial re-organization and regional development. With nearly half
of the country's research establishments also in the southeast (Buswell
and Lewis, 1970), that region is afforded an outstanding advantage in
fostering new enterprises in both the service and manufacturing
sectors of the economy, and especially those exploiting knowledge on
the frontiers of technological and scientific advance. It is not without
reason that the south-east region has come to be regarded as the
country's premier seed-bed of new economic growth (Taylor, M. J.,
1969).

Industrial movement
An outstanding facet of geographical research into the locational
behaviour of industry has been the exploration of the spatial 'trickle-
down' or 'spread' effects of investment and growth in the south of the
country, in the form of the movement of firms away from the south-east
and the west midland regions into other parts of Britain. Encouraged
by various government policies, there can be little doubt that this
movement has been and remains a central feature of the changing
economic geography of the country. For some time, evidence on the
mobility of industrial firms was largely confined to data generated from
surveys conducted by individuals and on an *ad hoc* basis—surveys by
Keeble (1969) and Spooner (1971) of manufacturing industry in
north-west London and south-west England respectively being cases
in point. More recently, however, data released by the erstwhile Board
of Trade (Howard, 1968) have provided a generous if incomplete data

set upon which much valuable interregional research has been conducted. Analysing the hundreds of moves made by industry since the end of the Second World War, Keeble (1971) has proposed his 'dual population hypothesis' which states that most industrial movement falls into one of two categories. Each is defined by the distance of the move, the nature of the destination and the size of the organization or firm. Shorter distance intraregional movement has been dominated by relatively small firms which provide the driving force for metropolitan expansion and overspill, and which shift to sites where close links with activities in their parent conurbation can easily be maintained and attendant external economies are not foregone. On the other hand, interregional movement streams have been dominated by larger firms (or the branches of larger firms) which have relocated in response to the more ready supplies of labour in the Development Areas, sometimes with the encouragement and assistance of government subsidies. These firms naturally tend to internalize many of their related services and activities—transport and accounts, for example—and as a result are indifferent to the relative absence of external economies in their new locations.

In the service sector of the economy, however, movement has proceeded over much shorter distances. The 'dual-population hypothesis' still stands to the extent that smaller firms, continuing to hold on to much of their existing labour force and valuing easy access to the central city of their origin, have tended to move only a short distance from their initial location. Larger firms, on the other hand, have been able to contemplate longer distance moves, accepting the need to recruit a replacement labour force in their new location and to choose a suitable place from this point of view. Predictably, it has been the more routine types of activities that have been decentralized over these longer distances. However, unlike manufacturing industry, which has been prepared to move several hundred kilometres in its search for adequate supplies of labour (and government aid), private office employers have been reluctant to shift more than about 125 kilometres from the centre of London—the exceptions tending to be moves to such outstandingly attractive urban environments as Cheltenham and Exeter. Only government offices have made a genuine contribution to the interregional problem in recent years (Daniels, 1969; Hall, R., 1970), at a cost which is by no means clear but which could quite well be surprisingly modest by comparison with the expense of moving manufacturing jobs (Rhodes and Kan, 1971). It nevertheless remains uncertain just how much office employment could be steered

away from southern England even if financial inducements in the
assisted areas were added to the floorspace controls currently existing
in the South East region. To the economies afforded in London and
the Home Counties by a large pool of skilled labour and relatively
easy linkages to other firms in the same office industry has to be added
the absence of any significant rent economies beyond the Outer
Metropolitan Area, plus the obvious personal disinclination of many
office executives to move their homes and workplace any great distance
from London.

The contribution of mobile (manufacturing and service) industry to
both intraregional and interregional development has been only too
obvious in the past. Intraregionally, the movement of activities in
search of space, lower land values and frequently pleasanter environments appears likely to persist in the future. The rate at which it takes
place, however, may well need to be governed by public as well as
private considerations. Amongst the many fundamental economic
issues raised in connection with the proposals of the Greater London
Council (1969) in their *Development Plan*, one of the more profound
concerns the future of dispersal planning. Undoubtedly too fast a rate
of decentralization could cause spatial imbalance of jobs and homes,
of people and social facilities. Research has yet to demonstrate, however, just how a satisfactory balance can be planned and maintained.
An even greater problem is increasingly evident in the matter of interregional movement. There is little doubt that, over the next decade and
more, the less prosperous industrial economies of the north and west
will continue to experience fairly rapid structural change and a loss of
employment opportunities. Some of these can be replaced by the
expansion of the many firms steered into these areas in recent years,
but it is unlikely that they will generate enough replacement jobs to
arrest high levels of unemployment and outmigration. At the same
time, all the evidence points to the fact that employment in manufacturing industry in the country as a whole is unlikely to grow particularly rapidly in the near future. Indeed, it seems likely to represent
over future years a declining share of total national employment, the
more so as rising wage demands and the increasing real cost of manpower encourage a substitution of capital equipment for labour in
most areas of manufacturing enterprise. Whilst a faster national rate
of economic growth would without doubt permit the government to
steer some new investment and growing enterprises into the Development and Intermediate Areas, thereby helping to create new and viable
activities there, it appears unlikely that such a movement could totally

offset the prospective loss of jobs in such industries as coal mining, iron and steel, shipbuilding, textiles and the like. Meanwhile, it is not at all clear whether large numbers of service jobs could be moved into the Development Areas, as they lie beyond the threshold of 125 kilometres, which seems to be the current limit for most long-distance moves. Perhaps such jobs will be located in the Development Areas on a significant scale only as a result of decisions to move additional central government departments from London and by the offer of powerful financial incentives to the private sector (Rhodes and Kan, 1971).

Public policy and regional development

The addition of a public component to the many forces shaping the geography of regional development has naturally generated a set of research activities by geographers at all scales from the small community and the sub-region (Daysh, 1958) to the conurbation and large region (Hall P., 1963; Keeble, 1972). Occasionally, a broader view has been taken of regional planning issues of the country as a whole (Caesar, 1964; Chisholm, 1964; Manners, 1972), but more usually interest has focussed upon the evaluation of policies in either the more prosperous central regions of the country or the less prosperous peripheral economies separately. In the case of the more dynamic city regions in the south of Britain, the writings of P. Hall (1963), Keeble (1972) and Powell (1961) have been among the more outstanding in the case of Greater London, while the names of Rodgers (1972), Wise (1950) and Lomas and Wood (1969) have been particularly associated with the West Midlands. All these studies have pointed to the strength of spatial economic forces in regional development and the (changing) constraints within which historical planning procedures and future planning options must operate. They have also indicated the contribution which both the more traditional (Thomas, D., 1970) and the more quantitative (Goddard, 1971) styles of geographical analysis can make to an understanding of public policy issues.

It has however been the evolution of the less prosperous regions of Britain and the governmental response to their problems which have generated most research and interest. Not only were some of the earlier students of the regional problem in the 1930s and 1940s, such as Daysh (1936, 1949; Daysh and Symonds, 1953), W. Smith (1949) and Caesar (Caesar and Daysh, 1949) spurred on by the difficulties of the coalfield industrial areas; but a number of more recent writers also, such as House (1969), Manners (1964), D. M. Smith (1969) and Rodgers

(1964), were inspired by the persistence of these problems and the
continuing need for various forms of public assistance and subsidy.
In these studies, not only has the relative weakness of the peripheral
zone as a whole been exposed in such matters as the ability to generate
new employment and to attract new investment, but the limited
number of options open to the planners of these regions outside the
framework of a national programme of regional assistance has been
repeatedly stressed.

Some attention has been given to the costs of this intervention in the
space economy. However, the total public and private costs involved
in seeking the benefits of a more balanced pattern of regional development are somewhat elusive. The public expense of assisting private
enterprise to move to or establish itself in one of the assisted areas is
of course known with some precision, since funds are voted under
clearly specified Parliamentary estimates—either under general regional
development legislation (such as the Location of Industry Acts, the
Local Employment Acts and the Industrial Development Act) or
under more specific legislation relating to particular industries (such
as the Cotton Industry Act of 1962 or the Shipbuilding Industry Act
of 1967). However, money spent in the assisted areas on the nationalized
industries—such as the support persistently given by the national
exchequer to the National Coal Board or British Rail—is much more
difficult if not impossible to quantify, since the aid affects the whole
industry and its geographical impact is not readily identified. Furthermore, expenditure on regional infrastructural improvements are highly
elusive, except when special grants are voted under exceptional circumstances such as occasioned the White Papers on *North East England*
and *Central Scotland* in 1963. Even if full data were available, of course,
their evaluation would pose enormous intellectual difficulties in the
absence of clear criteria for interregional public resource allocation
(Foster and Smith J. F., 1969), and given the imponderables surrounding
the measurement of the associated benefits.

To the public costs have to be added the many private expenses
associated with regional development policies. Empirical work by
economists (Cameron and Clark, 1966; Luttrell, 1962) has been largely
responsible for indicating the relatively small locational cost differentials
for a wide range of established and routine manufacturing industries.
Certainly, after the initial expense of movement and settling into a new
location, the costs of which can frequently be passed on to the public
purse, the average firm moving to a Development or Intermediate Area
would appear likely to have costs which are only marginally different

from those it would have experienced in southern England. For some industries, however, there is *prima facie* evidence for believing that there would be an increase in costs. These industries fall into two groups. The first comprises that range of large, raw-material processing enterprises that are concerned with the production of semi-finished goods and energy; the iron and steel, aluminium, oil refining and electricity generating industries, for example, are four activities whose costs are singularly sensitive to differences in location and the associated contrasts in transport inputs; these industries, it has been argued, might most appropriately be excluded from location of employment policies (Manners, 1970). The second group consists of the metropolitan industries *par excellence*, which are to be found in both the manufacturing and service sectors of the economy. These are characteristically relatively small firms that serve a fluctuating market, have a wide range of connections with suppliers and customers, and in effect share some of their costs with other 'local' firms in the same industry or with the metropolitan communuty as a whole. These external economies, in the form of purchased transport services, shared inventories, flexible sub-contracting arrangements and the like, are the real economic strength of the metropolitan firm. The magnitude of these advantages has yet to be quantified, although recent geographical research has thrown some light on their size and nature in the case of two important industries, paper making and iron founding (Parsons, 1971). Using standard costing procedures to overcome the problem of technological contrasts between different plants, this work develops for the first time a sound methodology for exploring spatial differences in costs and productivity, and—once extended—will add a further dimension to our understanding of the private costs of government intervention in the space economy.

The generally accepted need for government to supervise—if not actually provide—major transport investments, and the close relationship between these investments and regional development, has generated yet a further cluster of geographical research activities. The urban transport network (Hall, P., 1967a), the railway modernization programme (Patmore, 1965), seaport investment (Bird, 1963; Tanner and Williams, 1967) and airport planning (Adams, 1971; Sealy, 1967) have all attracted attention and have been studied from a number of useful standpoints. Especially noteworthy has been the recurring interest in whether the plans and investments generally serve the broader goals of regional and sub-regional planning. Some of the more immediate effects of, say, building a bridge (Manners, 1966) or of closing a railway

(Clayton and Rees, 1967) are relatively easy to trace in general terms. The employment effects of a new port facility or railway liner train terminal can be ascertained with a reasonable degree of accuracy, as can their most likely effects upon the patterns of transport and communication. It is, however, the indirect and medium term results of various transport developments which are much more difficult to trace and yet which are in many instances the more important. Gwilliam (1970) has summarized the many uncertainties in seeking to measure the indirect effects of highway investment. The questions surrounding the secondary effects of airport investment were more than adequately exposed in the work of the Roskill Commission (Parry Lewis, 1971). Progress in the reduction of these uncertainties would be one of the more valuable outputs of future research.

CONCLUSIONS

A concluding statement on the prospective directions of academic research within a particular discipline must of necessity blend personal interpretations of recent work and progress with an equally personal set of interests and preferences. Nevertheless, it is today quite widely recognized that the monitoring of spatial change, traditionally the most important rôle of the geographer in the field of regional development, will increasingly be performed by government at the national, regional and local levels. Not only have various public bodies the responsibility to perform this task, but in addition they have the financial resources to organize and develop the necessary information systems most effectively to this end—data banks in particular. Whilst specialized monitoring activities *per se* with no more than a descriptive objective will obviously continue to be pursued by some geographical workers, increasingly it seems inevitable and proper that monitoring exercises will come to be associated with either model building or problem-oriented analysis.

Most models of spatial change developed by geographers during the last decade or so have been based upon empirical data, and a steady improvement in these inductive paths to valid generalizations needs to be encouraged. In the future, however, with the advantage of greater interdisciplinary communication, it seems likely that deductive models, which in retrospect have been strangely neglected by the discipline, will assume a greater importance. Many of these models will inevitably have a level of resolution which is somewhat remote from the questions raised in the day-to-day study of regional development and especially the planning process. Hence they will have relatively little *immediate* practical value. In turn this could mean that public funds, which are likely to shape the emphasis of much future research, will be used particularly to sponsor enquiries which are characterized by a more direct approach towards, and analysis of, issues of regional development.

In the field of problem-oriented analysis, three clusters of problems seem likely to receive early attention. First, research will seek to examine more fully than hitherto the private and public costs of alternative regional developments and strategies, noting in particular the cost transfers between the two sectors. Second, geographical enquiries will be focussed upon larger scale problems, shifting the emphasis of research towards the much-neglected issues of inter-regional resource allocation. And, third, researchers will increasingly be concerned with an analysis of British problems within the context of north-west Europe. In embarking upon this 'research for a generation', confidence can be gained from the solid foundations that have already been laid by geographers and other social scientists in the understanding of regional development.

REFERENCES

Adams, J. G. U. (1971) 'London's third airport', *Geographical Journal*, **137**, 468–504.

Allen, K. J. (1969) 'The regional multiplier—some problems in estimation', Chapter 4 in Orr and Cullingworth (1969).

Appleton, J. H. (1962) *The Geography of Communications in Great Britain*, Oxford University Press.

Balchin, W. G. V. (Ed.) (1971) *Swansea and its Region*, University College of Swansea on behalf of the British Association.

Beaver, S. H. (1944) 'Minerals and planning', *Geographical Journal*, **104**, 166–193.

Berry, B. J. L. (1967) *Geography of Market Centers and Retail Distribution*, Prentice-Hall.

Best, R. H. (1959) *The Major Land Uses of Great Britain*, Wye College.

Best, R. H. and Coppock, J. T. (1962) *The Changing Use of Land in Britain*, Faber.

Bird, J. (1963) *The Major Seaports of the United Kingdom*, Hutchinson.

Britton, J. N. H. (1967) *Regional Analysis and Economic Geography*, Bell.

Brown, A. J. (1969) 'Surveys of applied economics; regional economics with special reference to the United Kingdom', *Economic Journal*, **74**, 759–796.

Buswell, R. J. and Lewis, E. W. (1970) 'The geographical distribution of industrial research activity in the United Kingdom', *Regional Studies*, **4**, 297–306.

Caesar, A. A. L. (1964) 'Planning and the geography of Great Britain', *Advancement of Science*, **21**, 230–240.

Caesar, A. A. L. and Daysh, G. H. J. 'The North-East Region of England', in Daysh (1949).

Cameron, G. C. (1971) 'Growth areas, growth centres and United Kingdom regional policy', paper presented to conference on growth poles, hypotheses and policies, United Nations Institute for Social Development, Madrid, September 24–30.

Cameron, G. C. and Clark, B. D. (1966) *Industrial Movement and the Regional Problem*, University of Glasgow, Social and Economic Studies, Occasional Papers No. 5, Oliver and Boyd.

CSO (Central Statistical Office) (1965 and subsequent years) *Abstract of Regional Statistics*, HMSO, London.

CES (Centre for Environmental Studies) (1970) *Urban and Regional Research in the United Kingdom*, CES Information Paper No. 22.

Chisholm, M. (1964) 'Must we all live in southeast England?', *Geography*, **49**, 1–14.

Chisholm, M. (1971) 'In search of a basis for location theory: micro-economics or welfare economics?', *Progress in Geography*, **3**, Arnold.

Chisholm, M., Frey, A. E. and Haggett, P. (Eds.) (1971) *Regional Forecasting*, Butterworths.

Chisholm, M. and Manners, G. (Eds.) (1971) *Spatial Policy Problems of the British Economy*, Cambridge University Press.

Chisholm, M. and O'Sullivan, P. (forthcoming), *Freight Flows and Spatial Aspects of Britain's Economy*, Cambridge University Press.

Clark, C. (1966) 'Industrial location and economic potential', *Lloyds Bank Review*, **82**, 1–17.

Clark, C. *et al.* (1969) 'Industrial location and economic potential in Western Europe', *Regional Studies*, **3**, 197–212.

Clayton, G. and Rees, J. H. (1967) *The Economic Problems of Rural Transport in Wales*, University of Wales Press.

Coates, B. E. and Rawstron, E. M. (1966) 'Regional variations in incomes', *Westminster Bank Review*, February, 28–46.

Coates, B. E. and Rawstron, E. M. (1971) *Regional Variations in Britain*, Batsford.

Conkling, E. C. (1964) 'The measurement of diversification', Chapter 6 in Manners (1964).

CTLA (Commission on the Third London Airport) (1970), *Papers and Proceedings*, **8**, HMSO.

Cripps, E. L. and Foot, H. D. S. (1969) 'A land use model for sub-regional planning', *Regional Studies*, **3**, 243–268.

Cyert, R. M. and March, J. G. (1963) *A Behavioral Theory of the Firm*, Prentice-Hall.

Daniels, P. W. (1969) 'Office decentralisation for London—policy and practice', *Regional Studies*, 3, 171–178.

Darwent, D. F. (1969) 'Growth poles and growth centres in regional planning —a review', *Environment and Planning*, 1, 5–31.

Daysh, G. H. J. (1936) *A Survey of the Industrial Facilities of the North East Coast*, North East Development Board.

Daysh, G. H. J. (Ed.) (1949) *Studies in Regional Planning*, Philips.

Daysh, G. H. J. (Ed.) (1958) *A Survey of Whitby and the Surrounding Area*, The Shakespeare Head Press.

Daysh, G. H. J. and Symonds, J. S. (1953), *West Durham*, Blackwell.

Department of the Environment (1971) *Long Term Population Distribution in Great Britain—a study*, HMSO.

Drewett, J. R. (Ed.) (1969) 'Urban and regional models in British planning research', Special Issue of *Regional Studies*, 3.

Economic Associates Ltd (1966) *A New Town in Mid-Wales*, HMSO.

Edwards, K. (1949) 'The East Midlands', in Daysh (1949).

First Secretary of State and Secretary of State for Economic Affairs (1965) *The National Plan*, Cmnd, 2764, HMSO.

Foster, C. D. and Smith, J. F. (1969) 'Allocation of central government budgets over city regions', *Urban Studies*, 6, 210–226.

Freeman, T. W. *et al.* (1966) *Lancashire, Cheshire and the Isle of Man*, Nelson.

Friedman, J. and Alonso, W. (1964) *Regional Development and Planning: A Reader*, MIT Press.

Fullerton, B. (1963) 'The localisation of service industries in England and Wales', *Tijdschrift voor Economische en Sociale Geografie*, 54, 126–135.

Goddard, J. B. (1970) 'Functional regions within the city centre; a study by factor analysis of taxi flows in Central London', *Transactions of the Institute of British Geographers*, 49, 161–182,

Goddard, J. B. (1971) *Office Linkages in Central London*, unpublished report for the South East Economic Planning Council.

Gordon, I. R. (1970) 'Activity rates; regional and sub-regional differentials', *Regional Studies*, 4, 411–424.

Greater London Council (1969) *Development Plan—report of studies*, GLC.

Gwilliam, K. M. (1970) 'The indirect effects of highway investment', *Regional Studies*, 4, 167–176.

Hall, P. (1963) *London 2000*, Faber.

Hall, P. (1967a) 'New techniques in regional planning: experience of transportation studies', *Regional Studies*, 1, 17–21.

Hall, P. (1967b) 'Planning for urban growth: metropolitan area plans and their implications for South East England', *Regional Studies*, 1, 101–134.

Hall, P. (1971) 'Spatial structure of metropolitan England and Wales', Chapter 4 in Chisholm and Manners (1971).

Hall, P. (Ed.) (1972) *Megalopolis Denied: the containment of urban England, 1945–1970*, Allen and Unwin.

Hall, R. (1970) 'An estimate of office decentralisation', unpublished paper read to Location of Offices Bureau Seminar, 30 June.

Hart, R. A. (1970) 'A model of inter-regional migration in England and Wales', *Regional Studies*, 4, 279–286.

Hauser, D. (1971) 'System costs and the location of new generating plan in England and Wales', *Transactions of the Institute of British Geographers*, **54**, 101–121.

Hirshman, A. O. (1958) *The Strategy of Economic Development*, Yale University Press.

Hoover, E. M. (1948) *The Location of Economic Activity*, McGraw-Hill.

House, J. W. (1969) *Industrial Britain: the North East*, David and Charles.

Howard, R. S. (1968) *The Movement of Manufacturing Industry in the United Kingdom*, HMSO.

Humphrys, G. (1962) 'Growth industries and the regional economies of Britain', *District Bank Review*, **144**, 35–56.

Hunt, A. J. (Ed.) (1968) 'Population maps of the British Isles 1961', special issue of *Transactions of the Institute of British Geographers*, **43**.

Isard, W. (1956) *Location and Space- Economy*, MIT-Wiley.

Isard, W. *et al.* (1960) *Methods of Regional Analysis*, MIT-Wiley.

Isard, W. *et al.* (1969) *General Theory: social, political, economic and regional*, MIT Press.

Kantorowich, R. H. (1964) *Regional Shopping Centres: a planning report on North West England*, University of Manchester Press.

Keeble, D. E. (1969) 'Local industrial linkage and manufacturing growth in outer London', *Town Planning Review*, **40**, 163–188.

Keeble, D. E. (1971) 'Employment mobility in Britain', Chapter 2 in Chisholm and Manners (1971).

Keeble, D. E. (1972) 'The South East' and 'East Anglia', Chapters 2 and 3 in Manners *et al.* (1972).

Klassen, L. H. (1965) *Area Economic and Social Redevelopment*, OECD.

Lasuen, J. R. (1969) 'On growth poles', *Urban Studies*, **6**, 137–161.

Lawton, R. (1968) 'The journey to work in Britain', *Regional Studies*, **2**, 27–40.

Lawton, R. and Cunningham, C. M. (1970) *Merseyside: social and economic studies*, Longmans.

Leontief, W. W. (1966) *Input-Output Economics*, Oxford University Press.

Lewis, P. and Jones, P. N. (1970) *Industrial Britain: the Humberside Region*, David and Charles.

Lichfield, N. (1970) 'Evaluation methodology of urban and regional plans: a review', *Regional Studies*, **4**, 151–165.

Lomas, G. M. and Wood, P. (1969) *Employment Location and Regional Economic Planning*, Cass.

Lowry, I. S. (1964) *A Model of Metropolis*, Rand Corporation RM–403–RC.

Luttrell, W. F. (1962) *Factory Location and Industrial Movement*, National Institute of Economic and Social Research, 2 vols.

Mackintosh, J. P. (1968) *The Devolution of Power*, Penguin.

Manners, G. (1959) 'Recent changes in the British gas industry', *Transactions of the Institute of British Geographers*, **26**, 153–168.

Manners, G. (1966) *The Severn Bridge and the Future*, TWW, Cardiff.

Manners, G. (1970) 'Research after Hunt', *SSRC Newsletter*, **8**, 17–19.

Manners, G. (1971a) 'Some economic and spatial characteristics of the British energy market', Chapter 6 in Chisholm and Manners (1971).

Manners, G. (1971b) *The Geography of Energy*, 2nd edition, Hutchinson.

Manners, G. (Ed.) (1964) *South Wales in the Sixties*, Pergamon.

Manners, G. *et al.* (1972) *Regional Development in Britain*, Wiley.

Martin, J. (1966) *Greater London: an industrial geography*, Bell.

McLoughlin, J. B. (1969) 'Simulation for beginners: the planning of a sub-regional model system', *Regional Studies*, 3, 313–323.

Mitchell, J. (Ed.) (1962) *Great Britain: geographical essays*, Cambridge University Press.

Morrison, W. (1971) 'Input-output analysis and urban development planning: some applications of the Peterborough model', unpublished paper read to Conference on Input-Output and Throughput, University of East Anglia, September 13–16.

Myrdal, G. (1957) *Economic Theory and Under-Developed Regions*, Duckworth.

NEDC (National Economic Development Council) (1963a) *Growth of the United Kingdom Economy to 1966*, HMSO.

NEDC (National Economic Development Council) (1963b) *Conditions Favourable to Faster Growth*, HMSO.

Norcliffe, G. B. (1970) *Industrial Location Dynamics*, unpublished Ph.D. thesis, University of Bristol.

Odell, P. (1965) *Oil: the new commanding height*, Fabian Research Series, **251**.

Odell, P. (1970) *Oil and World Power*, Penguin.

Ohlin, B. (1933) *Interregional and International Trade*, Harvard University Press.

Orr, S. C. and Cullingworth, J. B. (1969) *Regional and Urban Studies*, Allen and Unwin.

Parry Lewis, J. (1971) *The Forecasts of Roskill*, Occasional Paper No. 11, Centre for Urban and Regional Research, University of Manchester.

Parsons, G. (1970) *Some Comments on the Structure and Spatial Distribution of Corporate Manufacturing Industry in the United Kingdom*, Occasional Paper No. 14, Department of Geography, University College London.

Parsons, G. (1971) 'Manufacturing and agglomeration', paper presented to the annual conference of the Institute of British Geographers, University of Sussex, January.

Patmore, J. A. (1965) 'The British railway network in the Beeching era', *Economic Geography*, **41**, 71–81.

Patmore, J. A. (1970) *Land and Leisure*, David and Charles.

Perroux, F. (1955) 'Note sur la notion de pôle de croissance', *Economie Appliquée*, **8**, 307–320.

Pilgrim, B. (1969) 'Choice of house in a New Town', *Regional Studies*, **3**, 325–330.

Powell, A. G. (1961) 'The recent development of Greater London', *Advancement of Science*, **17**, 76–86.

Pred, A. (1967 and 1969) *Behavior and Location* (2 parts), Lund Studies in Geography, Series B, **27** and **28**, University of Lund.

Rawstron, E. M. (1955) 'The salient geographical features of electricity production in Britain', *Advancement of Science*, **12**, 73–82.

Rawstron, E. M. (1957) 'Some aspects of the location of hosiery and lace manufacture in Great Britain', *East Midland Geographer*, **9**, 16–28.

Rawstron, E. M. (1958) 'Three principles of industrial location', *Transactions of the Institute of British Geographers*, **25**, 132–142.

Rhodes, J. and Kan, A. (1971) *Office Dispersal and Regional Policy*, Cambridge University Press.

Rodgers, H. B. (1964) 'Recent industrial changes in North West England and their social consequences', in *Problems of Applied Geography II*, Polish Scientific Publishers.

Rodgers, H. B. (1967 and 1969) *Pilot National Recreation Survey* (2 vols.), British Travel Association and University of Keele.

Rodgers, H. B. (1972) 'The North West and North Wales', Chapter 7 in Manners *et al.* (1972).

Salt, J. (1969) 'Post war unemployment in Britain: some basic considerations', *Transactions of the Institute of British Geographers*, **46**, 93–103.

Sant, M. (1967) 'Unemployment and industrial structure in Great Britain', *Regional Studies*, **1**, 83–91.

Sealy, K. R. (1967) 'The siting and development of British airports', *Geographical Journal*, **133**, 148–170.

Secretary of State for Economic Affairs (1969) *The Intermediate Areas* (Hunt Report), Cmnd. 3998, HMSO.

SEJPT (South East Joint Planning Team) (1970) *Strategic Plan for the South East*, HMSO.

SEJPT (South East Joint Planning Team) (1971) *Studies Volume 5 (Report of Economic Consultants Ltd.)*, HMSO.

Simpson, E. S. (1966) *Coal and the Power Industries in Postwar Britain*, Longmans.

Smailes, A. E. (1960) *North England*, Nelson.

Smith, D. M. (1966) 'A theoretical framework for geographical studies of industrial location', *Economic Geography*, **42**, 95–113.

Smith, D. M. (1968) 'Identifying the grey areas—a multivariate approach', *Regional Studies*, **2**, 183–193.

Smith, D. M. (1969) *Industrial Britain: the North West*, David and Charles.

Smith, D. M. (1971) *Industrial Location*, Wiley.

Smith, W. (1949) *An Economic Geography of Great Britain*, Methuen.

Spence, N. (1968) 'A multifactor uniform regionalisation of British counties on the basis of employment data for 1961', *Regional Studies*, **2**, 87–104.

Spence, N. and Taylor, P. J. (1971) 'Quantitative methods in regional taxonomy', *Progress in Geography*, **2**, Arnold.

Stamp, D. (1948) *The Land of Britain: its use and misuse*, Longmans.

Stamp, D. and Beaver, S. H. (1933) *The British Isles: a geographic and economic survey*, Longmans.

Stilwell, F. J. B. (1969) 'Regional growth and structural adaptation, *Urban Studies*, **6**, 162–178.

Stilwell, F. J. B. (1970) 'Further thoughts on the shift-share approach', *Regional Studies*, **4**, 451–458.

Spooner, D. J. (1971) 'Industrial movement and the rural periphery—the case of Devon and Cornwall', paper presented to conference on the movement of industry, Regional Studies Association, Cambridge, September 25.

Tanner, M. F. and Williams, A. F. (1967) 'Port development and national planning strategy', *Journal of Transport Economics and Policy*, **1**, 3–10.

Taylor, E. G. R. *et al.* (1938) 'Discussion on the geographical distribution of industry', *Geographical Journal*, **92**, 22–39.

Taylor, M. J. (1969) *Industrial Linkage, Seed-bed Growth and the Location of Firms*, Occasional Paper No. 3, Department of Geography, University College London.

Thomas, D. (1970) *London's Green Belt*, Faber.

Thomas, R. (1969) 'London's New Towns', Political and Economic Planning, *Planning*, **35**, 373–473.

Townroe, P. M. (1971) *Industrial Location Decisions: a study in management behaviour*, Occasional Paper No. 15, Centre of Urban and Regional Studies, University of Birmingham.

Turnock, D. (1970) *Patterns of Highland Development*, Macmillan.

Warntz, W. (1959) *Towards a Geography of Price*, University of Pennsylvania Press.

Warren, K. (1970) *The British Iron and Steel Industry since 1840*, Bell.

Warren, K. (1971) 'Growth, technical change and planning problems in heavy industry with particular reference to the chemical industry', Chapter 7 in Chisholm and Manners (1971).

Watson, J. W. and Sissons, J. B. (Eds.) (1964) *The British Isles: a systematic geography*, Nelson.

Weber, A. (1929) *Theory of the Location of Industry*, University of Chicago Press.

Willatts, E. C. (1971) 'Planning and geography in the last three decades', *Geographical Journal*, **137**, 311–338.

Williamson, J. C. (1965) 'Regional inequality and the process of national development: a description of the patterns', *Economic Development and Cultural Change*, **13**, 3–45.

Wilson, A. G. (1968) 'Models in urban planning: a synoptic review of recent literature', *Urban Studies*, **5**, 229–276.

Wilson, A. G. (1971) 'On some problems in urban and regional modelling', in Chisholm *et al.* (1971).

Wilson, A. G. *et al.* (1969) 'Calibration and testing of the SELNEC transport model', *Regional Studies*, **3**, 337–350.

Wise, M. J. (1950) 'On the jewellery and gun quarters of Birmingham', *Transactions of the Institute of British Geographers*, **15**, 59–72.

Wood, P. A. (1969) 'Industrial location and linkage', *Area*, **2**, 32–39.

8 Geographers, decision takers and policy makers

JOHN HOUSE

Geography as an academic discipline was established about the turn of the present century but did not experience rapid development until the period between the two world wars. In many respects, the fact that the early rapid phase of growth coincided with a long period of economic recession, in which regional disparities were starkly evident, was formative for the subject. In particular, there developed a strong and abiding interest in the spatial allocation of resources (as discussed in Chapter 7) and this interest led to direct involvement in both the policy-making and policy-implementing activities of government. The purpose of this chapter is to explore the nature and degree of this involvement of British geographers in the public affairs of this country. Some geographers consider the search for distinctively geographical inputs to be somewhat sterile, if not pedantic in a present climate of increased ecumenical thinking and working in the social sciences, where common goals, overlaps in techniques and movable frontiers in research transcend older, more sharply defined disciplinary methods and objectives. The great majority of geographers, however, both within governmental service and in academic life, still sees merit in maintaining an identity for the discipline within an interdisciplinary framework in research or applications. Indeed there is concensus that the total fusion or merging of the contribution of applied geography within non-stratified social sciences would be to the detriment both of the development of the subject and the overall utility of its applications.

THE PROBLEM OF ASSESSMENT

The problem of evaluating contributions to decisions and policy in any one instance is inevitably elusive, for several reasons. First, the need to preserve confidentiality often shrouds parts if not the whole of the process from the outside observer; at times it seems unnecessarily so. This frequently impenetrable screen cloaks the direct professional participation by geographers within central and local government, but also much consultancy work, not least that for commercial bodies such as retailing groups. Secondly, it seems that even the contributors find it hard at times to trace the effects of their work along the decision-taking, policy-making continuum, since it has been rare indeed for the geographer to carry his advocacy throughout the spectrum from commissioning or initiation of research, through presentation of results with recommendations, to the decisions on policy, its execution, and the final evaluation and feedback therefrom. The partial view even from within thus makes assessment from without the more conjectural and necessarily more generalized, in any measurement of geographical inputs against apparent outcome.

Furthermore, decisions and policies manifestly do not originate either solely or directly from research inputs; indeed they may on all-too-many occasions have little to do with specialist or technical advice tendered, either by geographers or others. Thus, the attempt to assess the geographical contribution against the outcome in policy terms is often neither fair nor realistic, and separate evaluation may be needed for the nature and quality of the inputs, as far as these may be open to scrutiny, and for tracing the effects of the recommendations in influencing the final decisions or policies. This need for dual perspectives of interpretation accentuates a major issue of long standing, the continuing and mutually weak liaison and understanding between researchers and the decision takers or policy makers. This may be a shortcoming on the part of researchers, ill-trained academically for problem solving or action orientation in an operational rôle, or it may result from an inadequacy on the part of the decision-takers to appreciate the potential offered by individual disciplines, in either an academic or an applied context. Particularly disadvantageous to geography is the widespread inability or disinclination by administrators to view problems, decisions or policies in a spatial framework, or even as having an important spatial implication. More than any other reason this may account for the contraints on the geographer's contribution hitherto as researcher, advocate, commentator or critic. These limitations must be set alongside the balance sheet of strengths and weaknesses arising from the nature of the discipline itself. In general, the present state of affairs is especially frustrating to geographers in that research achievement and potential in the subject over the past decade have moved rapidly ahead of immediate applications and even the possible applications of earlier, simpler techniques have often remained beyond the perception of decision-takers or policy-makers. During the past decade marked changes have also taken place in the nature and quality of decision taking and policy making, to the benefit of both academics and administrators. Presently, the relationship remains underdeveloped and to that extent the requirements of the economy and society are inadequately catered for.

Selection of those geographical contributions which may have influenced decisions or policy implies, in principle, consideration of the entire cycle from pure research to executive action and feedback. This is a somewhat impracticable task and highly subject to personal interpretation, not least because of the at times subtle, elusive or fleeting evidence of the practical outcome from research findings. At one extreme, seminal ideas or concepts from pure research, in regional or systematic geography, may prove capable of direct application or they may fertilize the thinking of those, not necessarily only geographers, in planning, administration or commerce. Such general concepts have included Smailes' urban fields (1947) or urban hierarchy (1946), Green's accessibility areas defined by public bus services (1950, 1952), Gilbert's boundary studies of local government areas (1948), or Taylor's axial zone (1938).

More directly, specific studies in applied geography of industrial concentration in Britain have been either sponsored or commissioned or they may be the work of 'in-house' researchers. Consultant reports offer a further type, whilst within local or central government research may be followed by situation reports or memoranda with recommendations. These in turn may become committee papers, laid before decision-taking or policy-making groups, and may (or may not) afford the basis for later executive action. The process is complex, often two-way in character, with research sometimes hard to distinguish from compilation and *ad hoc* comment; at all events little of the process can readily be detected by an outsider. In due course more of this aspect will come to light in the history of ministries, councils, or other statutory bodies.

More research continues to be generated from below and moves upwards for comment and recommendation, than is calculatingly commissioned from above as part of some overall programme by policy makers. Occasionally, in new institutions such as the rural development bodies or the economic planning councils, a fresh start on the relationships between research, administration, decision taking and policy making becomes at least theoretically possible. Elsewhere, as in the latest proposals for preparing regional strategies, similar 'breakthrough' possibilities may exist for a time. All-too-widespread, however, remains the unfortunate dichotomy between research carried out by academics and the needs of those taking decisions or making policies. It was to help bridge this kind of intellectual gap, among other purposes, that the Centre for Environmental Studies was set up, but there is still an urgent need for rapid and more extensive diffusion of such thinking. The gap is often wide, with research needed not commissioned, existing research findings inadequately utilized, so that policies are based on inadequate research; in a reverse sense, much research that could be utilized is often not in a suitable form and lacks a problem focus or action orientation. Above all, feedback from the application of research findings continues to be both limited and tardy. A step towards closer liaison is seen in the representation of certain ministries, including the Department of the Environment, by assessors on some of committees of the research councils, whilst a number of ministries now also have academic liaison officers. A further instance of co-operation between academics and policy-makers is that of the social research committee at Telford New Town, with oversight of the entire spectrum from research needs, through research programmes to policy changes.

THE CONTEXT OF GEOGRAPHICAL INVOLVEMENT

The development of an applied geography is of long standing in Britain, growing logically by extension from the study of population and employment, towns, industries, the use of land and the structure of regions to a sharper focus on the problem aspects of those same topics. In pre-war years pioneering work was called forth by the needs of the times and the growing sense of involvement by a small number of geographers with problems of the local region or the national space. Such work is typified by that of G. H. J. Daysh on Tyneside and in north-east England, where from the early 1930s not only was he continuously active in research in the conurbation and coalfield but also took a leading part in local development organizations there and in Cumberland, whilst from time to time also advising local and central government committees. Wilfred Smith was active on Merseyside, and the first Land Use Survey, organized and carried through by L. D. Stamp in the 1930s and early 1940s, was a major feat of stock-taking for a vital national resource, to be followed thirty years later by an equally massive Second Land Use Survey. The evidence, in memorandum

and cartographical form, put forward by geographers to the Barlow
Commission on the Distribution of the Industrial Population, 1937–40,
marked another turning-point and was a precursor of the vigorous,
growing and widespread involvement of geographers in the wartime
years, a most formative period in the development of planning. The
establishment of the Ministry of Town and Country Planning in 1943,
with a geographer as its first principal research officer and other
geographers acting as research officers in the regions, also included a
Maps Office, thus following up the proposals by E. G. R. Taylor for the
publication of a National Atlas.

In a rather different field, geographers in wartime formed the greater
part of the Naval Intelligence section which produced Handbooks for
most of the maritime countries of the world. These volumes interpreted
the basic physical, social and economic geography and included
sections on the major ports and towns. They were a counterpart to the
similar but much more restricted range of Handbooks produced in
the 1920s for the briefing of naval officers visiting foreign lands.

In the early post-war years the development of coherent and nation-
wide Town and Country Planning under the 1947 Act, together with
the shaping of regional industrial location policies, following upon the
1945 Distribution of Industry Act, set the stage for a burgeoning
professional involvement by geographers within the planning machinery,
at all levels and in its successive phases; other geographers acted within
consultant groups on the preparation of the basic series of advisory
plans. From the same period there grew a commitment to the applications of geography, as Stamp put it, 'for the benefit of society'. The
following sections treat of the main post-war achievements by geographers in these applied fields and attempt both an assessment of the
present situation and prospects for the immediate future.

REGIONAL AND URBAN PLANNING

Two recent review statements (Powell, 1970; Willatts, 1971) permit an
overall assessment of the achievements and shortcomings of the
geographer in planning, perhaps the major field of British applied
geography, and some forecast of future prospects. Both were written
by geographers occupying senior positions in the Department of the
Environment, with wide and continuing experience of research and of
the interface between research, decisions and policy making within the
Department. In both cases, the balance-sheet is essentially similar; it is
critical, yet on the whole congratulatory and cautiously optimistic in

tone. On the one hand there has been a cumulative and widening involvement of geographers in planning since the war, at both central and local government levels, not without its setbacks, but with achievements well outweighing shortcomings; on the other hand both the nature of planning and the character of geography as a discipline have so evolved in the 1960s that their relationships have needed re-interpretation and harmonization, to mutual advantage. As Willatts puts it: 'In the past thirty years the geographer has advanced from survey-making to involvement in policy, but at the same time planning has become more complicated and, with team work, the contribution by the geographer has become more difficult to identify'. Powell's message is rather that the geographer needs to sharpen his technical competence, adopt a more dynamic, quantitative approach, and develop his ability to forecast future space/time relationships if he is to remain a basic participator in the new planning. At the same time Powell sees great and continuing merit in the catholic overview characteristic of traditional geography, with the possibility thereby for the geographer, as for few other contributors to planning, to be both specialist and generalist with advantage.

The contribution by geographers to decisions and policy in post-war years has also been wider than that of direct professional employment in governmental planning (House, 1965). Academic geographers have served as chairmen for two Departmental Committees, those concerned with Smallholdings (M. J. Wise) and with Allotments (H. Thorpe); J. R. James, formerly Chief Planner at the then Ministry of Housing and Local Government, was a member of the Hunt Committee on Intermediate Areas, whilst no less than six academic geographers, perhaps the largest disciplinary sub-group, are currently members of the Regional Economic Planning Councils; D. E. Keeble, East Anglia; K. C. Edwards, East Midlands; P. Haggett, South West; P. Hall and G. Manners, South East; and J. W. House, Northern. H. C. Darby is a member of both the Water Resources Board and the Countryside Commission, whilst at an earlier date the late Sir Dudley Stamp had been Vice-Chairman of the Scott Committee on Land Utilization in Rural Areas and a member of the Royal Commission on Common Land. J. T. Coppock has been a member of the Hughes Committee on Tourism and J. W. House a member of the short-lived Northern Pennines Rural Development Board, 1969–71.

These appointments at the policy-recommending or policy-formulating levels are more readily identifiable than the perhaps more characteristically indirect contributions by a much larger number of geographers. These include the submission of evidence, individually or collectively by the representative bodies of British geography (Royal Geographical Society, Institute of British Geographers and Geographical Association) to Government Commissions or Committees, from the Barlow Commission of 1940, through occasional Select Committees on Estimates, to the Maud and Wheatley Commissions on Local Government and the Ashby Commission on Pollution in more recent times. Another distinctive contribution has been by geographers acting as consultants, either in an individual specialist capacity or as a member of an inter-disciplinary or planning group or organization, ranging with some versatility over fields as diverse as tourism and recreation; service industry, particularly the retailing sector; impact studies of prospective industrial developments; land use; migration and mobility; New Towns; derelict land; amenity issues and environmental management. Finally, in this initial broad review of involvement, geographers have advised and acted as members of private or semi-official local or regional development associations, as in Scotland, North East England, the West Midlands and the North West. On the debit side, it has been difficult to detect any widespread contribution by geographers as such to either decisions or policy in manufacturing industry, in nationalized corporations or to the problems of trades unions or management.

The prime and most substantial heading covers the work of geographers professionally within planning and also the contributions made by academic or consultant geographers to the plan process, at national, regional and local levels. Any categorization of such work risks being arbitrary, but perhaps the most convenient division is between central and local government involvement, since the rôles of geographers within each have been distinct but complementary, and there has been a prime focus at different scales of work; furthermore, as between central and local scales, there has been some difference in the type of planning training required and in subsequent relationships with corporate planners. A division according to social, economic, urban and physical planning would be overlapping and may tend to confuse the geographical contribution; even in the separate assessment of work in central and local government there must remain some overlap, since the work of geographers at each level often transgresses different stages of the same process. The rôle of geographers on regional economic planning boards and councils is appropriate for consideration in this section.

Contributions by geographers to commissions and committees are treated separately, even though such bodies are almost universally serviced by technical groups composed of seconded civil servants, often including geographers in a research or advisory rôle. Those rural development bodies set up by government, on which geographers have served, deserve particular mention and, finally, general assessment is made of other fields in which geographers have interacted with decision takers and policy makers, notably in the service industries, but in limited, specific ways over a broad frontage.

Central government planning
Though geographers have been recruited to the research classes in several ministries their contribution has been most substantial, in numbers and character, to the ministry concerned with town, regional and urban planning, currently the Department of the Environment in England and Wales, and the Scottish Development Department north of the Border. Smaller numbers have been appointed to the Joint Intelligence Bureau, responsible for strategic, economic and world-wide stocktaking and analysis. Geographers have served, too, in the old Board of Trade and the present Department of Trade and Industry.

The work of geographers in the planning ministry has been fully chronicled by Powell (1970) and Willatts (1971), a participation which has been substantial, widespread and versatile, ranging from the person of the Chief Planner (J. R. James) 1961–67, through all levels of the technical hierarchy, and with rôles changing as the planning process matured and became more fully inter-disciplinary. Fields of involvement, in structured groups or in *ad hoc* commitment, have been as widely diverse as: the Maps Office; New Towns; regional and urban plans and strategies, including the review of Development Plans from local government and the more recent phase of strategies for the economic planning regions; resource management and the resolution of land use conflicts (James, Scott and Willatts, 1961); impact studies of the siting of major new facilities, such as airports or shopping centres; the reform of local government units; together with contributions to the theory and application of plans, and contributions to the drafting of legislation.

The achievements of geographers within the Ministry may be most aptly pointed up by a brief evolutionary account, set within the context of the development of applied geography over the same period and touching on the work of academic geographers as well as those in consultant groups. Three phases may be distinguished since 1945, corresponding roughly with changes in the general political attitudes to planning. The years from 1945 to 1954 were a period of the rapid development and implementation of a comprehensive plan process, particularly in land use and industrial location, arising from the principles formulated in wartime years and embodied in wide-ranging early post-war planning legislation. There followed, from 1954 to the early 1960s, a period when planning was less in fashion, with the keynote on consolidation and preparation for fresh advances. The third period may most appropriately be dated from the reinvigoration of planning after 1963, starting with the formation of the Department of Economic Affairs, the abortive National Plan of 1964 and the inception of a new phase of regional planning with the establishment of regional Economic Planning Councils and Boards for eight regions of England and Wales.

The period to the mid-1950s was one of pioneering by geographers in planning, leading, though not without problems *en route*, to a well-defined rôle and general acceptance of the discipline (Caesar, 1964). The geographers moving into planning were academics trained in pre-war traditions, strong on regional method, on broad resource evaluation and on tracing and interpreting sequences of change in past times; their skills were mainly descriptive, with a strong cartographical leaning. These skills found logical employment in regional and urban stock-taking, typified in the early post-war years, in one respect, by geographical contributions to consultant plans, as in those for the West Midlands conurbation, Middlesbrough, the Clyde Valley and South East Scotland. Within the Ministry, the preparation of planning summaries for each region (Daysh and O'Dell, 1947) was an essential and orthodox geographical provision for policy makers (Daysh, 1949b), a part of what Willatts has termed 'the build-up of operational capital'. Groups were established to study particular themes such as New Towns, London, or the physical, social, economic and demographic aspects of urban and regional planning; in the regional offices of the Ministry geographers worked at first hand on the problems of their regions, often developing their own lines of research, in close touch with interested local academic geographers. The widespread and varied nature of planning problems, the importance of the regional scale and the need for a broad spatial framework for analysis coincided well with the generalist outlook of traditional geographers and the then orthodox methods of investigation and interpretation. Few social scientists from other disciplines had entered planning and the geographer had to expand his interests to fill the gaps, using also economic and social interpretations. The interaction with planning professionals, trained as architects, engineers or directly as town planners improved only slowly, though the Royal Town Planning Institute came to recognize the merits of contributory disciplines.

From 1954 to 1963 the regional officers of the Ministry were based in the metropolis. A major feature of their work was concerned with approval of local authority Development Plans, both at the initial presentation and at the review stage, but there were also preoccupations with other problems, including the siting and development of further New Towns; the problems of administrative regionalism, including the Royal Commission on Local Government in Greater London (1960); city centre redevelopment; and with the entire range of spatial problems emerging from the regions, the cities and the countryside. The rôle of the geographer became less clear-cut, with the growth of planning teams, but the emphasis on general regional, resource and cartographical skills remained paramount. The consolidation phase saw a greater number of geographers drawn into employment in the Ministry, a maintenance of their broad range of research and advisory work, but also the emergence of specialists such as Powell on Greater London (1960), Vince on rural population (1952), or R. T. White on population patterns and structure. The Local Government Commission, set up in 1958 and referred to later, opened a major field to geographers, who comprised the senior professional staff.

As in the discipline of geography, so in the work of geographers in the Ministry, the 1960s were a period of rapid and structural change. From 1961–67, J. R. James, a first-degree geographer, was Chief Planner and during these very formative years was at the heart of the process of policy making. He was preoccupied with problems on the macro-scale, the economic and demographic foundations of the first generation of new Regional Studies, the infrastructure for a reformed Local Government, the trends towards the final legislation of the 1968 Town and Country Planning Act, and the entire range of relationships between research, decisions and policies. He was further instrumental in gaining support for the creation of the Centre for Environmental Studies, a national high-level forum for research and interchange between academics and decision takers, within an inter-disciplinary framework.

Individual geographers, including G. T. Warwick, in the West Midlands, also contributed to regional planning as part-time Administrative Officers in the regional groups of the former Ministry of Lands and Natural Resources, now within the Department of the Environment.

Though the wide range of involvement already touched on continued, perhaps the most significant development for geographers in the 1960s was the redefinition and strengthening of planning at the regional level, in the eight economic planning regions for England and, of course, also in Scotland and Wales. Regional planning had been active for some time in Scotland, where geographers had early been employed in what is now the Scottish Development Department. Contacts had been close with county planning groups and expertise developed notably in land use problems of the central lowlands, the growth point methodology, which figured strikingly in the 1963 White Paper (clearly more geographically orientated than its counterpart for North East England), and in the Glasgow overspill problem; moreover the difficulties of declining mining areas and the broad range of rural infrastructural problems figured more prominently in Scottish planning. A particularly valuable geographical contribution (Spaven, 1965) was the preparation and report writing of the 'Regional Studies' section of the White Paper on the Scottish Economy.

The *South East Study, 1961–81* (Ministry of Housing and Local Government, 1964) was the prototype for a series of regional studies in England, examining the structure and trends in population, employment, the use of land and development of resources. This foundation statement was a framework for local planning and was the work of an inter-disciplinary group in which geographers were dominant. It led in due course to other regional documents, and thus to one of the earliest responsibilities of the new planning councils, to assess the problems of their regions and to prepare recommendations for action.

Regional economic planning councils and boards
The author's service on the Northern Council permits some assessment of the achievements and potential for geographers, at Council and Board level, both as research adviser and policy-making participant. The tasks laid upon the Councils include fact-finding, survey, *ad hoc* decisions on matters of regional interest, and the two-way liaison, interchange and dialogue with central government, on the one hand, and the local authorities on the other. Lacking in powers, the Councils have a broad remit to advise and recommend, to interpret but also to initiate proposals for improvement and change. Geographers are currently serving, in a personal not a professional capacity, on five of the eight councils and geographers are also represented in the research and technical support groups of the boards.

The work of an Economic Planning Council proceeds at two levels;

by open Council discussion and in working parties concerned with particular sector problems. Both the main Council and the working parties receive committee papers, situation reports and drafts prepared by civil servants on the Board. Current working parties of the Northern Council include those on Strategy, Housing, Education, Manpower, Tourism, Ports and Communications. Working parties keep the sectors under continuing review and consolidate their work in published reports from time to time. Much of the work is of considerable social science interest, but the research inputs are necessarily constrained by the multiple other tasks undertaken by the government researchers, and the one or two academics who are council members. Moreover, here as elsewhere, research findings are only one of the ingredients in policy making.

The formulation and presentation of regional strategies may be used to illustrate a key concern to geographers in regional planning. The first stage strategies were completed by the Councils and Boards and it may be more than a coincidence that those with a strongly expressed spatial component came from councils with geographer-members. Other regional strategies are more sector-based, with sub-regional interpretations. There is a feeling from some of the earlier strategies that the spatial dimension has been seen as secondary in importance, or to be largely disregarded. One of the principal tasks of the geographer remains to convince his colleagues of the merits of a spatial approach, from survey and analysis, through presentation to eventual recommendations. Indicative of geographical inputs is the sector strategy for the South East (1967), in whose devising Peter Hall played a large part, and the graduated, interrelated growth and defensive strategy in the Outline Strategy for the North (1969). These proposals carried conviction in the Councils but, by reason of the hasty nature of compilation and limited research support, they are indications rather than final versions of where the geographer might more fully develop his art of spatial exposition.

The next series of regional strategies, typified by the *Strategic Plan for the South East* (South East Joint Planning Team, 1970), marks a major step forward in the continuing and deeper involvement of research workers, including geographers. In the first place, regional strategies have now become the product of a tripartite group of local planners, regional Board and Council, and a team of planners seconded from central government with a strong representation of geographers. The south-east team was required to 'test and evaluate alternative plans in both economic and physical terms and to recommend a preferred solution' (Powell, 1970). Geographer members of the planning team were responsible for the analysis of population, employment and economic structure, office growth, the economic structure and rôle of Central London and the study of journey to work. On social and environmental aspects, the geographers contributed especially to the chapters on housing, the countryside and minerals. It is not, however, possible to trace these contributions forward through the strategy formulations and patterns of development testing, since the summaries and conclusions reached by disciplinary groups at each phase of the analysis, pointing towards policy options, were consolidated at an early stage into a single set of proposals. The thread of geographical involvement is thus obscured but it is clear that, perhaps for the first time, it was continuous through all stages of the planning process; from contribution to provisional objectives, through trend analysis and forecasting, to the formulation and testing of alternative strategies for patterns of development, the selection of a preferred strategy and the final set of objectives. Furthermore, as and when the plan is approved by the Minister there will be a continuing responsibility to keep it up-to-date, to monitor progress towards the objectives at both regional and sub-regional level, to make further studies on strategy and to incorporate and evaluate major new developments, such as the third London airport.

Arising from the expectation that the population of Great Britain will increase by about one-fifth by the end of the century, and that mobility of both jobs and people will grow, the Government in 1966 commissioned studies of three major national estuarine growth areas. The feasibility studies for fast growth in these areas have now been published: Humberside (Central Unit for Environmental Planning, 1969), Tayside (Campbell and Lyddon, 1970) and Severnside (CUEP, 1971); the Dee barrage study (1971) should also be mentioned. The studies on Humberside and Severnside were carried out by an inter-disciplinary group drawn from the Central Unit for Environmental Planning, assisted by a Physical Planning Unit drawn from local planning authorities. The Humberside team was led by a geographer-planner; that for Tayside was the product of a consultancy team under the direction of an applied economist.

On the evidence of the Strategic Plan for the South East and the estuarine feasibility studies, the contribution of the geographer has evolved remarkably within a radically developed planning process. The hallmarks of contemporary involvement include, in addition to orthodox preoccupations, continuity through all stages of the process, merging of the geographers' work within the team, and greater ability to predict, using newer quantitative techniques and the aid of the computer. This is very much in keeping with the course and trend of academic geography within contemporary social science and with recent developments in geography curricula at University level.

LOCAL GOVERNMENT PLANNING

The rôle and status of the geographer within what has also been termed physical, or land use, planning presents something of a paradox. It is the principal field of employment for geographers in planning, since, in a recent year, some 40% of entrants to the Royal Town Planning Institute examinations held a first degree in geography, but there is progressive loss of identity, or even of rôle as a geographer, in the conversion to a corporate town planner. This contrasts with the Ministries where geographers tend to retain their professional identity unless transferred to the administrative ladder.

The recruitment of geographers to planning research work in the counties and boroughs goes back to the early days of the 1947 Planning Act. Geographers had indeed proved their usefulness in the earlier phase of consultant regional plans. Quoting a deputy county planning officer (Scarlett, 1971), currently one of two who were first degree geographers,

> the geographer can contribute [to the physical planning process] in two ways. First, by use of his direct geographical knowledge and techniques, e.g. his understanding of changing physical, social and economic influences on people and the way in which they live, and how to measure some of these influences. Secondly, through the discipline acquired in appreciating problems in the round and in assessing the relative importance of the various factors involved, to permit balanced decisions. Forward planning is the basic policy-making activity and a geographer can contribute to it in both the ways mentioned, particularly where the work covers an area with a variety of conditions. The weakness of the geographer in this work is his inability to move on from measuring and assessing influences and how they may change in future to formulating and testing 'real world' solutions in social, physical and cost terms. This is why geographers are sought with an added planning training for this kind of work.

Such a contemporary assessment of the rôle and status of the geographer should not disguise the widespread contribution made by the discipline during the past decades. This was perhaps at its height in orthodox geographical applications in the period of basic surveys for the initial Development Plans, with strong analytical and carto-graphical inputs. Since then geograpical work seems to have become much more diffused, though conventionally concentrated in the Development Plans group; in County Durham in the mid-1960s, twelve of sixteen geographers employed were in this group. From those authorities with a tradition of attracting geographers, including Durham, Lancashire, Staffordshire and Northumberland, a succession of published reports, as for example on rural growth points, tourism, coastal scenery classification and derelict land indicate both the scope and the practical nature of a continuing geographical contribution.

Furthermore, attitudes are changing within the Royal Town Planning Institute in respect of the further recognition of contributory skills in planning. Indeed, consideration of the most recent syllabuses for the Institute's examinations reveals a close and continuing relationship of some parts to the field and techniques of university geography. There is a useful degree of complementarity, even at times of seeming overlap, the more so in that common social science and computer-based techniques are today spreading rapidly in both disciplines. Similarly, in professional planning practice the requirements of the 1968 Planning Act open up, perhaps even require, new forms of collaboration and continuing relationships between disciplines, including that of geography. The 1968 Act requires a new hierarchy of plans at local planning level, suited to a change in the balance of responsibility from central to local government in local planning and to the larger, more coherent administrative units to be the basis of local government from 1974.

Broad sub-regional structure plans will replace the former detailed land use proposals of the Development Plans and will need to be fitted into the strategic framework at the level of the economic planning region, developed from the tripartite work of central and local government with the Economic Planning Council. The structure plans will thus 'call for a combined team effort by planners basically trained in economics, geography, economic geology, sociology, ecology and transport engineering' (Powell, 1970). In the light of this vision of increasing opportunities for geographers it is perhaps disturbing that they seem to have played so little part in some of the early sub-regional plans, sponsored by groups of local authorities (Leicester and Leicestershire, 1969; Coventry-Solihull-Warwickshire, 1971). On the other hand, but at a much less sophisticated level, sub-regional studies from Economic Planning Councils (e.g. Halifax and Calder Valley, 1968; Huddersfield and Colne valley, 1969; Doncaster, 1969) are more general trend evaluations, emphasizing strengths and weaknesses and postulating generalized objectives. These are the logical counterpart of the traditional work of geographers at central government level, but they fall short of the more ambitious purposes of sub-regional structure plans in which geographers have as yet made only a limited mark. At this sub-regional level the geographer needs a more quantified approach, both in the contribution of inputs to regional models and in measurement or evaluation of feedback from the operations of the model. However, in the short term, the flexibility and comprehensiveness of the traditional geographical viewpoint remains important in the formulations of the model.

A final example concerns the Greater London Development Plan to whose *Report of Studies* 'in-house' geographical work was contributed; in particular, Chapter 7, attempting to present London in the round, following a set of subject chapters, is a valuable context for the more technical appreciations.

Contributory work and consultancy by academic geographers

Comment is limited to instances where there was clearly service to a client or where the work was commissioned. This necessarily excludes several other ways in which the work of geographers has influenced the thinking of planners, as for example in the presentation of results or of concepts in book form or in forums, such as the Regional Studies Association, or by communications through the media, radio, television or the press. *London 2000* (Hall, 1963) rates particular mention as an example of an influential text.

Broadly different perspectives are indicated: on the one hand, the Aberdeen geographers have a vigorous and successful tradition of building outwards from staff research interests into applied work for the benefit of a wide range of clients; in contrast is the outlook of some members of the quantitative school, one of whom states, in this context, that 'relatively little of pre-existing research has been relevant to urban and regional planning, and policy problems have generated additional research. Indeed it may be possible to argue that much model-building activity has been generated in the first instance in this way' (A. G. Wilson, verbal communication, 1971). As a third category, there is the work by geographers as members of consultancy groups, both in the smaller groups with highly specialized inter-disciplinary expertise and within the large-project consortia capable of undertaking major planning consultancies. The tradition has been for the smaller groups to employ academic geographers for 'once-off' projects, whilst the latter have geographers among others on the permanent research staff. There is a general feeling that disciplinary boundaries in consultant groups have by now been substantially eroded, with the contributions by the geographers nowadays scarcely distinguishable in retrospect from those by economists, for example. This is to some extent the result of a growing convergence of research objectives and techniques within certain common fields in the social sciences.

Applied work developing from within University departments of geography may be illustrated from Aberdeen and Newcastle. The geographical inputs to the Gaskin Report (1969), an *Economic Survey of North East Scotland*, related initially to an Aberdeen thesis on central places and hierarchies of urban settlements in the area; a survey, requested by the Scottish Development Department, of the economy of Yell, Shetland Islands (Caird and Coull, 1964), and later the island of Westray in the Orkneys (Coull, 1965), followed upon a successful survey of the Island of Fetlar (Fraser and Coull, 1961), by a member of the staff of the Aberdeen Department, with a view to the reorganization of holdings for Zetland County Council. Other studies included a *Survey of Crofting in the Island of Skye* (Coull and Hamilton, 1963), a *Survey of the Social and Economic Effects of the Air Service in the North Isles of Orkney* (Coull and Willis, 1969), participation in the survey for the site of the smelter at Invergordon, the five-year study of the environmental effects of the Invergordon complex, together with work on resources and recreation, mentioned later.

At Newcastle, earlier stock-taking surveys of industrial facilities of the North East (Daysh, 1949a) and Cumberland (Daysh and Watson, 1951) were followed by the study of West Durham as a problem area (Daysh and Symonds, 1953) and the *Survey of Whitby*, by four geographers, an economist and a surveyor (Daysh, 1958). In 1960 an industrial and regional survey of Tees-side was completed (House and Fullerton, 1960), whilst in more recent times an analysis of the problems of migration and mobility in Northern England reviewed type problems, sectors, localities and key socio-economic groups (House *et al.*, 1965–68).

Indicative of the participation by geographers in consultant groups, little of whose work has been widely published, is that by Diamond at Swindon, the New Town at Livingston and in the Lothians Regional Survey; Emrys Jones, at the New Towns of Milton Keynes and Washington; Hall in the Canary Islands Regional Survey and the Central Wales New Town; and Manners, in his work with the Location of Offices Bureau. Manners, Hall, Goddard and Spence also contributed in one of the consultant groups working for the Roskill Commission, on urban forecasting, spatial allocation procedures and multiplier effects; Goddard also worked with the Economist Advisory Group on the City of London. These indications understate the extent of the involvement by geographers in consultancy, in which even the publication of findings, if it takes place at all, is no full assessment of the rôle played by individual specialists, in discussion, tendering advice, working through problems, recommending priorities or preferred alternatives, or in presentation of results.

A further valuable example of the direct linkage between Departmental work and consultancy is that of the Winsford Master Plan Survey (Rodgers and Old, 1960), in which a social survey was undertaken at the request of the local council and the consultants. The survey was drawn up to yield answers to a number of specifically relevant questions on demographic structure, journey-to-work, shopping habits and preferences, and public opinion on development of a family recreational centre.

COMMISSIONS AND DEPARTMENTAL COMMITTEES

The influence of geographers on decisions or policies is likely to be most difficult to detect in the work of official bodies. It may occur at successive stages: in the public debate, preceding the setting up of a Commission or Committee of Enquiry, as in contemporary interest in pollution questions or in the problems of rural areas; in the submission of evidence, individually or by representative corporate bodies; in membership of the official body, or as a technical contributor in a research support group; in the public debate which may follow publication of the official recommendations; and, finally, in aiding preparation of legislation.

Geographers have intermittently, but at times prominently, taken part in such deliberations and the sense of involvement at all stages has been growing, with a fuller exposition by individuals using the media or being directly and actively involved in the process itself. The tradition of participation was started by the submissions, on invitation, by the Royal Geographical Society to the Royal Commission on the Distribution of the Industrial Population (the Barlow Commission, 1937–40). Taylor was chairman of the committee which prepared the evidence for submission and she and Stamp also gave evidence orally. The memorandum presented was fully documented with a series of national maps, 'presenting a clear picture of the geographical distribution of industry and the industrial population as it is today, and in the second instance as affording some guidance in respect of any future policy of planning'. The Royal Geographical Society, however, resolutely declined, at that time, to address itself to the policy implications of a redeployment of the industrial population.

L. D. Stamp was vice-chairman of the Scott Committee on Land Utilization in Rural Areas, a fitting tribute both to his wide expertise in agricultural matters and to his particular contribution through the first land utilization survey of Britain in the 1930s. He remained an adviser to the Ministry of Agriculture and later became a member of the *Royal Commission on Common Land*, which reported in 1958. The need for careful stock-taking and evaluation of the fragmentary evidence on commons and its interpretation in the context of historical development on a nation-wide scale was a task particularly apt for geographical skills and advice (Stamp and Hoskins, 1963). In a more general sense, the influence of Stamp, through his writings, participation on committees and the breadth of his consultations was outstanding among the geographers of his generation; in particular, he was also one of the earliest protagonists in the cause of conservation (Stamp, 1964).

Perhaps the principal field of geographical participation has been in the work of successive bodies of enquiry into the structure, pattern and reform of local government. This had been a research field among academic geographers for some time, the work of Fawcett on the *Provinces of England* (1919) being followed by that of Gilbert (1948) on administrative regionalism, Freeman (1966) on the conurbations, Wise (1966) and Dickinson (1964) on city regions and regionalism. Within the Ministry there early developed a continuing concern with the problems of local government, through earlier Boundary Commissions, to the Local Government Commission for England (1958) and that for Wales. The senior staff of the Commission were always geographers, a discipline well-suited to studying the complex spatial and structural inter-relationships between community, population, employment, physical habitat, communications and accessibility. Problems ranged from those concerning the structure of local government most suitable for the Special Review Areas, which included several conurbations, to advice on changes in local government boundaries. Willatts (1971) draws attention to the geographical approach evident both in the accompanying maps and in the published reports, citing particularly Chapter II of the report on the York and North Midlands General Review Area, to indicate the nature of the geographical contribution.

Though not all the recommendations of the Local Government

Commission found favour and were implemented, the groundwork was laid for the next stages, the *Royal Commission on Local Government in Greater London* (1960), that on Local Government in England (Maud Report, 1969), and in Scotland (Wheatley Report, 1969). Geographical contributions to these were both in submissions of evidence, 'in-house' research and, subsequently, by critique and commentary on the recommendations made.

The Royal Commission on London deliberately sought the widest basis for submissions of evidence, circularizing, among others, every university in Britain. Much of the 'in-house' research has not been published, though the work of Carruthers on service centres (1962) involved original research with a specific outcome. Contributory submissions were made by the inter-disciplinary Greater London Group of the London School of Economics and Political Science, on which geographers have been consistently represented since its formation in 1958 and there is little doubt that its evidence was influential (paras. 188–195). The cartographical work and the Research Appendices (vol. III) of the Royal Commission on Local Government in England also well illustrate the 'in-house' geographical contribution, by S. W. E. Vince and others, most particularly Appendix 2 on 'Some aspects of the changing relationship of town and country'; 3 on 'Migration'; 4 'A profile of the conurbations' and 5 'Basic demographic trends'. As in the Strategic Plan for the South East (South East Joint Planning Team, 1970) the contributions by economists, sociologists and other specialists are now becoming more substantially apparent. Furthermore, since publication aspects of both the main report (vol. I) and the *Memorandum of Dissent* (vol. II) by Senior have been critically evaluated by geographers (James, House and Hall, 1970). For a group of Cheshire local authorities H. B. Rodgers prepared a consultant report on groupings alternative to the unit proposed in the Maud Report, recommendations which were overtaken by the rapidity of political change.

The Wheatley Commission on Scotland had a geographer in its Intelligence Unit; group discussions were held with Scottish academic geographers, an informal kind of consultancy. The working maps for the Population Distribution Map of Scotland, prepared in the Glasgow Department (1961 census) were used and some testing of the grid-square method was carried out experimentally in Glasgow ahead of the 1971 Census of Scotland (Robertson, 1969, 1970), whilst in England geographers were invited to form an Advisory Panel for the 1971 Census.

The advent of a Conservative Administration in 1970 introduced a different political evaluation of the problems of local government reform, within the area of general agreement that the number of local government authorities must be reduced and their size increased. The Bill presented to Parliament in 1971 and still passing through the committee stages at the time of final revision of this text in 1972, provides for all-purpose metropolitan districts in the major conurbations outside London (which is not affected by the Bill) and elsewhere two kinds of authority—counties and districts. The latter will share some powers with the former but are effectively the lower tier of a two-tier system. Under the Bill, a Local Government Boundary Commission for England has been established, with the initial task of defining the boundaries of the non-metropolitan districts and a longer term remit to review all local government boundaries. The only academic on this Commission is a geographer, M. Chisholm.

Two recent Departmental Committees of Enquiry are of particular interest since they had geographers, for the first time, as chairmen: M. J. Wise, Statutory Small Holdings (1966–67); H. Thorpe, Allotments (1969). The Smallholdings Enquiry was in essence an investigation of their economic position, management, and current problems with a view to recommendations on future provision, form of financing and structure of management. Though mainly a social and economic problem there was also a spatial dimension; much of Part I of the Report was embodied in Part III of the Agriculture Act, 1970. The recommendations of Part II, dealing with Land Settlement, did not find the same measure of acceptance, though substantial changes in the Land Settlement Association estates have followed, including the closure of a number of the less successful estates and an emphasis on horticulture as the main activity.

The Enquiry into Allotments had two further geographer-members (F. A. Barnes and E. Jones), in addition to its chairman, and is particularly strong in its historical and geographical content, cartography and spatial analysis. A massive questionnaire survey was made and the site and context of the allotment in the landscape were clearly established. The categories and sub-categories of allotments were analysed, together with the profile of allotment holders and the forms of their association; valuable comparative evidence was gathered from Europe and from both Scotland and Ireland. The recommendations are structural in character and the government has already given general approval to the concept of giving allotment gardens a new look. Meanwhile Thorpe has continued to research into this topic, with a

grant from the Social Science Research Council, studying the rational-
ization of urban allotment systems, particularly in Birmingham.

The Hunt Committee on the Intermediate Areas (1969) had J. R.
James, a trained geographer and former Chief Planner at the Ministry
of Housing and Local Government, as one of its members; another
member was a distinguished applied economist, A. J. Brown. The
problem of investigating areas, outside the Development Areas, which
gave or might give cause for concern in respect of economic growth
was crucial for the doctrine and policies of establishing regional balance
and equilibrium. The Committee made a thorough-going analysis of a
wide diversity of areas, with economic, social and geographical
perspectives, before concluding that no clear-cut category of grey (or
intermediate) area could be identified. Both the North West and
Yorkshire and Humberside were recommended for an intermediate
level of regional economic aid, together with scattered, smaller problem
areas; Merseyside was to be de-scheduled as a Development Area.
This latter recommendation was not accepted and, furthermore, much
more localized areas were finally granted Intermediate Area status.

RESOURCES PLANNING

The relevant research, consultant work, or membership of committees
covers a wide and disparate field of geographical participation, including
land use, beaches and coasts, environmental management, water,
amenity, sand and gravel, green belts, tourism and recreation; this
latter field for geographical applications is perhaps the fastest-growing
at the present time. Attention is confined to topics with a human
geographical content and to those with policy implications; the
subject grades off into problems more properly the concern of the
Natural Environment Research Council.

Rural development boards

The Highlands and Islands Development Board and that for the
Northern Pennines (1969–71) have both offered a rôle for the geographer
in research and policy-making. The Highlands Board is both regional
in scope and executive in power, set up to 'initiate, promote and assist
economic and social enterprise' over a broad region. The principal
qualifications needed for the staff were commercial and administrative,
in addition to professional or academic expertise. Geographers had
been active on the earlier Advisory Panel and in 1970 some six
geography graduates were employed by the Highlands Board, four of

them as Heads of Divisions. Two are in the Planning and Research Division, including its head (F. D. N. Spaven), working on regional intelligence, area development schemes and resource studies, along with two economists, an engineer, a cartographer and a consultant sociologist; another two are in the Fisheries Division, while others head the Industrial Development and Tourist Divisions respectively. The Board also employs geographers as consultants, notably on terrain and land resource capability, human resources, labour availability and aspects of tourism; and on industrial and urban growth. An example is the work of Aberdeen geographers in advising on Strath Kildonan and Glen Strathfarrar.

The short-lived Northern Pennines Board had a geographer (J. W. House) among its eleven members, the others being farmers and landowners, together with a rural transport specialist. The task of the Board was to operate the relevant provisions of the 1967 Agriculture Act, with powers relating to land transfer, the farming-forestry balance, the ability to improve communications and public services, and also to assist farmers and foresters to derive financial benefits from tourists. Within a short time the Board had to build up detailed knowledge of the structure, trends and problems of its two million acres and 6,246 farms. Policy had to be formulated in operational terms, from only general principles, and spatial aspects had to be interpreted at first in an *ad hoc* way. A programme for sponsoring research on the basic structure and potential of tourism in the area, the economics and profitability of hill farms and the social trends in villages was under way when the Board was dissolved. It had had the benefit of an excellent series of thematic maps of its area, provided by the Ministry of Agriculture. The operational needs for research, in the short and the longer term, had to be assessed and acted upon quickly, from very small beginnings.

Other resources

Pioneering work on the planning implications of natural resources includes that of Beaver and Wooldridge on the Advisory Committee on Sand and Gravel (1948–53). The geographical task was to assemble and assess all known data on these resources and the eighteen reports, most of them regional and covering the entire country, helped to clarify priorities where use of gravel resources involved potential land use conflicts. The report on derelict land in the Black Country (Beaver, 1946) was essentially geographical in that, additional to cartographic presentation, it involved geology, land use, economics and industrial history, and gave a holistic view of the problem; over two-thirds of the land surveyed has since been reclaimed. The same author also acted as consultant, on mineral resources and dereliction, for the West Midland and North Staffordshire Plan.

The survey of British coasts by J. A. Steers, for the Ministry of Town and Country Planning, was initially plotted on the 2½-inch scale and provided a rich source of data for later policy decisions. The high-grade category in the classification was made the basis of the Countryside Commission's later report on Heritage Coasts. Steers was also a member of the Wild Life Conservation Special Committee which, with its parent the Hobhouse Committee, contributed to the formation of the Nature Conservancy and the National Parks (later Countryside Commission). He established the importance of physiography in the study of coastal planning and pointed to the need for designating certain nature reserves.

Other planning work on the British coasts was carried out by C. Kidson as a member of the Scientific Civil Service, ranging from designation of physical features to be within nature reserves or sites of special scientific interest, to advice relating to pressures for coastal development. The reports of coastal conferences by the National Parks Committee will influence coastal development until the end of the century, not least in the designation of Heritage Coasts. Whilst at the Nature Conservancy Kidson was also concerned in decisions on coastal land use conflicts and priorities, amenity and conservation issues and impact studies of the siting of coastal nuclear power stations. Since leaving government service he has acted as consultant as, for example, on the proposed transfer of the Shoeburyness Ranges to Pembrey in South Wales and, secondly, on the possible conflicts between harbour development and the beaches at Teignmouth. Tanner (1970) was commissioned by the Sports Council to undertake a reconnaissance survey of the capacity of the coasts of England and Wales for physical recreation.

Geographical concern with water resources has ranged from the evidence by W. G. V. Balchin to the Central Water Advisory Committee of the Ministry of Housing and Local Government (1957–58), to the membership of H. C. Darby on the Water Resources Board and the National Parks Committee (1963), now Countryside Commission. The geographical view was valuable in the presentation of material regionally and spatially, and in clarifying the contentious relationship between amenity and water resources in National Parks; geographers are well represented on the technical staff of the Countryside Commission. On the contemporary issue of environmental management the British National Committee for Geography has submitted evidence, through the Royal Society, to the (Ashby) Royal Commission on Pollution.

Land use and potential conflicts among users has been a long-standing subject for geographical research (Best, 1958; Best and Coppock, 1962); the Land Use Survey of the 1930s (Stamp, 1962) has been followed by that of the 1960s (A. Coleman), both massive coverages of national land resources; furthermore, Aberdeen geographers have made land use appreciations for the Highlands and Islands Development Board. A compact, interdisciplinary land use evaluation is that for the Lower Swansea Valley Project (Hilton, 1967), on which several geographers served, one as chairman of the land-use committee. Many of the land use proposals then recommended, for an area with serious environmental problems, have since been implemented.

One of the fastest-growing fields of recent times has been the application of geographical techniques to the study of recreational and amenity use of land (Coppock, 1966; Rodgers, 1969), and also the geographical analysis of the problems of tourism (e.g. House, 1958). This novel field for social scientists involves presentation of basic material for the first time, but there is also a close and rapidly developing relationship between research and the needs of policy-making, given the pressure of current demands on recreational space. Substantive studies include those by J. T. Coppock and others, for the Scottish Tourist Board and local authorities, on the impact of Aviemore developments on Speyside, outdoor recreation in Lanarkshire, and also in Greater Edinburgh. The Aberdeen geographers have published a major survey, *Eastern Cairngorms: regional study* (Scottish Tourist Board, 1969) for the Scottish Tourist Board and had the remit to study depopulation problems on Deeside and Donside, in the context of the possible effects of the development of tourism. G. Humphrys prepared a report for the Welsh Tourist Board on the recreational pressures on the Gower peninsula.

Rodgers reported (Rodgers, 1967 and 1969) on the national pattern of outdoor recreation, with a particularly valuable contribution on regional contrasts in recreational behaviour in Great Britain; one major regional study, that for the Northern Region, has been published, whilst another (on the North West) is in progress. The national study was a large-scale pilot operation, based on stratified samples. Rodgers is also currently chairman of a Sports Council committee on research into recreation. Mention must also be made of the work of Wise (1968) on the Green

Belt, south of Birmingham, acting as an impartial adviser on land use problems, asked to provide a working solution to a problem of conflicting demands for land.

Other interesting geographical achievements are those by Appleton (1970) in producing, for the Countryside Commission, a nation-wide survey and evaluation of the possibilities for using the tracks of disused railway lines, an indication of the strengths and value of the historical geographer in planning matters; and secondly the contribution by Gentleman and Swift (1971) to the pioneer survey of Scotland's travelling people, the gipsies and tinkers.

OTHER POLICY AND DECISION-MAKING FIELDS

By the catholic nature of geographical interests other fields of contact with decisions and policies are necessarily widespread, but not the less important and effective for that. To avoid cataloguing the versatility of other geographical contributions attention is drawn only to one or two salient and evocative examples.

The successful assistance to commerce on its location problems contrasts with a general lack of effective geographical applications throughout manufacturing industry or in the transport fields. There are, of course, substantial research publications by geographers on these topics but consultancy or participation by geographers in policy recommendations seems to have been minimal. This difference in achievements may reflect the suitability of the service industries for geographical analysis or advice, with location of their establishments, as in retailing, often critical in profitability and their tendency to react to an increase in demand by multiplication of outlets. Such an industry is thus 'faced with a number of location decisions for which it will try to establish some analytical procedures to reduce risk' (D. Thorpe, verbal communication, 1971). Thorpe, a first degree geographer, is head of the Retail Research Unit of the Manchester Business School. For retailing, research of value does exist but it is limited in scale, and there is a need for more basic data sources, such as marketing maps or atlases. Much work is commissioned on markets, often with a fair geographical content, but frequently the spatial dimension is ignored. This may happen because of the difficulty and cost of incorporating breakdowns with this dimension, as well as the more usual market parameters of a demographic character.

Effective consideration of the consultant or applied work by British geographers overseas is beyond the scope of this chapter, but indicative of such widespread and effective participation is that of the Durham geographers, throughout the Middle East and Malta, in terrain and resource evaluation, social and development surveys and advisory work on urban problems. Similarly, the Liverpool geographers have worked in the tropical world, including the consultancy work of R. M. Prothero for the World Health Organization. In Srilanka (Ceylon) the work of B. H. Farmer as a member of the Ceylon Land Commission 1955–58, chairman of the Gal Oya Project Evaluation Committee and occasional consultant on agricultural development projects in Ceylon, is a further indication of substantial achievement. In the late 1960s, M. Chisholm was the senior field member of a team examining the economic and social aspects of transport investment proposals covering the entire territory of Papua and New Guinea, as part of a comprehensive evaluation of transport for the World Bank. Finally, the work of the Royal Geographical Society for the arbitration award on the Argentine-Chilean boundary (*Award of H.M. Queen Elizabeth*, 1966) is yet a further, and, for the present study, the last dimension to the geographer's advisory rôle on policies and decisions. L. P. Kirwan was leader of the Field Mission, which made a full and careful reconnaissance of all the areas under dispute, and was also a member of the Court under the Presidency of Lord McNair.

CONCLUSIONS

The essays in this book have illustrated the wide and expanding coverage of contemporary geographical research, an increasing volume and range of which is capable of application, and indeed in part has been generated by the social and economic problems of the times. This last chapter has shown the extent to which applications have taken place hitherto, in fields where decisions have had to be taken and policies made. The overall verdict must be that the utility of geographical findings has been remarkably widespread, but that penetrations in depth and a clear linkage to the formative elements of decisions and policies have been somewhat less common, though from time to time showing a dramatic and, on the whole, an increasing impact. In short, geography has fertilized extensively, but has rarely dominated in policy-making. In a sense, the weight of accumulated relevant research will always pay off in practical applications, but an important purpose in the shorter-term must be to increase the two-way interchange between researchers, decision takers and policy makers. In human geography the potential for a greater contribution has been well established in this group of essays. Indeed both the achievements and the further prospects for geography are probably among the most favourable within the social sciences: only economics has had a greater, if more narrowly-defined, success thus far at the policy-making level of consultation, whilst sociology is only now beginning to make its substantial mark in planning.

In assessing the record of applications in human geography since 1945 the successes must be attributed in the first place to the traditional breadth of co-ordinated vision over man and environment, allied with a strong empirical case-study approach and an ability to apply generic concepts developed within the systematic branches of the subject. During the past decade, however, both the nature of decision and policy fields and the objectives, techniques and topics within major branches of human geography have changed structurally and dramatically, becoming more specific, quantitative, capable of prediction as well as greater precision, and with closer theoretical and practical linkages to other social sciences. The research frontiers of human geography are thus currently more widely-ranging than the decision takers or policy makers either immediately dictate, require or can effectively incorporate and use. This must surely presage an even greater impact for human geography, among other social sciences, in relation to planning in all its forms over the next decade or so, providing decision takers and policy makers become more actively aware of the importance of the spatial dimension in social and economic affairs. In his turn the geographer can increase the significance of his contribution, without loss to traditional perspectives or applications, which should logically retain their long-established importance if the discipline of geography is to keep its identity within the social sciences. Important growth fields for applications lie, for example, in computer graphics, especially interactive systems, or in modelling spatial situations, especially in one or more parts of a system or sub-system, and hence in the ability to predict more meaningfully. The increasing requirement for planning forecasts, for evaluation of alternative strategies for regions, sub-regions and cities (Chisholm, Frey, Haggett, 1971; Bassett and Haggett, 1971) highlights both the social and economic need and the difficulties faced by all social sciences, including geography, when pressed into an hitherto unfamiliar forecasting rôle.

These problems are common to all social sciences actively re-defining their rôles in relation to the needs of the times. They necessarily carry implications for the rethinking of objectives and methods in the training of geographers, with desirably greater emphasis on problem solving and action orientation, resource perception and environmental evaluation, systems thinking and the need to deploy and refine better techniques of measurement, assessment and forecasting. Furthermore, greater attention should be focussed upon the large and growing areas of overlap with other social sciences, which often use similar techniques in pursuit of common objectives. Only thereby can human geography increase and render more fruitful its already considerable investment in operational capital and add to the existing, mutually beneficial links and bonds between academic researchers and those engaged in managing and legislating for the national, regional or local space.

REFERENCES

Adam, A. and Rankin, I. (1965) *Report of a Survey of the Parishes of Assynt and Eddrachillis*, Scottish Development Department.

Appleton, J. A. (1970) *Disused Railways in the Countryside of England and Wales*, Countryside Commission, HMSO.

Award of H.M. Queen Elizabeth II for the Arbitration of a Controversy Between the Argentine Republic and the Republic of Chile, Concerning Certain Parts of the Boundary Between their Territories (1966) HMSO.

Balchin, W. G. V. (1957) 'The nation's water supply', *Geography*, 42, 149–257.

Balchin, W. G. V. (1958) 'A water use survey', *Geographical Journal*, 124, 476–479.

Bassett, K. and Haggett, P. (1971) 'Towards short-term forecasting for cyclic behaviour in a regional system of cities', in Chisholm, Frey and Haggett (Eds.), 389–413.

Beaver, S. H. (1946) *Report on Derelict Land in the Black Country*, Ministry of Town and Country Planning.

Beaver, S. H. (1949) 'Surface mineral working in relation to planning', *Report of the Town and Country Planning School, Town Planning Institute*, 105–130.

Beaver, S. H. (1968) *The Geology of Sand and Gravel*, Sand and Gravel Advisory Committee for Great Britain.

Best, R. H. (1958) 'The composition of the urban area in England and Wales', *Journal of the Royal Town Planning Institute*, 44, 160–164.

Best, R. H. (1958) 'The loss of farmland to other uses in England and Wales', *Town and Country Planning*, 26, 426–431.

Best, R. H. (1959) *The Major Land Uses of Great Britain*, Wye College.

Best, R. H. and Coppock, J. T. (1962) *The Changing Uses of Land in Britain*, Faber and Faber.

Caesar, A. A. L. (1964) 'Planning and the geography of Great Britain', *Advancement of Science*, 21, 451–469.

Caird, J. B. and Coull, J. R. (1964) *Report of a Survey of the Island of Yell*, Shetland County Council and Scottish Development Department.

Campbell, A. D. and Lyddon, W. D. C. (1970) *Tayside: potential for development*, HMSO.

Carruthers, W. I. (1957) 'A classification of service centres in England and Wales', *Geographical Journal*, **123**, 371–385.

Carruthers, W. I. (1962) 'Service centres in Greater London', *Town Planning Review*, **33**, 5–31.

Central Unit for Environmental Planning (1969) *Humberside: a feasibility study*, HMSO.

Central Unit for Environmental Planning (1971) *Severnside: a feasibility study*, HMSO.

Chisholm, M., Frey, A. E. and Haggett, P. (Eds.) (1971) *Regional Forecasting*, Butterworths.

Chisholm, M., Frey, A. E. and Haggett, P. (1971) 'Regional forecasting; from prologue to epilogue', in Chisholm, Frey and Haggett (Eds.), 453–467.

Coates, B. E. and Rawstron, E. M. (1971) *Regional Variations in Britain*, Batsford.

Coppock, J. T. (1966) 'The recreational use of land and water in Britain', *Tijdschrift voor Economische en Sociale Geografie*, **57**, 81–96.

Coppock, J. T. (Ed.) (1971) *The Touring Caravan in Scotland*, Scottish Tourist Board.

Coull, J. R. (1965) *Report of a Survey of the Island of Westray*, Scottish Development Department.

Coull, J. R. and Hamilton, P. (1963) *Report of a Survey of Crofting in the Island of Skye*, Crofters Commission.

Coull, J. R. and Willis, D. P. (1969) *A Survey of the Social and Economic Effects of the Air Service in the North Isles of Orkney*, Department of Agriculture and Fisheries for Scotland.

Countryside Commission (1968) *The Coasts of England and Wales: use, protection and development*, HMSO.

Countryside Commission (1969) *Special Study Reports: Vol. I, Coastal recreation and holidays; Vol. II, Conservation at the coast*, HMSO.

Countryside Commission (1970) *The Coastal Heritage*, HMSO.

Countryside Commission (1970) *The Planning of the Coastline*, HMSO.

Coventry City Council *et al.* (1971) *Coventry–Solihull–Warwickshire. A strategy for the sub-region*.

Darby, H. C. (1963) 'British National Parks', *Advancement of Science*, **20**, 1–12.

Darby, H. C. (1967) 'The recreation and amenity use of water', *Journal of the Institution of Water Engineers*, **21**, 225–231.

Daysh, G. H. J. (1949a) *The North East Coast: a survey of industrial facilities*, North East Development Association.

Daysh, G. H. J. (Ed.) (1949b) *Studies in Regional Planning*, Philip.

Daysh, G. H. J. (Ed.) (1958) *A Survey of Whitby and the Surrounding Area*, Shakespeare Head.

Daysh, G. H. J. and O'Dell, A. C. (1947) 'Geography and planning', *Geographical Journal*, **109**, 1–3, 103–106.

Daysh, G. H. J. and Symonds, J. S. (1953) *West Durham: a study of a problem area*, Blackwell.

Daysh, G. H. J. and Watson, E. M. (1951) *Cumberland*, Cumberland Development Council.

Dickinson, R. E. (1947) *City, Region and Regionalism: a geographical contribution to human ecology*, Kegan Paul.

Dickinson, R. E. (1964) *City and Region*, Routledge, Kegan and Paul.

Fawcett, C. B. (1919) *The Provinces of England*. Reprinted in 1961 by Hutchinson.

Fraser, A. S. and Coull, J. R. (1961) *Fetlar Report*, Shetland County Council.

Freeman, T. W. (1966) *The Conurbations of Great Britain*, Manchester University Press, 2nd edn.

Gaskin, M. (Ed.) (1969) *A Survey of the Economic Potential of Northeast Scotland*, Scottish Development Department.

Gentleman, H. and Swift, S. (1971) *Scotland's Travelling People*, Scottish Development Department, HMSO.

Gilbert, E. W. (1948) 'The boundaries of local government areas', *Geographical Journal*, **111**, 4–6, 172–206.

Greater London Council (1969). *Report of Studies*.

Green, F. H. W. (1950) 'Urban hinterlands in England and Wales: an analysis of bus services', *Geographical Journal*, **116**, 1–3, 64–68.

Green, F. H. W. (1952) 'Bus services as an index to changing urban hinterlands', *Town Planning Review*, **22**, 345–356.

Hall, P. G. (1963) *London 2000*, Faber and Faber.

Hilton, K. J. (1967) *The Lower Swansea Valley Project*, Longmans.

House, J. W. (1958) 'Whitby as a resort', in *A Survey of Whitby and the surrounding area*, Shakespeare Head, 145–203.

House, J. W. (1965) 'Applied geography in Great Britain', *Applied Geography in the World*, Academia Prague, 178–194.

House, J. W. (1971) 'The geographer and long-term regional strategy: some recent British experience', *IGU Commission on Applied Geography*, Rennes, Brittany.

House, J. W. and Fullerton, B. (1960) *Tees-side at Mid-Century*, Macmillan.

House, J. W. *et al.* (1965–8) *Papers on Migration and Mobility in Northern England*, Nos. 1–9.

James, J. R. (1958) 'Land planning in an expanding economy', *Journal of the Royal Society of Arts*, **106**, 589–608.

James, J. R. (Member) (1960) *The Intermediate Areas: Report of a Committee under the Chairmanship of Sir Joseph Hunt*, Cmnd. 3998, HMSO.

James, J. R. (1967) 'Planning for the 1970s: a strategic view of planning', *Journal of the Royal Institute of British Architects*, **74**, 419–429.

James, J. R., House, J. W. and Hall, P. (1970) 'Local government reform in England', *Geographical Journal*, **136**, 2–23.

James, J. R., Scott, S. F. and Willatts, E. C. (1961) 'Land use and the changing power industry in England and Wales', *Geographical Journal*, **127**, 286–309.

Lea, K. J. (1965) *Report of a Survey of the Island of North Uist*, Scottish Development Department.

Leicester City and County Council (1969) *Leicester and Leicestershire sub-Regional Planning Study.*

Local Government Commission for England (1961–5). Reports 1–9, HMSO.

Ministry of Housing and Local Government. *Advisory Committee on Sand and Gravel* (1948–53). Reports 1–18, contributions by S. H. Beaver and S. W. Wooldridge, HMSO.

Ministry of Housing and Local Government (1964) *The South East Study, 1961–81*, HMSO.

Ministry of Town and Country (1947) *Conservation of Nature in England and Wales: report of wild life conservation special committee*, Cmnd. 7122, HMSO. J. A. Steers, member.

Northern Economic Planning Council (1969) *Outline Strategy for the North.* Contribution by J. W. House.

Powell, A. G. (1960) 'The recent development of Greater London', *Advancement of Science*, **17**, 76–86.

Powell, A. G. (1970) 'The geographer in regional planning', *Geographical Essays in Honour of Professor K. C. Edwards*, University of Nottingham, 224–232.

Report of the Committee on Land Utilisation in Rural Areas (1942). Cmnd. 6378, HMSO. Stamp, L. D. (Vice-Chairman).

Robertson, I. M. L. (1969) 'The census and research: ideals and realities', *Transactions of the Institute of British Geographers*, **48**, 173–187.

Robertson, I. M. L. (1970) 'The national grid and social geography', *Geography*, **55**, 426–433.

Rodgers, H. B. (1967) *Pilot National Recreation Survey*, Report 1. British Travel Association and University of Keele.

Rodgers, H. B. (1969) 'Leisure and recreation', *Urban Studies*, **6**, 368–384.

Rodgers, H. B. (1969) *Pilot National Recreation Survey*, Report 2. British Travel Association and University of Keele.

Rodgers, H. B. and Old, F. T. (1960) *The Winsford Master Plan Survey. A social survey of the town*, Department of Geography, University of Keele.

Royal Commission on Common Land (1958) Cmnd. 462, HMSO. L. D. Stamp, member.

Royal Commission on Local Government in England (1966–9) Report. Cmnd. 4046, HMSO.

Royal Commission on Local Government in Greater London (1960) Report. Cmnd. 1164, HMSO. See particularly paras. 188–195.

Royal Commission on Local Government in Scotland, (Wheatley Report) (1969). Cmnd. 4150, 2 vols., HMSO.

Royal Commission on the Distribution of the Industrial Population (1940). Cmd. 6153, HMSO.

Royal Geographical Society (1938) 'Memorandum on the geographical factors relevant to the location of industry', *Geographical Journal*, **92**, 499–526.

Scarlett, R. C. (1971) Private communication, March 24.

Scottish Tourist Board (1969) *Eastern Cairngorms: regional study (Royal Grampian Country).*

Smailes, A. E. (1946) 'The urban mesh of England and Wales', *Transactions of the Institute of British Geographers*, **11**, 87–107.

Smailes, A. E. (1947) 'The analysis and delimitation of urban fields', *Geography*, **32** (4), 151–161.

South East Economic Planning Council (1967) *A Strategy for the South East*, HMSO.

South East Joint Planning Team (1970) *Strategic Plan for the South East*, HMSO.

Stamp, L. D. (1962) *The Land of Britain: its use and misuse*, Longmans, Green.

Stamp, L. D. (1964) *Man and the Land*, Collins.

Stamp, L. D. and Hoskins, W. G. (1963) *The Common Lands of England and Wales*, Collins.

Steers, J. A. (1944) 'Coastal preservation and planning', *Geographical Journal*, **104**, 1–2, 7–26.

Steers, J. A. (1946) 'Coastal preservation and planning', *Geographical Journal*, **107**, 1–2, 57–60.

Steers, J. A. (1964) *The Coastline of England and Wales*, Cambridge University Press.

Tanner, M. F. (1969) 'Coastal recreation in England and Wales: a study prepared for the Sports Council', *Coastal Recreation and Holidays*, Countryside Commission, HMSO.

Tanner, M. F. (1970) 'Water resources and recreation: some problems of research', *Recreation, Land Use, Planning and Forecasting*, Seminar proceedings, Planning and Transport Research and Computation Co. Ltd.

Taylor, E. G. R. (1938) 'Discussion on the geographical distribution of industry', *Geographical Journal*, **92**, 22–39.

The Scottish Economy 1965 to 1970. A plan for expansion, Cmnd 2846, HMSO.

Thorpe, H. (Chairman) *Departmental Committee of Inquiry into Allotments* (1969) Cmnd. 4166, HMSO.

Vince, S. W. E. (1952) 'Reflections on the structure and distribution of rural population in England and Wales, 1921–31', *Transactions of the Institute of British Geographers*, **18**, 53–76.

Willatts, E. C. (1951) 'Some principles of land use planning', *London Essays in Geography*, Longmans Green, 289–302.

Willatts, E. C. (1962) 'Post-war development: the location of major projects in England and Wales', *The Chartered Surveyor*, **94**, 356–366.

Willatts, E. C. (1965) 'Geographical techniques in physical planning', in *Frontiers in Geographical Teaching* (Eds. R. J. Chorley and P. Haggett), Methuen, 266–293.

Willatts, E. C. (1971) 'Planning and geography in the last three decades', *Geographical Journal*, **137**, 3.

Wise, M. J. (1960) 'Some economic trends influencing planning policies', *Journal of the Royal Town Planning Institute*, **46**, 30–35.

Wise, M. J. (1966) 'The city region', *Advancement of Science*, **22**, 571–588.

Wise, M. J. (Chairman) *Departmental Committee of Inquiry into Statutory Smallholdings* (1966–7). First (Cmnd. 1936, 1966) and Final (Cmnd. 3303, 1967) Reports, HMSO.

Wise, M. J. (1968) *The Implications for Open Space and Recreational Land on the Conurbation [Birmingham] Fringe; a preliminary view*, Cadbury Brothers, Birmingham.

Yorkshire and Humberside Economic Planning Council (1969) *Doncaster: an area study*, HMSO.
Yorkshire and Humberside Economic Planning Council (1968) *Halifax and Calder Valley*, HMSO.
Yorkshire and Humberside Economic Planning Council (1969) *Huddersfield and Colne Valley*, HMSO.